LOOKING TO EUROPE

For Iris

Jens Henrik Haahr

LOOKING TO EUROPE

The EC Policies of the British Labour Party and the Danish Social Democrats

AARHUS UNIVERSITY PRESS

Copyright: Aarhus University Press, 1993
Word-processed by the author
Printed in England by The Alden Press, Oxford
Produced on permanent paper conforming to ANSI standard Z39-48.1984
ISBN 87 7288 449 5

The publication of this book was supported by the
Danish Social Science Research Council

AARHUS UNIVERSITY PRESS
Building 170, Aarhus University
DK-8000 Aarhus C, Denmark
Fax + 45 86 19 84 33

CONTENTS

FIGURES

TABLES

ACKNOWLEDGEMENTS

This book focuses on the British Labour Party's and the Danish SDP's attitudes towards the European Community. It has benefitted immensely from the comments, critique, advice and support of a large number of people. In particular I would like to acknowledge the importance of the discussions I have had with Jørgen Elklit, Niels Amstrup and Palle Svennson at the Institute of Political Science, University of Aarhus, during my work as a research fellow there in the period from 1990 to 1992. The comments of my colleague Karsten Skjalm on the economic aspects of European integration have also been very useful. In addition, I wish to thank William Paterson for his help and advice during my stay at the University of Edinburgh's Europa Institute in the Fall and Winter 1992-93, where Moshe Maor also offered valuable criticisms. A number of leading figures in both the Labour Party and the Danish SDP have been very forthcoming, both in terms of being accessible for interviews and in providing me with relevant unpublished documents.

Without the generous financial support of the Institute of Political Science, University of Aarhus, this study could not have been carried out. Furthermore, assistance from the Danish Research Academy and the Danish Institute of Foreign Policy (DUPI) has provided me the opportunity to make several visits to Britain in order to collect data and conduct interviews. A Schuman Research Grant for studies at the European Parliament's General Directorate for Research in early 1991 allowed me to supplement my material on the two partics' policies on the European Community's development in this setting.

Costs for publication of this study were provided by the Danish Social Science Research Council, and Steven Sampson's editing of the document was made possible by grants from the Danish Institute of Foreign Policy, the Danish Commission on Security and Disarmament (SNU), and Aarhus University's Fund of 1953. Where nothing else is indicated, translations from Danish into English have been carried out by myself.

J. H. H.   *Aarhus, August 1993*

ABBREVIATIONS

AES	Alternative Economic Strategy
CAP	Common Agricultural Policy (European Community)
CLV	Labour Campaign for Victory (Labour, Britain)
CLPD	Campaign for Labour Party Democracy (Labour, Britain)
COREPER	Committee of Permanent Representatives (European Community)
CSCE	Conference on Security and Cooperation in Europe
CSPEC	Confederation of Socialist Parties in the European Community
EC	European Community
ECOFIN	The Council of Economics and Finance Ministers (European Community)
ECSC	European Coal and Steel Community
ECU	European Currency Unit
EEC	European Economic Community
EP	European Parliament
EPC	European Political Cooperation
EFTA	European Free Trade Area
EMCF	European Monetary Cooperation Fund
EMS	European Monetary System
EMU	Economic and Monetary Union
ERM	Exchange Rate Mechanism
ETUC	European Trade Union Confederation
FRG	Federal Republic of Germany
GDR	German Democratic Republic
GATT	General Agreement on Trade and Tariffs
IMF	International Monetary Fund
LCC	Labour Coordinating Committee (Labour, Britain)
LO	Landsorganisationen (Confederation of Trade Unions, Denmark)
MEP	Member of the European Parliament
MP	Member of Parliament
MWU	Metal Workers' Union (Metalarbejderforbundet, Denmark)

NATO	North Atlantic Treaty Organization
NEC	National Executive Committee (Labour, Britain)
OECD	Organization of Economic Cooperation and Development
PLP	Parliamentary Labour Party
PS	Parti Socialiste (Socialist Party, France)
SCLV	Socialist Campaign for Labour Victory (Labour, Britain)
SDP	Social Democratic Party (Britain, Socialdemokratiet, Denmark)
SEA	Single European Act (European Community)
SPD	Sozialdemokratische Partei Deutschlands (Social Democratic Party, West Germany)
SID	Specialarbejderforbundet i Danmark (Manual Labourers' Union, Denmark)
SFIO	Section Française de l'Internationale Ouvrière (Socialist Party, France)
SPP	Socialist Peoples' Party (Socialistisk Folkeparti, Denmark)
TGWU	Transport and General Workers' Union (Britain)
TUC	Trades Union Congress (Britain)
VAT	Value Added Tax
WEU	Western European Union

Introduction

"British withdrawal from the Community is the right policy for Britain" (from the general election manifesto of the British Labour Party, "New Hope for Britain", May 1983).

"The European Community must become both deeper and wider in its membership. It should also have a more substantial agenda and a greater ability to act on it" (from the Labour Party policy review *Looking to the Future*, May 1990).

"... [W]e reject steps towards Union, we do not wish to abandon the right of veto, we do not want more powers for the European Parliament and we do not wish to shift the balance between Community institutions" (from the "preface" to *An Open Europe*, report of the Europe Committee of the Danish Social Democratic Party, July 1986).

"Everything indicates that the Social Democratic Party and the Government are about to agree on the contents of an EC union" (statement of the chairwoman of the Social Democratic Parliamentary Group, Ritt Bjerregaard, *Jyllands-Posten*, 6 August 1990).

This is a study of political parties and political integration in the European Community (EC). It compares the British Labour Party's and the Danish Social Democratic Party's (SDP) policies on the EC from the 1960s until today, and analyses the character and dynamics of these social democratic parties' respective relationships with EC institutions.

As the quotations above suggest, the positions of both the British Labour Party and the Danish SDP on the question of EC membership and of the EC's development have undergone important changes. This has been so primarily but not exclusively in the 1980s. Thus, open hostility towards British EC membership has at times characterised the Labour Party. Similarly, the Danish SDP has for long periods upheld significant reservations on the evolution of the European Community, even if it has never adopted the directly hostile positions of Labour. Yet by the beginning of the 1990s, both political parties had formulated policies on the EC which advocated a strengthening of the Community in various respects.

Why have the EC policies of the two parties developed in this way? The aim of this study is to provide some answers to this question. In doing so we formulate a number of more general propositions on factors influencing the relation of social democratic parties to a supranational institution as the European Community or, to put it more precisely, on factors influencing "political attitude integration".[1]

In the tradition of the neofunctionalist approach to regional integration, the level of attitude integration can be defined as the degree to which expectations and activities are directed towards EC institutions. Attitude integration would thus include (1) the degree to which support is expressed for national membership of the EC, and (2) the degree to which support is expressed for increased supranationality in the Community.[2] The level of supranationality in the EC is in turn defined by three variables: (1) the scope of regulation adopted at the Community level and accepted as binding by participating states, (2) the number of issue areas in which regulation is adopted following majority decision making procedures, and (3) the extent of authority in various issue areas conceded to international institutions.[3]

In examining the dynamics of the two parties' respective EC policies this study also seeks to demonstrate the fruitfulness of analysing party policies towards the European Community with outset in a number of basic assumptions about the character of political parties generally. Thus, when we later formulate our propositions regarding factors prompting changes in social democratic EC policy, we make the following assumptions: (1) parties have a national social basis, and parties' patterns of

---

1) Both the Labour Party and the Danish SDP will be referred to as social democratic parties. Furthermore, and as we shall discuss later, "party" refers to both the formal party leadership, the parliamentary party, and rank and file party activists. Trade unions with close formal or informal ties with one or more of these groupings and social groups whose electoral support for the party is particularly high constitute the parties' social basis.

2) An account of the neofunctionalist theory of international integration will be provided in Chapter 3. This definition of attitude integration approximates the definition of political integration in early neofunctionalist studies, cf. Ernst B. Haas, *The Uniting of Europe* (London: Stevens and Sons, Ltd., 1958), p. 12, and Leon N. Lindberg, *The Political Dynamics of European Economic Integration* (London: Oxford University Press, 1963), p. 6. Here and in the following, the terms "region" and "regional" will refer to groups of contiguous nation-states.

3) Supranationality is thus studied as a multidimensional phenomenon, an approach also applied by Haas, cf. Ernst B. Haas, *The Uniting of Europe*, pp. 32-59.

general policy goals reflect the perceived common interests of this basis; (2) the realisation of these general policy goals is sought only for this national social basis; (3) parties seek to achieve their general policy goals at the most efficient institutional level, i.e., at the level where goal achievement for the national social basis involves the lowest costs; and (4) political parties are guided by a real rather than a formal understanding of international political institutions, i.e., that such institutions are seen to be significant only to the extent they reflect real power structures or structures of interest.

We thus proceed from the assumption that social democratic parties are neither nationalist nor internationalist parties but, rather, national-instrumental political actors. They are not nationalist in the sense that they do not reject the pursuit of a given goal within a supranational framework simply because the framework is supranational. Neither are they internationalist, as they are expected to pursue goal realisation only for their national social basis and not for groups defined independently of nationality. These assumptions are compatible with a framework for analysis of party behaviour synthesising a "sociological" and an "economic" understanding of parties which will be developed in Chapter Two.

To sum up, this study has to two objectives: first, to examine the dynamics of social democratic parties' policies on the European Community, and, second, to evaluate the fruitfulness of a number of underlying assumptions about the nature of parties' EC policies, encapsulated in the concept of "national instrumentality".

The Research Context

The study of regional political integration in Western Europe has a long tradition. The functionalist and neofunctionalist theories have constituted two important alternative approaches to understanding processes of integration, even though functionalism is a normative rather than a falsifiable empirical theory.[4] Both traditions treat international integra-

---

4) The functionalist integration theory, which should not be confused with sociological functionalism, is outlined in David Mitrany, *A Working Peace System* (Chicago: Qudrangle Books, 1966), first published in 1943. See also A.J.R. Groom and Paul Taylor (eds.), *Functionalism. Theory and Practice in International Relations* (London: University of London Press, 1975). Classic neofunctionalist studies include Ernst B. Haas, *The Uniting of Europe* (London: Stevens and

tion as a process involving the relocation of political expectations, activities or loyalties from the national to some supranational institutional centre or, as in a number of neofunctionalist studies, as the process of gradual replacement of national political decision-making with supranational decision-making. Furthermore, both approaches view this replacement process as involving an internal dynamic which prompts the process to develop continually once initiated. Intergovernmentalism is a third approach to political integration in Western Europe. Developed primarily in response to the empirical inadequacy of the dynamic neofunctionalist theory, intergovernmentalism focuses on the persistent strength of the nation-state in the EC. The approach assumes that supranational decision-making will replace national decision making only to a very limited extent, as nation-states and national bureaucracies jealously defend their authority and because the nature of the international system works to increase fragmentation between states.[5]

However, the behaviour of political parties in the process of regional political integration has been the subject of fewer studies, and those studies which exist have generally not dealt with more comprehensive theoretical discussions of integration or the character of political parties in the context of integration. The most well-known studies which focus exclusively on political parties and political integration in the European context do not examine the nature of parties' relationship with supranational institutions in depth; nor do they discuss the dynamics of integration, as their analysis of factors underlying party policy changes typically remains unsystematic.[6] In the neofunctionalist tradition, the

Sons, Ltd.), and *Beyond the Nation State* (Stanford: Stanford University Press, 1964), Leon N. Lindberg, *The Political Dynamics of European Economic Integration* (London: Oxford University Press, 1963), Joseph S. Nye, *Peace in Parts: Integration and Conflict in Regional Organization* (Boston: Little & Brown, 1971), and Leon N. Lindberg and Stuart S. Scheingold, *Europe's Would Be Polity* (Englewood Cliffs, N. J.: Prentice Hall, 1970).

5) Although Stanley Hoffman in his "Obstinate or Obsolete? The Fate of the Nation-States and the Case of Europe", *Daedalus*, vol. 95 (Summer 1966), pp. 862-915, does not make use of the concept of intergovernmentalism, his article is normally counted as the first major contribution in the tradition. Other studies include Donald Puchala, "Of Blind Men, Elephants and Regional Integration", *Journal of Common Market Studies*, vol. 10, no. 3 (September 1972),pp. 267-284; Paul Taylor, "The Politics of the European Communities: the Confederal Phase", *World Politics*, vol. 27, no. 3 (April 1975), pp. 336-360, and Paul Taylor, *The Limits of European Integration* (London: University of London Press, 1983).

6) This is the case with Kevin Featherstone, *Socialists and European Integration: A Comparative History* (Manchester: Manchester University Press, 1988), which provides a descriptive overview of Western European social democratic parties' EC policies. Michael Newman's *Socialism and European Unity: The Dilemma of the Left in Britain and France* (London: Junction Books, 1983) is also a largely descriptive study. In his *The SPD and European Integration* (Farnborough: Saxon House, 1974), William E. Paterson analyses the West German

development of party positions towards the supranational institutions of the EC and the ECSC (the European Coal and Steel Community) has been of some importance. In what later became known as the first neofunctionalist study of European integration, Haas analysed the development of policies towards the ECSC in a number of nationally important political parties, including several social democratic parties.[7] Specifically regarding the latter category Haas concluded that the development of policies from the frequently very sceptical view of the ECSC in 1952 to a position calling for increased supranational authority to ECSC institutions in 1957 was evidence of "the expansive logic of sector integration", in which the evolution of the West German SPD's European policies constituted the clearest example.

However, in Haas' study and in neofunctionalist studies of European integration generally, there are few or inadequate attempts to understand such policy changes in depth and in the national context in which they take place. Haas limits himself to laconically stating that "[t]he case of the SPD is by far the most striking and the most significant in demonstrating the logic of sector integration in shaping new attitudes, if the ideology of the group fits the demands of the situation".[8] No satisfactory answers are provided to the questions of how such a "fit" between ideology and situation arises or of which specific circumstances produce changes in the positions of a political grouping towards supranational institutions.[9]

One of the conclusions from several decades of research on European political integration is that national governments continue to hold the key to any major developments within and around the EC.[10] If we accept this conclusion we must acknowledge a need to understand the dynamics which in the short or long term, directly or indirectly affect the policies of national governments toward European integration.[11] The

---

SPD's policies towards European supranational institutions more systematically, but West Germany in many respects represents a special case, as we shall argue later. Social democratic EC policies have been more thoroughly analysed than those of other categories of parties.

7) Ernst B. Haas, *The Uniting of Europe*, pp. 113-161.

8) Ernst B. Haas, *The Uniting of Europe*, p. 136.

9) The lack of attention directed to the domestic context in Haas' study is noted in William Paterson, *The SPD and European Integration*, p. ix.

10) This has been one result of the intergovernmental critique of the neofunctionalist approach to EC integration. The neofunctionalists tended to place national governments on roughly the same footing as other political actors.

11) This point has been noted by a number of scholars: e.g. Stuart A. Scheingold, "Domestic and International Consequences of Regional Integration", in Leon N. Lindberg and Stuart S. Scheingold (eds.), *Regional Integration: Theory and Research* (Cambridge: Harvard University

development of policies in major parties of the national political system here constitutes a fruitful object for research. Hence, studies of political parties and regional integration should be given more prominence. This study attempts to make a contribution to the needed research.

Why study precisely the EC policies of the British Labour Party and the Danish SDP? There are several reasons. First, the focus on two nationally important social democratic parties is motivated by an interest in the tensions which seem likely to emerge when the social democratic reform strategy, relying on comprehensive national state intervention in the market economy, confronts a supranational organisation which to a great extent promotes market regulation of society on an international basis. Do social democratic parties view the European Community as a threat to the desired national regulation of society? And how do social democratic parties envisage the evolution of the EC once a fundamental national dependency on membership of the Community is perceived and acknowledged? The potential tension between the social democratic desire to regulate the market economy and a basically market liberalist EC can lead to the formulation of several theoretical propositions.

Furthermore, there are good empirical reasons to analyse precisely the British and the Danish Labour parties as cases. Ever since EC membership became a reality for these two states in 1973, Denmark and Britain have constituted the two must reluctant member states. Almost regardless of the actual political composition of the two governments, both Denmark and the UK have opposed most measures entailing a strengthening of the supranational elements in EC cooperation. A development as the one suggested by the quotations above, in which two nationally important political parties increasingly come to favour a strengthening of the EC framework in certain areas, may therefore have important effects on Danish and British EC policies. Given the traditional positions of Denmark and the UK, it could potentially also be

---

Press, 1971), pp. 374-398; Steven J. Warnecke, "The Study of the European Community: A Critical Appraisal", in *Research Resources: The European Community* (New York: Council for European Studies, 1977), Donald J. Puchala, "Worm Cans and Worth Taxes: Fiscal Harmonization and the European Policy Process", in Hellen Wallace, William Wallace and Carole Webb (eds.), *Policy Making in the European Community* (Chicester: John Wiley, 1983), pp. 237-264; Simon Bulmer, "Domestic Politics and European Policy Making", *Journal of Common Market Studies*, vol. 21, no. 4 (December 1983), pp. 349-363; Carsten Lehmann Sørensen and Karen Siune, "Is the Theory of European Integration Dead or Alive? The Case of Danish Political Parties", paper presented at the European Consortium for Political Research meeting in Louvain, April 1976; Henry R. Nau, "From Integration to Interdependence: Gains, Losses, and Continuing Gaps, *International Organization*, vol. 33, no. 1 (Winter 1979), pp. 119-147.

significant for the course of the overall European integration process.

Both the Danish SDP and the British Labour party have been out of office for long periods. Labour lost office in 1979 and has not returned to power. The Danish SDP was out of office in the entire period from 1982 to 1993. However, even when not forming the government, both parties have constituted the major national opposition party, and one cannot understand national policy making without including them. Denmark's social democrats, being the largest single party despite being in opposition, have exerted considerable direct influence on national policy formulation in a number of issue areas. In the British political system, with its mode of representation and its two-party system, the opposition party has much fewer direct opportunities to influence policy. Yet the main opposition party can still exert influence on the national political agenda and, depending on the concrete circumstances, can pose such an electoral threat to the government in office so as to indirectly force it to adopt new policies.

Finally, focusing on the Danish SDP and the British Labour has methodological advantages as well. Both parties have experienced significant changes of policy on the EC, to some degree in the 1970s and to an even greater extent during the 1980s. Thus, the value of the dependent variable, previously defined as "attitude integration", varies considerably over time, providing relatively good possibilities to observe those factors prompting such variation. The extent of variance enables us to analyse the dynamics of attitude integration, allowing us to go beyond a purely static analysis.

SOCIAL DEMOCRACY AND REGIONAL INTEGRATION

As mentioned, this study attempts to formulate and examine some general propositions about the nature of social democratic parties' relationship with EC institutions and about the dynamics of this relationship.

The lack of previous theory-building in this area, however, does not mean that the analysis of the two parties' EC policies will take place in a complete theoretical vacuum. Existing propositions about the behaviour of political parties, on the one hand, and on the nature and dynamics of regional political integration, on the other hand, allow us to formulate three propositions about those factors which could influence the level of attitude integration for social democratic parties. The contents of these propositions are outlined briefly below and shall be elaborated in more detail later.

The Internal Dynamic of Integration

The neofunctionalist preoccupation with the dynamics of regional integration led to the formulation of a number of hypotheses about the "internal dynamics" of integration. The integration process was seen to contain an internal dynamic, insofar as the establishment of a supra-national bureaucracy and initiation of regional market liberalisations would create problems solveable only by further strengthening of this bureaucracy or by further market liberalisations. Alternatively, this would affect the balance between different political forces and release more intensive integrative pressures. Even when insufficient attention is directed to political parties in this approach, as we have argued above, it is possible to formulate propositions in the neofunctionalist tradition concerning the importance of regional market liberalisations for social democratic EC policies.

Here, we may take as a starting point the fact that social democratic parties have certain general policy goals, the realisation of which requires comprehensive state intervention in the national market economy. Furthermore, we note that the EC always has constituted a predominately market liberalist project, which imposes limits on the degree and nature of state intervention exerted by its member states.

On this basis, we can formulate the proposition that social democratic parties will reject the establishment of supranational decision-making on regional market liberalisations. However, if such decision-making is established in spite of this rejection or extended to cover the nation-state of the parties in question, they will gradually increase their support for EC membership and for the adoption of binding EC regulation which if implemented would take the Community beyond the exclusive promotion of regional market liberalisations. In the same way, we could expect a social democratic rejection of an increase in EC decision-making capacity aimed at regional market liberalisations, while the implementation of such measures would result in social democratic calls for a strengthening of the EC's capacity to adopt and carry out market intervening measures.

The proposition that social democratic parties will initially reject EC membership is plausible as an extension of such parties' mistrust of market regulation of society and the corresponding reliance on national state intervention as an instrument for reform. For social democratic parties, regional market liberalisations adopted in the EC framework may constitute a threat to the possibility of national state intervention. However, once EC decision-making on regional market liberalisations has been established or come to include the state of the party in question, it may mean that this state grows economically dependent on continued membership of the Community, as regional market liberalisations cause a restructuring of economic relationships among the member states.

This restructuring could have profound consequences. Thus, at the point where the party in question acknowledges a fundamental national economic dependency on EC membership, the supranational level becomes an arena for the political struggle over regulation of society. This means that social democratic parties will attempt to shape the predominately market liberalist EC according to social democratic visions and perceptions, thus implying a high level of attitude integration. The Community will be pushed to pursue interventionist policies where in the perceptions of the party such policies will support the achievement of general policy goals at the national level. Furthermore, social democratic parties will pursue the goals of having the EC equipped with sufficient decision-making capacity for intervention in the market, to the extent that this would not stand in the way of intervention at the national level.

Domestic Determinants of Attitude Integration

Propositions about the internal dynamics of integration cannot stand alone. As mentioned, Haas' early study of parties and regional integration was flawed in its neglect of the domestic context within which party positions vis-à-vis supranational institutions develop. It is a clear possibility that domestic national conditions and developments have decisive effects on the evolution of parties' attitude integration.

In keeping with the assumption that parties have certain general policy goals, we can cite various national developments which would appear to be plausible explanations for changes in attitude integration. Hence, in one scenario, developments initiated at the national level would alter the efficiency of national regulation in an issue area in a way which is difficult or costly to reverse. This would in turn prompt changes in the positions of national political parties towards EC institutions and EC regulation. Where the efficiency of national intervention in an issue area has diminished, attitude integration could be expected to grow. Here social democratic parties may favour increased EC intervention in the market and possibly also a strengthening of EC decision-making capacity in the area as a compensation for the lost national possibilities of regulation.

A second way in which domestic developments could entail changes in attitude integration might be via a given party's changed perceptions of the political possibilities for achieving general policy goals in the national arena. Thus, a party's reduction in influence on national policy formation, as occurred with the Danish SDP or the British Labour Party after they became opposition parties in the 1980s, could lead to a re-evaluation of supranational institutions and supranational regulation: The party in question, if it perceives its national channels for influence to be blocked, may increase its support for that binding supranational regulation which in its perception would contribute to the achievement of its general policy goals at the national level. Support for an increase in EC decision-making capacity in issue areas where regulation is seen as desirable by the party in question could also be motivated in this way.

Finally, while political parties, as we have argued, have certain general policy goals, the realisation of such goals in representative democracies depends on support for the party by the electorate. Here it is possible that a political party's change of attitude towards the EC is motivated instrumentally, as a means of increasing the party's electoral appeal to the electorate: Greater appeal of this kind may indirectly improve the party's possibilities of achieving general and intrinsically valued policy goals. However, if such changes in attitude integration are to be seen as domestically motivated, the preceding evolution of public opinion should not result from the actions of supranational institutions or the effects of progressing regional market liberalisations.

External Determinants of Attitude Integration

Neofunctionalist propositions have been subjected to other criticisms than the downgrading of the national context in which processes of integration may develop. Neofunctionalist approaches have been accused of ignoring the external international surroundings within which integration occurs. Thus, developments external to the state in question and not prompted by actions of supranational bureaucracy or regional market liberalisations may be seen as influencing parties' EC policies.

We can single out two possible trajectories of development here. First is the possibility of national exclusion. Other important states may wish to undertake reforms of the European Community, prompting changes in a party's attitudes. Thus, a stern refusal to accept the wishes of these states can rarely prevent them from following their own desired course of action, in the most radical scenario within a different formal framework than the Rome Treaty. To the extent that decisions made in the framework of supranational institutions will also affect excluded states and political actors within these states, this kind of development would entail a loss of opportunities for significant political influence. This may in turn endanger the realisation or protection of the general policy goals of a party within an excluded state inasmuch as the positions of the party are not represented in the necessary supranational fora. In this situation, the party may find it in its interest to seek a compromise and to attempt to influence developments in putting forward its own proposals for EC reforms, proposals which in the perceptions of the party would promote the protection or achievement of one or more of its general policy goals. For this type of dynamic to be categorised as an external development, however, the emerging desire of important EC states to undertake reforms cannot be based on previous actions of supranational institutions, nor on advancing regional market liberalisations. If this were the case, a given political party's "reactive" change of its EC policy would be part of an "internal" dynamic of integration.

As the second type of externally induced development, a party's changing attitude towards the EC's evolution may result from developments which, in terms of national security, increase the security political importance of institutionalised international cooperation. In a situation where external constraints on the reemergence of traditional national conflicts disappear from a region, as has been the case in Europe since 1989 following the partial superpower retraction, the security dimension may move to the centre of the political stage. Thus, strengthening the EC's decision-making capacity or extending its areas of competence may constitute a means of enhancing flexible structures of balance between states, structures which, within an agreed upon institutional framework, reflect the real relation of strength between these states. Reinforcing the

EC framework may thus enhance a stable power balancing structure in Europe without allowing the continent to retreat to the conflict-prone counteracting type of coalition-building of earlier decades and centuries. Furthermore, when the security political development entails the emergence of a potentially dominant state in Europe, *in casu* the unified Germany, other European states and political actors within those states would findt it advantageous to encounter the greater state in a strengthened multilateral framework rather than having to deal with the larger state in a bilateraal encounter.

METHODOLOGY

While the explanatory strength of the above propositions will be examined in a comparative framework, this study also contains important hermeneutic elements. To the extent that behavioural comparative methods are employed, we pursue two different research strategies. For both political parties we utilise the classical "comparable cases strategy", and in comparing the national political systems of Great Britain and Denmark we apply the "most different systems design". The fruitfulness of our underlying basic assumption - that parties in relation to the EC constitute what we have termed national-instrumental actors - will be evaluated through the analysis of the various specific propositions on factors influencing attitude integration. Since these propositions all rest on the assumption that parties are national-instrumental actors, this starting point is fruitful to the extent the propositions provide a covering understanding of the development of the two parties' EC policies.

Comparable Cases and Most Different Systems Design

The comparable cases strategy seeks to isolate the effect of the independent and explaining variable on the dependent and explained variable, comparing units which ideally are similar in all respects except for the values of the independent and dependent variables. In principle it is, thus, possible to control for third variables by observing only a small number of units. The most important problem posed by this research strategy is the identification of "comparable cases", that is, units of research which differ on the independent and dependent variable but are similar in all other ways. A prominent, though partial, solution to the problem is the employment of diachronic comparisons where the same unit is observed at different points in time and where the independent, explaining variable displays different values at different times.[12] This strategy will be applied here. Thus, the EC policies of the SDP and the Labour Party are observed over time. When changes of policy occur, we may look to the environment of the party in order to identify which of the independent variables contained in the propositions developed above has changed its value prior to this policy change.

What are the methodological advantages of comparing parties in two distinct national settings? By comparing systems following the "most different systems design" we are able to control for variables which display different values between systems.[13] A relationship between two variables within a specific system, such as Great Britain for example, may be shaped by characteristics particular to this system. However, if an identical relationship between variables is found in different systems, we can exclude the explanatory power of variables with different values between these systems, variables which we could not *a priori* dismiss as irrelevant. If, on the other hand, no such identical relationship can be established, it means that variables differing between systems must be of importance.

Hence, if the hypothesised relations are found in both Britain and Denmark, it means that variables with different values between Britain and Denmark, such as size, party system or mode of representation, are irrelevant to these relationships. Correspondingly, it suggests that one or more of these variables is important if a relationship between variables differs in Britain and Denmark.

Hermeneutic Elements

In the context of the current study, behavioural research strategies cannot provide the final answers as to which independent variables have caused changes in the dependent variable of "attitude integration". The comparable cases strategy, applied through diachronic comparisons,

---

12) E.g. Arendt Lijphardt, "Comparative Politics and the Comparative Method", *American Political Science Review*, vol. 65, no. 3 (September 1971), pp. 689-690.
13) The most different systems design is developed in Adam Przeworski and Henry Teune, *The Logic of Comparative Social Inquiry* (London: John Wiley, 1970).

constitutes but a partial solution to the problem of control for third variables, as no context can strictly speaking be considered the same at different points of time. A number of relevant variables may change their value over time, and some variables may change their value in a manner so as to render particularly difficult the isolation of their effect on the dependent variable. For example, where a given variable measures what could be termed structural characteristics and therefore changes its value only over a long period of time, its effects will be interwoven with the effects of other relevant variables changing their value during this period.

In this context, well-founded and well-documented interpretation in the tradition of historical research and Weberian sociology plays an important role. The analysis will seek to place the observer in the positions of important political actors, attempting to understand action from their point of view, while it in the Weberian tradition assumes that they operate with instrumental rationality. This perspective facilitates the assessment of the relative importance of factors underlying specific changes of party policy. That is, we will seek to show how a given change of policy is *understandable* as a reaction to one or another change in the party's environment.

The evaluation of the explanatory strength of the propositions formulated above, and of the underlying analytical framework's fruitfulness, will thus entail a considerable amount of interpretation of the behaviour, the statements, and perceptions of the party leaderships in the concrete context.[14]

The Possibilities of Generalisation

Naturally, we cannot arrive at statistically generalisable conclusions on the basis of the study of two political parties not chosen at random from the universal population of social democratic parties. However, there is evidence of a certain non-statistical representativeness of the observed parties; both the Danish SDP and the British Labour Party undoubtedly

---

14) In this sense, the methodology of this study is a comparative *approach* rather than a comparative *method*. Prominent recent examples applying a comparative approach include Peter A. Hall, *Governing the Economy. The Politics of State Intervention in Britain and France* (Cambridge: Polity Press, 1986) and Gösta Esping-Andersen, *Politics Against Markets. The Social Democratic Road to Power* (Princeton: Princeton University Press, 1985).

share many important characteristics with other social democratic
political parties. Electoral support for these parties comes predominantly
from blue collar and lower white collar strata of the population. Several
organisational similarities exist, just as clear affinities in terms of
general policy goals are expressed through membership in the Socialist
International held by most social democratic parties. In other words,
there is reason to believe that the conclusions of this study can be
applied to other social democratic parties than those examined here.

Furthermore, statistical generalisations are far from the only sort of
generalisations which contribute to our understanding of a given field of
study. Valuable knowledge is generated, as the exploration of events
contributes to our theoretical understanding of the social world, and
generalisation to theoretical propositions does not require the observation
of any specific number of units.[15] A single case study can contribute
more to our understanding than a host of statistical studies involving a
large "n", but only if this case study leads to new theoretical developments or the reformulation of existing theory.

THE STRUCTURE OF THE STUDY

Having introduced the study's research question, the propositions
following it, and the methods to be applied in evaluating the explanatory
strength of these propositions, Chapter Two will address the question of
the party as a political actor. Heretofore we have proceeded from the
argument that social democratic parties have certain general policy goals
which help guide specific policy developments. This implies a particular
view of the nature of political parties which will be discussed, resulting
in a framework for the analysis of party behaviour. Chapter Three
narrows the focus to party behaviour towards the European Community,
and the propositions formulated above will be elaborated in more detail.

Chapters Four through Nine contain the case studies of the British
Labour Party's and the Danish SDP's EC policies. In Chapter Four and
Seven attention is focused on the positions of Labour and the SDP
respectively towards EC membership as this question became topical in
the 1960s and early 1970s, and on the parties' policies on the EC's

---

15) Robert K. Yin, *Case Study Research*, (London: Sage, 1984). See also H.A. Scarrow, *Comparative*
   Political Analysis. An Introduction (New York: Harper and Row, 1969), pp. 7-8.

development once membership had become a reality in 1973. Chapter Five describes and analyses the British Labour Party's approach to the European Community in the wake of the recessions of the 1970s and the party's adoption of the policy of British withdrawal from the EC in the early 1980s. It also focuses on the party's positions towards the Single European Act, the 1986 reform of the Rome Treaty which instigated the drive towards a Single Market in the EC. Chapter Six analyses the party's reactions as the Single Market programme got under way and describes the Labour Party's approach to the plans for Economic and Monetary Union in the EC, as this question reentered the European political agenda in the late 1980s and early 1990s. Chapter Eight contains the analysis of the Danish SDP's EC policies before and after the adoption of the Single European Act and the February 1986 advisory referendum in Denmark on the reform, just as attention is focused on the party's reactions to the advancing Single Market programme, to the question of a socalled social dimension to the Single Market, and to the question of environmental protection conerns in the Single Market. Chapter Nine describes and discusses the EC policies of the Danish SDP in the period from 1989 to the start in December 1990 of the intergovernmental conferences which resulted in the Maastricht Treaty. The SDP's role in the formulation of the Danish Government Memorandum on EC reforms is particularly important here.

Chapter Ten sums up the analysis, evaluating the explanatory strength of the propositions on the dynamics of social democratic EC policy and appraising the fruitfulness of the underlying assumptions on the character of political parties. Finally, Chapter Eleven relates the findings of this study to studies of other social democratic parties and to the ongoing debate on the nature of the European integration process.

PART I

Social Democracy and Regional Integration: Theories and Propositions

2

Party Behaviour and
Social Democracy

The object of analysis here is the development of two political parties' policies on the European Community. This chapter will examine in more detail the assumptions underlying the propositions on party attitudes towards the EC introduced in the previous chapter. It thus relates the current study and the propositions which guide it to the literature on the nature of political parties.

In doing so, it describes two dominant alternative understandings of the character of political parties and of party behaviour: the "sociological" and the "economic". We will discuss the relevance of these approaches and some attempts at synthesis between them for the study of party policy change. We then turn our attention to the two political parties in question, the Danish SDP and the British Labour Party, as well as the national political systems in which these parties operate. This leads to the formulation of a framework for the analysis of social democratic party behaviour.

APPROACHES TO THE STUDY OF POLITICAL PARTIES

While the social sciences exhibit a long tradition for the study of political parties, a survey of the existing literature reveals only a limited degree of comprehensive theory building. This may be due to the fact that theory construction on political parties is particularly problematic, since parties constitute a distinct type of organisation operating in a unique environment. As political parties are supposed to represent the general preferences of the electorate or to reflect the social conditions for society as a whole, as well as to influence the development of society, it is difficult to envisage a comprehensive theory on parties which is not at the same time a general theory of society.[1] Even though there exists no comprehensive theory of political parties, we can nevertheless distinguish between two different approaches to political parties which are relevant in the context of this study.

The sociological approach focuses on the consequences of the unique characteristics of parties, attempting to understand them primarily as expressions of general underlying phenomena of society. Consequently, this approach is macrotheoretical, and propositions specifically concerning party behaviour tend to constitute a by-product of theoretical efforts seeking to understand society in general. The alternative economic approach abstracts from the general societal conditions surrounding political parties in order to undertake deductive model analysis. On the basis of a few assumptions primarily regarding the motivations of candidates for election, the economic tradition attempts to develop precise microlevel hypotheses about for example party behaviour in elections and the effects of electoral laws. The core of this understanding of political parties is not that parties reflect social cleavages of different sorts, but rather, that parties are competitive organisations created with one objective: to defeat opposing parties in elections.

The Sociological Approach

The sociological approach to political parties has one of its most important foundations in Marxist theory, but the Marxist tradition does not provide any elaborate theoretical understanding of parties. Marx's writings often apply the concepts of class and party synonymously, understanding the party as the political form of classes' organisation.[2] As class is defined in terms of its relation to the forces of production, the party is derived directly from the existing social formation. This "class reductionist" conception of parties leaves little room for political parties as an object of study in itself, just as it is implied that parties play no independent role in the continuing development of society. Yet this is not the only understanding of political parties which appears in Marx's writings. The role of parties in the shaping of working class conscious-

---

1) Cf. Klaus von Beyme, "Theoretische Probleme der Parteienforschung", *Politische Vierteljahres-schrift*, vol. 24, no. 3 (October 1983), pp. 241-252.
2) E.g. Karl Marx and Friederich Engels, *Werke*, vol. 7 (Berlin: Dietz Verlag, 1964), p. 401.

ness is implicit at other points. Thus, in the Communist Manifesto the proletarian party is "the organisation of the proletariat to class".[3]

Much non-Marxist research on political parties of the postwar period has proceeded on the basis of fundamental Marxian conceptions, even if the revolutionary perspective has evidently vanished. In a classic early study in political sociology, Lipset claims that

> "[i]n every democracy conflict among different groups is expressed through political parties which basically represent a 'democratic translation of the class struggle'. Even though many parties renounce the principle of class conflict or loyalty, an analysis of their appeals and their support suggests that they do represent the interests of different classes".[4]

Sartori has criticised this understanding, as these propositions cannot be falsified. That a party appeals to class interests may thus indicate that class support is dwindling, and the support of a particular class for a party does not entail that the party represents that class - it may indeed betray or misrepresent it. Furthermore, the claim that parties represent class interests presupposes a general theory of politics as a struggle between classes. However, a theory like this cannot be clear, since the interests of one class may coincide with those of other classes. Finally, the notion of "objective class interests" is problematic, just as the concept of class representation is seen to overlook the problems of collective action for entire classes.[5]

Perhaps partly as a result of problems stemming from the class understanding of political parties, Lipset and Rokkan introduced the "cleavage approach" to parties and party systems. The characteristics of party systems described as specific party configurations in different national and historical contexts constitute the primary object of study here. Party systems are studied as a "translation of conflict" and parties are seen as "alliances in conflicts over policies and value commitments within the larger body politic".[6] The number of potentially relevant sociocultural cleavages in understanding parties and party systems is considerable,

---

3) The emphasis on the active and creative role of parties comes to the fore in the works of Lenin and Gramsci and in the Gramscian concept of the "hegemonic party", contrasted to the "class party" often implied in classical Marxism. For an analysis of Marxist understandings of parties, see Wieland Elfferding, "Klassenpartei und Hegemonie. Zur impliziten Parteientheorie des Marxismus", *Argument Sonderband AS 91* (Berlin: Argument Verlag, 1983).

4) Seymour Martin Lipset, *Political Man* (New York: Doubleday, 1960), p. 220.

5) Giovanni Sartori, "The Sociology of Parties: A Critical Review", 1968, reprinted in Peter Mair (ed.), *The West European Party System* (Oxford: Oxford University Press, 1990), pp. 150-182.

6) Seymour Martin Lipset and Stein Rokkan, "Cleavage Structures, Party Systems, and Voter Alignments", 1967, reprinted in Peter Mair (ed.), *ibid.*, pp. 91-138.

and includes factors such as geographical location, language, ethnicity, class and religion. In their subsequent efforts, Lipset and Rokkan compared the development and outlook of national party systems, concluding that the party systems of Western Europe froze in the 1920s and that the party systems in the period from 1945 to the 1960s, when Lipset and Rokkan wrote, reflected very much the same cleavages as in the early part of this century.

Their claim was immediately challenged, as electoral volatility and upheaval in party systems appeared to contradict many of Lipset's and Rokkan's propositions. Kirchmeimer introduced the concept of "catch-all parties", compared to traditional political parties characterised by (1) a drastic reduction of the party's ideological baggage, (2) a further strengthening of the top leadership groups, (3) a deemphasis of the *classe gardeé*, specific social class or denominational clientele in favour of recruiting voters from among the population at large, and (4) an increasing emphasis on securing access to a variety of interest groups.[7] Thus, modern catch-all parties increasingly cut the traditional organisational ties with the society of which they are a part and begin to operate at a distance from their constituencies. Parties become "top-down" instead of "bottom-up" organisations and choose to operate on the electoral market rather than to narrow the market through close links with and appeals to specific groups, just as electoral achievements are built upon conditional voter support rather than on a sense of identification.[8]

The Economic Approach

The economic approach to the study of political parties is not concerned with inductively derived generalisations of the kind generated in the

---

7) Otto Kirchheimer, "The Transformation of the Western European Party Systems", in Joseph Lapalombara and Myron Weiner (eds.), *Political Parties and Political Development* (Princeton: Princeton University Press, 1966), pp. 177-200. See also Otto Kirchheimer "The Waning of Opposition in Parliamentary Regimes", *Social Research*, vol. 24, no. 2 (1957), pp. 127-156. Additional elements which may be said to have furthered the emergence of catch-all party characteristics since Kirchheimer's original analysis include public funding of political parties, the impact of new technology and mass media changes, and the availability of new marketing techniques.

8) It should not go unnoticed that the thesis of increasing dominance of catch-all party characteristics has also been challenged, partly because it is difficult to test empirically. See Karl Dittrich, "Testing the Catch-All Thesis: Some Difficulties and Possibilities", in Hans Daalder and Peter Mair (eds.), *Western European Party Systems: Continuity and Change* (London: Sage, 1983), pp. 257-266.

sociological tradition. As a part of the rational choice tradition of social theory, this approach proceeds deductively following the methodology of neoclassical microeconomic theory; abstract agents operate in an abstract environment defined by narrow assumptions. The aim is the construction of parsimonious models with predictive force.

Paradoxically, however, the assumptions underlying the development of hypotheses in the economic approach lead to party characteristics which would be rather close to an ideal type catch-all party. In one prominent formulation, a party is defined as "a team seeking to control the governing apparatus by gaining office in a duly constituted election".[9] Individual voters and candidates for elections are assumed to be "self-interested rational actors", rationality being defined as a purely instrumental rationality of means. The "self-interest axiom" is in turn the condition that "each has a greater regard for his own safety and happiness than for the safety and happiness of others".[10] In Downs' understanding it follows that parties and candidates for elections have only one goal: to win elections. "Parties formulate policies in order to win elections, rather than win elections in order to formulate policies".[11] The individual self-interest of politicians explains this, as the lust for power, prestige, and wealth motivates the quest for office.

Assuming that (1) political preferences of voters can be ordered spatially along a left-right dimension, (2) that voters vote for the party whose policies are closest to their own preferences, and (3) that only two political parties are present, Downs concludes that the preferences of the median voter will be decisive for party policies. The median voter will determine the outcome of the election, since his or her vote decides which party will be given the majority of all votes. Consequently, it is the expectation of the model that political parties in two-party systems will converge around the same policies, for in order to win the election, both will have to appeal to the median voter.[12] However, parties can only

---

9) Anthony Downs, *An Economic Theory of Democracy* (New York: Harper and Row, 1957), p. 25.

10) *ibid.*, pp. 6, 27. To Downs, rationality means that an individual (1) is always able to make a decision when confronted with alternatives, (2) order all alternatives according to preference, (3) chooses the most preferred alternative, (4) chooses the same alternative whenever confronted with the same situation, and (5) that preference orderings are transitive.

11) *ibid.*, p. 28.

12) *ibid.*, pp. 115-22. This conclusion presupposes that each voter will in fact vote, regardless of the absolute distance between the "closest" party's policy and the voter's preferences. Furthermore, this is the simplest scenario in Downs' analysis. He also considers a multiparty system, cf. *ibid.*, pp. 125-27, but only in a situation of equally distributed voters along the scale. With voters normally distributed and assuming that there are no abstentions, the model implies

change their policies gradually and consistently, as other patterns of behaviour would damage their credibility in the eyes of the electorate.[13]

Social cleavages play no direct role for the behaviour of parties in Downs' model, as parties pursue votes, and as individual voters in choosing between parties are simply assumed to maximise their expected utility. On the other hand, these assumptions do not in themselves preclude cleavages having an effect on voter preference distributions and, hence, indirectly party behaviour.

The expectations of the "vote maximising" behaviour of political parties derived from Downs' model have encountered significant empirical problems. Hirschman notes the blatant contradictions between the expectations derived from Downs' model and the actual conduct of parties adopting unpopular platforms.[14] The continued existence in multiparty systems of parties appealing to small and declining social groups also defies the logic of vote maximising behaviour. As Hirschman sees it, Downs has overlooked the possibility of "voice" in explaining party behaviour. In a situation where voters or party activists have no party closer to their own policy preferences to which they can turn, it remains an obvious possibility for these individuals to try and influence the party line directly, inside the party organisation, and to push the party policies in the direction of own preferences.

The economic approach to political parties has generated two alternative models of party behaviour: the office-seeking party and the policy-pursuing party. The focus here is on the legislative behaviour of political parties rather than on electoral competition. Thus, early versions of the office-seeking approach view political parties in isolation not only from the general societal conditions surrounding them, but also from the fact that parties must take part in elections with regular intervals. As the term indicates, the fundamental assumption of this model is that political parties attempt not to maximise votes and win elections but to maximise office benefits, i.e. private goods awarded to recipients of governmental

---

that parties in a multiparty system will also converge around the same policies. The more complicated versions of Downs' model relax the assumptions of certainty and zero information costs and include the possibility of multi-issue situations, leading the author to argue that party ideologies simplify voters' choice between parties and reduce the costs of obtaining necessary information, just as they enable parties to spread their political appeal, cf. pp. 96-103 and 133-37.

13) *ibid.*, pp. 103-11.

14) Albert O. Hirschman, *Exit, Voice, and Loyalty* (London: Harvard University Press, 1970), p. 71.

or subgovernmental appointments. On this basis, it is predicted that in multiparty systems winning coalitions of a minimum size can be expected to form, a proposition seemingly contradicted by the frequent presence of minority governments.[15]

The policy-pursuing party, on the other hand, is assumed to maximise its effect on public policy. Developed primarily in response to the problematic assumption underlying office-seeking models that any party is willing to join any other in forming a coalition, the policy-based analysis of coalition behaviour assumes that coalitions form between parties which are connected in policy space.[16] Policy pursuit, then, influences party behaviour in this approach, but parties may still pursue government portfolios instrumentally.[17] Until recently, however, no theoretically founded propositions on this trade-off between office-seeking and policy-pursuit have been formulated. Consequently, the policy-pursuing model of party behaviour has been more difficult to refute than the office-seeking model. Prior to Kaare Ström's contribution, which we shall discuss below, the policy-pursuing model of the party should therefore be seen as the least well developed framework in the economic approach to political parties.[18]

Party Policy Formation: Attempts at Syntheses

Some efforts in the study of political parties have sought to synthesise the sociological and the economic understandings of how parties' policy positions form. In 1965 Björn Molin developed an interpretive framework

---

15) The office-seeking model was first formulated in William Riker, *The Theory of Political Coalitions* (New Haven: Yale University Press, 1962). For an elaborate version of the model and an empirical testing of it, see Lawrence C. Dodd, *Coalitions in Parliamentary Government* (Princeton: Princeton University Press, 1976).

16) Robert Axelrod, *Conflict of Interest* (Chicago: Markham, 1970), pp. 165-185.

17) Ian Budge and Michael Laver, "Office Seeking and Policy Pursuit in Coalition Theory", *Legislative Studies Quarterly*, vol. 11, no. 4 (November 1986), pp. 485-506. See also Michael Laver, "Party Competition and Party System Change. The Interaction of Coalition Bargaining and Electoral Competition", *Journal of Theoretical Politics*, vol. 1, no. 3 (July 1989), pp. 301-324.

18) To the extent that policy influence is seen as an end in itself, it should be noted that the policy-pursuing model of party behaviour belongs only to the rational choice tradition in a broad methodological sense. If policies are valued intrinsically, this runs counter to the assumption of self-interested rationality which underlies other rational choice approaches. The implicit concept of rationality in the policy-pursuing model is close to being empty, implying only that parties or individuals are "utility-maximisers", which means nothing more than that "they do what they want to do".

for the study of party behaviour in multiparty systems which, while somewhat inspired by rational choice approaches, incorporates the importance of social cleavages.[19] This approach considers a party's decision between alternative standpoints to be a product of an opinion factor, a coalition factor and an interest factor.

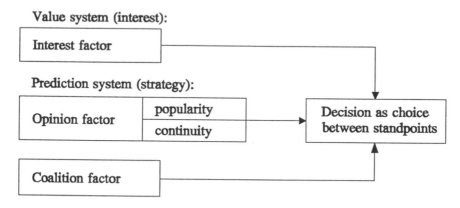

Figure 2.1: Molin's Framework for the Study of Party Decision-Making as Interpreted by Sjöblom.

Together, the opinion factor and the coalition factor constitute the party's "strategy" or prediction system. "Strategy" is in turn defined by Molin as the factor motivating standpoints that maximise the probability of attaining or preserving control of the government apparatus.[20] This can be achieved either by gains in a duly constituted election or by the formation of a coalition with a majority in parliament. In taking Down's arguments on the importance of parties' reliability into account, Molin argues that the opinion factor can be divided into two elements, popularity and continuity, where the latter indicates that party policy positions must be consistent with previous actions and statements.

The opinion factor and the coalition factor correspond to the categories of vote-seeking and office-seeking behaviour in the economic approach. This is true in the sense that if, for instance, the opinion factor were the only factor determining party policies, the party in question would

19) Björn Molin, *Tjänstepenionsfrågan: En studie i svensk partipolitik* (Göteborg: Akademiförlaget, 1965), esp. pp. 141-147. See also Gunnar Sjöblom, "Analysis of Party Behavior", *Scandinavian Political Studies*, vol. 2 (1967), pp. 203-222, and Gunnar Sjöblom, *Party Strategies in a Multiparty System* (Lund: Studentlitteratur, 1968), esp. chapters 5 and 6.
20) Björn Molin, *ibid.*, pp. 143-145.

behave as a pure vote-seeker. The interest factor is in turn related to a party's policy-seeking behaviour, with the qualification that policy-seeking in the policy-pursuing model of party behaviour concerns behaviour in the formation of governing coalitions.

As opposed to what is implied in rational choice approaches, however, Molin's framework relates party policies to material interest in the surrounding society and takes into account the fact that various groups with perceived common interests have organised or are closely tied to specific parties and play important political roles. Hence, in Molin's approach, "interest" is defined as the determining factor motivating the realisation of the demands of the parties' major groups. The major groups are seen to constitute the "hard core" of parties. Writing in a Swedish context, Molin views these groups as defined by their socio-economic characteristics; that is, in terms of factors such as the occupational status of their members. The interest factor in Molin's framework is, in other words, closely related to cleavages in the parties' societal surroundings, connecting the framework to the Lipset-Rokkan approach.[21]

Ström's more recent contribution evidently belongs within the rational choice tradition, but nevertheless attempts to integrate distinct elements of the vote-seeking, the office-seeking and the policy-pursuing models of party behaviour. Ström also formulates a number of arguments on when which type of party behaviour is likely to dominate, primarily emphasising the importance of institutional and internal party organisational constraints on party leaders.[22]

In simplifying his analysis, Ström limits himself to the study of two trade-offs: between policy influence and office benefits on the one hand, and between short-term and long-term realisation of these goals on the other. This simplification can be made since votes are assumed to be purely instrumental to parties and party leaders. Present vote-seeking therefore equals office-seeking or policy-pursuit at a later point of time.

As to the institutional factors affecting the time horizons of party leaders, Ström's study stresses, first, the uncertainty of electoral contests, defined as the degree to which electoral results are expected to vary

---

21) Molin's "interest factor" concerns parties' motivations for adopting a policy position, for which reason the demands of the parties' major groups are presumed to be internalised by the party decision-makers. This does not, however, affect the conclusion that the "interest factor" ties the decision on party policy positions to societal cleavages.

22) Kaare R. Ström, "A Behavioral Theory of Competitive Political Parties", *American Journal of Political Science*, vol. 34, no. 2 (May 1990), pp. 565-598.

across the set of feasible policy positions. The greater the perceived competitiveness, the more parties are forced to focus on electoral survival.[23] Second, electoral institutions may influence the degree to which party leaders pursue votes. Thus, the more unpredictable the relationship between electoral and legislative weights following an election, the less incentives for parties to maximise votes. Third, party behaviour will be influenced by institutions affecting legislative bargaining power. Legislative bargaining power is not the same as relative legislative weight, as it is exemplified by a party "tipping the scale". The more strategic interaction enters into the picture, the less predictable the benefits of electoral strength. Hence, the less strategic interaction and the lower the number of parties in the legislature, which is most often the same, the more parties will value votes. In a pure two-party system, legislative weight will equal bargaining weight, as a majority always emerges here and strategic interaction disappears.

Finally, the organisational characteristics of a party are viewed as influencing the degree to which votes are valued as well. Thus, the more decentralised the party, the less it is likely to value votes. Giving activists a direct voice in decisions on policy will reflect the activists' frequent preference for short-term policy benefits and will constrain party leaders in their vote-seeking.

PARTY BEHAVIOUR IN BRITAIN AND DENMARK

In this study, we intend to analyse two parties' policy development in a specific issue area. In evaluating the utility of the general propositions on party behaviour outlined above we must therefore take into account what we know about these two parties and about the contexts in which they operate.[24] In this connection the economic approach to party behaviour is inadequate in not paying attention to the social basis of parties, dipicting political parties as simply competitors for votes or office benefits. Even if the rational choice tradition does not in itself preclude

---

23) Institutions are here defined broadly and includes both organisational structures and patterns of behaviour.
24) In elaborating our framework for the analysis of the British Labour Party and the Danish SDP, we do not imply that this framework is equally valid for all political parties in all settings. For instance, it may in some cases prove difficult to identify the social basis of a party as this term is understood here.

the existence of clearly identified social groups with special ties to certain parties, it is implied that these phenomena are irrelevant to an understanding of the true characteristics of political parties.

On the other hand, the sociological understanding through its emphasis on the importance of classes or societal cleavages tends to play down the competitive nature of political parties. In studying the formation of party policy positions in a policy area, the competitive determinants of party behaviour should be taken into account. Thus, even if parties have close ties to distinct social groups, they obviously cannot escape the concern for votes, since electoral support is a necessary precondition for the realisation of the intrinsic goals parties or their social bases may possess. This is the case at least as long as these intrinsic goals are either office benefits or the initiation of certain public policies.

Third, we must acknowledge the possibility pointed to by Ström and implicitly also by Molin that electoral or legislative institutions may influence party behaviour. This point is particularly relevant since we compare two parties operating in two different political systems.

In considering these arguments our point of departure for the analysis of party behaviour here will be that the development of specific policies of political parties is conditioned by, on the one hand, policy interests in the form of the general policy goals of the party's social basis, and on the other hand by the party's pursuit of electoral support.[25] Furthermore, following Ström's propositions, we argue that institutional factors are likely to influence the relative importance of each of these conditioning factors. As it appears, we do not distinguish between interests and values, as both concepts contain a normative element: a proposition on

---

25) Formulated in Ström's terms, there is a constant tension between short-term and long-term realisation of intrinsic party goals. However, Ström does not relate intrinsic party goals to the existence of parties' social bases. In criticising Epstein's argument that parties are increasingly divorced from social movements and institutions, Ware also argues that many party leaderships continue to be constrained by the existence of a social basis. See Alan Ware, "Introduction: Parties under Electoral Competition", in Alan Ware (ed.), *Political Parties: Electoral Change and Structural Response* (Oxford: Basil Blackwell, 1987), pp. 10-12; and Leon D. Epstein, *Political Parties in Western Democracies* (New Brunswick, N. J.: Transaction Books, 1980), pp. 233-260. Finally, Kirchheimer has himself pointed to the limits of "catch-all vote-seeking", as some parties have distinct ties to specific groups. See Otto Kirchheimer, "The Transformation of the Western European Party Systems", *op. cit.*, pp. 185-87. Both Molin and Ström imply that party leaders value office-holding, intrinsically or instrumentally, for which reason the office-seeking concern could be treated as a third conditioning variable. However, the question of office-seeking vs. policy-pursuit concerns parties bargaining over policies and portfolios in governing coalitions. This is a special situation which is not very relevant in the current context.

what ought to be done. The conceptual difference between value and interest relates to the "ultimate motive" underlying a position; i.e., whether a goal is perceived as having instrumental or intrinsic value. This question need not concern us much here. We proceed, however, from the assumption that to political parties and political leaders electoral support is only an instrumental goal.

The Social Basis of the British Labour and the Danish SDP

The argument that a social basis is identifiable for both the parties studied here and that this is likely to have bearings on their behaviour does not mean that they should be conceived as "class parties". However, neither the British Labour Party nor the Danish SDP can be understood as political actors flowing freely in the policy space on the prowl for electoral victories. Rather, their behaviour is constrained by the perceived common interest of members of their social basis. Hirschman would argue that it is the "voice"-option of party activists that constrains party leaders' vote-seeking. This may be true, but it does explain why the substantial contents of policies advocated by party members and activists take the form they do. The position here is that these policy positions to a high extent reflect social cleavages.

A party's social basis is most usefully identified by various characteristics of the party's relationship with its social environment.[26] In proceeding along this pragmatic road, we wish to avoid reductionist conceptions of political parties. Thus, we specify a party's social basis as constituted by the societal groups or the parts of societal groups which organisationally and in terms of electoral support have, and have had, the strongest formal or informal ties with the party. Societal groups may in turn be identified on the basis of socio-economic or other characteristics, as the Lipset-Rokkan cleavage model argues.

In the current case, it is evident that socio-economic factors distinguish the social bases of both the British Labour Party and the Danish SDP from those of other parties. Historically, both parties originated as the political expressions of the labour movements in Britain and Denmark, coinciding with the organisation of trade unions for

---

26) This is why we prefer the term "social basis" to Molin's concept of "cores" in political parties: It makes little sense to define a "core" of a party in terms of relations to its environment.

manual workers in the late 19th century, just as the steadily increasing political strength of both parties in the first half of the 20th century corresponded to the growth of organised labour. The close links between both parties and blue- and lower white-collar trade unions are reflected in various organisational features. Traditionally, the British Labour Party has been characterised as an "indirect" party, a party whose members are other organisations rather than individuals, and this structure is evidently identical with very close formal connections between the trade unions and the party.[27] Trade union block votes have thus played a very important role at Labour Party conferences. Recent developments in the Labour Party have been in the direction of increased decentralisation and intraparty democracy.[28] Nevertheless, large elements of indirect organisation remain, both with respect to party conferences and the National Executive Committee (NEC), where trade union representatives in 1989 held 13 of 32 seats.

The Danish Social Democratic Party's formal ties to trade unions are weaker but nonetheless clearly present. The party and the trade union movement were formally separated in 1878, but ever since the creation of the Confederation of Trade Unions (LO) in 1898, both the party and the confederation have retained rules on mutual representation at executive boards. To this must be added the numerous informal ties existing between party and trade unions, in the form of various co-operation committees, as exemplified in recruitment patterns, and as illustrated by the fact that trade unions continue to provide considerable economic support for the party's activities.

Finally, voting patterns may be helpful in identifying the social basis of the parties. Here the largest voting support for both parties is found among blue-collar and lower white-collar employees. Hence, in the first half of the 1980s almost 50% of blue-collar voters cast their votes for the Danish SDP, whereas the party's share of the total vote was just above 30%.[29] However, there is widespread agreement that "class voting" has been declining over the past decades in Denmark, one result of which is

---

27) Maurice Duverger, *Political Parties* (London: Methuen and Company, 1954), pp. 6-17.

28) See for example Dennis Kavanagh, "Power in British Political Parties: Iron Law or Special Pleading", *West European Politics*, vol. 8, no. 3 (July 1985), pp. 5-22.

29) Ingemar Glans, "Langtidsudviklingen i dansk vælgeradfærd", in Jørgen Elklit and Ole Tonsgaard (eds.), *To folketingsvalg* (Aarhus: Politica, 1989), p. 56, and Søren Risbjerg Thomsen, "Udviklingen under forholdstalsvalgmåden (1920-1984)" in Jørgen Elklit and Ole Tonsgaard (eds.), *Valg og vælgeradfærd: studier i dansk politik* (Aarhus: Politica, 1984), pp. 46-47.

a decline in the working class share of the SDP's total vote from 68% to 52% in the period from 1968 to 1988.[30] In the British case, 69% of all manual workers but only 26% of all non-manual workers voted for Labour in 1966. In 1983, 42% of all manual workers and only 17% of all non-manual workers voted Labour. Furthermore, in 1983, 55% of the Labour Party's total vote came from the working class, defined narrowly as rank and file manual employees in industry and agriculture.[31] Thus, for both parties, electoral ties to the working class have loosened, but the overall importance of the working class vote remains significant. The Danish SDP and the British Labour Party continue to receive the greatest share of their support from the lower and lower middle classes.

General Policy Goals of Social Democratic Parties

The identification of the parties' social basis is important, as the existence of this basis corresponds to the existence of a pattern of general policy goals, the basis' perceived common interests as expressed in its images of desired general societal conditions.[32]

A political party's general policy goals are likely to influence the shaping of specific party policy in two respects. The pattern of general policy goals serves as a constraint on the formulation of specific party policy, as party policy must be broadly consistent with the general goals of the party. Neglecting this consistency will bring those sections of the party formulating specific policy positions into conflict with the social basis of the party and risks endangering the party's credibility with the broader electorate.

Furthermore, the pattern of general policy goals serves as a guideline for the formulation of policies in a changing environment. Confronted with new situations, party representatives are able to look to the general policy goals of the party in order to formulate a specific position. By

---

30) Ingemar Glans, "Langtidsudviklingen i dansk vælgeradfærd", p. 68.
31) Polling data quoted from Anthony Heath et al., *How Britain Votes* (Oxford: Pergamon Press, 1985), p. 21 and p. 30. The class distinction is between white-collar non-manual workers and blue-collar manual workers.
32) Sartori's critique of the argument that parties represent class interests referred to on p. 21 is not seen to affect this proposition, as it relates primarily to the contents of the two concepts of "representation" and "interest". The first of these terms has been avoided entirely here. Furthermore, "interest", "value" and "general policy goal" are seen as subjectively defined concepts.

definition, the pattern of general policy goals provides no specific answers, but it will furnish some basic clues as to which values and interest should be considered in specific circumstances.

The British Labour Party and the Danish SDP differ in many respects, but their political similarities are also manifold, as both parties belong to the broad social democratic movement. A precise formal definition of social democracy as a pattern of general policy goals or in other ways is difficult to arrive at,[33] but it is sufficient to emphasise the existence of a number of common basic goals which historically have been fundamental to social democratic policy formation. Thus, the social citizenship and thereby the comprehensive welfare state undoubtedly constitute substantial general policy goals of the social democratic movement. The concept of the welfare state may include various connotations. In limiting ourselves to propositions with a normative content, we may distinguish at the most general level between ideal-typical models which are conservative, liberal, or social democratic.[34]

The "etatist" conservative welfare state seeks social integration in order to uphold traditional class boundaries, authority, and privileges. In this model, social rights are attached to class and status. The ideal-typical liberal welfare state limits public social assistance to situations where the market has failed. Social rights are therefore qualified by a criteria of basic needs, as any extension of such rights beyond this level is seen to inhibit both efficiency and freedom. Market solutions dependent on individuals' ability to perform on the labour market are favoured in order to solve social problems, and non-market income is reserved for those who are unable to participate in the market at all.

The social democratic vision of the welfare state differs fundamentally from both these models, as it revolves around the idea of emancipation from individual market dependency and the corresponding goal of a society of equality, where the individual is guaranteed a decent living simply in the capacity of being a citizen.[35] The social democratic

---

33) Cf. Gösta Esping-Andersen, *Politics against Markets*, pp. 4-11.
34) The following account is inspired by Gösta Esping-Andersen, *Three Worlds of Welfare Capitalism* (Cambridge: Basil Blackwell, 1990).
35) The concept of "social citizenship" was developed and analysed in Thomas H. Marshall, *Class, Citizenship, and Social Development* (London: The University of Chicago Press, 1977, first edition 1950). See also Gösta Esping-Andersen, *Politics Against Markets*, pp. 145-165. As the following brief account is intended as an ideal typical description of basic social democratic goals, the current and historical differences between the ideologies of the British Labour Party and the Danish SDP are ignored.

objective in this respect has been the extension of universal social rights such as old age pensions, health care, education, sufficient unemployment and other social benefits, and in general material rights which viewed as providing a life of dignity.

The social democratic commitment to full employment in a growing economy, a goal which throughout the postwar era was thought to be attainable through the application of Keynesian macroeconomic policies as well as some measure of economic planning, is understandable as the devotion to a further universal right: the right to work. However, it is also a logical consequence of the commitment to the previously mentioned universal rights. The costs of guaranteeing universal and sufficient social transfers and services simply requires the minimisation of employment problems as well as a working economy. Similarly, the redistributive tax practises promoted by social democratic parties are understandable in light of the quest for a high degree of economic equality, but it must also bee seen in connection with the expenditure levels necessitated by the establishment of the comprehensive welfare state.

The realisation of the basic social democratic vision of the good society inevitably involves a high degree of state intervention in the functioning of the economy and in the lives of citizens, even if the specific form of state involvement may take numerous forms. The guarantee of universal social rights does, however, presuppose both relatively high levels of public sector spending on services and transfers and a comprehensive legislative and administrative regulation of the private sector. This last point may be modified where trade union organisation is extensive, in which case a part of state regulation may be left for trade unions and employers' organisations to negotiate.

Institutions and Party Behaviour in Britain and Denmark

In understanding specific policy developments of the two political parties, developments conditioned by the general policy goals of the parties' social bases and their interest in electoral support, attention should also be directed toward the institutional setting in which each party operates.

The British and Danish political systems display significant differences, and this is likely to affect the relative importance of the two major concerns seen to shape party policy positions. Ström's arguments on the significance of strategic interaction in legislatures for party leaders' time horizons, and hence their valuation of votes, are relevant here. As the British single member district electoral system produces for a number of reasons a two-party system, strategic interaction disappears.[36] In the British House of Commons, legislative weight therefore equals bargaining weight. In contrast, the Danish electoral system of proportional representation results in a multiparty system with a higher degree of strategic interaction. Hence, legislative weight does not necessarily correspond to bargaining weight.

This does not imply that parties in Britain only pursue votes whereas Danish parties limit themselves to the pursuit of policies and/or office benefits. Yet it certainly points to the fact that in the British political system, electoral support is the *sine qua non*. The ability of a party to directly influence public policy or to obtain office benefits is very limited unless the party possesses a parliamentary majority. This is not the case in Denmark, particularly as Danish governments tend to be minority coalitions. Except for the periods 1957-64 and 1968-71 this has been the case since the Second World War. Hence, opposition parties have the possibility to influence public policy.

In sum,a the differences between the electoral systems of Britain and Denmark therefore point to a larger propensity for parties to pursue votes in Britain than in Denmark, or to put it in other terms: compared to Denmark, the British system favours the quest for long term rather than short term realisation of intrinsic party goals.

It could be argued that the organisational characteristics of the two parties influence their policy development as well, since according to Ström, a decentralised structure increases a party's propensity to pursue short-term policy benefits rather than votes. Party activists tend to behave as policy pursuers rather than vote-seekers. However, even if the Labour Party's structure, as mentioned, must be characterised as relatively indirect, and even if the Danish Social Democratic Party is largely a direct party, this hardly in itself entails a higher degree of decentralisation in the Danish SDP in Ström's understanding of the term. Real decision-making powers on personnel and policies are not necessarily delegated to individual party activists in a direct party, and

---

36) Of course, the Liberal Party constitutes a viable third party in the British system. The real importance of this party, however, remains very limited, as one of the major parties has almost always had a controlling majority in the House of Commons. This has been the case for the entire period since the Second World War, except for a short time in 1974 and the years 1977-79.

a predominately indirect structure does not exclude a certain decentralisation of the same powers. Consequently, it is difficult to claim that one of the two parties here is unequivocally more decentralised than the other.

Starting with Ström's propositions on the effects of political institutions on party behaviour, there are thus good reasons to expect vote-seeking behaviour to be more significant in the British than in the Danish context. At the same time, however, we have stressed the importance of the two parties' social basis and corresponding pattern of general policy goals as a significant conditioning factor. This raises the question of how to determine the precise motivation underlying party policy developments.

Here the question of vote pursuit versus policy goal-conditioned behaviour in explaining specific policy change appears partly to be a question of different mechanisms reflecting the same underlying developments. This is the case to the extent that there is an overlap of general policy preferences between a party's social basis and its voters or potential voters. In this situation, changes in the societal environment of the party will entail the same changes of specific party policy, albeit through two different channels. Thus, the general policy goals of the party's social basis may constitute that factor which conditions the relation between changes in the party's societal environment and changes of specific party policy, while vote pursuit may also constitute this conditioning factor if changes in the societal environment are reflected in the preferences of the party's voters or potential voters. To the extent that party policy changes correspond to similar changes in public opinion regarding a policy issue, this will not necessarily mean that the party pursues votes and that the concern for general policy goals will have played no role. Furthermore, we may single out the situation where specific party policies change before voter preferences on the issue change or where public opinion has not changed at all. In this case, specific party policy development is unlikylty to have been conditioned by the pursuit of increased electoral support.

A similar situation emerges where the nature of the issue area at hand acts to preclude any substantial public involvement or interest in it. Hence, indirectly the content of a policy proposal or a specific change of policy may in itself reveal much about its underlying motivations. Explicit motivations about the reasons underlying policy changes should be considered as well. This element should not be granted too great an importance in isolation, as political leaders cannot always be expected to reveal their real motives. However, as a source of information possibly supporting the indications of other evidence, the contents of relevant public statements is clearly beneficial.

Finally, the settings in which calls for new policies on a given issue are formulated and the channels through which the party leadership is influenced may indicate which concerns have been of the greatest significance. Thus, in a situation where organisations representing larger or smaller segments of the party's social basis are the primary actors in initiating the movement towards policy changes, it suggests that the concern for the achievement of general policy goals has been the relatively most important conditioning factor.

In general, however, it is necessary to analyse the development of specific party policy in connection with the development of the parties' other policies and its overall political situation, present and past, in order to support claims as to the precise motivations underlying party policy change. Thus, the central questions are interpretive ones: can we, in the context of each political party, understand policy developments as being conditioned by vote-seeking? Do policy changes make more sense if understood in terms of vote-seeking than of general policy goals?

On the Dynamics of Policy Change

We have argued that political parties' specific policies are conditioned by concerns for electoral support and by the general policy goals of the party's social basis. We have provided a brief discussion of the most basic general policy goals of social democratic parties, and we have added that institutional characteristics of the political systems analysed may influence the relative importance of electoral support concerns, on the one hand, and general policy goals on the other. These points will serve to guide the analysis of actual party behaviour. The concerns for votes and policy goals act as as a "decisional filter", as constraints on and guidelines to specific policy development.

We should not stop here, however. If specific party policy development is seen as being explained by focusing exclusively on vote-seeking and policy interests, respectively, the analysis will remain static. A political party's concern for votes and/or policy goals in a specific situation may determine the party's choice of standpoint, but it tells us nothing about how the situation arose in the first place, or how and why the party came into a position to decide between different specific standpoints or to consider a change of previously advocated policies. This can be illustrated by the example of a pure vote-seeking party: Our argument here points to the fact that the Downsian model is inherently static, as voter preferences are simply assumed to display certain characteristics. Downs' model tells us nothing about how and why voter preference distributions develop over time.

The same argument applies to Molin's framework. His model simply adds a second variable with a fixed value in explaining parties' choice between different standpoints: the "opinion factor" is supplemented by an "interest factor", assumed to be constant over time. Molin's framework appears useful for the analysis of a party's choice of standpoint on an issue becoming politicised; i.e., entering the political agenda, but it remains silent on the reasons underlying this politicisation and says nothing about the causes underlying any development of both the "opinion factor" and the "interest factor".[37]

Our concern here lies in analysing two political parties' policy developments in a specific policy area. It is not primarily to analyse the parties' choices between different standpoints on an issue becoming politicised. The analysis of choice remains a static analysis, as the setting for the choice is taken for granted. In contrast, the analysis of change requires a broader approach which directs attention to the context in which the development of specific policies takes place. General policy goals and interest in electoral support condition parties' changes of policy, but this in itself does not tell us enough. Neither the general policy goals of the party nor its concern for electoral support translate directly into specific policy change.

In order to answer the question as to what factors underlie specific party policy developments, we must turn to an analysis of changes in the environment of the party, to the general societal setting which the party operates, and to changes in this setting. In a situation where the general policy interests of the party appear as the dominating factor conditioning

---

37) Kaare Ström, "A Behavioral Theory of Competitive Political Parties", pp. 580-582, attempts to introduce some dynamic elements in the rational choice tradition, the focus being on political parties within the electoral cycle. A party's positions at time t+1 is seen to depend on its positions at time t and on the party's electoral and legislative weights following elections at time t. The dynamic elements remain limited, however, as a party's electoral weight is assumed to depend exclusively on the party's policy positions. Voter preference distributions are therefore implicitly assumed to be constant.

the development of a specific policy, the focus must be on societal developments affecting the ways in which these general policy goals can be achieved or protected in the perceptions of a given party; or alternatively on societal developments which influence the extent and nature of problems signifying imperfect goal realisation. Where concern for electoral support conditions specific policy formation, we should focus our attention on those developments affecting voter preference distributions. In situations where concerns of both types may be important, the broadest contextual analysis appears necessary.

A FRAMEWORK FOR THE ANALYSIS OF POLICY CHANGE

We can order the above arguments into a framework for the analysis of party policy change. We have argued that for political parties such as the British Labour Party and the Danish SDP two factors condition the relationship between on the one hand the party's general societal environment and changes in this environment and on the other hand the party's policies in specific issue areas and changes in this policy.

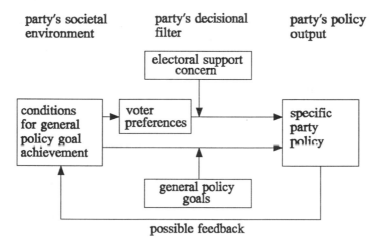

Figure 2.2: A Framework for the Analysis of Party Policy Change.

The two factors are (1) the party's general policy goals and (2) the party's pursuit of electoral support, electoral support constituting a necessary precondition for being able to achieve or protect general policy goals.

Taken together, the two fundamental conditioning factors constitute the political party's "decisional filter".

It is clear that what we have termed "conditions for general policy goal achievement" in the above and in figure 2.2 is a broad category, comprising such elements as the extent and perceived nature of societal problems signifying imperfect goal realisation and party perceptions of the availability and efficiency of policy instruments for achieving general policy goals. As mentioned, the analysis of party policy change in specific issue areas must consist primarily of an examination of developments in the conditions for general policy goal achievement, as well as of factors underlying changes in voter preferences. Thus, as emphasised in the figure, neither the general policy goals of a party nor the instrumental goal of electoral support translate directly into change of party policy in a specific area, and an adequate account of policy changes must therefore look to developments affecting ways in which the general policy goals of a party can be achieved or are threatened; or alternatively it must focus on developments affecting voter preferences about the applicability of specific policies.

This chapter has also argued that institutional characteristics of national political systems may influence the degree to which general policy concerns or pursuit of electoral support respectively affect the relationship between developments in the party's environment and changes in the party's policy in a specific issue area. In the cases of Britain and Denmark, Britain's electoral system seems to render vote-seeking behaviour more important in the British than in the Danish context. The way in which the analytical framework is illustrated in figure 2.2 does not reflect this proposition. However, it remains an objective of the current study to evaluate the extent to which specific party policy change in a given issue area has been conditioned by general policy goals and hence by the parties' social basis or by the instrumental goal of ensuring sufficient electoral support.

3

Social Democracy and European Integration

The previous chapter presented a general framework for the analysis of party policy change. However, understanding a party's EC policy poses particular problems, as it concerns the very institutional setting within which the two parties studied here operate. This is certainly the case where broader questions about the EC's overall development are at stake. The Community's evolution may affect both the ways and the institutional settings in which general policy goals can be protected or achieved.

This chapter takes these particular problems into account. In developing in more detail the propositions on social democratic parties' policies towards the EC as introduced in Chapter One we now discuss how the existence of the EC may change what we have termed the parties' "conditions for general policy goal achievement", causing social democratic parties to change their policies concerning extent and scope of regulation to be adopted in the EC framework, and concerning the EC's decision making capacity. This chapter also describes two other sets of potentially relevant factors which could affect the two parties' conditions for general policy goal achievement: (1) domestic developments affecting the efficiency of national policy instruments, altering the availability of domestic influence channels or changing public opinion on EC-related issues; and (2) external developments which might entail either a threat of exclusion from international decision-making fora or the emergence of potential security threats.

THE INTERNAL DYNAMIC OF INTEGRATION: REGIONAL MARKETS AND NATIONAL STATES

As mentioned in Chapter One a number of early studies on the development of international cooperation in the framework of the

European Coal and Steel Community and later the European Economic Community resulted in the formulation of a model for what has been termed the internal dynamics of integration.

In the neofunctionalist theory on regional integration, as developed in the late 1950s and early 1960s, the integration process was seen to be propelled forward by a dynamic internal to the process, in the sense that the creation of a supranational bureaucracy and the initiation of regional market liberalisations would cause problems, the solutions to which demanded further strengthening of the supranational bureaucracy or increased regional market liberalisations. Alternatively, the creation of a supranational bureaucracy and the release of market forces at a regional level would cause a change in the balance between different political forces, entailing increased pressures for further market liberalisations or for a further strengthening of the supranational bureaucracy.[1] The specific mechanisms cited as leading from the initiation of regional market liberalisations and the establishment of a supranational bureaucracy to renewed pressures for additional market liberalisations and bureaucratic strengthening were summarised in the concepts of "functional" and "cultivated spill-over".[2] The formation of regional interest groups and other transnational political actors, and increased transactions between states following market liberalisations were also seen to constitute "process mechanisms" spurring continuing integration.

To the extent that attention is devoted to political parties in this framework, parties are seen to respond to the problems and possibilities created by supranational bureaucracies or by regional market liberalisations. However, as argued previously, the one neofunctionalist study focusing the most on political party behaviour - Haas' early analysis of developments surrounding the ECSC - remains imprecise regarding those factors causing what we have defined as changes in the level of attitude integration. In this context, we should develop propositions about the

---

1) For an overview of early neofunctionalist integration theory, see Joseph S. Nye, "Comparing Common Markets" in Leon N. Lindberg and Stuart A. Scheingold (eds.), *Regional Integration: Theory and Research*, pp. 192-231. The problems and promises of both the functionalist and the neofunctionalist approach are discussed in my working paper "Regional Integration Theory: Contents and Current Relevance" (Aarhus: Institute of Political Science, 1991).

2) In one prominent formulation, "functional spill-over" refers to the "perceived linkages between problems arising out of their inherent technical characteristics". "Cultivated spill-over" is defined as "package dealing in the sense of coalition-building and deliberate linkage of issue areas"; this mechanism is seen to be particularly important in the context of the European Community, given the existence of the Commission as an institutionalised mediator. See Joseph S. Nye, "Comparing Common Markets", pp. 200-203.

internal dynamics of integration which specifically seek to understand changes in attitude integration in social democratic parties. When and why could we expect the actions of supranational bureaucracies or the effects of advancing regional market liberalisations to prompt social democratic parties to favour an extension of supranationality?

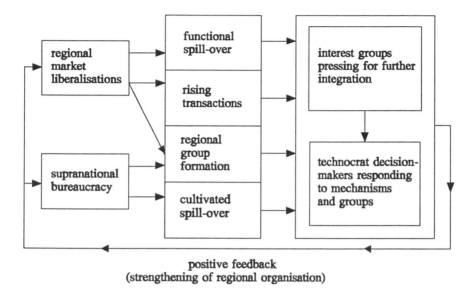

Figure 3.1: Early neofunctionalist process model, adapted from
Joseph S. Nye, "Comparing Common Markets".

As argued in the previous chapter, we may here proceed from the assumption that social democratic parties have a number of general policy goals including full employment, universal social rights within the state in question, equality, and prosperity. The realisation of these general policy goals inevitably requires comprehensive state intervention into or regulation of the national market economy. In addition, we note the fact that the supranational organisation of the EC, from its conception and onwards, has to a great extent constituted a market liberalist project, the core of which is the creation of a Common Market between the participating states, entailing specific legal obligations which set limits on national state intervention in the market.

Given these contradictions, we might hypothesise that social democratic parties will resist or reject the establishment of supranational decision-making on regional market liberalisations or oppose the extension of such decision-making to cover the nation-state within which a given social democratic party operates. However, if despite social democratic resistance, such decision-making is installed, social democratic parties will gradually increase their support for supranational decision-making and for the creation of binding supranational regulation, the implementation of which would take the EC beyond being an organisation which simply promotes and supervises regional market liberalisations.

Similarly, we could expect that an increase in supranational decision-making capacity aimed at extending the scope of regional market liberalisations would be initially rejected by social democratic parties. However, once such structures were established, they would be accompanied by social democratic calls for an increase in the supranational decision-making capacity regarding market intervention.

Why are these propositions plausible? The initial social democratic scepticism towards international market liberalising schemes or a strengthening of supranational decision-making in the area of market liberalisation would constitute a logical extension of social democratic parties' traditional mistrust of the efficiency and distributional effects of market regulation applied to national society. It would also reflect social democratic reliance on national state intervention as an instrument for societal reform. Hence, social democratic parties would tend to view regional market liberalisations established and implemented by supranational institutions as a threat to the possibility of national state intervention.

In the case of EC membership, the Rome Treaty, which was negotiated and implemented long before Danish and British EC membership, implies formal limits to national state intervention regarding trade- and tariff policies as well as aspects of agricultural and industrial policies. Furthermore, growing competitive pressures following EC membership and exposure to regional market liberalisations may also, in the perceptions of social democratic parties, involve an immediate and real as opposed to formal threat to the efficiency of required national regulation. This could be the case where these competitive pressures endanger national regulation, which is seen to constitute an international competitive disadvantage.[3]

---

3) Articles 9-17, 30-37, and article 95 of the Rome Treaty establish the principle of free movement of goods across borders in the EC, prohibiting the application of tariffs and excise duties with the same effect as tariffs, as well as quantitative restrictions on EC internal trade. Articles 18-29 establish a common external tariff, and articles 110-116 a common external trade policy.

Once supranational decision-making on regional market liberalisations has been established or has increased its geographical scope so as to include the nation-state of a specific social democratic party despite this party's initial resistance, the effects of the EC's Common Market on the state's structural external economic relations are activated. This entails that the state grows increasingly economically dependent on continued membership in the supranational organisation, as existing or ongoing regional market liberalisations implies a growing economic reliance on international trade and a restructuring of trade patterns via trade diversion and trade creation.[4] Growing national economic dependency on membership makes it increasingly costly for the state in question and the political parties of this state to ignore supranational rules and procedures, possibly in the form of leaving the supranational organisation altogether. Thus, a social democratic party which ignores supranational rules in order to achieve one of its general policy goals, full employent for instance, risks endangering another of the party's goals, namely increasing national wealth. This will be the case since such behaviour would provoke reactions in other member states, most likely damaging the now increasingly important economic relations with those states.

At the point when the social democratic party in question acknowledges the country's fundamental national dependency on membership in the EC, the supranational level will then become an arena for the political struggle over regulation of society. Acknowledged national dependency on membership can be said to exist when the perceived costs of insisting on the possibility of national state intervention despite or in conflict with supranational regulation exceed the expected future benefits from such intervention.

Article 92 prohibits state subsidies which distort competition by favouring specific companies or products, to the extent that these subsidies influence trade between the member states. Articles 38-47 lay down the principles of a Common Agricultural Policy. It could be argued that formal limits do not equal real constraints on policy making where they follow from international agreements. Accordingly, the initial social democratic scepticism towards EC membership should result not from the formal contents of the Rome Treaty but from the actual economic impact of EC membership which is viewed as leading to dependency on continued membership in the longer term as the Common Market alters the structure of economic interactions. It is thus only when real dependency emerges that the formal constraints of the Treaty become real, in the sense that no net-benefit can ensue from ignoring them. However, while this argument seems valid, it is irrelevant here. If no net-benefit is seen to ensue from membership, as is implied when it is argued that formal constraints can be ignored, then this may also constitute grounds to reject membership in the first place.

4) Trade diversion presupposes the existence or creation of a common external tariff of a size larger than tariffs between the member states of the supranational organisation.

Acknowledged national dependence on EC membership means that the social democratic party in question will attempt to shape the European Community according to its own visions and perceptions. In relation to a predominately market liberalist EC, this implies a high level of attitude integration. The Community should then pursue interventionist policies in those areas where such policies in the perceptions of the party support the achievement of general policy goals at the national level, particularly where national regulation is not sufficiently efficient, or where supranational regulation could improve the efficiency of national regulation.

Interventionist Community policies might also be approved of where they could guarantee the continued existence of national regulation. Thus, EC regulation is "stable" in the sense that more than the change of political majority in one national parliament is needed to reverse it. Furthermore, the party would seek that the EC be equipped with adequate decision-making capacity for intervention in the market to the extent that this would not hinder necessary intervention at the national level.

In a situation of national dependence on EC membership, social democratic parties could also be expected to reject any extension of supranational decision-making capacity regarding regional market liberalisations. Thus, with national dependency on continued EC membership, regulations adopted by supranational institutions and stipulating progressing market liberalisations could not be ignored and might therefore involve direct threats to the possibility necessary national state intervention in the market.

Where an extension of the supranational market liberalising decision-making capacity is implemented despite this resistance, it may in turn release new social democratic pressures for extended supranational market intervening regulation. Given national dependency on EC membership, the perception that regional market liberalisations in themselves pose a threat to the efficiency of national regulation could create an incentive for social democratic parties to promote supranational regulation, either as a replacement for threatened national regulation or as a means of reestablishing the efficiency of national regulation. Finally, supranational market liberalisations may also be perceived as creating or magnifying problems, whose solution would require new supranational regulation. Support for increased supranational decision-making capacity in specific issue areas may also be motivated by these factors.

To sum up, for social democratic parties, the EC membership of the nation-state within which they operate could be expected to lead to a perception of economic dependence on continued EC membership. Once such national dependency on EC membership is acknowledged, it could be expected to lead to increased social democratic support for extended supranational regulation and possibly also for increased supranational decision-making capacity aiming at implementing the necessary intervention in the market economy. Several mechanisms could be effective in this connection: (1) EC membership may be seen to provide access to institutions capable of establishing regulation heretofore not perceived to be efficient at the national level, or subsequently improving the efficiency of national regulation, (2) supranational regulation may be perceived to serve as a guarantee for existing national regulation, (3) EC membership and advancing EC market liberalisations may be perceived to threaten the efficiency of necessary national regulation, creating the need for supranational replacement regulation, or regulation reestablishing the efficiency of national regulation; or (4) EC market liberalisations may be perceived to create or magnify problems, whose solution requires new supranational regulation.

DOMESTIC DETERMINANTS OF ATTITUDE INTEGRATION

As mentioned, one weakness of Haas' early study of political parties and regional integration was the fact that it did not pay sufficient attention to the domestic context in which party policy positions towards supranational organisations develop. Propositions on the internal dynamics of integration must be supplemented, since it is a clear alternative possibility that domestic national conditions and developments influence political parties' attitude integration.[5]

Remaining with our assumption that political parties are actors striving to achieve certain general policy goals defined by their social basis, there are various national developments which could constitute plausible explanations for changes in a party's EC policy. Thus, in one possible scenario, developments initiated at the national level and not

---

5) Indeed, William E. Paterson, *The SPD and European Integration*, pp. 119-136, argues that domestic factors played a major role in shaping the West German SPD's attitudes towards regional integration in the 1950s.

caused by the actions of supranational bureaucracy or by regional market liberalisations alter the efficiency of national regulation in an issue area in a way which is difficult or costly to reverse.

This may again prompt changes of attitude integration in national political parties. If the perceived efficiency of national regulation viewed as important by the party in question is increased, then the development of attitude integration for a given political party could be expected to be negative. Correspondingly, if the efficiency of national intervention in the issue area is diminished in a hardly reversible manner as a result of the domestic development, attitude integration could be expected to grow: social democratic parties will in this situation favour increased supranational intervention in the market as a substitute for the lost national possibilities of regulation, and possibly also increased supranational decision-making capacity in the area for this reason. However, this could be the case only to the extent that supranational regulation would actually be seen by the party as constituting a potentially efficient replacement for national regulation.

For opposition parties such as the Danish SDP and the British Labour Party during the 1980s, it seems particularly relevant to point to the policies and administrative actions pursued and implemented by the governments of Denmark and the United Kingdom, respectively, as a factor which may have entailed the erosion of specific national policy instruments, again prompting changes in the two parties' EC policies in issue areas affected by this erosion.

A party's experience of changed political possibilities for achieving general policy goals in the national political arena may also affect its EC policy. Thus, a party's complete or partial lack of influence on national policy formation for shorter or longer periods of time could entail a re-evaluation of supranational institutions and supranational regulation. The party in question could then increase its support for that binding supranational regulation which in the party's view would contribute to achieving its general policy goals at the national level of, but which due to the party's lack of direct influence opportunities in the national political situation cannot be adopted nationally. An increase in supranational decision-making capacity in issue areas where regulation is seen as necessary by the party could be motivated in this way as well.

It is important to stress, however, the different institutional context in which the Danish SDP and the British Labour Party operate. As mentioned earlier, the Danish system of representation with its resulting multiparty configurations and frequent minority governments seems to give opposition parties, as was the SPD from 1982, better access to channels for national influence than what can be said of Labour in the British political system. Arguably, the blocking of national channels of influence as a factor underlying changes of attitude integration could therefore be expected to be of greater significance for the British Labour Party than for the Danish SPD.

An objection may be raised that a party which is in opposition at the national level has just as few or fewer possibilities to influence supra-national decision-making compared to national decision-making, given the fact that national governments dominate the EC system. Neverthe-less, there exists other channels for influence in the EC besides the Council of Ministers, as the European Parliament (EP) following the 1986 reform of the Rome Treaty, the Single European Act, has obtained a limited ability to influence EC legislation.[6]

Thirdly, even if the behaviour of political parties is guided by the general policy goals of their social basis, the realisation of such goals depends instrumentally on the degree of support for the party among the electorate, as we have emphasised in the previous chapter. Particularly for opposition parties striving to get back into office the concern for electoral support is fundamental. Here it seems a distinct possibility that a political party's change of EC policy may be motivated instrumentally, by a desire to convey greater electoral appeal to the party. Enhanced electoral appeal may thus indirectly improve the party's possibilities of achieving general and inherently valued policy goals.

A development such as this, however, can be said to constitute a domestic development only insofar as the changes in public opinion, which in this scenario may precede a party's change of EC policy, cannot be traced to effects of regional market liberalisations or actions of supra-national bureaucracies.

If the latter dynamic is present, it would be more appropriate to view changes in the party's attitude integration as evidence of an internal dynamic of integration, even if the precise mechanisms guiding the process are different than those lined out in the previous section. In

---

6) Thus, article 149 (c) of the Rome Treaty, amended by the ratification of the SEA in July 1987, enables the European Parliament to reject the "common position" adopted with a qualified majority in the Council of Ministers. If the Parliament rejects the common position, the Council can only decide with unanimity, opening up the possibility of a blocking coalition between the European Parliament and one member state.

terms of the general framework for analysis developed earlier, it would be an instance where the pursuit of electoral support rather than direct concern for achieving or protecting general policy goals constitutes the main factor conditioning the relation between changes in the party's environment and changes in its specific policies, cf. figure 2.2.

EXTERNAL DETERMINANTS OF ATTITUDE INTEGRATION

Neofunctionalist propositions have not only been criticised for ignoring the national political, economic, and social context within which processes of regional integration may develop. Neofunctionalism has also been accused of neglecting the external international surroundings within which integration may occur.

The arguments here are that the international environment in which the ECSC was founded and within which the EC developed was unique, since Europe in this period was subject to extensive superpower dominance, and that neofunctionalist studies have failed to take this into account. Ernst Haas, the very founder of the neofunctionalist approach, has himself conceded that the international environment is of crucial importance for integration processes.[7]

It therefore remains possible that developments external to the state in question and not prompted by actions of supranational institutions or advancing regional market liberalisations determine the EC policies of political parties of this state. Two quite different paths of development may appear.

First, starting from the experiences accumulated from studies of international cooperation in the EC framework we may point to the possibility that changes in a party's EC policy derive from the threat of national exclusion, in light of other states' wishes to undertake reforms of the Community.[8] Where several important EC member states wish to

---

7) The importance of the international environment was already emphasised in Stanley Hoffman, "Obstinate or Obsolete? The Fate of the Nation-State and the Case of Europe". Ernst B. Haas also acknowledged this point in a radical critique of own efforts, "Turbulent Fields and the Theory of Regional Integration", *International Organization*, vol. 30, no. 2 (Spring 1976), pp. 173-212.

8) The risk of exclusion as a factor prompting willingness to compromise in intergovernmental EC bargaining has been pointed out in Andrew Moravcsik, "Negotiating the Single European Act: National Interest and Conventional Statecraft in the European Community", *International Organization*, vol. 45, no. 1 (Winter, 1991), pp. 34-37; and in Paul Taylor, "The New Dynamics of EC Integration in the 1980s" in Juliet Lodge (ed.), *The European Community and the*

change the number of issue areas in which decisions are made at the supranational level, the supranational decision-making capacity, or other authorities of supranational institutions, a political party representing a given state risks being excluded from important supranational decision making fora.

An outright refusal to accept the wishes of other states can rarely prevent these states from pursuing their desired course of action on their own. Thus, in the most radical scenario, states seeking reforms may create a new formal framework for cooperation, thereby literally excluding those states who have opposed reforms. To the extent that decisions made in the framework of supranational institutions in new issue areas will also affect excluded states and political actors within such states, this sort of development entails a loss of opportunities for significant political influence. This may in turn pose a threat to the realisation or protection a party's general policy goals within an excluded state, since the views of the party are not represented in the suitable supranational fora. In this situation, a given political party may find it in its interest to seek a compromise and to attempt to influence developments by putting forward reform proposals which serve to achieve or protect one or more of its general policy goals.

As was the case with those changes in attitude integration prompted by changes in voter preferences, it should be stressed that for this type of dynamic to be labelled as an externally induced development, the emerging desire of important EC states to undertake reforms in the framework for cooperation cannot appear as the result of previous actions of supranational institutions, nor of advancing regional market liberalisations. If this were the case, a given political party's "reactive" attitude integration would be part of a dynamic internal to the integration process, even if it were to involve mechanisms different than referred to in our discussion of the internal dynamics of integration. Furthermore, it should be emphasised that the effectiveness of this mechanism is likely to be conditioned by the perceived level of dependency on continued EC membership. It amounts to a virtual truism that the threat of exclusion is no threat if a net benefit is seen to ensue from leaving the institution completely.

As a second possibility, changes in a political party's EC policies may result from developments which increase the security political importance

of institutionalised international cooperation. Up to after the end of
World War Two the European region could be termed a "security
complex", i.e. as a set of states whose major security perceptions and
concerns are so interlinked that their national security problems cannot
reasonably be analysed apart from one another,[9] and security considerations clearly played an important role in the creation of the ECSC and
its transformation into the European Community. Particularly for French
foreign policy the EC has constituted a new answer to an old problem:
that of power balancing in a Europe where Germany at the same time is
too small to be the dominant power and too large not to constitute a
potential threat to neighbouring states. However, Europe's traditional
character of a security complex was weakened significantly with superpower penetration of the region after 1945. Europe became subject to
"overlay", as the interests of the United States and the Soviet Union
came to dominate the region so heavily that the traditional regional
pattern of security concerns virtually ceased to operate.

Evidently, the breakdown of the centrally planned economies and the
ensuing accelerating process of political and economic reforms in these
societies have had profound consequences for this condition. One of the
most important effects has been the Soviet Union's diminished interest
in Eastern Europe and the political revolutions this allowed. Thus, in
Eastern Europe, overlay disappeared almost completely during 1989 and
1990, again causing the United States to cease viewing the Soviet Union
as a political and military adversary. This means that the European
region has again become a security complex, with the corresponding
threat that traditional European conflict lines will be reactivated.

This is particularly true because the disappearance of overlay made
possible the unification of the two German states, reactivating and
reactualising the traditional "German problem" of the European security
order referred to above. Hence, in a situation where the two German
states have united and where superpower interference in Europe is at its
lowest level since 1945, the non-German European states are confronted
with new challenges. The traditional answer to the emergence of a
potential security threat has been that of counteracting coalition-
building. In the Europe of the late 20th century, this could take place

---

9)   Barry Buzan, *People, States, and Fear: An Agenda for International Security Studies in the
     Post-Cold War Era*, 2nd ed. (Hemel Hampstead: Wheatsheaf, 1991). The following account
     relies on this study as well as on Barry Buzan et al., *The European Security Order Recast*
     (London: Pinter Publishers, 1990).

outside the framework of the EC, but also inside it, in the form of cooperation and policy co-ordination between those states confronting Germany.

Potential coalition-building within a strengthened formal Community framework, strengthened in terms of issue areas covered by supra-national decision-making, appears as the most efficient and least risky solution. This is because supranational principles of decision-making, e.g. by qualified or simple majority, by either the Council of Ministers or the European Parliament, enables smooth balancing processes, as they further the ability to form coalitions of a size and strength able to match that of any single state. Formal ability to block or overrule the positions of a large member state does not equal real ability, as the words of an important member state will always have considerable political weight. Other things being equal, however, an extension of EC supranationalism will increase the balancing capabilities of the Community.

To the extent that a political party reacts to external developments such as other important states' desires to undertake fundamental reforms of the EC framework or as the emergence of a potential security threat in increasing its support for strengthened supranationality in the EC, it acts as a statist political actor rather than as an actor reflecting on the perceived interests of its social basis. Or to put it in more precise terms: Ensuring national participation in important international decision making fora and stable and institutionalised international relations must be seen as quite fundamental preconditions for the political party's other general policy goals to be achieved or maintained.

If the above-mentioned kinds of external developments underlie the evolution of a party's attitude integration, those concerns should therefore be valid for and reflected in the EC policies of other political parties in the national context as well. Avoiding national exclusion and ensuring stable international relations seem likely to be goals shared by a very broad spectrum of parties.

In the following chapters we evaluate the explanatory strength of the propositions developed above. The next three chapters analyse the EC policy of the British Labour Party as developed from the initial discussions on British EC membership. What was Labour's policy on the question of British EC membership and on the extent of supranationality in the Community? How and under what specific circumstances has Labour's EC policy changed, and what does the context within which changes occur tell us about the explanatory strength of the three propositions regarding causes of change in attitude integration? We then direct our attention at the Danish SDP, its position on Danish EC membership, and the dynamics of its relation to EC institutions.

PART II

The British Labour Party,
the Danish SDP, and the
European Community

4

Labour and the EC Until 1980: Reluctance and Internal Disagreement

This chapter describes and analyses the British Labour Party's policy towards the EC in the period prior to 1980. In light of our proposition on the internal dynamic of integration, a major focus will be the tension between the party's reliance on state intervention for attainment of general policy goals on the one hand and evolving processes of regional market liberalisations in the EC on the other. The analysis will also direct attention to the external or domestic developments which may have influenced the party's position on the question of British EC membership and the evolution of the EC once Britain had become a member.

Taking the arguments of Chapter Two on the nature of social democratic parties into account, it will be useful to analyse the development of policy positions in three different settings. We shall therefore distinguish between the policy positions of the parliamentary party, the party activists, and the trade union movement.[1] The positions of the party leadership constitutes a fourth object of study, as the leadership takes the final decision on the party's policy stance and presents it to the electorate.

THE LABOUR PARTY AND THE EC BEFORE 1970

When in the summer of 1961 the Conservative Government of Prime Minister Harold MacMillan announced its intention to apply for membership in the European Community, it represented a major reversal of

---

1) Even if not all British trade unions are affiliated with the Labour Party, this is the case for the clear majority. As defined here, the trade unions form a part of Labour's social basis; strictly speaking they are not themselves components of the party. However, for both the Labour Party and the Danish SDP, ties between the trade union movement and the parties are so close so as to grant trade unions a significant role in specific party policy formation.

British foreign policy. The policies of the immediate post-World War Two years had been rooted in the "three circles" strategy, which sought to preserve British world power status through the Commonwealth organisation, the "special relationship" to the United States, and cooperation with Western European countries.

The "European circle" had originally been envisaged as the least important. This was also reflected in the Labour Party's policies. The Labour Government under Clement Attlee had welcomed the Schuman-plan for the creation of the ECSC in May 1950, but found itself unable to participate in the new body, instead establishing only tenuous associational links with it.

An official Labour Party pamphlet published in connection with the plan explicitly stated that the Commonwealth and the Atlantic relationship took precedence over European ties, also arguing that close economic cooperation with Europe was unnecessary, the economies concerned not being complementary.

Labour's deep mistrust of market regulation of society was reflected in the pamphlet's rejection of the very foundation of the ECSC, namely the common market for coal and steel. Far from leading to a more rational distribution of the factors of production, the pamphlet asserted that the common market was likely to result in chaos. It also argued that socialists would be in a permanent minority in a federated Europe, and that Britain could sacrifice neither her newly won social welfare benefits nor the sovereign power to plan her economy.[2]

Hence, in addition to the Labour Government's preoccupation with domestic reforms and Britain's non-European external ties, opposition to supranationalism and to regional market liberalisations in a supranational framework was clearly present at this point.

However, the increasing fragility of the Commonwealth, a number of foreign policy fiascos during the 1950s, and the fear of closer US-EC cooperation at the cost of the "special relationship" lead the Conservative Government to upgrade the European aspect. The failed attempts at creating an all-European free trade area in 1956-58 - a Conservative initiative supported by the Labour Party on condition that it rest on an

---

2)   Uwe Kitzinger, *The Second Try. Labour and the EEC* (Oxford: Pergamon Press, 1968), pp. 61 and 69, and Ernst B. Haas, *The Uniting of Europe*, p. 159.

intergovernmental foundation - constituted the triggering event here.[3]

Labour and the Macmillan Initiative

In the period from the Conservative Prime Minister's statement of intent to apply for EC membership in July 1961 to General de Gaulle's veto of British entrance in January 1963, the Labour Party struggled to define its position.

The trade union wing of the labour movement took a pragmatic stance, concentrating on specific union interests. Hence, a statement of the Trades Union Congress' (TUC) General Council in August 1961 was sympathetic to Macmillan's July announcement, even though it expressed some concern about specific problems.[4]

This position was further developed in a lengthy June 1962 memorandum to the Government, which held that the key to British entry hinged on the question of whether it would further economic expansion and rising living standards. The memorandum sought assurances that the implications of British Rome Treaty accession would not be curtailment of the British Government's economic planning powers. Assurances were also sought on the consequences of harmonisation of social services, while on the issue of unemployment the TUC suggested that "the Treaty itself should have written into it an obligation on each country to promote full employment and to report on what steps it has taken to achieve this", a proposal not included in the British position presented by the Government's negotiators.[5]

Even though the memorandum had demonstrated an interest in the issue of EC membership, it did not lead the TUC to adopt a clear stance for or against British entry. The September 1962 congress of the TUC agreed to postpone a final decision, and the trade unions maintained this "wait and see" policy despite the subsequent developments in the Parliamentary Labour Party (PLP) and the Labour Party at large.[6]

---

3) Cf. Miriam Camps, *Britain and the European Community 1955-63* (London: Oxford University Press, 1964), p. 109, and Robert J. Lieber, *British Politics and European Unity* (London: University of California Press, 1970), pp. 142-144.
4) TUC, *93rd Report 1961*, pp. 468-470.
5) Memorandum to the Lord Privy Seal, Edward Heath, TUC, *94th Report 1962*, pp. 261-266.
6) Robert L. Lieber, *British Politics and European Unity*, p. 113.

The PLP's initial response to Macmillan's EC-proposals was cautious. In the parliamentary vote in August 1961 following the Prime Minister's announcement, Labour abstained. Important differences existed, however, between the left-and the right-wing of the party. The majority of the left opposed entry, as the Community was seen as a capitalist "laissez faire"-device serving the interests of business and representing an obstacle to national economic planning. In this interpretation, the EC constituted the economic reflection of NATO, created so as to prevent the emergence of socialism in Western Europe.[7] The right wing of the PLP, on the other hand, viewed the EC as consistent with cherished values of social justice, political and personal freedom and internationalism. Furthermore, the EC was seen as an engine for economic growth, this being the precondition for the desired social reforms.[8]

The period until the annual Labour Party conference in October 1962 was characterised by a movement of party sentiment away from EC entry on the terms emerging in the negotiations. At the party conference in October 1961, a resolution which would have offered unconditional support for membership was overwhelmingly rejected. A resolution unconditionally opposing entry was also defeated, and instead the party adopted a composite motion stating that Labour would not approve EC entry unless guarantees were obtained for agriculture, EFTA, the Commonwealth, and Britain's right to retain the power of nationalisation and economic planning.[9]

In a June 1962 speech to the House of Commons, Harold Wilson, then a member of the shadow cabinet and widely seen as a potential future leader of the party, put a series of critical questions to the Government. Wilson in this connection judged the Treaty of Rome very critically in terms of its consequences for national planning of the economy:

"The plain fact is that the whole conception of the Treaty is anti-planning, at any rate anti-national planning in the sense that [we] understand it with

---

7) A document released by a group of left-wing EC opponents in May 1967 and signed by 74 Labour MPs summarises these views, cf. "Statement on the Common Market" reprinted in Uwe Kitzinger, *The Second Try*, pp. 136-140.

8) Michael Newman, *Socialism and European Unity*, pp. 170-172. Left-right divisions on the EEC question were not clear-cut; some left wingers were pro-marketeers and some right wingers opponents of EC membership, cf. Lynton J. Robins, *The Reluctant Party: Labour and the EEC, 1961-1975* (Ormskirk: G. W. and A. Hesketh, 1979), p. 15.

9) *Labour Party Conference Report 1961*, p. 211. See also party leader Hugh Gaitskell's statements in the Commons, *Hansard, Parliamentary Debates, (Commons)*, 6 June 1962, cols. 517-528.

the National Economic Development Council. ... The whole philosophy of the relevant articles [of the Treaty] shows a dedication to one principle, and that is the principle of competition. ... What planning is contemplated - a tremendous amount of planning is involved in the Common Market - is supranational, not national, but it is planning for the one purpose of enhancing free competition."[10]

Wilson went on to state that in his opinion the Treaty would stand in the way not of public ownership but of the use of the public sector for planning purposes, insofar as it would prohibit "anything that involves discrimination". Furthermore, the Treaty would impede national industrial- and regional policies, as state subsidies for relocation of industries would undoubtedly be regarded as illegal.

"Equally, our proposal ... for new publicly-owned industries based on new scientific research, extension of the powers of N.R.D.C.[11] to cover manufacturing, research and development contracts in the civil field, and so on, might very well fall foul of the provisions about subsidies and state intervention. ... Emergency action to control speculative capital movements would have to be subject to challenge in the Common Market, because in my view purposive direction of our national economic affairs without power to control capital movements is an illusion".[12]

Following this, a statement formulated by the Labour Party's National Executive Committee (NEC) and adopted by the party at the October 1962 conference made clear that support of EC entry would require the fulfilment of five broad conditions:[13] "Strong and binding safeguards for the trade and other interests of our friends and partners in the Common-wealth, freedom to pursue our own foreign policy, fulfilment of the Government's pledge to our associates in the EFTA, the right to plan our own economy, and safeguards for the position of British agriculture".[14]

These conditions are far from unambiguous. However, the address of party leader Hugh Gaitskell to the conference left no doubts about his own position on the EC. It contained a sweeping attack on the European case, primarily stressing the Commonwealth ties as a reason for

---

10) Mr. Wilson in *Hansard, Parliamentary Debates (Commons)*, 7 June 1962, col. 679.
11) National Research and Development Councils.
12) Mr. Wilson in *Hansard, Parliamentary Debates (Commons)*, 7 June 1962, col. 681. N.
13) The members of the NEC are appointed by the Party Conference. It therefore constitutes a forum where trade unions, constituency Labour Party organisations, and the PLP are all represented. The left wing of the party has dominated the NEC for long periods.
14) NEC, "Labour and the Common Market", London, 1962.

opposition.[15] Gaitskell's strong personal affection for the Commonwealth presumably played a role here, as well as his need to fight off the potential leadership challenge from EC critic Harold Wilson on the left.[16]

The Wilson Government's Application

General de Gaulle's veto of British EC membership effectively removed the issue from the British political agenda for several years. However, despite the setback of January 1963, "Europeanism" remained a latent force in British political life.

In 1964, the newly elected Labour Government headed by Harold Wilson initially kept its distance from the EC, but in February 1965 the Prime Minister stressed the Government's desire for closer cooperation between the EFTA and the Common Market.[17] This was followed by a similar statement by foreign secretary Michael Stewart in May of the same year.[18] When the results of this course failed to materialise, the Government in late 1965 began to show signs of softening the five conditions for entry which remained Labour's official policy. Subsequently, in December, Michael Stewart, adressing the House of Commons, said that the safeguarding of the EFTA-partners' interests had become easier to ensure than previously, and that the Government now viewed the major remaining difficulty to be the Common Agricultural Policy (CAP) and its implications.[19]

The general election of March 1966 considerably enlarged the Labour Government's majority. In the campaign, Labour had remained more reserved than the Conservatives on the EC issue, stressing the need for an agreement on Britain's relationship to the Common Agricultural Policy. However, a decisive turning point appears to be Harold Wilson's appointment, in July 1966, of George Brown as new foreign secretary.

---

15) For an analysis of Gaitskell's conference speech, see Michael Newman, *Socialism and European Unity*, p. 193.
16) This is the interpretation proposed in Lynton J. Robins, *The Reluctant Party*, pp. 27-34.
17) Prime Minister Harold Wilson in *Hansard, Parliamentary Debates (Commons)*, 706, 16 February 1965, cols. 1003-1004.
18) Secretary of State for Foreign Affairs Michael Stewart in *Hansard, Parliamentary Debates (Commons)*, 3 May 1965, cols. 909-910.
19) Secretary of State for Foreign Affairs Michael Stewart in *Hansard, Parliamentary Debates (Commons)*, 20 December 1965, col. 1724.

Brown had already made it clear in May, that for him the question was not whether Britain should join the EC but when and on what terms.[20]

In November 1966, the Prime Minister announced that informal negotiations on British EC entry had been resumed. After a series of meetings with the governments of the six EC states, Wilson, in April 1967, told a meeting of the PLP that "whatever the immediate economic effects of EC membership, there are vital long term advantages of economic dynamism and technology".[21]

On May 2nd, the Prime Minister then declared that Britain had decided to make a formal application under article 237 of the Rome Treaty. Some resistance to the announcement surfaced in the PLP and in the TUC, which stated that the five conditions had not yet been relieved, but there existed a majority for the application at all levels of the party hierarchy.[22]

On 10 May the House of Commons, with 488 votes to 62, approved the application, with 35 Labour MPs voting against it and 51 abstaining. Harold Wilson in his speech stressed the urgency of the application and the overwhelming advantages of membership, both in terms of economic and technological benefits in the longer run, and in terms of political advantages for Britain:

> "All of us are aware of the long-term potential for Europe, and, therefore, for Britain, of the creation of a single market of approaching 300 million people, ... and of the enormous possibilities which an integrated strategy for technology, on a truly Continental scale, can create. ... But the Government's purpose derives, above all, from our recognition that Europe is now faced with the opportunity of a great move forward in political unity ... Together, we can ensure that Europe plays in world affairs the part which the Europe of today is not at present playing."[23]

As opposed, he played down the relevance of the five conditions.[24] Following the parliamentary decision, the annual Labour Party

---

20) Michael Newman, *Socialism and European Unity*, p. 203, Robert J. Lieber, *British Politics and European Unity*, p. 246.

21) Quoted from Robert J. Lieber, *British Politics and European Unity*, p. 248.

22) Michael Newman, *Socialism and European Unity*, p. 213, and Cynthia W. Frey, "Meaning Business: The British Application to Join the Common Market November 1966-October 1967", *Journal of Common Market Studies*, vol. 6, no. 3 (September 1968), pp. 217-218. On the TUC's views see TUC, *99th Report 1967*, pp. 390-424.

23) Prime Minister Wilson in *Hansard, Parliamentary Debates (Commons)*, 2 May 1967, cols. 313-314. See also foreign secretary George Brown's statements in *Hansard, Parliamentary Debates (Commons)*, 10 May 1967, cols. 1504-1517.

24) E.g. Prime Minister Wilson in *Hansard, Parliamentary Debates (Commons)*, 2 May 1967, cols. 317-318.

Conference in October 1967 adopted by a ratio of 2:1 a statement welcoming the application for membership.[25]

Several developments appear to underlie Labour's reversal on the EC issue. Most important, external events weakened the viability of alternatives to EC membership. Britain's large balance of trade deficit in 1964 had demonstrated that the EFTA-option could not in itself provide a solution to this problem, and in October 1964 the Labour Government had itself weakened the organisation by imposing a 15% surcharge on EFTA imports clearly contraving the EFTA treaty. Furthermore, concern for an independent foreign policy had evaporated in light of the EC's 1966 Luxembourg compromise, and the Commonwealth option was undermined during 1965 and 1966 as political uprisings in the former colonies shook the fragile concept of "Commonwealth unity". Commonwealth trade as a percentage of Britain's total trade also continued to decline.[26] Finally, the right to independent planning of the economy remained a concern for the left wing of the party, but for the leadership the existence of French indicative planning within the EC appeared to have diminished its worries in this respect. The question of national planning was thus prevented from taking precedence over the structural longer term economic benefits which in Wilson's view followed from EC entry and from overshadowing the fact that credible alternatives to membership had gradually disappeared.[27]

Domestic developments also made EC membership seem more appealing. By 1966 Labour's economic programme had run into severe difficulties. Its centrepiece had been the adoption of French-style indicative national planning, which via increased investments in technology-based industries would produce an export led boom. The policy was doomed, however, by Wilson's (and London City financial interests') insistence on maintaining the international parity of sterling despite balance of payments deficits. By July 1966 the National Plan had been subordinated to an array of orthodox deflationary measures in order to restore external

25) NEC, "Labour and the Common Market" (London, 1967).
26) Michael Newman, *Socialism and European Unity*, pp. 204-205. The declining importance of Commonwealth trade was emphasised by Foreign Secretary George Brown in *Hansard, Parliamentary Debates (Commons)*, 10 May 1967, cols. 1510-1511.
27) As Wilson himself explained his change of opinion on EC membership, "[m]y experience of the working of the Community, the actual, practical working [...] renders unfounded the fears and anxieties which I certainly had [...] based on the literal reading of the Treaty of Rome and the regulations made under it". *Hansard, Parliamentary Debates (Commons)*, 2 May 1967, cols. 321-322. Wilson elaborated on this position in *Hansard, Parliamentary Debates (Commons)*, 8 May 1967, cols. 1074-1079.

balance.[28] This in turn spurred increased pressure from major interest groups to reconsider the EC option. Both the Confederation of British Industries and the TUC came out strongly in favour of British EC entry on economical grounds.[29] In the early 1960s, Wilson and indeed the mainstream of the Labour Party had exuded confidence about the possibility of transforming the British economy. After the failure of the National Plan, the Government and the trade unions looked to Europe for economic impetus.[30]

However, in May 1967 General de Gaulle had repeated his veto of 1963, leaving Britain back where it had started.

LABOUR AND THE EC 1970-80: RENEGOTIATION,
REFERENDUM AND INTERNAL RIFTS

Following de Gaulle's resignation, French resistance to British EC membership diminished. Thus, in addition to setting up economic and monetary union as a goal for the Community, the Hague summit of December 1969 confirmed that another veto on British membership was unlikely, and preparations for the opening of negotiations were resumed. This meant that the Labour Government developed a White Paper on the costs of entry into the EC. The White Paper was published in February 1970, and its conclusions were pessimistic. The immediate detrimental effect of EC entry on the balance of payments was estimated to lie between £ 100 million to £ 1.100 million a year, primarily since Britain's cheap overseas food imports would be subject to high tariffs or would be replaced by expensive EC imports.[31]

The Labour Government, having lost the general election, left office in June 1970, but the new Conservative Government under Edward Heath continued negotiations. Still limiting its analysis to mainly economic aspects, the TUC during 1970 displayed increasing concern with the balance of payments aspect of EC entry. The TUC's report on the EC from this year focused almost exclusively on whether the terms of entry negotiated could limit the balance of payments burden so that

---

28) Peter A. Hall, *Governing the Economy*, p. 51 and pp. 87-89.
29) Robert J. Lieber, *British Politics and European Unity*, pp. 268-269.
30) Michael Newman, *Socialism and European Unity*, p. 207.
31) The Labour Party, *Britain and the European Communities: An Economic Assessment* (London, 1970).

the prospects for faster growth would still be more favourable inside the Community than outside.[32] Trade union anxieties on the direct economic consequences of EC entry had already been revealed at the annual Labour Party Conference in 1969, where a resolution from the Transport and General Workers' Union (TGWU) demanding a tough stance in the negotiations with the EC was carried without a card vote.[33] The 1970-conference revealed increasing opposition to EC membership, as a motion from the same union openly rejecting membership was only narrowly defeated.[34]

Within the PLP, resistance to EC entry had also been mounting before the lost general election of June 1970. The economic burdens indicated by the February White Paper presumably constituted the single most important factor. However, after the election, opposition to EC membership gained momentum. The presence of a Conservative Government, which in a number of fields pursued policies aggravating the Labour Party, and which actively sought membership of an organisation imposing economic burdens on Britain in the short run, rendered the EC issue an attractive object of attack. This was especially the case because de Gaulle's second veto and the release of the 1970 White Paper had moved public opinion in a very EC-critical direction.[35]

Anti-EC sentiment grew during 1971 as a stream of decisions from trade union conferences revealed that a large majority of the unions had turned against EC membership. The trade unions were particularly aggravated by the Heath Government's industrial relations policies, and they saw the EC as an exploitable issue for campaigning against it, just as the balance of payments burden from EC entry on the negotiated terms led many unions to reject membership.[36] A special one-day Labour Party conference on the EC in July 1971, held in the wake of the

---

32) TUC, *102nd Report 1970*, pp. 468-474.
33) Michael Newman, *Socialism and European Unity*, pp. 219-220.
34) Lynton J. Robins, *The Reluctant Party*, p. 93.
35) James Spence, "Movements in the Public Mood: 1961-75", in Roger Jowell and Gerald Hoinville (eds.), *Britain into Europe: Public Opinion and the EEC 1961-75* (London: Croom Helm, 1976), pp. 23-31, finds a clear majority against EC membership in the electorate in the period from late 1969 to mid-1971. Anthony King, *Britain Says Yes: The 1975 Referendum on the Common Market* (Washington D.C.: American Enterprise Institute, 1977), pp. 19-21, reports a slight majority against membership already from June 1967 and onwards, but from November 1969 to April 1970 the majority against EC entry increased from 9 to 40 percentage points. Lynton J. Robins, *The Reluctant Party*, p. 111, contains evidence that the EC issue was used by some by-election candidates to rally support against Conservative candidates.
36) Michael Newman, *Socialism and European Unity*, pp. 221-222. For the views of the TUC's General Council see TUC, *103rd Report 1971*, pp. 308-328.

Heath Government's successfully concluded negotiations on terms of entry, further increased the impression of strong and growing opposition to EC entry in the trade unions. However, Harold Wilson succeeded in having the final decision on the question postponed.

These developments made it clear that to avoid defeat at the 1971 annual party conference, the NEC would have to assume some form of opposition to EC membership. Consequently, in July, by a vote of 16 to 6, it adopted a motion which opposed "entry into the Common Market on the terms negotiated by the Conservative Government" and called for a general election on the issue.[37] This formulation, as well as Wilson's ambiguous statements on the subject in the same period, evidently sought to bridge the widening rifts between left-wing EC opponents and right-wing proponents, personified by then deputy leader of the Labour Party Roy Jenkins.

At the annual party conference, the compromise motion gained widespread acceptance and was adopted with a 5:1 ratio. Following this, the PLP decided to reject the Parliamentary motion which approved the principle of British EC entry. However, as part of a deal to preserve a minimum of party unity, the party leadership allowed the proponents of EC membership to vote for entry in principle in the October 1971 debate if they in return opposed the Government's enabling legislation.[38]

The Compromise: Renegotiation and Referendum

Opposition to EC entry continued to occupy a salient position in the Labour Party in the following months. After a March 1972 meeting of the NEC, resistance took on a new form, as the Committee recommended that the PLP support left-winger Tony Benn's campaign for a referendum on Britain's EC membership. The NEC policy divided the Parliamentary Labour Party in two almost equally large groupings, and the shadow cabinet was able to endorse the idea only at the price of three shadow cabinet members' resignation.[39]

---

37) *Labour Party Conference Report 1971*, pp. 114-115.
38) 68 Labour MPs voted for entry in principle and 20 abstained. Peter Byrd, "The Labour Party and the European Community 1970-1975", *Journal of Common Market Studies*, vol. 13, no. 4 (June 1975), p. 475.
39) David Butler and Uwe Kitzinger, *The 1975 Referendum* (London: Macmillan, 1976), pp. 18-19, and Anthony King, *Britain Says Yes*, pp. 62-64.

In an attempt to repair the rifts, the NEC in July 1972 reemphasised a renegotiation of the entry terms as the most important basis for British EC membership. In addition, the results of a Labour Government's renegotiation would be subject to a subsequent consultative referendum. The 1972 annual party conference approved the NEC policy proposal, but at the same time it adopted, with NEC agreement, a resolution opposing parliamentary participation in the European Assembly (later the European Parliament) and setting up very strict conditions for the renegotiated terms of entry. The conference called upon a future Labour Government

> "to reverse any decision for Britain to join [the EC] unless new terms have been negotiated including the abandonment of the Common Agricultural Policy [...], no limitations on the freedom of a Labour Government to carry out economic plans, regional development, extension of the public sector, control of capital movement, and the preservation of the power of the British Parliament over its legislation and taxation".[40]

After Britain joined the EC in January 1973, the salience of the issue decreased, and the party leadership was able to maintain its position of renegotiation and a consultative referendum on membership in the February 1974 general election.

The election produced a marginal victory for the Labour Party, and in order to obtain a parliamentary majority the new Wilson Government needed the support of the Liberal party. James Callaghan, a pragmatic "EC-sceptic", became foreign secretary and was to lead the renegotiations on the terms of entry. Roy Hattersley, a long standing "pro-marketeer", was appointed minister of state for European affairs, but his presence in the negotiations was counter-balanced by the appointment of the passionately anti-EC Peter Shore to the post of secretary of state for trade.

James Callaghan made his first statement on Britain's demands to the EC Council in April 1974. Even if his speech was blunt, in reality it retreated from some of the Labour Party's previous implicit positions. Thus, it acknowledged that perhaps the Rome Treaty and the Treaty of British Accession could remain unchanged.[41]

In June 1974 Callaghan set out his demands in more detail, the tone being far more conciliatory than in April. At a meeting of the EC's Heads

---

40) *Labour Party Conference Report 1972*, p. 195 ff.
41) Anthony King, *Britain Says Yes*, pp. 74-75.

of State and Government in September 1974, a political deal which would ensure Britain a tolerable result of the renegotiations was then lined out. In return for an understanding with the French President that agreement would be reached on acceptable British terms of entry, Wilson in principle accepted a proposal to institutionalise the summit meetings as "the European Council", as well as a proposal that direct elections to the European Parliament should be scheduled.[42]

Shortly after the September 1974 election, which had returned the Labour Government with a small overall majority, James Callaghan then asked for the renegotiation to be completed by spring 1975. However, the party conference of November 1974 turned out to be a reminder to the Government of the strength of resistance to EC membership. The conference adopted a resolution demanding "complete safeguards" on each of eight points, including

> "the right of the British parliament to reject any EEC legislation, directives or orders, when they are issued, or at any time after, ... to control and regulate industry by financial and other means, ... to restrict capital inflows and outflows, [and] to determine its own taxation policy".[43]

Apparently, this did not impress the Prime Minister. In December 1974 he stated that if renegotiations were successful he would commend the terms to the British people and recommend that Britain "play her full part in the development of the Community".

At the December 1974 summit Harold Wilson even felt able to subscribe to a declaration stating that economic and monetary union in the EC remained the objective of the Community, while he reserved Britain's position on the proposed direct election to the European Parliament.[44]

At the first meeting of the recently established European Council in March 1975, only two topics were still outstanding: Market access for New Zealand dairy products and the future size of the British EC budget contribution. Regarding both points, the Prime Minister secured what he considered a satisfactory result,[45] and on 18 March 1975 the cabinet voted 16 to 7 in favour of recommending that Britain remain in the EC, the opposition again coming primarily from the left wing of the party.

---

42) This is the interpretation offered in Stephen George, *An Awkward Partner. Britain in the European Community* (Oxford: Oxford University Press, 1990), pp. 85 and 118.
43) *Labour Party Conference Report 1974*, pp. 249-260.
44) David Butler and Uwe Kitzinger, *The 1975 Referendum*, pp. 38-39.
45) Stephen George, *An Awkward Partner*, pp. 86-88.

The Labour MPs opposed to the Government's line acted swiftly as the cabinet had made its decision. An Early Day Motion opposing the Government's recommendation was organised and had attracted 140 signatures before the collection was abandoned. In the NEC a motion was tabled condemning the renegotiation results as falling "very far short of the ... objectives which have been party policy for more than ten years". Furthermore, seven dissident cabinet ministers including Michael Foot, Tony Benn, Barbara Castle and Peter Shore issued their own statement in opposition to the Government's recommendation. They declared that the CAP would mean higher food prices in Britain, and that EC membership would increase Britain's already large trade deficit with the EC states. Their main argument, however, was that staying in the Community meant denying the British people the right to democratic self-government.[46]

The TUC also opted for a "no" to continued British EC membership on the renegotiated terms of entry, the official motivation being that the renegotiation had not sufficiently altered the original entry terms. An additional reason appear to be the perception that EC membership would stand in the way of import controls, a measure deemed necessary by the 1974 TUC Economic Review in order to avoid the return of the British economic stop-go cycle in the wake of the first oil crisis.[47]

When the NEC met, it had to take these developments into account, but instead of supporting the motion calling for the party to campaign against its own Government it decided to neutralise the party apparatus in the referendum campaign. The Labour Party's deep internal disagreement on the issue was also reflected in the April debate on the EC in the Commons, where a majority of 145 to 137 Labour MPs voted against continued EC membership. Within the Government, however, a clear majority supported membership.[48]

This pattern was repeated at the second Special Labour Party Conference on the EC, also held in April: By a majority of almost 2 to 1, delegates voted to support the NEC motion opposing continued membership. The main issues for the EC opponents, here as well as in other

---

46) David Butler and Uwe Kitzinger, *The 1975 Referendum*, pp. 49-50.
47) TUC, *Economic Review 1974*, pp. 18-22. The importance of the question of import controls for the TUC's rejection of continued EC membership is discussed in Peter Gourevitch et al., *Unions and Economic Crisis: Britain, West Germany and Sweden* (London: George Allen and Unwin, 1984), p. 50. The TUC's general position on the EC in this period is explicated in TUC, *Renegotiation and the Referendum: The TUC View* (London, April 1975).
48) David Butler and Uwe Kitzinger, *The 1975 Referendum*, p. 52.

settings during the campaign, were the consequences of the CAP for British food prices as well as the implications of EC membership for formal British sovereignty.[49]

At an NEC-meeting in May, a second attempt was made by the party's EC opponents to activate the party apparatus in the campaign against continued British membership, but it failed. The overall picture in the weeks before the June 5th referendum comprised a clearly dominant pro-EC campaign supported by the majority of the Labour cabinet and virtually the whole Conservative and Liberal parties. EC opposition was very strong among Labour Party activists, but a clear majority of the leadership advocated continued membership. Finally, the trade unions were sceptical towards EC membership but did not want to involve the party apparatus in an anti-EC campaign.

The outcome of the referendum reflected this situation, as 67.2% of the votes supported continued membership and 32.8% rejected it. As a consequence, the PLP voted shortly after the referendum to end its boycott of the European Assembly which had been decided at the 1972 party conference.[50]

The EC and Labour's Economic Strategy in the 1970s

As we have seen it, it had always been a concern in the Labour Party that EC membership should stand in the way of neither national economic planning measures nor national industrial or regional policies. This was primarily but not exclusively a priority for the left wing of the party.

By the mid-1970s, British EC membership had led to only a few perceptible formal limits on the possibility to pursue nationally independent economic strategies. This is true in the sense that the policies which British governments had wanted to pursue had not conflicted fundamentally with EC legislation even though Prime Minister James Callaghan, who had replaced Harold Wilson in March 1976, acknowledged in September 1977 that EC regulation in some instances had been "stretched" as to allow state subsidies to be given to specific

---

49) David Butler and Uwe Kitzinger, *The 1975 Referendum*, pp. 97-115.
50) David Butler and David Marquand, *European Elections and British Politics* (Harlow: Longman, 1981), p. 10.

industries.[51] However, a situation such as the one emerging in the wake of the first oil crisis involving both high unemployment and inflation rates and accelerating balance of payments problems prompted a search for new policy instruments. Oil price hikes in combination with the mild reflation initiated by the new Labour Government in 1974 had caused to a massive balance of payments deficit and a currency crisis in 1976. Keynesian demand management, occupynig a key position in Labour's economic strategy since the Second World War, apparently could not guarantee full employment in a world of international free trade without being undermined by external balance problems or leading to currency devaluations which implied a risk of high domestic inflation rates and falling real wages.

Labour's left wing and a large part of the trade unions in this situation voiced increasing support for economic policies which later came to become known as the Alternative Economic Strategy (AES), and which were in fundamental conflict with British adherence to the Rome Treaty. Thus, in January 1975 the left wing Tribune Group of the PLP was advocating the introduction of selective import controls in order to

> "encourage the growth of firms concerned with import substitution, to ensure that key industries have the raw materials and the components they need, to see that the whole plan is not frustrated by excessive import bills and to maintain full employment".[52]

The TUC had, as mentioned already, been operating with import controls prior to the 1975 referendum. At the 1975 Trades Unions' Congress, resolutions incorporating a number of proposals from the Alternative Economic Strategy were tabled by important unions, but they were defeated in favour of a more moderate stance.[53] At the September 1976 Congress, however, the proponents of the AES were able to have a number of their ideas incorporated into the resolutions on economic policy passed by the TUC, as the composite motions 8 and 10 called for a "socialist economic and industrial strategy" involving selective import

---

51) Labour Party News Release: "The Prime Minister's Letter to the September 1977 Meeting of the NEC about the Common Market", Harvester Microfilms, "Britain in Europe" series. One prominent example was the Government's "temporary" employment subsidy for the textile and clothing industry. The state subsidy was curtailed when the EC Commission in 1978 insisted on it; cf. Peter Maunder, "International Trade", in Peter Maunder (ed.), *The British Economy in the 1970s* (London: Heinemann, 1980), pp. 256-258.
52) Quoted from David Coates, *Labour in Power?* (London: Longman, 1981), p. 236.
53) TUC, *107th Report 1975*, pp. 455-470, pp. 570-571, p. 590, and pp. 592-593.

controls and extended public ownership.[54] By 1977, the partisans of the Alternative Strategy had gained control of the floor, and they succeeded in passing a wide range of motions declaring the TUC's support for their basic ideas.[55]

These developments were gradually reflected in the policies promoted by Labour Party conferences: Labour's comprehensive 1973 programme had advocated interventionist industrial policies but at the same time it had expressed belief in the importance of multilateral free trade.[56] By 1976 the conference showed greater willingness to move in a protectionist direction. *Labour's Programme 1976* went a long way in the direction proposed by the Tribune Group, stating that the party "is committed to a new selective and discriminatory interventionist policy towards industry, involving the possibility of discretionary policies".[57] The main instrument for state intervention were to be the "planning agreement" which set out what a given firm should do to qualify for government assistance. Import controls also constituted a key element in the programme, as the widespread use of import penetration ceilings was deemed necessary in order to protect the balance of payments following reflation.

Partly as a consequence of the looming conflict between the 1976 programme and British EC membership, the conference also decided to have the NEC develop a background analysis of the relation between the Community-system and the party's economic strategies. The NEC document which was presented to the 1977 conference confirmed the dominance of anti-EC positions in this forum and explicitly analysed the Community in terms of the obstacles it posed to what was termed "socialist economic strategies". Thus,

> "our continued membership [in the EC] would be likely to add considerably to our burdens - whilst at the same time limiting our capacity to carry through the programme for radical socialist change needed to put Britain back on its feet".[58]

Concerning industrial policy, the document states that "the EC's approach to industry imposes significant constraints on the ability of a

54) TUC, *108th Report 1976*, pp. 526-529 and pp. 638-40.
55) TUC, *109th Report 1977*, pp. 478-486 and p. 582.
56) The Labour Party, *Labour's Programme 1973* (London, 1973).
57) The Labour Party, *Labour's Programme 1976*, London, 1976.
58) The Labour Party, *The EEC and Britain: A Socialist Perspective* (London, 1977), p. 7.

Labour Government to pursue such an interventionist policy".[59] The aspects of the Community's legal framework mentioned concern state-owned companies, where it is considered a possibility that the granting of concessions, grants or aids could be outlawed by the EC Commission. State aids are also discussed, as these could be prevented by articles 92 to 94 of the Treaty. Import controls constitute a third policy instrument, the use of which is hindered by EC membership, as such controls are prohibited by articles 30 to 37. Finally, the free movement of capital, foreseen in the Treaty's Article 67, is seen to pose a threat to the weaker economies and regions of the EC.

The Callaghan Government, on the other hand, found itself unprepared to embark upon a radical new strategy such as the AES as the balance of payments crisis was mounting in 1976. The Government clearly feared the international reactions which would ensue from an undisguised recourse to protectionism. Thus, at the 1976 annual Labour Party Conference, the Chancellor of the Exchequer, Dennis Healey, rejected the introduction of import controls as they would in his opinion provoke retaliations and touch off a tariff war reminiscent of the conditions in the 1930s.[60] Instead, the Government chose to negotiate with the International Monetary Fund (IMF) on a loan for the stabilisation of the currency. In December 1976 these negotiations resulted in an agreement which entailed sweeping public expenditure cuts in 1977-78 in return for foreign currency credits.[61]

The Government's subsequent response to the persisting economic problems was to call for an internationally coordinated effort. In March 1977 the Prime Minister presented German Chancellor Schmidt and American President Carter with a five-point plan, the centrepiece of which was a proposal for an internationally coordinated reflation where Germany would play a dominant role,[62] but the plan did not arouse much interest in Washington and the Prime Minister's meeting with Chancellor Schmidt failed completely.[63]

---

59) The Labour Party, "The EEC and Britain. A Socialist Perspective", p. 13.
60) *Labour Party Conference Report 1976*, p. 319.
61) Peter A. Hall, *Governing the Economy*, pp. 93-94. Edmund Dell, *Hard Pounding. Politics and Economic Crisis, 1974-76* (Oxford: Oxford University Press, 1991), examines the events surrounding the currency crisis in detail.
62) Jocelyn Statler, "The European Monetary System: From Conception to Birth", *International Affairs*, vol. 55, no. 2 (April 1979), pp. 206 ff.
63) Peter Ludlow, *The Making of the European Monetary System* (London: Butterworth Scientific, 1982), p. 76.

Prior to the 1977 Labour Party Conference, the Prime Minister issued a statement on the Government's EC policy. Here, withdrawal from the Community was firmly rejected, but Callaghan went on to acknowledge that "there are aspects of present Community policies which do not work in our interests". Six basic guidelines for British EC policy were then outlined, starting with the maintenance of the authority of national governments and parliaments, which involved the clear rejection of according increased powers to the European Parliament. As a second point, Britain would work toward improving national parliaments' EC scrutiny procedures and the introduction of open meetings in the Council of Ministers in some instances. The third point asserted that the EC system not be able to block national governments in achieving their economic, regional, and industrial policy objectives. A reform of the CAP and the development of a common energy policy constituted the fourth and fifth guidelines, and finally, enlargement of the EC was presented as having several benefits, among other things reducing the risk of "an over-bureaucratised and over-harmonised Community".[64]

Thus, in the wake of economic turmoil and persistent and growing hostility to EC membership in the party at large the Callaghan Government settled on an EC policy which even while rejecting British withdrawal nevertheless disapproved of any strengthening of the EC framework or extension of supranational regulation in all but very limited areas. Simultaneously, it reaffirmed the Government's will to prevent Community regulation from interfering with its economic, regional, or industrial policies.

Labour and the European Monetary System

Fom a number reasons, including French concerns about the consequences of fluctuating exchange rates for the CAP and German anxiety about damages to export earnings following an appreciating Deutsche Mark, President D'Estaing and Chancellor Schmidt launched the idea, in April 1978, of a European Monetary System (EMS). The Callaghan Government adopted a sceptical attitude, but the Prime Minister agreed to participate in the negotiations, and a "zone of monetary stability" was

---

64) Labour Party News Release: "The Prime Minister's Letter to the September 1977 Meeting of the NEC about the Common Market".

in principle not rejected. Thus, in a July 1978 debate in the Commons the Prime Minister argued that even if the EMS-scheme would limit the Government's powers to pursue the exchange rate policy it wanted, it could increase stability and prosperity, a deal Callaghan seemed willing to accept.[65]

During the autumn of 1978 the debate on Britain's relationship with the emerging EMS intensified, revealing substantial antipathy at all levels of the party. The 1978 Labour Party Conference turned out to be decisive in this respect. At the conference an attempt by EC opponents to secure a vote on an emergency motion denouncing the EMS was thwarted, but there was ample evidence of the depth of opposition to the scheme as speaker after speaker went to the podium to condemn the proposal. Moreover, the conference approved of a resolution on the EC which called for amendments to the 1972 legislation of British EC accession "so as to restore to the House of Commons the power to decide whether or not any EEC regulation, directive or decision should be applicable to the United Kingdom" as well as for reforms of the Rome Treaty "so as to curtail the powers of the Commission and give express recognition to the rights of the member States to pursue their own economic, industrial and regional policies".[66]

Within the PLP opposition to British membership of the EMS was also very strong. In November 1978, 120 Labour MPs, constituting over half the party's non-ministerial members, signed a motion rejecting "any attempt by the EEC, its institutions or its member states to assume control of domestic policies through a new monetary system for the Community".[67]

The NEC overwhelmingly opposed EMS membership. In an October 1978 statement, approved by a vote of 13 to 2, the NEC insisted on "freedom to determine our own budgetary policy and to control our own currency". It also asserted that moves to tie the value of the Pound to that of other EC currencies "could involve British acceptance of reactionary economic policies, low growth, and high unemployment for decades". In more general terms, the NEC declaration went on to state that its objective was

---

65) *Hansard, Parliamentary Debates (Commons)*, 10 July 1978, col. 1034.
66) The Labour Party, "Composite Resolution 42 as Approved by Annual Party Conference 1978", *Labour and Europe: Recent Statements of Policy* (London, 1978).
67) *The Guardian*, 10 November 1978.

"to create the conditions in which each member state is able to render [economic] power more closely accountable to its own people, with each member being able to bring about, at its own pace, and without impediment, its own programme of fundamental change in industry and society".[68]

The TUC's views on the EMS were stated in a paper submitted to a House of Commons subcommittee. Although the wording is more moderate than that of the NEC, the TUC position is clear: There are "grounds to believe that the EMS would operate in a fashion which would inhibit the growth of some of its members, particularly its weaker members".[69]

The concerns expressed by TUC and the NEC reflect the fact that the British inflation rate was significantly above the average EC level during this period. In a fixed exchange rate regime this entails the erosion of competitiveness and growing unemployment over time until inflation is reduced. Most likely, the concerns also reflect the presumption that the EMS would have a deflationary bias in the sense that the system's actual prescriptions for national economic policy in order to maintain exchange rate stability, would be deflation.[70]

Throughout late 1978, negotiations on the EMS continued, but in October Callaghan told Chancellor Schmidt that it would be impossible for the UK to join the new system. Mr. Callaghan subsequently hinted at a British "half-way house" when he stated that it was not necessary for all member states to adhere to every part of the plan.[71] The December 1978 European Council then agreed to include the UK in certain aspects of the system, even if it did not participate in the central Exchange Rate Mechanism (ERM).[72] At the at the same time, however, the Prime Minister announced that Britain would attempt to keep the Pound within a 2.25% fluctuation margin vis-à-vis the other EMS

---

68) NEC policy statement, here quoted from *The Times*, 25 October 1978.
69) First Report from the Expenditure Committee, Session 1978-79, The European Monetary System, HMSO, pp. 138-143.
70) Both positions mentioned above are found in The Labour Party, "The European Monetary System", background paper (London 1978). The economic argument for the deflationary bias of a "parity grid" exchange rate system such as the EMS is as follows: A state's intervention in currency markets to protect its currency from depreciation implies a falling money supply in this state, as the central bank buys its own currency. Conversely, a state's intervention to avoid appreciation involves an expansion of the money supply, but this expansion can be greatly sterilised by for instance tightening reserve deposit demands.
71) *International Herald Tribune*, 25 November 1978, here quoted from Peter Ludlow, *The Making of the EMS*, p. 245.
72) Peter Ludlow, *The Making of the EMS*, pp. 262-263.

currencies.[73] Together with the fact that the British also took part in
the partial pooling of foreign currency reserves to create the European
Currency Unit (ECU), this policy meant that although Britain was
formally not a full member of the system, it acted as though it were. A
glimpse of the analysis underlying this policy was given in the
Government's Green Paper on the EMS, which argued that the counter-
inflationary benefits of a "high" exchange rate outweighed the
competitive gains from movements in the reverse direction.[74] This
suggests that within the Government, concerns about strong opposition
to full British EMS-membership within the Labour Party played a
greater role than the alleged deflationary bias of the system.[75]

The course of the EMS negotiations thus indicates that in the cabinet
and perhaps also in the Government generally, the belief in exchange
rate realignments as an effective policy instrument was weak and
perhaps indeed eroding. In connection with the Government's five-point
plan for international economic recovery, the negotiations therefore
strengthen the impression of a political leadership which has increasingly
lost faith in the possibility of pursuing nationally independent
macroeconomic strategies. However, the EMS negotiations also serve as
evidence of the presence of the same faith in national economic strategies
within the larger Labour Party. The NEC's 1977 background analysis of
Britain and the EC, the NEC statement of late October 1978 and the
TUC's statement all exuded a confidence that Britain could solve its own
economic problems if only allowed sufficient freedom from formal
international constraints.

The 1979 Direct Elections to the European Parliament

By mid-1976, the issue of direct elections to the European Parliament
had reentered the political agenda. James Callaghan felt obliged by
Wilson's commitment on this issue; as mentioned, it had been part of the

---

73) *Financial Times*, 7 December 1978, here quoted from K. Johnson and C. Painter, "British
    Governments and the EMS", *The Political Quarterly*, vol. 51, no. 3 (July-September 1980), p.
    321.
74) HMSO, *The European Monetary System*, Cmnd. 7405, November 1978, p. 12, here quoted from
    K. Johnson and C. Painter, "British Governments and the EMS", p. 321. See also Christopher
    Allsopp, "The Political Economy of EMS", *Revue Economique*, vol. 30, no. 5 (1979), p. 869.
75) This is also the interpretation proposed by Stephen George in his *An Awkward Partner*, p. 130-
    131.

deal on the renegotiation. Consequently, the European Council, in July 1976, had agreed that direct elections to the EP should be held in 1978.

Due to resistance to the proposal in the cabinet, however, the bill enabling the elections to take place was not introduced in the House of Commons in due time.[76] Moreover, in October 1977, the Labour Party Conference rejected direct elections by a vote of almost 2 to 1. It was not until December that the Commons was able to approve an amended version of the bill, and because of administrative problems this meant that the elections could not take place until June of 1979.[77]

Although opposition to the elections remained strong in the party, the NEC decided that Labour should participate, and all sections of the party chose to campaign actively. Due to the novelty of the situation, to the PLP's desire to avoid confronting the National Executive on the issue, and perhaps also because Callaghan wished to exploit the electoral advantages of the unpopularity of the Community, the NEC found itself able to dominate the formulation of the election manifesto during late 1978 and early 1979.[78]

As a result, Labour's first European manifesto reflects the anti-EC left-wing dominance within the NEC, restating the highly critical resolutions adopted by the 1977 and 1978 party conferences. The manifesto thus declares that the objective of the Labour Party in the European Parliament and elsewhere is to "work towards the creation of a wider but much looser grouping of European states".[79] This in turn requires amendment of the British 1972 European Communities Act and fundamental reforms in the Rome Treaty. Moreover, the 1979 manifesto confirms the commitment of the 1976 Party Conference toward radical economic and industrial policies, declaring that Labour "will seek specific derogations (i.e. exemptions) from Community requirements on industrial and regional policies", and that Labour is opposed to the free movement

---

76) Michael Newman, *Socialism and European Unity*, p. 240.
77) David Butler and David Marquand, *European Elections and British Politics*, pp. 39-40.
78) David Butler and David Marquand, *European Elections and British Politics*, pp. 48 and 57, and Michael Newman, *Socialism and European Unity*, p. 243. Clause Five of the Labour Party Constitution stipulates that Labour manifestos in general elections are discussed between the NEC and the PLP. In practice, this means that when the election is carried out under a Labour Government, its contents are determined by the Prime Minister and the Cabinet. On the general implications of Clause Five see Leon D. Epstein, *Political Parties in Western Democracies*, pp. 294-305. Polls indicate a majority against British membership in the EC in the electorate in the last years of the 1970s; see, for example, the Commission of the European Community, *Eurobarometer*, 1981.
79) The Labour Party, "Labour's Manifesto for the 1979 European Elections" (London, 1979), p. 2.

of capital in the EC, Community interference in national exchange rate policy, and any movement in the direction of economic and monetary union.[80] To make things abundantly clear, the penultimate paragraph states that

> "if the fundamental reforms contained in this manifesto are not achieved within a reasonable period of time, then the Labour Party would have to consider very seriously whether continued EEC membership was in the best interests of the British people."[81]

The NEC's highly critical stance on the EC conflicted with the positions of both the Callaghan Government and a large part of the PLP. It also brought the party into conflict with the Comunity's other socialist or social democratic parties, which since 1974 had attempted to develop Europe-wide strategies within the Confederation of Socialist Parties of the EC (CSPEC). The Labour Party had joined the CSPEC in March 1976 but had not been fully participated when, at a June 1977 meeting in London, the Confederation at adopted a draft manifesto for the upcoming EP elections. With Labour participation lacking, the resulting document was strongly federalist, recommending a dramatic strengthening of the European Parliament. This went much too far for Labour, and in December 1977 the International Sub-Committee of the NEC rejected the draft without discussion.[82]

During the first half of 1978, negotiations continued in the CSPEC-framework, culminating with a June 1978 conference of party leaders in Brussels. Among the participants were Willy Brandt of the German SPD, Francois Mitterrand of the French Socialist Party PS, the leader of the Italian Socialist Party Bettino Craxi, and Danish Prime Minister Anker Jørgensen. Labour, however, chose to represent itself by its General Secretary Ron Hayward. By then it had become clear that it would be impossible to produce a manifesto acceptable to all nine parties. The meeting therefore resulted in a draft declaration, which in fairly general terms set out a socialist approach to the problems faced by the Community and its member states, stressing the need for "common policies agreed between the main industrial nations" in order to fight the economic crisis. Virtually no mention was made of the EC as such, though there were a few references to "Europe" and to "European

---

80) The Labour Party, "Labour's manifesto for the 1979 European elections", pp. 5-6.
81) The Labour Party, "Labour's manifesto for the 1979 European elections", p. 11.
82) David Butler and David Marquand, *European Elections and British Politics*, pp. 52-53.

solidarity". Following a January 1979 meeting of the CSPEC in Brussels, a slightly modified version of the draft declaration became an official "appeal to the European electorate".[83]

As occurred with Labour's manifesto, the opponents of EC membership dominated the party's campaign.[84] In general, the EP failed to arouse much interest, clearly being overshadowed by the general election on 3 May 1979. Unsurprisingly, the result was a turnout of only 32.1%. Following Margaret Thatcher's victory in the May general election, the Conservatives secured the awaited victory, with the party winning 60 of the 78 contested seats. Labour, on the other hand, secured a mere 17 seats.[85]

LABOUR AND THE EC UNTIL 1980: CONCLUSIONS

We have previously formulated three broad propositions on factors influencing social democratic parties' attitude integration, defined as the degree to which a given party directs its activities and expectations towards a supranational organisation, including (1) the degree of support expressed for national membership of such organisations, and (2) the degree of support expressed for increased supranationality in the organisation.

According to the first proposition, social democratic parties will resist national membership in an organisation such as the European Community since the EC primarily constitutes a market liberalist project which in a number of areas sets formal limits on national state intervention in the economy. However, once a dependency on EC membership has been acknowledged by the social democratic party in question, it will attempt to shape the Community according to its own visions: EC institutions will be pushed to pursue interventionist policies in those areas the party perceives will support or further the achievement of general policy goals at the national level.

---

83) The Labour Party, "Appeal to All EEC Electors. Declaration Agreed to at the Brussels Congress of the Confederation of Socialist Parties of the European Community" (London, 1979). At the meeting Labour was represented by Tony Benn.
84) EC opponents claimed that approximately 60 of the 81 candidates standing for election would be hostile to British membership; cf. Michael Newman, *Socialism and European Unity*, p. 243. David Marquand and David Butler in *European Elections and British Politics* (p. 64) estimate that 30 of the candidates represented pro-EC positions.
85) David Butler and David Marquand, *European Elections and British Politics*, p. 133.

The second propositions stresses the possibility that purely domestic developments may underlie changes in a party's level of attitude integration: the EC issue may be used as a means of broadening electoral appeal, domestic developments may change the perceived efficiency of national policy instruments or the party's perception of the political possibility of goal realisation in the national political system.

Finally, the third proposition stresses the role of external events in changing attitude integration. Thus, changes may occure as a result of a threat of national exclusion from important supranational decision-making fora or due to alterations in the international security political context.

The Labour Party and British Accession to the Rome Treaty

The British Labour Party's approach to the European Community offers considerable support to the proposition that social democratic parties will initially adopt a sceptical attitude towards national membership of a supranational organisation which seeks primarily to foster regional market liberalisations. As the plans for the establishment of the ECSC were formulated in the early 1950s, the Labour Government under Clement Attlee rejected the invitation to take part, and the Labour Party pamphlet published in this connection displayed hostility towards the idea of a common market for coal and steel, arguing that it would result in chaos rather than a more efficient allocation of resources.

Similarly, following Macmillan's application in 1962, Labour ended up adopting a very sceptical position on British membership in the EC, stressing that membership could be acceptable only if a number of conditions were fulfilled, including "the right to plan our own economy". At the same time, Harold Wilson judged the Rome Treaty very critically, as its entire conception was seen to be "anti-planning" and to rest solely on the principle of competition.

It should be acknowledged, however, that the perception of the EC and its predecessor, the ECSC, as constituting basically market liberalist enterprises was not the only reason for Labour's initially very sceptical attitude. Robins has stressed the dominance of anti-German and of pro-Commonwealth attitudes in the party during the early stages of European integration, as well as the need to formulate policies different from the Conservative Government's in a way which would not threaten the unity of the party.[86] This last point suggests that purely domestic developments, here the coming to power of the Conservative Macmillan Government, may have influenced Labour's position taking, as the party leadership may have seen a sceptical policy on EC membership as a means of broadening Labour's electoral appeal.

Despite the initially sceptical stance, Harold Wilson, supported by the majority of his party, in 1967 actively pursued British EC membership. How should this be understood? The most plausible explanation is found in a combination of external and domestic developments. External developments gradually removed or weakened the alternatives to EC membership, such as an all European free trade area or "the Commonwealth course", just as the evolving EC posed a potential threat to Britain's "special relationship" with the US.

These external developments can be seen as involving a threat of British exclusion from important formal or informal international decision-making fora. This threat of exclusion was not prompted by the desire of important EC member states to undertake reforms of the Community, as the previously formulated proposition on external determinants for attitude integration would have it. Rather, it dericed from the diminishing real importance of other international decision-making fora where Britain was represented. With the gradual weakening of the Commonwealth during the 1960s, the importance of this forum was reduced, thus causing other international settings to become increasingly central to Britain's political actors. Similarly, for the Wilson Government, a dynamically evolving European Community which did not have the United Kingdom as a member posed the threat of reducing the real importance of the close informal relations between Britain and the United States, replacing it with close relations between the EC and the USA. This would, again, imply the effective exclusion of the British Government from those decision-making fora in which questions of considerable importance to Britain were being dealt with, regardless of British membership. As Wilson was stressed in his May 1967 Commons speech, Britain needed to be a part of the EC in order to maximise its influence.

We may also note the fact that the Labour Party's approach to the EC in 1964-67 mirrored developments in the Macmillan Government's

---

86) Lynton J. Robins, *The Reluctant Party*, pp. 18-24.

European policy.[87] This is certainly the case insofar as Labour's EC
policy constituted a reaction to the disappearance of alternatives, or - as
we have termed it in the above - to the threat of real exclusion from
international decision-making fora. This suggests that national exclusion
from influential international decision-making fora is perceived as a
threat by a broad spectrum of political parties.

Regarding the threat posed by an evolving EC to Britain's "special
relationship" with the United States, however, its influence on the Wilson
Government's decision to apply for EC membership must to a certain
extent be characterised as evidence of an internal dynamic of integration.
The economic and political dynamism of the EC in the 1960s was thus
not least a result of the progressive regional market liberalisations which
came with the creation of the Common Market. It is, however, another
type of "internal dynamic" than that outlined out in the first proposition
on social democracy and supranational institutions: Even though
involving the effects of advancing regional market liberalisations, it
operated by enhancing a threat of national exclusion.

Domestic events also influenced the Labour Party's approach to the
EC. Labour's National Plan for restructuring the British economy had
failed, prompting the party leadership and trade unions to look to the
Common Market for new economic impetus. In terms of the propositions
formulated previously, these efforts could be seen as expressing the
realisation that a national policy instrument - namely, the National Plan
- had shown itself to be inefficient, i.e. to have side effects, which would
outweigh the perceived benefits from implementing it. In the perceptions
of the Government and of the City finance interests,' the devaluation
necessary to keep the Plan alive posed a threat to the Pound's status as
an international reserve currency.

However, it was not - as implied in our proposition on domestic
determinants of attitude integration - a domestic development as such
which caused the Wilson Government to view the National Plan as
ineffective. Rather, the attempt to introduce comprehensive national
economic planning in the British context resulted in experiences which
lead the Government to emphasise the economic benefits of joining the
Common Market. It is, thus, more accurate to speak of a learning process

---

87) The pattern of policy development is indeed similar for the Macmillan and the Wilson
Governments: an initial flirtation with Commonwealth and EFTA alternatives followed by
cautious acceptance of entry on certain conditions; cf. Miriam Camps, *Britain and the
European Community 1955-63*, p. 194.

rather than a particular domestic development diminishing the perceived effectiveness of a national policy instrument.

A learning process was most likely also involved in Mr. Wilson's personal change of his initially very critical evaluation of the contents of the Rome Treaty. Wilson's experiences with the real functioning of the EC and the actual consequences of Community regulation may have been important in suggesting that the problems seen to follow from British EC membership were less insurmountable than first thought. This was indeed suggested by Wilson himself in the House of Commons in May 1967.

Finally, it should also be mentioned that instrumental use of the EC issue to broaden the Labour Party's electoral appeal appear to have been of some importance for the Wilson Government's EC policy. Labour's persistent emphasis on the technological advantages of EC membership fitted in with the party leadership's overall commitment to "rejuvenate Britain in the white hot heat of technology". This slogan again served to modernise the party's image, to present it as the party fit to govern a modernising economy rather than as a traditional working class party.[88]

The course of developments from the early 1960s to the Wilson Government's application for British membership of the EC in 1967 hence leads us to a reformulation of the first part of the proposition on the internal dynamic of integration. A combination of external developments, involving a threat of British exclusion from important decision-making fora, and domestic events, involving learning processes on the limits to national planning in the British economic context, led the Labour leadership to support and promote British EC membership. This occurred in spite of the fact that EC membership implied formal and in the longer term presumably also real limitations on national state intervention in the economy in a number of areas.

This suggests that to the party leadership the political and economic benefits of membership outweighed the perceived costs of international constraints on national state intervention. The case of the Wilson Government therefore serves to illustrate that for social democratic

---

88) The importance of the question of technology in shaping Labour's attitude to the EC in the mid-1960s is pointed out by Lynton J. Robins, *The Reluctant Party*, pp. 47-51. The article by Letje Lips, "The Labour Party and the Common Market", in A. Boxhoorn, J. Th. Leersen and M. Spiering (eds.), *Britain in Europe*, Yearbook of European Studies no. 1 (Amsterdam: Rodopi, 1988), pp. 109-110, also directs attention to the emphasis on technology in the party's EC policy as a means of modernising the party image.

parties, the possibility for the nation-state to intervene in national markets unimpeded by international constraints is not an absolute imperative. Rather, the possibility of intervention is held up against other concrete political or economic benefits when deciding to enter into binding international frameworks. For Harold Wilson, his cabinet and the majority of the parliamentary party, renouncing the possibility of pursuing independent trade, tariff, agricultural and certain types of industrial policies was not so costly so as to justify rejecting EC membership.

The Labour Party in the European Community

Nevertheless, it was evident that the depth of feeling in the Labour Party in favour of British EC membership had remained very limited when the question of EC entry reappeared on the agenda in 1969. The growing opposition in the trade unions and the Labour Party in 1970-71 indicate that the calculus which appears to have underlain the Wilson Government's position towards the EC was far from being shared by everybody in the party.

Yet why did the apparent change of opinion against EC entry occur, and why at that particular point of time? Surely, the change of Government in 1970 did not in itself change the situation which had justified the Wilson Government's application: neither the declining real importance of international decision-making fora with British partici-pation, nor the experiences learned from the attempt to implement the National Plan had been altered with the change of Government. Rather it was the release of the 1970 White Paper on the immediate costs of British EC entry which appears to have provided new knowledge and, subsequently, to have changed the perception of the situation for a number of important actors in the Labour Party.

For the trade unions and the left wing of the PLP, the White Paper's statements regarding price increases and the related balance of payments burden which would follow from EC membership tipped the balance against EC entry. From the onset of discussions on the British relation to the EC, the trade unions had been persuaded to support membership only on the grounds that it would enable higher living standards and improve the employment situation. Consequently, support for member-ship for purely political reasons could not be expected from this side.

Similarly, many Labour MPs who had supported the Wilson application changed their opinion following the release of the White Paper's economic estimates. In combination with the initial scepticism towards the EC on the grounds that it would hamper the British Government's ability to apply the forms of state intervention it found necessary, description of the immediate economic burdens following from membership appear to have tipped the scale against EC entry. A different mechanism also seems to have been at work, as the White Paper and other assessments of the immediate economic effects of EC membership most likely contributed to the electorate's growing opposition to British entry. In combination with the change of Government in mid-1970, this provided many Labour MPs, rank and file activists and trade union representatives an incentive to oppose membership instrumentally in order to increase the party's electoral appeal vis-à-vis the Conservatives.

Whether directly or indirectly, new knowledge in the form of new assessments of the immediate economic consequences of membership was therefore the single most important factor underlying the growing opposition in 1969-71. This factor is not part of the framework for analysis developed earlier, nor of the propositions contained in this framework. However, it is appropriate to view new knowledge as a factor to be placed alongside the learning processes, as an element related to purely cognitive developments.

The uneasy compromise between proponents and opponents of British EC membership, a compromise which underlay Harold Wilson's policy of renegotiation and referendum, characterised the Labour Party's position in the EC question for the remainder of the 1970s. As the 1975 referendum demonstrated, resistance to membership in the European Community among trade unions and party activists as well as in the PLP was quite considerable. Even though the referendum resolved the question of Britain's relation to the EC, at least for a time, it did not have the same effect within the Labour Party: British EC membership remained a highly controversial issue.

The proposition on the internal dynamic of integration expects that social democratic parties will exhibit increasing attitude integration once national dependency on EC membership has been acknowledged. However, the Labour Party's EC policy prior to 1980 neither resulted in support for extended binding supranational regulation, nor for a strengthening of supranational institutions' decision-making capacity. The only instance where there occurred a development similar to the one suggested by the proposition on the internal dynamic of integration was when the TUC in 1962 demanded that British EC entry be conditioned on adding an amendment to the Rome Treaty, obliging the member states to promote full employment, a position which was later replaced by full-blown opposition to EC membership.

The fact that Labour Party support for supranationality did not develop following British EC membership can be ascribed to the fact that a fundamental British dependency on membership was not acknowledged by a substantial body of the party. The PLP's EC opponents had persistently rejected the economic and political rationale for membership, and most of the trade unions joined the opponents' rank following the economic crisis of the mid-1970s and onwards.

For most of the trade unions and for a growing part of the PLP, EC membership in the period from 1975 and onwards came to be seen as a straitjacket and, hence, as an economic and political liability rather than as a means of improving the party's possibilities of realising its policy goals. The TUC's and the Labour left wing's gradual formulation of the Alternative Economic Strategy thus indicates a strong and growing belief in the possibility of an independent solution to Britain's economic problems. The developments surrounding the establishment of the European Monetary System in 1979 also serve as evidence of the widespread position in the Labour Party at large that the fewer formal international constraints in which the British state is entangled, the better the possibilities of solving British economic problems.

In the second half of the 1970s, the Labour leadership did not hold such views. On balance, the Callaghan Government still supported British EC membership, and it did not see the same possibilities of independent British solutions to economic problems as did the left wing and many trade unions. This is clearly evidenced by the Chancellor of the Exchequer's rejection of managed trade as a useful policy instrument, and by the Callaghan Government's subsequent efforts to establish an internationally coordinated reflation as a response to the recession.

Furthermore, Callaghan and a large part of his cabinet would presumably have opted for full British membership of the EMS had resistance in the larger party not been so strong.

This is indicated by Callaghan's own remarks in the Commons, suggesting that he was willing to sacrifice formal exchange rate independency in exchange of achieving the general Labour goal of increasing welfare, and by the exchange rate policy pursued by the Government following the establishment of the British "half way house". However, the strong and growing hostility towards the Community among the trade unions, party activists, and in the PLP forced Callaghan to adopt a sceptical stance towards the EMS and the European Community in general, and towards the principle of supranationality in particular, a sceptiscism indicated in his 1977 statement to the NEC.

By the 1979 elections to the European Parliament, Callaghan seemed reseigned to a policy position which came very close to recommending British withdrawal from the EC. The desire to make use of the Community issue in order to broaden the Labour Party's electoral appeal may also have been of some importance here, inasmuch as opinion polls during the late 1970s have suggested a majority against continued British EC membership.

5

From Withdrawal to the Rejection
of the Single Act

During the final months of 1978 and the first months of 1979 there occurred a wave of public service strikes in Britain. "The winter of discontent" led to the downfall of the Callaghan Government on 28 March 1979 and signalled the beginning of the Thatcher decade, as the general election of May 1979 resulted in a clear Conservative victory.

The question of the European Community took up a relatively prominent position in Labour's 1979 election manifesto. Among other things, it stated that Labour "once again [will] be the only major political party to offer the British people the prospect of fundamental and much-needed reform of the EEC". The suggested reforms included proposals for a fundamental restructuring of the CAP and of the Community's budget, enabling Britain to escape its status as a net contributor to the EC. As to the future of the EC, the manifesto argued that Labour's aim was

> "to develop a Europe which is democratic and socialist, and where the interests of the people are placed above the interests of national and multinational capitalist groups, but within which each country must be able to realise its own economic and social objectives, under the sovereignty of its own Parliament and people."

On trade and industry policy, the manifesto stressed the party's will to preserve and enhance formal national independency and the possibility of national intervention in the economy:

> "Working with our Socialist colleagues, we will defend the ability of each member state to determine its own industrial policies. Our policy is to encourage such measures as import penetration ceilings and orderly marketing arrangements where they are necessary to protect vital national economic interests."[1]

---

1) The Labour Party, "Labour's Manifesto for the 1979 General Election, The Labour Way Is the Better Way" (London, 1979), p. 32.

In many ways, the EC policy advocated in the general election manifesto resembled the 1979 manifesto for the EP elections. The tendency is clearly towards a more EC-critical Labour policy and an increased insistence on the desirability of protectionist or quasi-protectionist measures in the overall economic strategy. However, whereas the 1979 EP manifesto explicitly cited the possibility of British withdrawal from the EC, the general election manifesto sidestepped this question. This fact probably reflects the relative strength of the PLP leadership vis-à-vis the NEC in the formulation the general election manifesto. The PLP's electoral concerns and the left wing's weaker position here resulted in a more cautious approach. Nevertheless, it was not long before this policy was forced to give way to a much more radical strategy at all levels of the party.

LABOUR'S POLICY OF EC WITHDRAWAL 1980-1984

Labour's defeat in the 1979 general election entailed the coming to power of a Conservative government with the most radical programme for liberalist political change in modern British history. Moreover, the year of 1979 and early years of the 1980s witnessed the evident, albeit temporary, victory of the Labour Party's left wing over the revisionist right, a development which again caused the Labour Party to officially adopt a policy of British withdrawal from the EC. Within the Labour Party antipathy towards the EC had been strong and increasing before the left wing's dominance became manifest. By 1980 the the policy of withdrawal had become explicit.

The Left's Ascendance: 1979-81

The ascendance of the Labour Party's left wing was a gradual development which culminated in the first years of the 1980s. It was not, as has often been conveyed by the press, a sudden development occurring exclusively in 1979-1981. Rather, Labour Party conferences had been moving in a more radical direction during the entire period from 1973 to 1979, with the conferences of 1976-1978 constituting particularly unmistakable evidence in this respect.

The conferences of 1979, 1980 and 1981, however, marked a new round in the struggle between the party's left and right wings. Thus, in addition to the dispute over the actual contents of the party's policies, the controversy increasingly came to focus upon the means by which the conference and the NEC could ensure that the PLP adhered to the policies adopted here. For many left wingers, the experiences with the Callaghan Government had been traumatic in this respect, the typical argument being that the government had "betrayed the socialist cause".

The frustration generated by the Callaghan Government gradually spurred increased opposition to the party leadership. It also led to the strengthening of so-called "Outside Left" groupings in the party, groups such as the Campaign for Labour Party Democracy (CLPD), the Socialist Campaign for Labour Victory (SCLV), the Trotskyist Militant Tendency, and the Labour Co-ordinating Committee (LCC).[2]

The CLPD was the most important of these groups. As the name suggests, its primary aim was to install a new type of democracy in the Labour Party, increasing the rank and file activists' influence over key aspects of party activity such as the election of the party leader, formulation of the election manifesto, and the behaviour of Labour MPs. At the same time, however, the substantive political objectives of the CLPD overlapped with those of other Outside Left-groups; the organisation favoured radical economic and industrial policies, withdrawal from the EC, and unilateral British nuclear disarmament.

The CLPD was founded in June 1973 following party leader Harold Wilson's rejection of the relatively radical statement of party policy *Labour's Programme 1973* which had been adopted by the party conference. Initially the CLPD was weak, and at the 1974 annual party conference the group's main campaign issue - mandatory reselection of Labour MPs by their Constituency Labour Party at least once during the term of a parliament - was proposed by only a single constituency. By 1975 the CLPD had increased its strength and mandatory reselection was proposed in 12 constituency resolutions at the conference. In 1976, 1977 and 1978 the respective numbers were 45, 79, and 67.[3]

---

2) The "Tribune Group", referred to previously, is a group of the "Inside Left" comprising left wing Labour MPs.
3) Patrick Seyd, *The Rise and Fall of the Labour Left* (New York: St. Martin's Press, 1987), p. 103, and David Kogan and Maurice Kogan, *The Battle for the Labour Party* (London: Kogan Page, 1982), pp. 27-28.

However, since the constituency Labour parties at that time had less than 10 per cent of the votes cast at conference, CLPD success was dependent on footholds in the trade unions. Inroads were made here from 1975 and onwards, and in 1980 161 branches and other trade union institutions were affiliated to the CLPD. By 1977 the CLPD felt confident of a majority of conference votes for mandatory reselection, but procedural matters postponed the issue. In 1978 the vote on mandatory reselection was lost by just a few votes, and at the 1979 conference the CLPD won its first major conference victory on intra-party democracy with almost 60% of the delegates voting in favour of mandatory reselection of Labour MPs in principle.[4] This gave constituency Labour party organisations the power to replace sitting MPs if local party activists were dissatisfied with their performance.

By the end of the 1970s, the CLPD had begun to focus on two other questions: control over the party's election manifesto and the election of the party leader. The CLPD proposal to transfer control over the party manifesto from the leader of the party to the National Executive Committee was first considered at the 1979 conference, but the issue was not resolved until two years later, when a narrow majority first decided that the NEC should have control over the election manifesto only to retreat from this decision following an appeal by party leader Michael Foot.

Until 1981, the leader of the Labour Party had been chosen exclusively by the PLP. Proposals for changes in this procedure had surfaced in 1976. At the 1978 conference, three different formulas were considered, with a proposal of an electoral college being defeated by a ratio of approximately 2 to 1. At the October 1980 conference and the special January 1981 conference at Wembley, however, the Outside Left movement mustered a conference majority for replacing the PLP's power to elect the leader of the party with an electoral college in which trade unions and Constituency Labour Parties were also represented. The end result was a solution where the unions held 40% of the votes and the PLP and the Constituency Labour Parties 30% each.[5]

Following the October 1980 conference James Callaghan resigned as party leader, temporarily throwing the Labour Party into confusion as

4) Patrick Seyd, *The Rise and Fall of the Labour Left*, pp. 108-109. David Kogan and Maurice Kogan, *The Battle for the Labour Party*, pp. 32 and 42.
5) Patrick Seyd, *The Rise and Fall of the Labour Left*, pp. 116-123, and David Kogan and Maurice Kogan, *The Battle for the Labour Party*, p. 118.

the precise formula for the composition of the electoral college had not been agreed upon. Nevertheless, the PLP decided to go ahead with the election of a party leader and elected the compromise candidate advocated by the "soft" left, Michael Foot.

The Call for Withdrawal and the Secession of the SDP

As a consequence of the tide of left-wing radicalism in Labour, the possibility of a break with the party and the creation of a new social democratic party surfaced repeatedly among party moderates in the end of 1979 and the beginning of 1980. Observing the growing radicalism of Labour with increasing uneasiness, the moderates had sought to reverse the development. The Campaign for Labour Victory (CLV), created in 1977, was an immediate response to the growing strength of the CLPD and other Outside Left groups, but it had not obtained any significant support from the party leadership.[6] The CLV was also hampered by internal disagreement on many issues, including Britain's relationship with the EC.[7]

As Labour continued to drift towards the left, the right-wing's critique became more outspoken. One important factor underlying this development and contributing significantly to the breakaway of the social democrats was Labour's adoption of a new defence policy, a policy change discussed at a special party conference on 31 May 1980.[8] Perhaps equally important, however, was the Labour Party's move towards a formal policy of British withdrawal from the EC. This tendency was also witnessed at the May conference and amply confirmed when Labour's industry spokesman John Silkin at the same time announced to a meeting of the anti-EC Labour Common Market Safeguards Committee that a motion would be put to the next party conference committing a Labour government to withdrawing Britain from the EC.[9] The radicalism of party conferences on the EC issue was not new, but the apparent acceptance of this radicalism by influential sections of the leadership -

6)   G. L. and A. L. Williams, *Labour's Decline and the Social Democrats' Fall* (London: Macmillan, 1989), pp. 104-105.
7)   David Kogan and Maurice Kogan, *The Battle for the Labour Party*, pp. 68-69.
8)   On the importance of the defence issue, see G. L. and A. L. Williams, *Labour's Decline and the Social Democrats' Fall*, pp. 67-78.
9)   Ian Bradley, *Breaking the Mould? The Birth and Prospects of the Social Democratic Party* (Oxford: Martin Robertson, 1981), pp. 75-76.

John Silkin was a member of the Shadow Cabinet - was a different matter.[10]

The willingness of some Labour leaders to endorse the policy of EC withdrawal resulted in a joint statement issued on 7 June 1980 by the "gang of three": the Foreign Secretary until 1979 and member of the Shadow Cabinet David Owen, NEC member and former MP Shirley Williams, and former Minister of Defence and Transport Bill Rodgers. The statement denounced the left's EC policy and made clear that if Labour officially adopted British withdrawal from the Community as party policy, the "gang of three" and their followers would leave the party.[11] Nevertheless, at this point all three remained sceptical about the idea of forming a new party stating that their aim was to remain in Labour and bring the party back on course.

However, the evolution towards the secession of the social democrats went further in August 1980 when Owen, Williams and Rodgers in a carefully worded letter reprinted in *The Guardian* publicly hinted, for the first time, of the need for a new centre party. In light of the mounting left-wing pressure preceding the annual party conference, the letter castigated the Labour Party for pursuing policies "based on bureaucratic centralism and state control, policies that offer no improvement in the quality of life", and it accused the NEC of flirting with "extremists who regard democracy as a sham". The letter's penultimate paragraph stated that "if the Labour Party abandons its democratic and internationalist principles, the argument may grow for a new democratic socialist party to establish itself".[12]

The 1980 annual Labour Party Conference only accelerated the centrifugal trends. As regards substantial policy issues, the conference marked a clear victory for the left. A resolution demanding unilateral British nuclear disarmament was adopted, and with a ratio of 5 to 2 the conference called for "the Labour Party to include the withdrawal of the United Kingdom from the EEC as a priority in the next general election manifesto [and] to disengage Britain from the EEC institutions", meaning that Labour should take Britain out of the Community without a referendum.[13] Clive Jenkins of the Association of Scientific, Technical

---

10) The importance of Silkin's action is emphasised by David Owen himself in Kenneth Harris, *David Owen* (London: Weidenfeld and Nicholson, 1987), p. 165.
11) Ian Bradley, *Breaking the Mould*, p. 76.
12) Quoted from Ian Bradley, *Breaking the Mould*, p. 78.
13) *Labour Party Conference Report 1980*, p. 126.

and Managerial Staffs (ASTMS), who moved the motion, motivated it by
pointing to the considerable direct economic costs of British membership,
while stressing the constraints imposed on British policies by EC
membership:

> "We cannot have [import controls] if we stay in the EEC. We cannot use our
> North Sea oil revenues for financial assistance to industry if we stay in the
> EEC. Really, we cannot introduce exchange controls if we stay in the EEC,
> and £3 or £4 billion has left the country already."[14]

Peter Shore, who at the time was considering to stand for the party
leadership, supported the resolution and declared that EC membership
had meant a "rape of the British people and of their rights and constitution". That was why Labour had resorted to the extraordinary procedure of the referendum, but according to Shore another referendum was
unnecessary if the party clearly stated its policy in the next manifesto.[15]
David Owen, by contrast, declared it a constitutional outrage "first to let
the British people decide in 1975 and now not even to give them the
chance to determine their own destiny." In rejecting the call for withdrawal, Owen emphasised the growing economic importance of British
EC membership:

> "We have to face certain realities. The Community is now our dominant
> trading partner. Seven out of ten of our biggest export markets are in the
> European Community. ... In 1984 jobs are going to be the massive issue
> that faces this country after the devastation of Thatcherism, and it will be
> a very serious decision as to whether this movement feels that we should
> withdraw from the EC."[16]

The 1980 party conference thus revealed that conflict between proponents
and opponents of British EC membership had grown to its widest gap
since 1975, and in general, the split between the right and the left wing
of the party seemed deeper than at any period since the Second World
War.

Before the conference, the "gang of three" had agreed to remain in the
party if the conference were to vote for unilateral British nuclear
disarmament and withdrawal from the EC but to leave if it also voted for
an electoral college to elect the party leader. As this last issue was left
unresolved, it was decided to put all efforts into trying to secure a defeat

---

14) *ibid.*, p. 127.
15) *ibid.*, p. 130.
16) *ibid.*, p. 128.

for the left at the Wembley conference in January 1981 and, failing this, to secede.[17] As a further step towards secession, the "gang of three" in the wake of the conference contacted Roy Jenkins, former Labour MP and Cabinet Member and, until January 1981, President of the EC Commission. Jenkins had publicly distanced himself from the leftward drift of the Labour Party and had expressed sympathy for the idea of a new party. He thus welcomed the contact, and the "gang of three" had become the "gang of four".

While no final decision had been made on a break with the Labour Party, the formal secession became inevitable after the special one-day conference at Wembley in January 1981, in which the left wing achieved its policy regarding the election of the party leader. Hence, on 26 January 1981 David Owen, Shirley Williams, Bill Rodgers, and Roy Jenkins announced that together with 20 Labour MPs, they had broken with the Labour Party in order to found the British SDP.

Labour's Radical Strategies

The left wing's victory in the Labour Party in 1980-81 lead directly to the party's official adoption of radical strategies for Britain's future economic, social and political development, a component of which was British withdrawal from the European Community.

Many of the positions which became Labour Party policy in the aftermath of the left's victory, derived from ideas traceable to the infancy of the British Labour movement, lying at the core of the ideological concept of democratic socialism. This is especially true for the left's preference for a high degree of public control over the means of production as a strategy for democratising capitalist society.

Other elements of Labour's radical strategies, however, were, closely tied to a more recently developed understanding of the problems of modern society. This is the case for the left's analysis of the economic crisis which was affecting most of the Western countries from the mid-1970s onwards. It also goes for the left's understanding of the international environment in which the economic crisis was to be fought.

In a study analysing the EC in the context of economic recession Stuart Holland thus argued that the structural causes of the "stagflation"

---

17) Ian Bradley, *Breaking the Mould*, p. 82.

crisis of the late 1970s were to be found in a deficiency of aggregate demand combined with inflationary pressures feeding on the non-competitive behaviour of an increasingly monopolised private capital. Another left wing policy document of the period, developed by Francis Cripps and his associates, adopted a more political view as to the causes of the economic crisis pointing first of all to the private capital's "loss of confidence" in any government pursuing reflationary policies. Thus, the preoccupation with "sound money" had spread through the whole international managerial class, eventually leading governments to adopt orthodox economic policies involving destructive processes of public budget cuts and private sector company closures.[18]

The left-wing assessment of the international environment in which national policies must be carried out saw the EC-system as biased towards non-interventionist economic strategies, preventing national governments from developing adequate policy responses. The Rome Treaty was seen as fostering negative integration such as the removal of barriers to trade and international production. In contrast, the Treaty stated the development of common policies only in vague terms, as distant goals, and only in a very restricted number of areas.[19] Correspondingly, the overall international economy was seen as dominated by intergovernmental institutions such as the GATT (the General Agreement on Trade and Tariffs), and the IMF, the functioning of which reflects the preferences of the liberal or conservative governments establishing them, as well as the strength of multinational capital in the shaping of international economic policy.[20]

Regarding the specific situation of Great Britain, the analyses of the left wing point emphasise the tendencies of unequal development inherent in the capitalist economy. "De-industrialisation" (defined as the long-term shrinkage of manufacturing as a component of national output, investment and employment) was a concept frequently applied in the debate on the British economy of the late 1970s and early 1980s. In this connection, one of the largest repercussions in the public was probably created by the group of left-wing associated economists publishing the

---

18) Stuart Holland, *Uncommon Market. Capital, Class and Power in the European Community* (London: Macmillan, 1980). Francis Cripps et al., *Manifesto. A Radical Strategy for Britain's Future* (London: Pan Books, 1981), pp. 27-28.
19) E.g. Stuart Holland, *Uncommon Market*, pp. 3-43; Tony Benn, *Arguments for Socialism* (London: Jonathan Cape, 1979), pp. 93-107 and 164-169; and Austin Mitchell, *The Case for Labour* (London: Longman, 1983), pp. 123-135.
20) Francis Cripps et al., *Manifesto. A Radical Strategy for Britain's Future*, p. 21.

1978 Cambridge Economic Policy Review. Thus, the Economic Policy Review argued that the free-trade regime of the Western World had been an important factor in Britain's industrial decline insofar as it had prevented effective responses to structural balance of payments weaknesses, imposing limits on demand stimulating macroeconomic policies with adverse consequences for the level of private investment. The Policy Revies went on to state that

> "it is our contention that there is no solution to the problems of structural trade imbalance through free trade unless it were really to be accepted that whole countries and whole regions of individual countries should be permitted to become impoverished and derelict."[21]

Cripps et al. similarly conclude that "our present international relationships lock us into destructive patterns of trade and investment in many other countries and commit us to supporting an anarchic 'free world'. The international system's prescriptions for our economy are deflation or devaluation."[22]

Thus, underlying these analyses is a recognition of policy constraints derived from the international agreements entered into by the British state. In the view of the left, these constraints stand in the way of effective responses to the economic crisis in general and to Britain's relative economic decline in particular. In this context, the Alternative Economic Strategy championed by the left aimed at strengthening public control of capital and at enabling a Keynesian economic expansion in Britain within a hostile international environment.

In concrete terms and as outlined by Cripps et al., the strategy comprised, first of all, of an expansion of the economy in order to raise output and growth, the centrepiece of which was large increases in public spending. A second element was the introduction of exchange controls to prevent international finance from undermining the strategy through capital flight. A third point consisted of the introduction of import penetration ceilings to prevent an immediate trade deficit from arising and to allow the British government time to plan its trade in negotiation with its foreign partners. Fourth, the strategy called for public control over investment policies of the pension funds and other semi-socialised

---

21) Cambridge Department of Applied Economics, *Cambridge Economic Policy Review*, no. 4 (March 1978), p. 4 and p. 29. Francis Cripps, co-author of the left-wing policy document *Manifesto. A Radical Strategy for Britain's Future*, was also co-author of the economic policy review.
22) Francis Cripps et al., *Manifesto. A Radical Strategy for Britain's Future*, p. 21.

wealth in the hands of private finance institutions as a preparation for converting them into public ownership. Finally, and more generally, the strategy involved greatly increased public intervention in private investment planning in the form of compulsory planning agreements negotiated between the government, large companies, and their employees as well as in the form of extended public ownership of large companies.[23]

Withdrawal from the European Community constituted an integral part of the AES. Through the repeal of the Rome Treaty, the left sought to escape the Treaty's formal constraints on policy-making. In particular, the possibility of reshaping British trade policies outside the EC was seen to carry considerable economic benefits with it. Thus, in the 1978 Economic Policy Review, it is estimated that the direct balance of payment costs of British EC membership in 1980 would amount to about £1.2 billion in 1978 prices. When taking into account the constraints this imposes on demand expansion the conclusion is that real national income could be about £3 billion higher outside the EC.[24] In addition, the introduction of capital and import controls would make possible a further Keynesian expansion of the economy with a wider range of favourable effects on the economy.[25]

However, the question of foreign economic retaliation is not considered in this scenario. Neither are the structural longer term costs resulting from the shielding off of the national economy from international competitive pressures, something indicative of the left's faith in national planning as the primary instrument for stimulating growth. Where the question of foreign economic retaliation following the imposition of import controls is addressed at all in the analyses of the left, the magnitude of the problem is scaled down: Cripps et al. claim that following the introduction of import controls

"Western governments could not threaten direct intervention in Britain's affairs without incalculable risks. Indeed, the danger of 'retaliation' and pressure for overt economic sanctions against Britain would be tempered

---

23) Francis Cripps et al., *ibid.*, pp. 133-134. See also the Conference of Socialist Economists, London Working Group, *The Alternative Economic Strategy* (London: CSE, 1980), for an elaborate account.

24) Richard Bacon, Wynne Godleay and Alister McFarquhar, "The Direct Costs to Britain of Belonging to the EEC", *Cambridge Economic Policy Review*, no. 4 (March 1978), pp. 44-49.

25) See Francis Cripps, Martin Fetherston, and Terry Ward, "The Effects of Different Strategies for the UK Economy", *Cambridge Economic Policy Review*, no. 4 (March 1978), pp. 5-21, for some estimates.

by the need to avoid an excessive punitive posture. Most likely, other governments and international institutions would take symbolic action, threatening worse unless the issues were resolved."[26]

The authors go on to argue that "interdependence is a two-way affair", and that Britain thus has a valuable negotiating lever in constituting a market for foreign export goods: "Once the British government had declared its intention of leaving the EEC in order to pursue independent policies, there would be plenty of scope for a realistic negotiation in which both sides took account of the other's vulnerabilities."

Labour Party EC Policy Development 1980-1983

In the first instance, the secession of part of Labour's right wing to the SDP meant a strengthening of the left. Indirectly, however, the SDP breakaway proved an asset to the remaining moderates of the party as any further radicalisation of Labour immediately threatened to release a full scale defection of MPs and voters to the SDP. This clearly weakened the left's position during 1981 as the SDP produced impressive by-election results, generally polling over 40% of the votes and causing spectacular defeats to both Labour and the Conservatives.

The left's retreat into a defensive posture became explicit at the 1981 annual party conference. Here, the threat from the SDP was probably decisive in dividing the left and in ensuring the tactical coalition between the right and the "soft" left, primarily consisting of the Tribune group headed by Neil Kinnock. This coalition managed to prevent the victory of the left wing's champion Tony Benn over Denis Healey in the contest for the post of deputy party leader, just as it meant that the left, for the first time in almost 30 years, lost its overall majority in the NEC. Thus, in a strict sense, left wing dominance of the Labour Party lasted for only a brief period of time and was always constrained. Tony Benn was never close to becoming party leader, and the right wing maintained strong positions in the party leadership especially after the 1981 conference, where for the first time the left was divided into fundamentally dissenting factions.

Nevertheless, the policies advocated by the party remained dominated by left wing strategies. On the issue of British EC membership, the NEC

---

26) Francis Cripps et al., *Manifesto. A Radical Strategy for Britain's Future*, pp. 141-142.

presented the 1981 conference with a series of research papers on the consequences of British EC withdrawal, the conclusions of which continued to insist on the net advantages of leaving the Community and that practical problems could be overcome. In its assessment of the EC, the NEC statement places particular emphasis on the immediate economic disadvantages for Britain and corresponding advantages of withdrawal, repeating many of the arguments used in the early 1970s. The conflict between EC membership and the AES also figures as an argument for withdrawal. The document acknowledges that "there is an increasing interdependence between nations, and if the Labour movement is not to stand on the sidelines, while the multinationals and their political allies gain control, we must co-operate to survive". However, it goes on to argue that EC withdrawal will not diminish the possibilities of international cooperation.[27] The party conference subsequently adopted the NEC's policy statement by an overwhelming majority of nearly 6 to 1, just as it endorsed a resolution urging the NEC to continue to find solutions to the practical problems posed by EC withdrawal. A resolution calling for a referendum on the EC issue was defeated.[28]

In parliament, the PLP during the same period acted to make clear its opposition to British EC membership. Hence, in February 1982, the great majority of Labour MPs voted to support a private bill demanding that the UK shed the supranational elements of British EC membership by repealing the 1972 European Communities Act.[29] Furthermore, in June 1982 the party's EC spokesman, Eric Heffer, rejected the so-called Genscher-Colombo proposals on European Union as "totally irrelevant for the needs of this country" and as containing "serious dangers for the future of our sovereignty".[30]

Within the trade union movement, left wing positions also continued to dominate. The 1980 TUC conference had adopted a motion which called on a future Labour government to put the question of Britain's EC membership to another referendum. However, at the 1981 TUC conference the strict anti-EC line then championed by the Labour Party

---

27) The Labour Party, "Withdrawal from the EEC", Statement by the National Executive Committee to the 1981 Conference, p. 5.
28) *Labour Part Conference Report 1981*, pp. 236-239.
29) *Parliamentary Debates (Commons)*, 3 February 1982, cols. 314-320.
30) *Parliamentary Debates (Commons)*, 17 June 1982, col. 1111. The German-Italian Genscher-Colombo initiative proposed certain limits to the use of the political veto in the Council, an improvement of EC foreign policy cooperation, and a certain very limited strengthening of the European Parliament.

was echoed by the overwhelming majority of the trade unions, and the Conference adopted a motion stating that a future Labour government should take Britain out of the Community without a referendum.[31]

The 1982 annual Labour Party conference adopted as its basic statement of policy *Labour's Programme 1982*. The left's influence on substantial policy issues continued to be considerable, the programme reiterating the party's commitment to the Alternative Economic Strategy and to take Britain out of the EC. With respect to the controversial rejection of a new EC referendum, it argued that since withdrawal from the EC is not an issue which can be separated from the party's overall strategy, it cannot be decided by a separate decision. The principal arguments for EC withdrawal were repeated: the considerable direct costs for Britain of belonging to the Community, and the conflict between the AES and the articles 12, 67-73, 90 and 92 of the Rome Treaty. In addition, the programme claimed that "the simple fact of withdrawal, at worst, [would] have a neutral effect on both investments and jobs". However, in order to lend credibility to the argument that Britain's increasingly close trade relations with its European partners would not be affected adversely by withdrawal, the Programme argued that negotiations with other EC member states would make possible the establishment of new favourable trading agreements.[32]

The Election of 1983 and the Decline of the Hard Left

Labour's radical strategies were submitted to the voters sooner than most had expected. The Conservative Government's booming popularity in the wake of the Falklands War (May-June 1982) led Prime Minister Thatcher to dissolve Parliament in early May 1983 and to call general elections on 9 June. Apparently caught by surprise by the timing of the election, the Labour leadership decided to promote an abbreviated version of *Labour's Programme 1982* as the party's general election manifesto.[33]

The manifesto thus retained the AES, renaming its first expansionary phases as an "emergency programme of action", and retained the call for

31) Paul Teague, "The British TUC and the European Community", *Millennium*, vol. 18, no. 1 (Spring 1989), p. 35.
32) The Labour Party, *Labour's Programme 1982* (London, 1982), pp. 229-233.
33) David Butler and Dennis Kavanagh, *The British General Election of 1983* (London: Macmillan, 1984), pp. 61-63.

British withdrawal from the EC without a referendum. At the same time, it reiterated that Labour's objective was a "gentle rupture" with the EC, a break which would free Britain from the Community's institutional framework without impairing her trade relations with the other EC states:

> "[We are] committed to bringing about withdrawal in an amicable and orderly way, so that we do not prejudice employment or the prospect of increased political and economic co-operation in the whole of Europe."[34]

The party leadership's inability to convince the electorate that EC withdrawal and the imposition of import controls would not trigger any foreign economic retaliation presumably contributed to the party's vulnerability preceding the 1983 election. During the campaign, the party indeed chose to ignore its own pledge to withdraw Britain from the EC after a series of polls had shown the Conservatives as "having the best policy on the Common Market" leading Labour by 17 to 23 percentage points.[35] Other factors than Labour's EC policy, however, appear as more important in explaining the Conservative victory: the impact of the Falklands War, Labour's controversial policy of unilateral nuclear disarmament, and the availability of the SDP-Liberal alternative.

The elections were devastating for Labour. Despite the Conservative Government's evident responsibility for the deep British recession and over 3 million unemployed, Labour secured a mere 27.6% of the vote, the lowest share since the 1918 election, and only 209 of 650 seats in Parliament, the lowest number since before the 1945 election. The Alliance won 25.4% and the Conservative government 42% of the total vote.

Inside the party, the left generally blamed the right wing's and the party leadership's lack of commitment to the party's policies for the result, whereas the right wing saw the electoral disaster as a consequence of the radical strategy's poor appeal to the voters. Shortly after the election, both Michael Foot and Denis Healey resigned from the party leadership, and the 1983 annual party conference, with clear majorities, elected as new party leader Neil Kinnock of the now clearly profiled "soft" part of the left wing and Roy Hattersley, a dedicated right winger, as new deputy leader.

---

34) The Labour Party, "Labour's Manifesto for the 1983 General Election, New Hope for Britain" (London, 1983), p. 33.
35) David Butler and Dennis Kavanagh, *The British General Election of 1983*, p. 143.

The emergence of distinct "soft" and "hard" factions of Labour's left had already begun before the 1981 conference, but the split was consolidated from 1983 and onwards. The soft left, headed by Neil Kinnock, distanced itself from the strategies of the hard left, reiterating a commitment to the left's general policy objectives. Yet it also argued that the means of achieving societal reform required a reexamination of some past policy commitments, of prevailing social and economic forces, and of the current state of public opinion. For its part, the hard left maintained its commitment to both its original strategies and objectives, continuing to emphasise working class mobilisation and public ownership of the means of production.

The prolonged coal miners' strike in 1984-85 and the disputes between local hard left-controlled authorities and the central government on local expenditure levels further aggravated the strains between the soft and hard left and weakened the hard left. The 1985 party conference signified Kinnock's open rejection of the hard left, as he in a much publicised speech denounced the practices of the hard left dominated Liverpool City Council.[36]

FRAGILE PRAGMATISM: LABOUR'S EC POLICY, 1983-86

The general election of 1983 clearly marked the onset of a fundamental revision of Labour's EC policies. Since the 1983 manifesto "New Hope for Britain", Labour has continued to evolve in the direction of increased acceptance of British EC membership, of EC institutions, and eventually of strengthening the European Community in a number of areas. However, this evolution was a gradual one.

Critical Pragmatism and Coordinated Reflation

The first phase in the party's policy development on the EC was marked by the leadership's retreat from the commitment to British withdrawal. As was the case with other of the 1983 manifesto's positions, Neil Kinnock distanced himself from this policy in the campaign preceding his election as party leader, declaring that withdrawal could only be a "last

---

36) Patrick Seyd, *The Rise and Fall of the Labour Left*, pp. 166-169.

resort" if renegotiation of the CAP failed.[37] Prior to the 1983 annual party conference, Kinnock's research team also presented a document, "Campaigning for a Fairer Britain", which took the first steps in re-evaluating the party's past policies. The document was extraordinarily vague on topics as the British nuclear force and nationalisation. On Britain's future relationship with the EC, it stated laconically that Labour intended to "retain the option of withdrawal" if fundamental reforms of the EC could not be achieved.[38]

This trend continued in the following months as the party developed its positions for the 1984 election to the European Parliament. One of Neil Kinnock's close aides, Robin Cook, had been appointed Labour's spokesman on EC affairs and came to play a leading role in the 1984 campaign. In a December 1983 strategy paper, Cook reflected on the emerging consensus that withdrawal of the EC was out of the question for the next few years. Following this analysis, the party's aims in the upcoming elections to the EP should be to recapture as much as possible of what had been lost in the 1983 elections. This meant attempting to restore the party's overall image as well as establishing Labour as the clear alternative to the Conservatives, something which could only be achieved by leaving the Liberal-SDP Alliance in a clear third position at the polls. As for policy, the paper stressed that the campaign should focus on both domestic and European issues. Regarding Europe, Labour should make it clear that it would protect British interests against threats from EC institutions, just as the party should emphasise Labour's desire to coordinate a collective response to European problems such as the arms race and unemployment.[39]

As mentioned, the call for an internationally coordinated response to mass unemployment had for a period been part of the Callaghan Government's economic policy in the 1970s. As a counterweight to Labour's policy of EC withdrawal, the 1983 election manifesto also pointed to the idea of coordinated response as an illustration of the party's allegedly internationalist nature.[40] However, the strategy of coordinated reflation was gradually given more emphasis in the Labour

---

37) *The Economist*, 1 October 1983, p. 27.
38) NEC, "Campaigning for a Fairer Britain" (London, 1983). The statement was carried by the conference without a card vote.
39) Here quoted from David Butler and Paul Jowett, *Party Strategies in Britain. A Study of the 1984 European Elections* (London: Macmillan, 1985), p. 60.
40) The Labour Party, "Labour's Manifesto for the 1983 General Election, New Hope for Britain", p. 34.

Party's economic thinking from 1983 and onwards. In the Western European labour movement, the strategy of joint reflation had been discussed in various fora from 1979, primarily under the auspices of the trade unions. In the early 1980s, the Labour Party had become more deeply involved in these discussions. The economist and Labour MP Stuart Holland had been appointed coordinator for a study, "Out of Crisis", under the Forum for International Political and Social Economy, an organisation which brings together parliamentarians and members of the executives of Western European social democratic or socialist parties. In addition, the Labour-attached left wing economist Francis Cripps was appointed advisor to the group.

The group's report, at that time the most detailed study of policy coordination published by the European left, was released just as the French socialist government abandoned its attempts at an internationally uncoordinated Keynesian expansion, a policy which in a number of respects closely resembled the Labour Party's AES.[41]

In its analysis of the economic crisis, the report largely parallels the Labour left's emphasis on the consequences of multinational capital and increasing monopolisation. Its policy prescriptions are essentially captured by the three concepts of restructuring, redistribution and reflation. Thus, the necessary restructuring of the capitalist economies requires reshaping the relationship between the public and the private sector as well as expanding public sector intervention to the benefit of small- and medium-sized enterprises. It also entails the general introduction of planned trade so as to make reflation more sustainable. Redistribution in the form of shorter working hours and increased social transfers is seen as an aim in itself as well as a means of increasing demand and reduce unemployment. The key element in the plan, however, is a coordinated reflation of the Western European economies: the study presents a model analysis of a cumulative reflation in 4 stages projected to result in the creation of about 9 million new jobs in the period from 1983 to 1991.[42]

---

41) Stuart Holland (ed.), *Out of Crisis: A Project for European Recovery* (Nottingham: Spokesman, 1983). On French economic policy in 1981-83, see e.g. Peter A. Hall, *Governing the Economy*, pp. 192-227, Peter Holmes, "Broken Dreams: Economic Policy in Mitterrand's France", in S. Mazey and M. Newman, (eds.), *Mitterrand's France* (London: Croom Helm, 1987), pp. 33-55, and Hans-Peter Fröhlich, "Die französische Wirtschaftspolitik unter Präsident Mitterand aus europäischer Perspektive", *Europa-Archiv* vol. 41 no. 3 (February 1986), pp. 79-87.

42) Stuart Holland (ed.), *Out of Crisis. A Project for European Recovery*, abridged version (Roskilde: Institute of Economics and Planning, 1983), p. 60.

The "Out of Crisis"-project's emphasis on internationally coordinated responses to the economic crisis was reflected in an article by Neil Kinnock on Britain's relationship to the other Western European countries published in the *New Socialist* in February 1984. In the opening statement, Kinnock makes clear that "Britain's future, like our past and present, lies with Europe". The subsequent paragraphs, however, argue that Europe is not the same as the European Community and that "for us as socialists [Britain's future] will still only lie within the EEC if the Common Market can be transformed to measure up to our wider vision of Europe's own future".[43]

The leader of the Labour Party then emphasises the desirability of coordinating national policies in a number of areas and proposes joint European action. This goes for macroeconomic policies, for policies on multinational corporations, for joint international planning of trade, for policies on the Third World, and for nuclear disarmament in Europe. In the realm of international macroeconomic coordination, Kinnock suggests the establishment of a "Euro Bretton Woods" system. Thus, "a new Euro Bretton Woods should take initiatives to harness multinational finance capital, and it should aim to achieve the conditions for modern full employment policies in Europe and positive policies for the rest of the world".[44]

The specific policies advocated here include coordinated European reflation at the national level, supplemented by an expansion of EC activities which also work in a reflationary direction, such as an increase in the lending activities of the European Investment Bank.

Kinnock argues that "in the age of multinational capitalism, democracy must become multinational too". Accordingly he proposes, "joint policies for economic democracy and for the control of multinational corporations so that the economic strength they represent can be used constructively to help in the economic, social and cultural regeneration of our countries." Sceptical about what could actually have been achieved had the so-called Vredeling-proposal for an EC directive on employee participation and information not been blocked in the EC Council of Ministers, Kinnock nevertheless emphasises the significance of striving to secure any progressive changes in this field and to support policies by

---

43) Neil Kinnock, "New Deal for Europe", here quoted from the reprint in James Curran (ed.), *The Future of the Left* (Cambridge: Polity Press and New Socialist, 1984), pp. 231-242.
44) *ibid.*, p. 232.

like-minded left governments in Europe for the accountability of multi-national capital.[45]

Joint planning of trade constitutes the third proposal for internationally coordinated action. Kinnock argues that "[w]e have to acknowledge the right of a country which pursues policies for full employment to protect itself against the effects of policies in other countries which do not". Contrary to evidence, Kinnock denies that the function of planned trade is to prevent the outflow of growth and employment effects to other states than precisely the one which is reflating: "The purpose of planned trade is to ensure that each country which benefits its own people through the stimulation of demand at the same time benefits its partners."[46]

The desirability of joint European action is, thus, stressed in a range of areas, but with the cornerstones of the AES remaining intact and the introduction of measures such as import penetration ceilings therefore continuing to play an important role in the party's economic policies, no role for the European Community appears in Kinnock's visions. Labour's continued scepticism towards the EC is also underlined by the fact that his proposals in the article for reforms of the EC involve measures which would clearly replace the existing Community with a loose intergovernmental framework organisation. Kinnock calls for the convening of a new Messina Conference (the conference which in 1957 negotiated the Rome Treaty). This conference should fundamentally reform or reject the Paris and Rome treaties, among other things thereby depriving the Commission of its right of initiative, enabling all European parties to send representatives to an Assembly of Europe, and correspondingly allowing all European governments to join a European Council.

The 1984 Elections to the European Parliament

In March 1984, the Confederation of Socialist Parties of the European Community agreed to a lengthy common programme for the European elections, notably centering around the same themes as Labour's overall

---

45) The first version of the Vredeling-proposal (named after the Commissioner presenting it) on "procedures for informing and consulting employees for undertakings with complex structure" was published in November 1980, cf. *Official Journal of the European Communities*, C 297 1980.
46) Neil Kinnock, "New Deal for Europe", p. 243.

policy objectives: commitment to substantial cuts in unemployment and, even if it occupies a less salient place than in Labour's programmes, to East-West détente. Most of the arguments of the "Out of Crisis" study take up prominent positions in the CSPEC manifesto. Hence, alongside initiatives for restructuring the EC economies and for redistributing for the benefit of unemployed, lower income groups, and Third World countries, the Manifesto - as the centrepiece in a joint recovery strategy - proposes a coordinated public investment push in the West European countries amounting to 1% of GNP. However, as a significant exception from the "Out of Crisis" document, the CSPEC manifesto does not include calls for the introduction of managed trade.[47]

For the British Labour Party, the CSPEC agreement was constrained by a series of reservations. Labour was unable to subscribe to the manifesto's call for strengthening the European Monetary System in order to protect the European economies from fluctuations in the dollar, its call for strengthening the European Parliament, and its proposal for an increase in the Community's own resources.

Nevertheless, the Labour Party's adoption of the CSPEC manifesto signified its partial return to the strategy championed for a period by James Callaghan in 1977. Even if the AES, as we have seen, continued to play an important role in the party's overall economic strategy, it appears that the difficulties of the French socialist government were making themselves felt in Labour policy making circles. The evident problems of internationally uncoordinated Keynesian growth strategies in an environment giving priority to the attainment of low inflation were forcefully illustrated by the experiences of the Mitterrand-administration, gradually leading the Labour Party to adopt a more internationally oriented strategy.

The final version of Labour's own manifesto for the European elections was adopted in May 1984 by the NEC and the Shadow Cabinet. It adheres to the recommendations put forward by Robin Cook in his December 1983 strategy paper and to the policies outlined in Kinnock's 1984 article. Thus, the manifesto focuses on domestic issues, calling for effective measures to stimulate the economy and demanding the preservation of welfare state institutions.

---

47) CSPEC, "Manifesto Adopted by the XIIIth Congress of the Confederation of the Socialist Parties of the European Community" (Luxembourg, March 1984), pp. 10-16 and 23-26.

Regarding the EC, it insists on a reduction in Britain's budget contribution and a fundamental reform of the CAP.[48] Although the manifesto does not explicitly demand British EC withdrawal, it calls upon the British Parliament to repeal the 1972 European Communities Act and hence to shed the supranational elements of EC cooperation. Laconically, it acknowledges that Britain will remain a member of the EC for the term of the next European Parliament, and it opens up the possibility of further developments in Labour's EC policy by then. Thus,

> "[a]t the end of that time Britain will have been a member of the EEC for 15 years - and this will be reflected in our pattern of trade, the way our economy works and our political relations overseas."

Nevertheless, the following section reiterates the continuing conflict between the party's visions of European cooperation and the existing European Community:

> "[We] recognise the fundamental nature of the changes we wish to see made in the EEC and that its rules may stand in the way of a Labour Government when it acts to cut unemployment. It is in this context that we believe that Britain, like all member states, must retain the option of withdrawal from the EEC".[49]

The second direct election to the European Parliament resulted in a victory for the Conservative Party: with 39.9% of the total cast vote, it won 45 of 81 seats whereas Labour's 36% of the total vote secured 32 seats. However, compared to the 31.6% of the vote and 17 seats won in the 1979 EP election, the results marked a partial come back for Labour. As Labour's candidates in most instances had been selected on grounds of strong anti-EC credentials, approximately twice as many opponents as proponents of British EC membership were elected.[50]

On the surface, the Labour Party's EC policies in the period from the 1983 election defeat to the 1984 European election give the impression of reform and retreat from earlier commitments. Analysed in more detail, substantial changes in the party's strategies seem less significant. The policy of EC-withdrawal had been replaced by a more vague policy of "keeping the options open". In light of the French experiences and its involvement in the "Out of Crisis" project, the party increasingly put

---

48) The Labour Party, "Labour's Manifesto for the 1984 European Elections" (London, 1984), pp. 1-8.
49) *ibid.*, p. 9.
50) David Butler and Paul Jowett, *Party Strategies in Britain*, p. 117.

emphasis on the need for internationally coordinated responses to the problem of mass unemployment. However, the two factors which had been of greatest importance in leading to the call for withdrawal from the Community, the direct economic costs of British EC membership and the Alternative Economic Strategy, remained intact as fundamentals in shaping the party's attitudes towards the EC. Consequently, Neil Kinnock's February 1984 call for joint European efforts to solve common problems virtually circumvents the structures and institutions of the EC, and his proposal for fundamental reform of the Community amounts to nothing less than a proposal to dissolve it. Similarly, the 1984 EP manifesto implies that the party will enact the policies it deems necessary, regardless of the Rome Treaty obligations.

The Labour Party and the Single European Act

The movement towards the reforms of the Rome Treaty, which were later to become known as the Single European Act, was initiated by French president Mitterrand. In May 1984, Mitterrand, in his capacity as president of the EC's Council of Ministers, announced his willingness to consider fundamental changes in the EC's functioning. In a context where the European Parliament recently had adopted its Draft Treaty for the European Union, he stressed the need for more efficient decision-making mechanisms in the Community and an increased use of majority decisions. Accordingly, the President suggested commencing consultations which could lead to an intergovernmental conference.[51] At the meeting of the European Council in Fontainebleau, the French presidency subsequently gained the approval of the other EC governments for the creation of a committee which should examine ways to improve the functioning of the Community. The Council also reached a partial solution to the problem of Britain's disproportionate contribution to the EC budget. The report of the reform-committee was presented at the meeting of the European Council in December 1984. Among other things, it called for an intergovernmental conference to negotiate reforms entailing the increased use of majority voting in the Council. In June

---

51) Bulletin of the EC, 5-1984, p. 138. See also Helmut Wagner, "Neues im Westen. Frankreichs späte Hinwendung zu Europa", *Zeitschrift für Politik*, vol. 31, no. 4 (December 1984), pp. 351-364.

1985 a majority of the European Council then agreed to convene an intergovernmental conference. The British, Danish and Greek governments opposed the decision, but according to article 236 of the Rome Treaty only a simple majority is required to call such a conference.

In Britain, the Labour Party was accorded the possibility to clarify its position on the EC reform proposals in a House of Lords committee set up in 1984, the committee's purpose being to investigate the European Parliament's Draft Treaty for a European Union as well as the reform-committee's report. The Labour Party's newly appointed spokesman on the EC, George Robertson, here argued that he thought there was a general view that the EC should be working more effectively. At the same time, however, he objected to the idea that "institutional tinkering" would advance solutions to the serious problems facing the Community, among which unemployment was seen as the most important. Thus, the question of a more effective EC was "really a question of political will and using the institutions which exist now rather than desperately searching round for new institutions".[52] Robertson expressed scepticism as to whether the use of the political veto in the EC Council could effectively be limited, and the extended use of majority voting was not seen as fostering an acceleration of EC decision-making. However, Robertson argued that

> "[f]rom the point of view of the labour movement ... it is not necessarily a self-interest argument for the veto. The trade union movement in Britain and Europe has argued for some time for a number of major measures, which have suffered from veto: Proposals on reduced working hours, quality of treatment in work, and so on."[53]

The final remarks of George Robertson appear to testify to a new pragmatism in the Labour Party's relationship with the EC. Thus,

> "we want to see the European nations dealing with the problems of growth, unemployment, the recession and the challenge of technology; and we will make use of any institutions which exist at the moment to make sure it happens."[54]

In the following months, however, this seemingly very workman-like approach was not followed up by any specific initiatives to further the

---

52) George Robertson in House of Lords Select Committee on the European Communities, "European Union" Session 1984-1985, 14th Report, HL 226, July 1985, p. 220.
53) *ibid.*, p. 225.
54) *ibid.*, p. 233.

said objectives within the given institutions. Rather, the approach of the party turned out to be little more than a continuous repetition of the call for a common European reflation.

Labour's persisting problems in painting a fundamentally new picture of its European policies is also exemplified by the fact that the party retained strong reservations on the future role of the European Parliament. Thus, in the Select Committee, both George Robertson and the then Labour spokesman on foreign affairs George Foulkes implied that direct elections to the EP were causing a number of problems.[55] At the end of 1985 George Foulkes proposed that Labour include in its general election manifesto the ending of direct elections to the EP and a return to the previous indirect system of nominated national parliamentarians.[56]

The intergovernmental conference on reforms of the Rome Treaty was officially convened in September 1985. The European Council met in December 1985 to discuss the proposals and surprisingly agreed on a draft Treaty reform package, the Single European Act, even though the final resolution of the summit was sprinkled with exemptions. Important in this respect was the British government's acceptance of Treaty reforms connected to the establishment of a Single Market in the EC. It appears that the British negotiators had been persuaded by the fact that London City financial enterprises stood to benefit significantly from the completion of a Single Market for financial services.

The SEA reform package contained Rome Treaty amendments in four main areas. First, qualified majority decision making procedures were introduced in the EC's Council of Ministers regarding the completion of the internal market; that is, the achievement of free movement in the Community of goods, services, capital, and persons, the last point including the removal of physical border controls (the amended Rome Treaty's article 100A). With respect to decisions on fiscal matters and the free movement of persons, however, the Council continued to decide by unanimity. In addition, article 8A of the amended Treaty set up 31 December 1992 as official deadline for the completion of the project. Transition to Council decision making by qualified majority was also

---

55) George Foulkes and George Robertson in House of Lords Select Committee on the European Communities, "European Union" Session 1984-1985, pp. 232-233.
56) *The Times*, 27 December 1985, here quoted from John Grahl and Paul Teague, "The British Labour Party and the EEC", *The Political Quarterly*, vol. 59, no. 1 (January-March 1988), p. 79.

made with respect to minimum workplace health and safety directives (article 118A) and regarding aspects of Community research programmes. Second, the role of the European Parliament was enhanced, as the EP in the "cooperation procedure" was to be heard twice regarding measures aiming at the completion of the internal market, questions of workplace health and safety, and on aspects of EC research programmes. If after the second hearing the Council wanted to decide with a qualified majority, those Parliament's proposals accepted by the Commission must be accepted by the Council as well (article 149 in the amended Treaty). Third, Community technology research programmes as well as the EC's environmental activities are codified (the amended Treaty's article 130 F-Q and R-T). Finally, the existing foreign policy cooperation of the EPC-system (European Political Cooperation) is codified and incorporated into the Treaty.

In the context of Labour's initial scepticism towards institutional reforms in the EC, it was hardly surprising that the party, in December 1985, rejected the Single European Act. In the first parliamentary debate on the SEA Neil Kinnock criticised the agreement for "yet again evading the obligation of [EC] members effectively to tackle unemployment in Europe and promote Europe's role in international affairs". Kinnock also castigated the government for having performed a U-turn on the desirability of Rome Treaty reform.[57]

The same viewpoints were expressed by Labour spokespersons during the spring 1986 parliamentary debates on the Amendment Bill incorporating parts of the SEA into British law. In March 1986, George Robertson condemned the Single Market plans as being a wholly inadequate response to the problem of mass unemployment:

> "The idea that reform of the internal market will inspire confidence among the 4 million unemployed in this country, never mind the 10 million others out of work across the Community, leaves me in mystification, and will give no hope to the people of Europe".[58]

The party's EC spokesman emphasised Labour's support for a cooperative growth strategy in the EC and criticised the Government for not having properly analysed the consequences of an internal market for British industry. On the specific contents of the SEA, Robertson argued that the Commission's programme for 1986 had made it clear that completion of

---

57) Neil Kinnock in *Parliamentary Debates (Commons)* 5 December 1985, col. 430.
58) *Parliamentary Debates (Commons)*, 5 March 1986, col. 343.

the internal market must not be allowed to compromise the Community's social priorities. However, precisely that EC legislation with a social content had been blocked by the British government. This was the case for the proposed directive on employee consultation and information procedures as well as a directive on parental leave. Moreover, in the SEA, British pressure had ensured that directives affecting the rights and interests of employees would remain subject to unanimity. George Robertson went on to state that

> "[if] the European Community is to be credible ... and is to benefit the peoples of the Community, surely it must be allowed to be used in these areas where it can be of use. In recent months we have heard much about multinational companies that have the freedom to play off against each other the workers in their various subsidiaries, but many of these abuses can be curbed only by measures that can be applied on a European basis, such as those that are proposed in the directive on worker information. However, they have all been vetoed by this Government."[59]

However, when asked directly whether Labour favoured the granting of more powers to the EC in these areas, he retreated, repeating Labour's continued wish to reform the EC fundamentally, that is: to upgrade its regional policy and to reform its budget and the CAP.

In April 1986, the House of Commons voted to incorporate the SEA into British law. The Labour Party's critique of the Treaty Reforms was by then clearly formulated. Firstly, the measures aiming at completion of the internal market of the EC were judged insufficient to stimulate European growth: "Nowhere", Robertson declared, "are we told when or how this is all to take place, or how, in a recession-battered continent, fewer barriers will not just mean shared misery and not increased prosperity".[60] Secondly, the specific constitution of the Single Market project was criticised in various respects. Labour's EC-spokesman stated that the party is not opposed to moves towards a more genuine internal market, but that the Government had failed to analyse the effects of the internal market on Britain's economy. Furthermore, the proposed harmonisation of VAT rates in "project 1992" was rejected, just as the need for accompanying social measures in the process of completing the internal market was stressed and the Government criticised for vetoing progress in this field. In conclusion, the Labour Party

---

59) George Robertson in *Parliamentary Debates (Commons)*, 5 March 1986, cols. 345-346.
60) George Robertson in *Parliamentary Debates (Commons)*, 23 April 1986, col. 330.

"agreed with the Prime Minister when she said that Treaty amendments were unnecessary, undesirable and a time-wasting diversion. Labour has not done any somersaults and still believes that this is the case."[61]

CONCLUSIONS: LABOUR AND THE EC 1980-1986

From the party's defeat in the 1979 general election to the vote in the House of Commons on British ratification of the Single European Act, the Labour Party's EC policy developed significantly. Labour's position on the question of British EC membership and on future development of the Community went from being critical towards the nature of the EC in 1979 to a policy of British withdrawal from the Community in the period from 1980 to 1983. From the 1983 election defeat and onwards, Labour policies on the European Community reverted towards a pragmatic, albiet clearly "EC sceptical" position: supporting internationally coordinated measures in the fight against unemployment, while keeping options open in the question of continued British EC membership. Finally, the party's continued scepticism towards the EC was illustrated by the fact that in early 1986 Labour voted against British ratification of the SEA. How do these developments correspond with the previously formulated propositions on the behaviour of social democratic parties towards market liberalising regional institutions such as the EC?

The Policy of EC Withdrawal

The Labour Party's long standing scepticism towards British membership of the EC has been analysed in the previous chapter. The party's adoption of a policy of withdrawal from the EC in many respects built on a deep-rooted hostility towards the Community, a scepticism traceable to the considerable direct and tangible economic costs for Britain of belonging to the EC, as indicated in the 1970 White Paper and reemphasised by among others the Cambridge Economic Policy Review group. Labour's sceptiscism also derived from the formal limitations on the nature and extent of state intervention in the economy following from Rome Treaty accession, a point repeatedly stressed by the left wing of the party.

---

61) *ibid.*, col. 332.

However, the radicalisation of Labour's EC policy in the late 1970s and early 1980s clearly reflected the ascendancy of the party's left wing. The left's growing strength again presumably resulted from a number of factors, especially Britain's continuing economic problems in the 1970s and the apparently inadequate political responses to these. For the left, the experiences of the Callaghan Governments and, prior to that, of the Wilson Governments had revealed the necessity of pursuing radically different economic and political strategies in order to prevent the continuing spread of industrial wastelands and the deepening of social problems.

In terms of our previously developed propositions, it seems clear that the ascendancy of the left wing in the Labour Party was a domestic development, a specifically British development significantly affecting the party's perceptions of the problems it was confronting in the British society as well as the ways in which it thought these problems should and could be solved. Thus, in many ways, the growing strength of left positions in the party constituted a cognitive development which reflected on the failed policies of the past and sought on this basis to formulate new strategies.

As viewed by the Labour left, the extension of the Common Market's legal framework to include the British political system meant damaging limits to the types of state intervention perceived necessary for solving Britain's economic problems. This prompted the left to call for withdrawal from the EC in order to increase the possibilities of implementing such intervention. On first sight, this appear as a straight-forward and convincing political strategy. On closer examination, however, the policy of withdrawal from the European Community in order to enable the implementation of the AES rests on a weak rationale. Hence, if a net economic-political benefit for the national regime in question is seen to ensue from pursuing a policy which conflicts with the Rome Treaty, then there is no reason to formally apply to and negotiate leaving the Community. The most significant threat possessed by other EC states in a situation of systematic and comprehensive violation of the Treaty is *de facto* expulsion of the violating state, perhaps supplemented with retaliatory economic sanctions. However, if leaving the EC yields a net benefit, then expulsion is no threat. Furthermore, the possibility of economic retaliation remains regardless of whether a given state is a member of the Community or not. It is an imminent possibility whenever there exists a degree of mutual economic dependency between states.

The weak economic-political rationale for the Labour Party's policy of withdrawal from the EC was reflected upon by one of the party's prominent MPs and MEPs, the long-standing opponent of British EC membership Barbara Castle, in an influential commentary already in September 1982. Castle argued that a future Labour Government should simply implement the measures it deemed necessary for the achievement of its priority objective of reducing unemployment. This would lead Britain into conflict with the EC and would prompt the British Government to call for reforms of relevant EC legislation. If sufficient reforms were not obtained, a Labour government could then let the other EC member states expel Britain if this eventually proved to be the only remaining possibility.[62]

The point not addressed by Barbara Castle, however, is the risk of other states' economic retaliation following measures such as import penetration ceilings, which undoubtedly would damage foreign export interests.

As we have seen, this possibility was either toned down or neglected in the writings of the proponents of the AES, or it was argued that negotiations with other member states of the EC would prevent the increasingly close trade relations between Britain and the remaining members of the EC from being adversely affected by withdrawal and the implementation of the AES. Thus, "negotiated withdrawal" as proposed by the party in *Labour's Programme 1982* as well as in the 1983 general election manifesto would allegedly remove Britain from the straitjacket of the Rome Treaty and at the same time make possible the establishment of new favourable trading agreements.

If withdrawal from the EC was sought in order make possible the implementation of the AES, however, then the establishment of new international agreements on matters such as trade and industry policy would sacrifice precisely the freedom from formal external constraints on economic policy which the withdrawal aimed at achieving. As Grahl and Teague have stated, "negotiated withdrawal" meant that the main rationale for British departure from the EC - the restoration of Parliament's freedom to deploy import and investment controls - had to be relinquished in order to facilitate the departure itself.[63]

---

62) Barbara Castle, "Let Them Throw Us Out", *New Statesman*, 17 September 1982.
63) John Grahl and Paul Teague, "The British Labour Party and the EEC", pp. 73-74. See also John Palmer, "Britain and the EEC: The Withdrawal Option", *International Affairs*, vol. 58, no. 4 (Autumn 1982), pp. 638-647.

In sum, to the extent that the Labour Party in the period from 1980 to 1983 sought British withdrawal from the EC instrumentally in order to enable the implementation of the AES, it did not constitute a logically coherent policy. Moreover, genuine national economic dependency on access to the markets of the European Community cannot be eliminated through changing what must be seen as purely formal relations. The increasing British dependency on EC market access, which was pointed out by David Owen in his rejection of the withdrawal policy and which presumably contributed to the electorate's rejection of Labour's 1983 manifesto, constitutes a basic structural condition which would remain regardless of formal British secession from the Community institutions.

Elimination of an economic dependency of this sort would, thus, require a fundamental change in the international economic structures of Western Europe, a change likely to be so costly that any economic benefits would be virtually ruled out. Nevertheless, proponents of the AES believed that a net benefit for British society could follow from a recourse to undisguised protectionism, a position which seems to rely on optimistic assumptions and a long term horizon, even if it must be conceded that Britain, in formally leaving the EC, would clearly escape the direct economic cost of its net budget contribution.

If Labour's policy of formal British withdrawal from the EC is to be understandable as instrumental-rational in the sense that withdrawal, in the views of the party leadership, constituted the best instrument for achieving intrinsically valued goals, it thus seems necessary to proceed from the assumptions that either 1) freedom from formal international constraints on national policy making was seen as such an intrinsically valued goal by the dominant part of the party, regardless of the fact that the elimination of formal constraints would not remove the actual structural constraints, as argued in the above, or 2) the direct benefits of escaping the net-contribution to the EC's budget constituted the only reason for the withdrawal policy.

If, however, freedom from purely formal international constraints on policy-making is seen as an end in itself, we transcend the analytical framework which underlies the study and the basic propositions guiding it. It means departing from the assumption that the institutional level at which a given general policy goal is pursued is not intrinsically important to social democratic parties, and that social democratic parties are therefore not "nationalist" and do not accord importance to national symbols of purely formal significance.

It seems a distinct possibility that the symbolic freedom from formal international constraints on national policy-making has been an intrinsically valued goal in parts of the Labour Party, and that this has constituted a motivation for the policy of formal British withdrawal from the EC. Hence, the importance of a nationalistic motivation is suggested by the fact that some of Labour's most outspoken critics of British EC membership, Peter Shore for instance, did not belong to the left wing of the party and consequently placed little emphasis on the implementation of the AES as a justification for withdrawal.

Similarly, the question of Britain's net-contribution to the EC budget clearly played a role for the party's policy of withdrawal. Witness the analyses of the Cambridge Economic Policy Review group and the NEC research papers presented to the 1981 conference.

An overall evaluation of the process leading the Labour Party to adopt its policy of EC withdrawal does not, however, support the claim that a nationalist valuation of symbolic freedom from international constraints has provided its main rationale. Neither is it plausible that the direct economic benefits of leaving the EC have been the dominant motivation for the policy of withdrawal.

Nationalist objections to British EC membership were voiced in the party, and the direct costs of membership certainly played a role, but the emergence of a policy of EC withdrawal remains closely correlated with the growing strength of the party's left wing. For the left wing, the most important objection to EC membership was that membership prevented the implementation of the Alternative Economic Strategy. This thread runs through the arguments for EC withdrawal in *Labour's Programme 1982*, Clive Jenkin's justification for moving the motion for withdrawal at the 1980 party conference, the analyses of the 1978 Cambridge Economic Policy Review, as well as Francis Cripps' and other writings developing the AES.

We can conclude that in the period from 1980 to 1983 the Labour Party pursued a policy which in several respects was logically incoherent, a policy which therefore cannot be seen as instrumentally rational in the sense that formal EC withdrawal constituted the most effective means of achieving intrinsically valued general policy goals. In other words, political parties cannot always be expected to formulate coherent policies, and a factor such as misperceptions may influence the content of specific party policies.

Coordinated Reflation and the Single European Act

In the aftermath of the 1983 election defeat, the Labour Party leadership turned the party's EC policies in a more pragmatic direction. Thus, the official approach to the question of continued British EC membership became one of "keeping the options open" in the event that EC membership came to stand in the way of a Labour government's policies. This policy line most likely reflected Barbara Castle's arguments regarding the excessive formalism contained in the policy of EC withdrawal. Furthermore, the 1983 election and the opinion polls preceding it had shown the party to be at odds with the majority of the electorate on the question of continued British EC membership. For this reason, it seems likely that the party leadership was adjusting its EC policies in order to broaden the party's electoral appeal.

At the same time, Labour increased its emphasis on the need for internationally coordinated measures to cope with mass unemployment, as evidenced by Neil Kinnock's 1984 article in the *New Statesman* and by the party's active involvement in the Western European socialist and social democratic parties' campaign for coordinated reflation. This development may be explained by two factors. First, the French socialist government's internationally uncoordinated economic expansion in an environment stressing the attainment of low inflation rates seems to have accentuated the need for international macroeconomic cooperation for the Labour leadership. We may thus identify a learning process in which the Labour Party's understanding of the existing state of affairs regarding internationally uncoordinated macroeconomic management gradually changes due to the experiences from other states.

The second factor relates to the steadily growing British economic dependency on access to the markets of other EC states, a development mentioned in the party's manifesto for the 1984 elections to the European Parliament. Thus, there is some evidence that Britain's growing dependency on EC membership was reflected upon by the party leadership, leading it to implicitly emphasise that an internationally coordinated reflation was preferable to a unilateral British reflation which, in light of the French experience, would have to involve import controls in order to be sustainable and therefore entailed grave risks of damaging Britain's foreign trade relations.

As mentioned, learning is not a factor constituting an integral part of the propositions on social democratic parties' EC policies formulated previously. However, to the extent that the second factor - Britain's growing economic dependency on continued EC membership - derives from British membership in the Common Market and the EC custom union and had led the party to increase its emphasis on the need for internationally coordinated action, this development appears to be in accord with our proposition on the internal dynamic of integration. British membership of a regional trade liberalising scheme gradually leads to increased economic dependency on continued membership, causing changes in the attitudes of a social democratic party.

However, this proposition predicts acknowledged dependency on membership of the EC to result in support for increased supranationality in the Community in areas where it could further the achievement of general social democratic policy goals. This does not occur in the Labour Party's EC policy following the 1983 elections. Although Kinnock's 1984 article and the Labour Party's subscription to the main parts of the 1984 CSPEC manifesto testified to the perceived need for international coope-ration, and although Kinnock's article also emphasised the need for "joint policies" to control multinational corporations and pursue economic democracy, any strengthening of the EC framework for furthering these goals is rejected; and indeed the proposal for a new Messina conference indicates that the leader of the Labour Party would have prefered to abolish the EC altogether.

This fact points to the Labour Party's enduring belief in the Alter-native Economic Strategy at this point in time, but also to the importance of the seemingly equally persistent "nationalist" rejection of the principle of supranationality *per se*. Hence, while the Mitterrand Government's experiences suggested that unilateral reflation was a difficult road to proceed, the Labour Party had not at this point in time developed any new economic strategy to replace it, and the belief that the existing character of the EC would lead a future Labour government into conflict with it thus continued to dominate the party leadership's approach.

Whereas the Labour Party's reaction to growing British dependency on EC membership fails to confirm out proposition regarding the internal dynamic of integration at this point in time, the party's rejection of the SEA accords more with the first part of this proposition, which states that social democratic parties will reject any strengthening of supranational decision-making capacity on regional market liberalisations. Hence, Labour's spokesmen on the EC repeatedly stressed their mistrust of regional market liberalisations as a solution to Western Europe's enduring economic problems.

However, the predominant attitude towards the Single Market plans appears as one of indifference rather than outright hostility. The position of the Labour Party seems to be that the Single Market constitutes an irrelevant project rather than a potential threat to the achievemet of national regulation of the market economy or the party's general political goals, as would be expected by the proposition on the internal dynamics of integration. Furthermore, George Robertson, in the April 1986 Commons debate, stated that the party was in principle not opposed to a more genuine internal market in the EC, a statement which moved the party line away from the Alternative Economic Strategy's emphasis on managed international trade.

The attitude of indifference reflects the fact that the Single European Act's provisions for majority voting on the establishment of an internal market did not pose an immediate threat to the existing national regulation perceived as necessary by the Labour Party or by its social basis. Thus, as the British regulation of relevance in the process of creating a Single Market does not generally deviate from most other member states in terms of being significantly more restrictive, the harmonisation or mutual recognition of standards which forms the main part of the 1992-process seemed unlikely to have immediate detrimental effects on highly valued regulation. Furthermore, it seems as if Labour's EC spokesman George Robertson was not convinced that the SEA would actually improve decision-making on regional market liberalisations in the Community; his remarks in the House of Lords committee pointing in this direction appear a consequence of the many years of stalemate and paralysis in the Community system preceding the SEA.

The acceptance in principle of moves towards a more genuine internal market in turn signifies the EC spokesman's diminishing belief in an independent British trade policy as an instrument for achieving general policy goals. However, in 1985 and early 1986, it did not seem as if this was an opinion widely shared in the party at large.

Robertson's indications during the parliamentary debates on the SEA in March 1986 of what the Labour Party would do within the Community framework had the party been in power at the same time testifies to a growing willingness to make practical use of EC institutions for furthering the party's general policy goals. This change most likely reflects the first concrete results of an increasing awareness that any fundamental restructuring of Britain's relations with the EC had become increasingly unlikely and increasingly costly.

As touched upon previously, an external development in the form of a threat by other major EC states' to exclude Britain from important international decision making fora seems to have influenced the Conservative government's willingness to compromise in the SEA negotiations. The same was not the case for Labour. This fact seems to be the result of two factors. First, Labour had low direct involvement in the negotiations, reflecting opposition parties' meagre possibilities of influence in the British political system. The fact that the next general election could not be expected to take place until 1987-88 probably weakened the party's interest in the concrete negotiations additionally, as this situation diminished the immediate concern for portraying the party as capable of pursuing a credible and plausible foreign policy. Since the party's prospectives for taking responsibility for British foreign policy were hardly imminent, it could more readily allow itself a distanced attitude to the SEA negotiations. Second, the fact that Labour was not significantly affected by the threat of national exclusion may serve as evidence of a continuing disaffection in the party with the EC as such. Hence, to the extent that it was not yet entirely clarified whether EC withdrawal or conflict with other EC states was an imminent possibility, the threat of exclusion may not be perceived as a threat at all, a point we made in the discussion of the strategy of withdrawal.

6

Towards Maastricht: Labour and the EC 1987-1990

In the period following the ratification of the SEA, the question of Britain's relation to the EC initially played a very small role in Labour Party rhetoric. The party's general election manifesto for the June 1987 election laconically stated that "Labour's aim is to work constructively with our EEC partners to promote economic expansion and combat unemployment". The explicit policy of withdrawal from the EC had been abandoned, but enthusiasm for the Community was still lacking: "[W]e will stand up for British interests within the European Community and will seek to put an end to the abuses and scandals of the Common Agricultural Policy. We shall, like other member countries, reject EEC interference with our policy for national recovery and renewal."[1]

The European question took up but a single paragraph in the manifesto, and in general the EC was not an issue in the election campaign, as only the Alliance of Liberals and the SDP seriously attempted to put it on the agenda.[2] One reason why the Labour Party ignored the EC issue may have been the wish to avoid exposing internal disagreements. The election resulted in a clear victory for the Conservatives, who retained the more than 42% of the total vote won in 1983. However, Labour gained almost three percentage points at the cost of the SDP-Liberal Alliance, securing 30.8% of the vote and winning an additional 20 seats in Parliament. Following the election defeat, the third in a row, the annual Labour Party conference overwhelmingly decided to support Neil Kinnock's and the NEC's proposal to instigate a thorough review of party policies prior to the next general election, taking into account the economic and social changes in British society following a

---

1) The Labour Party, "Labour's Manifesto for the 1987 General Election, Britain Will Win" (London, 1987), p. 15.
2) Cf. Andrew McEwen, "Only Steel and Owen Want Europe in Election Debate", *The Times*, 30 May 1987.

decade of Conservative rule.[3] Among other things, the review would entail a reformulation of the party's policies on the EC.

LABOUR, THE SINGLE MARKET, AND THE SOCIAL DIMENSION

The 1986 on agreement the Single European Act did in itself produce any fundamental new dynamism in the EC. The SEA did not take effect before June 1987, when it was ratified by last member state, Ireland. Furthermore, in order to obtain political agreement on the SEA, the Treaty amendments had deliberately left open a number of questions and avoided specifying policies and resources allotted to these policies in an additional number of areas. One such area was the strengthening of the Community's regional policy, a commitment which had been essential in order to obtain support for the SEA among the weaker industrial economies. In the period following the political agreement on the SEA, the EC also faced more immediate problems, primarily in relation to the Community budget and the ever growing expenses of the CAP.

The EC Commission addressed these problems in a proposal of January 1987.[4] The fundamental objectives were clear here: funds had to be provided for the structural funds of the regional policy, and the continuing problems with the CAP had to be solved so as to remove the issue from the political agenda. The European Council first debated the proposal at its meeting in June of 1987. Negotiations were resumed in October 1987, but a final compromise was not reached until February 1988 when a special summit meeting resulted in a 4 year agreement on the EC budget and the CAP.[5]

Thus, it was not until the beginning of 1988 that "project 1992" could reach the top of the EC's agenda and that the SEA had been supplemented with the political bargains necessary to lend credibility to the whole undertaking. Credibility was further strengthened when the European Council, at its June 1988 meeting, agreed on a directive which formalised the comprehensive liberalisation of regulation on capital movements in the Community.

---

3) The Labour Party, "Moving Ahead", NEC Statement to the Labour Party Conference (1987).
4) Commission of the European Community, "Requirements for the Implementation of the Single Act" (Brussels, 1987).
5) Lars Kolte, "Beslutningsprocessen i EF 1985-89", *Politica*, vol. 21, no. 4 (November 1989), pp. 376-395.

The Labour Party, however, had paid some attention to the issue of the evolving EC already at its 1987 annual conference. One of the Party's MEPs, David Martin, had called attention to the importance of "project 1992":

> "The Tories have set their agenda for Europe and are carrying it out. They are exporting Euro-Thatcherism. That agenda is the agenda of the multi-national companies and international capital. It is the agenda that heads for the completion of the internal market by 1992, a programme which will sweep away all controls to the movement of capital in relentless pursuit of profits for the minority. It is our job to work with our socialist allies in Europe to oppose the internal market. Yes, we would use the large market of 320 million people, but we have to use it in a planned, constructive way that leads to a co-operative growth strategy."[6]

A week prior to the February 1988 EC summit, Neil Kinnock then commented on "project 1992" during a visit to Brussels. Among other things he stated "we are no more prepared to leave the field of Europe to the operations of an unrestrained market capitalism than we are willing to leave Britain to the operations of Thatcherism."[7]

Furthermore, the Single Market "should not merely be a hunting ground for an unbridled market economy which only benefits an already privileged minority of the population."

Continuing in the same line, Kinnock made the clearest statement since the 1983 election that British withdrawal from the EC was no longer part of Labour's policies. In his view, the prospects for withdrawal were nil. Coincidentally, however, he implied a vision of the European Community very similar to that espoused by him in 1984, as he stated that Britain should demand exemption from relevant EC regulation so as to be able to follow the national recovery policies it considered necessary.[8]

The impression conveyed by Kinnock's February 1988 statements, therefore, is one of a party leadership which increasingly wishes to influence the direction in which the EC develops, but which also maintains its by now long standing insistence on exemptions from important parts of the Community's legal framework in order to enable a sustainable and internationally uncoordinated reflation in Britain.

---

6) David Martin in *Labour Party Conference Report 1987*, pp. 112-113.
7) "Strong Labour support for EEC", *The Times*, 4 February 1988, p. 2.
8) *Europe. Agence Internationale D'Information Pour la Presse*, 4 February 1988, p. 3.

The 1988 TUC Congress

During 1988, Labour's gradually changing approach towards the European Community was echoed by the British trade union movement. The trade unions had remained committed to an explicit policy of British withdrawal from the EC longer than the Labour Party itself. At the 1983 TUC Congress several months after the general election, a resolution calling for a revision of the policy of EC withdrawal was overwhelmingly defeated, even though supporting voices pointing to the growing economic importance of the EC's markets for UK exports were heard.[9] As late as late 1984 the TUC remained dominated by anti-EC positions.

However, divisions on how to approach the EC became increasingly manifest, the main cleavage being between the TUC secretariat, which is made up of full time staff members, and the TUC General Council and Congress, representing affiliated trade unions. The secretariat wanted the TUC to align its positions to the Labour Party, while the General Council wanted to maintain the status quo. From 1985 and onwards the balanced tipped, and the Secretariat was gradually given space to argue for more positive European policies in various fora.[10] Nevertheless, the General Council in November 1986 issued a statement criticising the EC's Single Market plans for "greatly restricting the freedom of national governments to pursue independent policies.[11]

The TUC's emphasis on a more positive position on the Community increased dramatically in 1988. In May, TUC Assistant General Secretary David Lea, speaking in Stockholm to the European Trade Union Confederation (ETUC), opined that there would be great support for the Community's 1992 programme if it were accompanied by employment creating measures. Lea made clear that unless trade unions took the initiative, harmonisation of workers' rights and conditions would be based on the lowest common denominator in the Single Market.

At the congress, the ETUC, supported by the British TUC, adopted resolutions advocating minimum legal standards for workers' rights in the EC and for a coordination of economic policies in Western Europe.[12]

In August of the same year, the TUC then released a report on the

---

9) TUC, *115th Report 1983*, pp. 493-497 and p. 618.
10) Paul Teague, "The British TUC and the European Community", pp. 35-36.
11) TUC, *118th Report 1986*, p. 281.
12) Michael Dynes, "TUC Aim is Cross-Frontier Collective Bargaining", *The Times*, 20 May 1988.

effects of the Single Market. The very fact that an analysis like this was put forward signifies a clear increase in the attention the trade unions directed to developments within the institutions of the European Community. Furthermore, the report effectively buried the TUC's policy of British withdrawal from the EC and stressed the challenges posed by "project 1992".The introductory section, for example, noted that "the Trade Union Movement in Western Europe needs to identify precisely the effects of the open market and to work out a strategy and develop the means to deal with them".[13]

The "social dimension" of the Single European Market occupies a prominent position in the TUC report. The social dimension has various meanings, but as it was promoted by the EC Commission in general and the EC Commission President Jacques Delors in particular since 1988, it refers to the need for legally guaranteed fundamental workers' rights in the Market, as well as to the need for supplementary EC measures to maximise the employment effects of the Single Market; i.e., measures aimed at increased mobility of workers and at investment in training and infrastructure.[14]

The need for a number of fundamental workers' rights to be guaranteed in the Single Market has been motivated from the side of many trade unions in the EC by their fear that an increase in the real mobility of capital in the EC could release pressures on employee rights. To the extent that capital, goods, and services flow freely between states, companies obtain a broader range of choice as to where to locate production. It is thought that some states may lower social standards in order to increase cost competitiveness and attract foreign investments. This may again put pressure on other states, entailing a downward spiralling of social benefits and employee rights as member states attempt to outdo each other in creating a "healthy business climate", a process often referred to as "social dumping". In addition, the corporate dynamics

---

13) TUC, *Maximising the Benefits. Minimising the Costs*, Report on Europe 1992 (London, 1988), p. 2.
14) The proposal for a set of guaranteed workers' rights in the Single Market was first put forward by the Belgian Government in the fall of 1987. Together with an ETUC-proposal for an EC system of social rights, advanced in February 1988, it became the basis for the Commission's proposals for a Social Charter and a social action programme, as announced by Jacques Delors at the May 1988 ETUC meeting in Stockholm, cf. Paul Teague, *The European Community: The Social Dimension* (London: Kogan Page, 1989), pp. 74-86, Europe. Agence Internationale D'Information Pour La Presse, *Europe Documents*, 11 March 1988, p. 1, Kåre Hagen, *Nasjonalstat, Velferdspolitik og Europeisk Integration* (Oslo: FAFO, 1990), pp. 88-89 and *Financial Times*, 9 May 1988.

released by regional market liberalisations involving growing numbers of mergers and take-overs across borders has been seen, by organised labour, as posing a threat that employers would utilise "divide and rule" strategies against employees in different member states, necessitating EC regulation to guarantee certain rights.

The question of the social dimension may also be seen, however, as involving the question of the entire model for future economic development in Western Europe, a question as to whether labour market flexibility should be "defensive" or "offensive". A defensive strategy relies on wage flexibility for attaining full employment with the risk of demand deficiencies and low productivity growth. "Offensive flexibility" uses public regulation and fundamental social rights as a means to increase labour productivity.[15] This argument, however, evades the question of why precisely a supranational organisation such as the EC should adopt the regulation. If strict labour market regulation is seen to have positive effects on productivity levels and thereby on international competitiveness, there is no risk that national standards are undermined by regional market liberalisations and competitive pressures from low-standard economies.

Finally, liberal economists generally argue that a "social dimension" is unnecessary, since national labour market regulation must be seen as an element of total labour costs, and as changes in this regulation are reflected in employment levels and, subsequently, in real wages. Assuming constant productivity, employees themselves therefore "pay" for the level of labour market standards, as illustrated by an increase in the level of standards which will entail rising unemployment and falling real wages until a new equilibrium emerges.

It follows that "social dumping" is no threat, as low labour market standards will be offset by high demand for labour and subsequently by higher real wages. It also follows that the imposition of supranational standards higher than the lowest existing country standard in the EC will serve only to increase unemployment in the regions with the lowest previous standards until real wages have been depressed so as to allow for the establishment of a new equilibrium. If the supranational regulation in question produces a minimum wage higher than the lowest

---

15) Cf. e.g. Martin Rhodes, "Labour Market Regulation in Post-1992 Europe", *Journal of Common Market Studies*, vol. 30, no. 1 (March 1992), pp. 27-35, and Robert Boyer, "Defensive or Offensive Flexibility?" and "The Search for New Wage/Labour Relations" in R. Boyer (ed.), *The Search for Labour Market Flexibility* (Oxford: Oxford University Press, 1988), pp. 222-273.

wage level in the Community, the result will be higher employment in high wage regions at the cost of higher unemployment in low wage regions, at least as long as productivity levels in the low wage regions are lower than what is needed to clear markets at the minimum wage level. This effectively means a different sort of protectionism from the side of high wage economies.[16]

The social dimension to the Single Market takes up a very prominent place in the TUC's document on the EC's 1992-programme. Thus,

> "[if the] benefits [of the Single Market] are to be maximised for the Community as a whole, it is important that they are distributed to working people as well as for companies. Indeed they make possible the achievement of the social dimension of the internal market, which is integral to the 1992 process and to making it work. The social dimension is not, therefore, an additional cost for industry, but an element in improving its competitiveness."[17]

The report calls attention to what it views as a backlog of social legislation in the EC framework, and identifies the Thatcher Government as the main obstacle in this respect. It also emphasises, however, the possibilities offered by the adoption of the Single European Act, as the SEA permits new directives for "improvements, especially in the working environment, as regards the health and safety of workers, to be adopted by a qualified majority, thus bypassing the UK veto."[18]

Regarding specific proposed EC directives, the report supports elements which restrict the extent to which market mechanisms alone will determine the nature and location of production. With respect to the proposed liberalisation of public procurement in the 1992 programme, the TUC wants labour conditions and regional policy programmes to be safeguarded.

In the conclusions of the document, the TUC General Council calls for a mobilisation of the trade unions in order to influence the development of "project 1992". It is recommended that all affiliated unions appoint at least one full time officer with specific responsibilities for European matters, just as it calls for strengthening European trade union cooperation in specific areas within the framework of the ETUC.[19]

---

16) Kåre Hagen, *Nasjonalstat, Velferdspolitik og Europeisk Integration*, pp. 65-78, and Det Økonomiske Råd, *Dansk Økonomi* (Copenhagen, December 1989), pp. 77-108.
17) TUC, *Maximising the Benefits*, p. 7.
18) TUC, *Maximising the Benefits*, pp. 14-15.
19) TUC, *Maximising the Benefits*, p. 24.

The fact that the TUC perceived a need to react to the process towards the completion of a Single Market is also evidenced by the fact that the president of the EC Commission, Jacques Delors, was invited to address the TUC's annual conference in September 1988.

Delors' speech emphasised the significance of the Single Market process, terming it a peaceful revolution in which everyone must participate. According to Delors, there were many ways of reacting to "project 1992". Some were sceptics, and enthusiasts saw the internal market as the answer to all problems. Yet, there were also architects, like Delors himself, who saw the opportunities and were ready to tackle difficulties. Delors invited the British trade unionists to join this process, in this respect paying particular attention to the social dimension of the Single Market: It would be unacceptable for Europe to become a source of social regression, and the Commission had already advanced proposals to safeguard and improve working and living conditions (the first proposals for an EC Social Charter and a social action programme to supplement to the 1992 programme).[20]

Delors' address, reported by the major television networks in prime time, won a standing ovation from the delegates, and at the symbolic level the TUC's reception of Delors undoubtedly marked a turning point in the British labour movement's relations to the EC, especially so in the eyes of the public.[21]

Norman Willis, general secretary of the TUC, commented upon Delors' speech, stating that the EC was not going to go away, and that 1992 could not be deferred. Hence, the TUC had to make the most of it. The TUC had a vital, influential role to play. Ron Todd, chairman of the TUC's International Committee, added that there was nothing to be gained by approaching the Government: the only card game in town was in Brussels.[22]

The Congress subsequently voted in favour of the TUC's report on the Single Market, just as it adopted a composite motion on Europe ending the movement's opposition to British EC membership, calling for "project 1992" to be accompanied by parallel measures to safeguard jobs and

---

20) TUC, *120th Report 1988*, pp. 568-570.
21) This view is affirmed by interviews in October 1990 with George Robertson, Labour's spokesman on the EC, and Mike Gapes, then Labour's Senior International Secretary. Delors' speech was also referred to by Neil Kinnock at the Labour Party's Conference a month later, cf. *Labour Party Conference Report 1988*, p. 61.
22) TUC, *120th Report 1988*, pp. 571-572. See also "Workers in Unions Will be Only Ones Ready for 1992'", *The Times*, 9 September 1988.

working conditions, and for the General Council to work through the ETUC toward increased cooperation with unions in other EC states, and for the establishment of Europe-wide bargaining.[23]

Labour's Social Offensive 1988-1989

The Labour Party's spokesman on EC affairs, George Robertson, was quick to draw his conclusions from the general atmosphere of the TUC congress. In a political commentary, he stated that "the TUC has changed the whole direction of Britain's Labour Movement". He continued:

> "The union approach to the Single Market involves coming to terms with two real pressures. First is the relentless Europeanisation of companies and markets which is marginalising the effect of purely national unions. Second is a dawning awareness that Community institutions may provide a rare escape from the Thatcherite social offensive in Britain. ... The trade unions have, therefore, an awakened self-interest in plugging into a European dimension - an interest which the Labour Party shares".

According to Robertson, Labour would follow this course, and in the period up to the European Parliament elections in June 1989 would emphasise the demand for harmonised employee rights and adequate social and regional funds to offset unbalanced growth. "And, after years when antipathy to the Common Market has downgraded the issue, the Labour Party can have a position on Europe which will be positive and clear".[24]

The Labour Party's own definite and formal dissociation from the policy of British withdrawal from the EC came shortly after this, at the October 1988 annual party conference. Thus, according to the Party's Shadow Foreign Secretary, Gerald Kaufman, "we have accepted that nearly 20 years after Britain joined, withdrawal is no longer a practical proposition. Those like myself who opposed British membership came to that conclusion reluctantly. But we decided that we had to come to terms with inescapable facts and make the best of membership."[25]

Subsequently, the conference without a card vote adopted a resolution on Britain and the EC which acknowledged not only that "Britain politi-

---

23) Composite 16, "Europe 1992: Trade Union Strategy, TUC, *120th Report 1988*, pp. 573-576.
24) George Robertson, "Forward from Delors", *The Times*, 26 September 1988.
25) Gerald Kaufman in *Labour Party Conference Report 1988*, p. 126.

cally and economically is integrated into the EC", but also that "the Labour Party, in conjunction with the other socialist parties of the EC, must seek to use and adapt Community institutions to promote democratic socialism". It also made clear that

> "the completion of the Single European Market will present a major challenge to the socialist parties of Europe. Unless the Community is committed to implementing social provisions and a complementary social programme to the Single European Market to ensure that the benefits of the unified Market are shared by all people in the EC, it will only benefit the business community. Conference recognises the need to devise a strategy to overcome these problems".[26]

Neil Kinnock pursued this theme in his speech. He highlighted the importance of the 1992-programme and the inadequacy of Government measures to prepare British industry for its competitive challenges. Similarly, he pointed to the necessity of a social dimension in the Single Market, just as he contrasted the positions of the Labour Party with the Thatcher Government's rejection of guarantees for social rights within the EC, a position underlined two weeks earlier when Mrs. Thatcher attacked EC supranationality and social regulation in speeches at Bruges and Luxembourg:[27]

> "Our attitude is very different. We want Europe to be a community as well as a market. ... If a Single Market is created that extends across half the continent and the requirements of social justice are not installed as a central component in that venture, then the fruits of economic efficiency will be scooped up by a few [regions]. ... That is why we say that the social dimension of the Single Market must be central to the prospectus and to the practice of the EC. Social Europe must mean getting the highest standards of working conditions and workers' rights across that Single Market. ... It must mean, in this multinational market, tough anti-trust laws firmly enforced by domestic governments and by the Community itself. It must mean substantial social and regional funds to counteract the market's inevitable pull of wealth, production and jobs towards the centre. And Social Europe must mean the root and branch reform of the Common Agricultural Policy which is unsustainable. ... It is clear, too, [that] Social Europe must mean Community action to safeguard, to protect and conserve the environment: land, sea and air. ... We insist upon all that."[28]

Kinnock elaborated on these views in his contribution to a booklet

---

26) Composite motion 58, *Labour Party Conference Report 1988*, p. 180.
27) See e.g. Nicholas Wood, "Europe Fears Battle Ahead With Thatcher", *The Times*, 22 September 1988.
28) Neil Kinnock in *Labour Party Conference Report 1988*, pp. 61-62.

containing the views of prominent social democrats on the EC's 1992-programme. The leader of the Labour Party here stated that

> "[t]he concept of the 'social dimension' of the Community is one which must be widely and effectively applied ... We must vigorously assert, therefore, that the Social and Regional funds must be substantial enough to offer support to those parts of the [EC] which will most feel the disruptive effects of the new market arrangements. ... [Furthermore,] we have to offer instruments for balance that will include ... a) the acceptance of the principle and practice of government or EC intervention for the purpose of ensuring development in regions, that do not have the advantages of location in the central area of the Single Market, b) the encouragement of productive and competitive industry by targeted investment and research and training, c) the achievement of a European strategy for the development of science and technology, d) upward harmonisation in rights and conditions at work, including decision-making structures in industry, and e) a genuine intra-EC trade policy that prevents one country from acquiring a massive surplus at the expense of another".[29]

As foreseen by George Robertson, the Labour Party's efforts prior to the June 1989 elections to the European Parliament subsequently focused on social rights in the EC framework. Hence, the manifesto of the CSPEC, adopted in February 1989 with the support of Labour, reiterated the importance accorded to social measures accompanying the 1992 process. Furthermore, the call was repeated for common European expansionist economic policies, albeit in less concrete terms than in the 1984 manifesto, along with proposals for a strengthened EC industrial and regional policy. The Labour Party could not, however, subscribe to the contents of the manifesto proposing a strengthening of the European Parliament and fiscal harmonisation in the internal market.[30]

Labour's own manifesto for the 1989 European elections enthusiastic supports "progress on the social dimension in Europe", understood as "an upward harmonisation of all social standards across the Community to the highest possible level". The manifesto castigates Mrs. Thatcher for blocking social legislation in the EC framework, stating that for the Conservatives, "the future is in deregulation without social obligation". It also calls upon the EC to develop a coherent industrial strategy for Europe, involving a strengthening of common research and training programmes. The traditional calls for reform of the CAP and the EC

---

29) Neil Kinnock, "Facing the Future of the European Community", in Piet Dankert and Ad Kooyman (eds.), *Europe Without Frontiers. Socialists on the Future of the European Economic Community*, London: Mansell Publishing, 1989, pp. 6-7.
30) CSPEC, "Manifesto Adopted at the XVIth Congress of the Confederation of Socialist Parties of the European Community" (Brussels, 10 February 1989).

budget are present as well.[31] During the campaign, particular support was voiced for the European Social Charter, the Commission's proposal having been unveiled on 17 May, and the Government's hostility towards the charter was criticised.[32] Domestic issues, however, took up a very prominent role in the campaign, as the Labour Party in the context of rising inflation rates, the Government's introduction of an unpopular poll tax, and a growing trade-deficit attempted to turn it into a popular verdict on ten years of Thatcherism.[33]

The result of the election was a Labour victory, the party winning 46 of the UK's 81 seats in the European Parliament, an increase of 14, whereas the Conservatives secured 32 seats. In contrast to the 1984 European elections, the majority of the new Labour MEPs had a positive attitude towards the EC. Shortly after the election they chose to replace Dr. Barry Seal with Glyn Ford as leader of the Labour EP group.[34]

The NEC's report to the 1989 annual Labour Party conference argued that the result of the EP election was "a clear endorsement of Labour's positive approach to the EC and its attitude to the social dimension of the internal market. The Labour Party has now shown itself to be the party of Europe. It is now far more committed and enthusiastic in its attitude to the Community than the Conservative Party". It also stated that the newly elected Labour EP group would build on the electoral success and act as a "second front" to fight the Conservative government in Britain.[35]

At the same time the party conference approved the Policy Review Group's comprehensive final report for new Labour policies in a range of areas, the report being entitled "Meet the Challenge, Make the Change". The report marks the official approval of Labour's EC approach, as formulated by the party leadership from the 1988 conference and onwards. Hence,

"Britain's future is in the European Community as it develops. But we have a very different vision from the present government of what that future should be. Mrs. Thatcher persists in trying to impose her free market dogmas on the rest of the EC, seeking to thwart or evade every measure for

---

31) The Labour Party, "Meeting the Challenge in Europe, Labour's Manifesto for the European Elections" (London, 1989).
32) E.g. The Labour Party, Campaign Briefing, 9 June 1989.
33) The Labour Party, "Neil Kinnock's Statement at the Launch of Labour's Campaign for the European Parliament Elections", London, 23 May 1989.
34) Nicholas Wood, "Moderates to Lead Labour in Europe", The Times, 21 June 1989.
35) NEC, Report to Conference 1989, p. 59.

social progress. She wants Europe to be a Market, with minimum regulation for big business and finance. We want it to be a Community too - not just because it is more desirable in human terms, but because it also is a precondition for durable economic success. We want Britain to take a lead in building social Europe".[36]

A later section of the policy review went on to state that this entailed "a Community which promotes economic growth, creates jobs and fosters industrial and technological advance; a Community which gives a strong priority to social and regional concerns; ... whose policies protect and enhance our environment; ... which strengthens consumer rights [and] which overcomes the barriers which divide East and West."[37] Concretely, this meant that a future Labour Government would lift the British veto on EC regulation to improve employee co-determination, just as it would work for EC environmental protection measures such as a far more rapid improvement in vehicle emission standards, creation of an EC environmental charter, and EC research programmes into the job creating effects of environmental regulation.

The policy review stated that consumer protection should be given a greater emphasis in EC harmonisation regulation, that EC consumer legislation should "build on the best of the law enjoyed by the United Kingdom and the rest of Europe". Furthermore, "it may be necessary to give the European Court of Justice jurisdiction over consumer rights and protection".[38] Finally, on social and labour market policies, the review reiterated the party's commitment to a social dimension to the Single Market:

> "If wages remain higher, environmental standards tougher or employees' benefits more generous in other countries, then British companies will try to compete by undercutting and Britain will end up as a social dumping ground. This is precisely what the present government wants and why they are so opposed to the idea of Social Europe, rising standards. They will continue to encourage a deregulated labour market, by abolishing minimum wages, reducing maternity rights, weakening trade unions, and removing legal protection for employees."[39]

The policy review thus marks the practical and concrete integration of the EC and of existing EC regulation into the party's political strategies.

---

36) The Labour Party, *Meet the Challenge, Make the Change: A New Agenda for Britain. Final Report of Labour's Policy Review for the 1990s* (London, 1989), p. 7.
37) The Labour Party, *Meet the Challenge, Make the Change*, p. 79.
38) The Labour Party, *Meet the Challenge, Make the Change*, pp. 13, 25, 42, 68, 75, and 78.
39) The Labour Party, *Meet the Challenge, Make the Change*, p. 17.

It also marks a perhaps even more basic change of general attitude on behalf of the party as well, a change of attitude as to what "European" stands for. The review repeatedly refers to the need for and wish to achieve "European standards" of public regulation, as contrasted to the perceived inadequacies of the Thatcher Government's reliance on market regulation.[40]

Endorsing Institutional Reforms

Up to this point, the Labour Party's EC-offensive had manifested itself as an unprecedented focusing on the possibilities for and necessity of adopting regulation in the EC framework with a social content and aimed at areas such as consumer and environmental protection. Compared to earlier statements, the Labour Party's EC policy in 1988-89 differs in being more positively worded.

Particular importance is attached to opportunities offered by the EC for the adoption of binding regulation with a content which in the party leadership's perception would further achievement of the party's general policy goals. The emphasis on failures and inadequacies of the Community's functioning and the limits EC membership entails for national policies has similarly been toned down.

This very important development seems to have several causes: (1) a recognition of fundamental British dependency on continued membership of the EC; (2) the Community's evolution towards the completion of a genuine Single Market, and (3) the Thatcher Government's obstinate rejection of adopting any EC legislation not explicitly linked to regional market liberalisations.

By autumn, however, 1989 little willingness had been shown to endorse any institutional reforms of the EC, as the 1989 policy review had found institutional changes in the Community to be unnecessary.[41] This changed during the winter 1989-90 and the spring of 1990, with the dramatically enlarged Labour group in the European Parliament appearing to have played a certain role in this respect.

---

40) This applies to policies on education (pp. 18 and 48), on competition and mergers (p. 11), on consumer protection (p. 42), labour rights (p. 25), local and regional government powers (pp. 45 and 57), immigration (p. 62), environment (pp. 67 and 69), infrastructure (p. 71), and energy (p. 76).

41) The Labour Party, *Meet the Challenge, Make the Change*, p. 80.

As will be discussed later, French President Mitterrand, in October 1989, in a situation of accelerating breakdown of the Communist regimes in Eastern Europe, called for the convening of a new EC intergovernmental conference whose aim would be to discuss Rome Treaty reforms for the creation of an Economic and Monetary Union (EMU) in the Community. In this context Carole Tongue, deputy leader of the Labour EP group, in November 1989 opined that the party according to her own opinion would be willing to transfer formal national sovereignty to the EC in areas such as social policy and industrial relations.[42]

Following this, in December 1989 the leader of the Labour EP Group, Glyn Ford, made clear that the forthcoming intergovernmental conference on an EMU also should allow for the use of majority decisions in the Council of Ministers in matters concerning environmental protection and social rights. Thus, "it is absurd to operate with two different types of decision making procedures: that the Single Market which benefits industry can be completed with a majority in the EC whereas it takes unanimity in areas benefitting the working classes".[43] Apart from this, Glyn Ford hinted that a new Labour position on a strengthening of the European Parliament could be on its way.

In early February 1990, however, these viewpoints had not yet penetrated the party leadership: At a meeting of the CSPEC in Berlin, Neil Kinnock rejected the introduction of general majority decision-making procedures within this organisation. His motivation stressed Labour's resistance to a strengthening of the European Parliament and to EC constraints on a Labour government's tax policies. The party thus objected to general majority procedures for reasons of principle.[44]

Then, in March 1990, the European Parliament adopted a resolution which as a goal for the coming intergovernmental conference stressed the need for the introduction of systematic majority voting in the Council on social and environmental policies in order to "provide for a balanced and equitable development of the Single Market and the Monetary Union". The resolution also emphasised the EP's support for economic and monetary union between those EC members states wishing to pursue this objective, just as it proposed a significant strengthening of the European

---

42) Interview with Carole Tongue, Radio Denmark, 22 November 1989.
43) Lars Olsen, "Britisk Labour regering ville være tæt på Danmark i sin EF-politik", *Information*, 23 December 1989.
44) Martin Kettle, "Socialists Pave the Way for All-Europe Federation", *The Guardian*, 9 February 1990.

Parliament's authority in the EC's legislative process, among other things in the form of the introduction of parliamentary co-decision with the Council of Ministers on Community legislation.[45]

The interesting point in this connection, however, is that the report adopted by the resolution was developed by a subcommittee chaired by David Martin, Labour MEP, and that a clear majority of the Labour EP group voted in favour of the resolution.[46] As Ian White of the EP group explained in the plenary debate,

> "[A] Single Market without barriers cannot operate without a common approach in all those areas in which it is necessary or desirable for the public authorities to set the rules or intervene, including: policies for economic and social cohesion and, above all, social policy to ensure there is no competitive undermining of minimum standards."[47]

The Labour EP group's support for the resolution generated a certain tension between the EP group and the Westminster party, as Labour's Campaign Coordinator, Jack Cunningham, and General Secretary, Larry Whitty, meeting with Labour MEPs on 15 March, pointed out that the Martin report went "significantly beyond the position of the Labour Party" and might cause problems with the PLP of Westminster.[48]

However, the meeting did not persuade the Labour EP group to change its policies. Rather, it was the Westminster leadership which reformulated its positions. Thus, at the end of March 1990, the views of the EP group were to some extent agreed to by parts of the party leadership in the form of a draft policy review by a special subcommittee of the NEC, the work of which constituted a part of the ongoing process to reformulate the party's policies before the next general election. The subcommittee consisting of EC spokesman George Robertson, Glyn Ford of the EP group, and Gwyneth Dunwoody of the party's women's section recommended that the Labour Party should support, firstly, the introduction of majority decision-making procedures in the Council of Ministers in matters of social and environmental policy and, secondly, a strengthening of the European Parliament, enabling the EP to initiate legislation

---

45) The European Parliament, "Resolution on the Intergovernmental Conference in the Context of Parliament's Strategy for European Union", 14 March 1990.

46) The European Parliament, "Interim Report of the Committee on Institutional Affairs", Doc. A 3-47/90.

47) Ian White in *Debates of the European Parliament*, no. 3-388, March 1990, p. 115. See here also David Martin, *European Union and the Democratic Deficit* (West Lothian: John Wheatley Centre, 1990), pp. 13-18.

48) John Palmer, "Labour MEPs Warned Off Federalism", *The Guardian*, 16 March 1990.

for consideration in the Council, appoint the Commission, and together with the Council of Ministers pass laws on social and environmental policy. At this point, Glyn Ford would comment on any details of the document, stating only that "the Labour Party will have to come to terms with the realities of European integration and progress towards European union if we are to achieve our political goals".[49]

In a context where, in April 1990, German Chancellor Kohl and French President Mitterrand following the accelerating breakdown of the GDR and moves towards German unification, had proposed the summoning of a second intergovernmental conference on a "political union" in the EC, a meeting on 1 May 1990 in the NEC policy review group on foreign and defence policy then agreed to support the main conclusions of the EC-report.[50] It endorsed the proposal to extend majority voting procedures in the Council to areas of social and environmental policy, but the proposals for an extension of EP authority were diluted, as any reference to co-decision procedures had disappeared.

The new policy on institutional change in the EC reached the official stage as it was included in the abbreviated campaign version of the comprehensive Labour Party policy review released on 24 May 1990. As the policy document stated it:

> "The European Community must become both deeper and wider in its membership. It should also have a more substantial agenda and a greater ability to act on it".

The proposal to extend majority voting in the EC was motivated by the "asymmetry" of decision-making in the Community following the adoption of the Single European Act:

> "As a result of the Single European Act, the EC's Council of Minsters can now decide on measures to implement the 1992 Single Market by a qualified majority vote. Perversely, however, qualified majority voting does not apply to the measures needed to ensure a balanced 1992 programme. Labour therefore supports the extension of majority voting to those decisions where it would help to improve social policy and raise environmental standards."[51]

Regarding environmental protection, the document explains that "[w]e

---

49) John Palmer, "Labour Move for European Union", *The Guardian*, 30 March 1990.
50) Patrick Wintour and Michael White, "Labour Looks to Europe as PM Digs In", *The Guardian*, 2 May 1990, and Patrick Wintour, "Labour to Back European Credentials With Policy", *The Guardian*, 3 May 1990.
51) The Labour Party, *Looking to the Future*, Labour Party Policy Review (London, 1990), p. 45.

will ensure that decision making is done at the most appropriate level - whether tackling ozone layer destruction at the global level, acid rain at the European level, or other environmental problems at the national, regional or local level."

The document also endorses a certain limited strengthening of the European Parliament, calling for the EP to be granted the right to initiate proposals for legislation and for the "cooperation procedure" involving a second EP reading to be extended to social and environmental areas.[52] In the same connection, however, it is stated that the EC is not a unitary state and should not develop towards a European superstate. Hence, "the European Parliament should be given the powers it needs to complement - not to replace - national parliaments".

In addition, the policy document makes clear Labour's support for increasing the number of EC member states, declaring that "[a]n enlarged European Community, with the united Germany firmly entrenched within it, will provide the best framework for building new relations across our continent."

By mid-1990, then, the Labour Party had formulated a policy on the institutional development of European Community which differed markedly from the positions defended in the years immediately after the adoption of the Single European Act, not to mention in the late 1970s and the first half of the 1980s.

LABOUR AND EUROPEAN MONETARY INTEGRATION, 1989-90

In the European Community, the period from 1988 to 1990 was not just characterised by the progressing completion of a Single Market and by the political pressures linked to this process. From mid-1988 onwards, the question of a deepening of monetary integration in the form of the gradual creation of an Economic and Monetary Union gradually moved to the top of the agenda. EMU had been discussed in the late 1960s and early 1970s. The 1969 Hague EC summit meeting had produced a state- ment of intent to move forward in this direction. Subsequently, the Commission developed the "Werner Plan" to establish an Economic and

---

52) The proposal to allow the EP a right of initiative is not of great importance, as the EP granted itself this right years ago and as the Commission most often adheres to the EP's proposals. However, stipulating the right may lend extra muscle to the EP vis-à-vis the Commission, cf. David Martin, *European Union and the Democratic Deficit*, p. 24.

Monetary Union by stages before 1980, some of the first steps including
the creation of a "centre of decision for economic policy" and a
Community system of central banks. The Council, however, could not
agree on these reforms at its meeting in March 1971, and a few months
after this, the Breton Woods monetary regime broke down, leading to
sharply increasing global exchange rate volatility. Together with the
other economic problems which gripped the West from 1973 onwards, this
meant that the Werner Plan slid into oblivion.

In combination with a strong dollar in the early and mid-1980s the
establishment of the European Monetary System gradually furthered
increasing exchange rate stability as well as a convergence of inflation
rates in the EC member states. This development in turn rendered the
idea of monetary union less unrealistic, just as the progressing
completion of the Single Market may be said to have constituted an
economically necessary precondition if economic and monetary union
were to result in welfare gains.[53]

However, the political factor of most immediate importance for the
revival of the EMU-plans appears to be the political implications of the
Single Market's full liberalisation of capital movements in a system of
fixed exchange rates. In combination with the Deutsche Mark's status as
international reserve currency and high credibility as a "hard" currency,
the liberalisation meant that the monetary policies of all members of the
EMS were effectively determined by the German Bundesbank.[54]
Presumably, this was the fact which motivated the French Finance
Minister Balladur's proposal of January 1988 to create a European
system of central banks, the presence of which would eliminate the
Bundesbank's dominance.[55]

After some hesitation, the West German Government responded
favourably to Balladur's initiative, and in June 1988 the European

---

53) Cf. R. A. Mundell, "A Theory of Optimum Currency Areas", *American Economic Review*, vol.
51, no. 4 (September 1961), pp. 657-665.

54) Cf. e.g. Det Økonomiske Råd, *Dansk Økonomi* (Copenhagen: May 1991), pp. 131-133. Tommaso
Padoa-Schioppa in his *Efficiency, Stability, and Equity: A Strategy for the Evolution of the
Economic System of the European Community* (Oxford: Oxford University Press, 1987), pp. 23-
24, states in more general terms that free trade, capital mobility, fixed exchange rates and
national control over monetary policy constitute an inconsistent quartet. On the imortance of
the German Mark in the international financial system see George S. Tavlas, "On the
International Use of Currencies: The Case of the Deutsche Mark", *Essays in International
Finance*, no. 181 (March 1991), pp. 1-41.

55) E.g. Francois Renard, "M. Balladur veut accelerer la construction de l'Europe monetaire", *Le
Monde*, 8 January 1988, and Jens Pagter Kristensen, "Den Europæiske Centralbank",
Samfundsøkonomen, no. 6 (1988), pp. 31-37.

Council was able to agree on the creation of a "committee for the study of economic and monetary union", the "Delors Committee". The report of the study group, the "Delors Report", was presented in April 1989. Resembling the Werner Plan in many ways, the Delors Report suggested the establishment of an Economic and Monetary Union in stages, the first stage consisting of relatively cautious measures, primarily full EMS membership to all EC states. The second stage envisaged in the report involved the creation of a system of European central banks and a gradual narrowing of exchange rate fluctuation bands on currencies participating in the EMS system. Finally, in the third stage, exchange rates were to be locked completely and national foreign currency reserves pooled, eventually leading to a common currency. At the same time, and through all three stages of the plan, coordination of finance policies was to be strengthened with the objective of increasing economic convergence.[56]

The conclusions of the Delors Report were discussed at the Madrid June 1988-meeting of the European Council, and despite resistance from the British Government, it was agreed to make the Report the basis of subsequent EMU activities. Furthermore, it was decided to implement the first stage of the plan before June 1990.

Labour and the Exchange Rate Mechanism, 1989-1990

For the British Labour Party, however, a policy on EMU was not immediately topical when the issue became prominent in early 1988. At this point, any constructive involvement in the debate on Economic and Monetary Union from the side of Labour had necessarily to be preceded by a clarification of the question of British membership of the Exchange Rate Mechanism in the EMS.

As noted, the Labour Party while in opposition could have a substantial interest in British membership of the ERM. As a political party traditionally regarded unsympathetically by financial markets, it

---

56) Committee for the Study of Economic and Monetary Union, *Report on Economic and Monetary Union in the European Community*, pp. 34-40. For a currency union to be stable, inflation rates of the participating states must converge in the longer term, entailing a need for finance policy coordination. Furthermore, currency union in most analyses requires rules on the size of national budget deficits. The costs of excessive national deficits financed by borrowing on the capital markets, namely rising interest rates, would be paid by all borrowers, whereas benefits from a budget deficit are concentrated in the deficit state.

could contribute to short term stabilisation of the currency in the event of a Labour victory in a general election.[57] Full membership of the EMS would not shift the balance of payments constraints on the British economy and is not compatible with a major British reflation which would necessitate capital controls. However, large scale British reflation is incompatible with continuation of free trade relations with the EC anyway since, as argued by the AES proponents, it presupposes the introduction of import controls to make it sustainable.

Even if ERM membership could contribute to greater currency stability in the case of a Labour Government, the Labour Party during most of the 1980s remained in disarray over the question. This was also true after the AES and British EC withdrawal had ceased to be the cornerstones of Labour economic strategy; The party's trade and industry spokesman Bryan Gould had flatly rejected full British EMS membership in 1984 as it "would not benefit the real economy by enabling us to regenerate industry and tackle unemployment". Notably, Gould repeated this standpoint as late as September 1987.[58] Other sections of the party, such as deputy leader since 1983 Roy Hattersley, had long expressed sympathy for the idea of ERM membership.[59]

Neil Kinnock's contribution to the debate in late 1986 was to link the acceptability of membership to coordinated reflation in Western Europe and the introduction of controls on EC internal trade. Four essential conditions were to be fulfilled before Labour could recommend British ERM entry: (1) The right exchange rate, (2) a far more comprehensive system of mutual financial support, (3) a Community commitment to coordinated economic expansion, and (4) a "rational" approach to EC-internal trade, meaning a policy of managed trade discriminating in favour of economically weaker regions.[60] These are very comprehensive conditions to be met, and since they could not conceivably be fulfilled within the existing EC, the argument amounts to discarding the value of currency stabilisation because it is not the desired but unobtainable coordinated economic expansion.

In Labour's policy review, published in May 1989, this pattern of argument is largely repeated, as the review points to the need to remove

---

57) John Grahl and Paul Teague, "The British Labour Party and the EEC", p. 81.
58) *The Financial Times*, 7 May 1984, and *The Times*, 28 September 1987.
59) John Grahl and Paul Teague, "The British Labour Party and the EEC", p. 80.
60) Neil Kinnock, *Making Our Way: Investing in Britain's Future* (London: Basil Blackwell, 1986), pp. 165-179.

the allegedly deflationary bias of the ERM prior to British entry. At the same time, however, the potential benefits of stable exchange rates are also stressed:

> "We see clear advantages in returning to a more stable and predictable system of exchange rates, but we believe that the EMS ... suffers from too great an emphasis on deflationary measures as a means of achieving monetary targets and that it imposes obligations which are not symmetrical."[61]

In June 1989, prior to the European Council meeting on the Delors Report and in the context of high and increasing domestic inflation and interest rates, Prime Minister Margaret Thatcher's continued rejection of ERM-entry, and Conservative disarray over the issue, Kinnock restated these views, saying he would be "eager" to join the Exchange Rate Mechanism provided there existed a Community-wide commitment to economic expansion, entry at a competitive rate for sterling and agreement by the European central banks to defend the Pound.[62] Yet, the call for introduction of "managed trade" within the EC was not reiterated. Nor does it appear in Neil Kinnock's comments on the EMS in the statement launching the campaign for the EP elections.[63]

The commitment to the original preconditions for full EMS membership weakened further throughout the autumn of 1989. In the trade unions, the chairman of the TUC Economic Committee, speaking at the annual TUC Congress in September, stated that early entry into the ERM at a competitive exchange rate was the preferable policy, and constituted a valuable piece in the jigsaw of needed policies, and in October Gordon Brown, then the Shadow Chief Secretary to the Treasury, demanded a rapid entry into the ERM as a response to an accelerating inflation rate.[64]

---

61) The Labour Party, *Meet the Challenge. Make the Change*, p. 14.

62) Nicholas Wood and John Lewis, "Thatcher is Accused of Reneging on European Treaties", *The Times*, 24 June 1989.

63) The Labour Party, Neil Kinnock's Statement at the Launch of Labour's Campaign for the European Parliament Elections, 23 May 1989, p. 4.

64) "Bickerstaffe Demands Early UK Moves to Join the European Monetary System", *The Times*, 7 September 1989. John Lewis, "Labour Urges Move to EMS", *The Times*, 14 October 1989. The argument for ERM entry as a move against inflation holds that a switch to a credible policy of a fixed exchange rate reduces the "sacrifice ratio", the increase in unemployment necessary to obtain a given decrease in inflation. With a fixed exchange rate, employers and employees bear the costs in terms of falling competitiveness and unemployment themselves if wage increases exceed those of other states in the fixed rate system; i.e., they are not accommodated by a currency depreciation. If the fixed rate is more credible, economic agents are assumed to adjust more rapidly. The ERM has in turn been seen as increasing the credibi-

In conection with the Queen's Speech debate in November 1989, Neil Kinnock furthermore argued that the existing situation entailed considerable costs for Britain:

> "We are in [the EMS] but not of it. The result is that we bear all the pressures of having a currency measured against the Deutsche Mark, without having any of the benefits of stability and credibility for the currency that could be secured by participation in the exchange rate mechanism.[65]

Speaking at a Labour policy conference with the German SPD the then Shadow Chancellor of the Exchequer, John Smith, said in April 1990 that the case for negotiating British entry into the ERM was now overwhelming, arguing that Labour's four preconditions were close to being met.[66] Shortly hereafter, Neil Kinnock stressed that ERM participation would "provide a monetary sheet anchor for the British economy with the potential for the greater exchange rate and interest rate stability, which are the critical ingredients of sustainable growth". ERM membership would cause some adjustment difficulties, but staying outside would damage the pursuit of Britain's long-term interests.[67]

These views were reflected in the May 1990 policy document which argued that "a Labour government will negotiate Britain's entry into the ERM at the earliest opportunity on the basis of the prudent and reasonable conditions which we have frequently outlined." The conditions are stated as an exchange rate avoiding competitive disadvantage but also furthering an anti-inflationary policy, just as entry must be accompanied by "closer monetary and fiscal co-operation designed to maintain steady economic growth". Finally, ERM entry must be followed by a strengthening of the EC's regional policies, and by effective collaboration between the EC central banks to combat speculation.[68]

On the surface, few fundamental changes have been made in the conditions Labour requires to be fulfilled in order to take Britain into the ERM. A noticeable exception is the disappearance of the call for managed

---

lity of a fixed rate policy. See, for example, Francesco Giavazzi and Marco Pagano, "The Advantage of Tying One's Hands", *European Economic Review*, vol. 32 (June 1988), pp. 1055-82. For a critique of this argument, see John T. Woolley, "Policy Credibility and European Monetary Institutions", in Alberta M. Sbragia (ed.), *Europolitics* (Washington DC: The Brookings Institution, 1992), pp. 157-172.

65) Neil Kinnock in *Hansard, Parliamentary Debates (Commons)*, 21 November 1989, col. 17.

66) Patrick Wintour, "Labour Ready to Negotiate Entry Into the Exchange Rate Mechanism", *The Guardian*, 3 April 1990.

67) Patrick Wintour, "Kinnock Says ERM Vital for the Economy", *The Guardian*, 5 April 1990.

68) The Labour Party, *Looking to the Future*, p. 7.

internal EC trade, last voiced in Labour's May 1989 policy review. The wording of other conditions, however, have changed subtly in the course of 1989 and 1990. Hence, a "coordinated EC-wide growth policy" became "closer monetary and fiscal cooperation", just as the criticism of the deflationary bias of the EMS was toned down in the 1990 review.

On 8 October 1990, Britain entered the Exchange Rate Mechanism in the wider 6% fluctuation band and became a full member of the EMS. In the Commons debate, Labour's spokespersons accepted the decision as correct, but called for measures to strengthen the competitiveness of British industry within the ERM. When asked whether Labour's conditions for taking Britain into the ERM had been met, John Smith castigated the Government for not having demanded a strengthening of the EC's regional policy prior to entry,[69] just as Neil Kinnock professed that Labour had never demanded a Europe-wide reflation as a pre-condition for ERM entry.[70] Furthermore, both Neil Kinnock and John Smith sharply criticised the motivations underlying ERM entry. Since June 1990, the Prime Minister had made entry into the ERM conditional on falling British inflation rates. Inflation had since risen, but for political reasons the annual Conservative party conference had required a cut in the very high interest rate levels. This could not be achieved outside the ERM without causing a depreciation of the Pound on the currency markets.[71]

Labour and the Economic and Monetary Union

The Labour Party's policy on the plans for economic and monetary union was closely intertwined with the question of British membership of the ERM. During 1989 and particularly in 1990, however, the EMU to an increasing extent came to constitute a question in its own right for the party leadership.

Labour's initial policy line on the EMU was clear. As late as in the May 1989 policy review, the idea is rejected out of hand: "We oppose

---

69) John Smith in *Hansard, Parliamentary Debates (Commons)*, 23 October 1990, cols. 272-273.
70) Neil Kinnock in *Hansard, Parliamentary Debates (Commons)*, 23 October 1990, col. 206.
71) E.g. Neil Kinnock, *Hansard, Parliamentary Debates (Commons)*, 23 October 1990, cols. 204-205. On the Conservative's political-economic rationale for ERM entry at that particular point of time, see C. Goodhart, "An Assessment of EMU", *The Royal Bank of Scotland Review*, no. 170 (June 1991), pp. 11-14.

moves towards a European Monetary Union which would impede progress [in reforming the EMS]".[72] Nevertheless, a modification of this position occurred a few weeks after the release of the policy review, when the Shadow Chancellor of the Exchequer John Smith, in connection with the June 1989 European Council stated, in a BBC interview, that

"[i]ncreasingly, I think that independent sovereignty in economic matters is an illusion for countries in Europe. The basis upon which you pool your sovereignty, though, is quite important."[73]

Asked in the same interview about the prospects for the European economic picture in a longer time perspective, he said that economic policies were bound to converge, and that "[i]n order to have sovereignty over some economic events, it will have to be a pooled sovereignty".[74]

The autumn of 1989 was, of course, marked by the political upheavals in Eastern Europe, events which culminated in the fall of the Berlin wall on 9 November. Within the EC the French presidency of the European Council reacted to these developments by calling for a speed-up of the deliberations on reforms of the Rome Treaty. In October 1989, President Mitterrand proposed that an intergovernmental conference on Economic and Monetary Union be convened. In spite of British resistance, the European Council, in December 1989, subsequently agreed to follow the proposal, deciding to hold an intergovernmental conference before the end of 1990.

The rapidly developing situation in Eastern Europe and the prospect of an upcoming intergovernmental conference failed to initially lead the Labour Party leadership to adopt any fundamentally new positions on the subject. Nevertheless, the party gradually edged towards conditional acceptance of British membership of an EMU: The party leadership's criticism of the Prime Minister's complete rejection of surrendering any formal national sovereignty in monetary affairs was voiced with increasing strength. Thus, in a November 1989 Commons debate, Neil Kinnock portrayed the Thatcher Government's insistence on formal national sovereignty in the area of monetary policy as having little relation to the reality:

"Sovereignty ... is a fine thing. But what sovereignty was the Government exercising on 5 October? When the Cabinet met that Thursday morning, it

---

72) The Labour Party, *Meet the Challenge, Make the Change*, p. 14.
73) Interview with John Smith in "Today", BBC Radio Four, 27 June 1989.
74) *ibid.*

had to wait to see what the directors of the Bundesbank would do to their interest rates before [it] could decide what it was going to do to our interest rates. On that day our sovereignty lasted for about half an hour."[75]

Labour's policy document of May 1990 in several ways took these views into account. Thus, "[g]iven the effect of the Single Market and Britain's likely participation in the ERM, closer co-operation on monetary policy between the EC countries is both inevitable and desirable".[76] However, the document went on to argue that Labour would "oppose the proposals for an all-powerful, but unaccountable European Central Bank, as outlined in the Delors Plan for Economic and Monetary Union. As the central banks of the EC countries gain experience of working more closely together ... it may be that the need for a new institution will emerge. But any new European system of central banks must be politically accountable."[77]

During the Commons debate following British ERM entry in October 1990, Neil Kinnock elaborated on this position, appearing to state the conditions which would make British participation in a currency union acceptable to the Labour Party:

> "As there is a strong and developing consensus in several other Community countries in favour of currency union, I repeat [...] that a community of democracies should never support the creation of a so-called independent central bank [and that if] the Community seeks to achieve currency union, ... then, whatever the implications for Britain, it will have to make arrangements for joint growth strategies, fiscal co-ordination and regional polices on an unprecedented scale."[78]

In November 1990 Prime Minister Margaret Thatcher was confronted with revolt from within the Conservative Party. The looming recession, very low Conservative ratings in the opinion polls, and strong resistance to the approach of Mrs. Thatcher towards the upcoming intergovernmental conferences lead to her downfall and the election of the former Chancellor of the Exchequer John Major as Prime Minister.

Shortly thereafter, deputy leader of the Labour Party Roy Hattersley, in a speech to the Labour EP Group, argued that entry into an EMU would possess substantial advantages as it would establish monetary stability, encourage investment, eliminate currency speculation, and

---

75) Neil Kinnock in *Hansard, Parliamentary Debates (Commons)*, 12 November 1989, col. 18.
76) The Labour Party, *Looking to the Future*, p. 8.
77) *ibid.*
78) Neil Kinnock in *Hansard, Parliamentary Debates (Commons)*, 23 October 1990, col. 213.

enable the Community to play a for more powerful international role. As to the question of sovereignty, Hattersley stated that

> "sometimes by pooling sovereignty, we increase it. It is at least arguable that a country within a monetary union - able to influence the level of interest rates and the supply of money - is more sovereign than a nation which, by remaining outside, has no choice but to wait and see what the union decides and then follow slavishly."[79]

Hattersley also declared that it would be "madness" for Britain to pretend it could deflect the rest of the EC from "social and monetary union". If Britain did not join the talks, the other 11 Community countries would simply go ahead, and some years later Britain would be forced to make a belated application to join on the Community's terms. In referring to the consequences of the original British refusal to join the EC in the late 1950s, he said that this would mean that "once again we would be forced into participating in systems and institutions which we had not helped to create".[80]

The same line of argument was put forward by Labour's foreign policy spokesman Gerald Kaufman. In the Commons' final debate on the EC prior to the start of the intergovernmental conferences on 13 December 1990 in Rome, Kaufman castigated the Government for failing to have a policy on EMU, and for thereby putting Britain's interests at risk:

> "If the United Kingdom does not put forward proposals for others to consider, accept modify, vary and compromise with ... that will not stop the other countries from agreeing and going forward, leaving the United Kingdom not only isolated but damaged"[81]

On 10 December 1990 in Madrid, the Labour Party, together with the other EC socialist parties in the CSPEC framework issued a joint declaration on Economic and Monetary Union in the European Community.

The declaration had the character of a compromise document, being vague on the European Parliament's role in the future Community: The EP's right of initiative over legislation vis-à-vis the Commission and a strengthening of its control over the implementation of EC legislation was endorsed, whereas the document merely stated that co-decision

---

79) Anthony Bevins, "Hattersley Backs Monetary Union: Labour Party Policy on Europe", *The Independent*, 4 December 1990.
80) Patrick Wintour, "'Madness' to Buck EC intergrationist Trend, Says Hattersley: Labour's Conditions for Monetary Union", *The Guardian*, 4 December 1990.
81) Gerald Kaufman in *Hansard, Parliamentary Debates (Commons)*, 6 December 1990, col. 494.

between the EP and the Council "could" take the form of a procedure where final approval of both institutions is necessary.[82]. This ambiguity presumably reflected the British Labour Party's reluctance to go very far in the area.

The declaration's commitment to a strengthened EC in the areas of economic and monetary policy is clear, however:

> "The ever increasing internationalisation of the economy and the interdependence of our societies at every level means that it is increasingly difficult to respond on a national level to the new challenges which arise. Democratic control of the future remains possible, provided that those elements of sovereignty which can no longer be exercised in a purely national framework are pooled".[83]

In this connection, the document, as a precondition for monetary union to "benefit the peoples of the Community", places much emphasis on the "economic" side of an EMU, advocating a strengthened EC regional policy and increased coordination of the economic policies of the member states. Thus, "the Community should develop adequate instruments in order to be able to pursue an anti-cyclical economic and budgetary policy and/or to react to sudden international economic developments."[84]

The document remains unclear on the question of the independence of a European central bank, however, reflecting divergencies of opinion between the German SPD and other socialist parties: "The overall aim should be to combine a clear and decisive level of accountability with the freedom of the bank in implementing monetary policy".

The Labour Party's own definitive stand on the question of economic and monetary union was formulated in the NEC statement published on 14 December in the party's weekly.

The opening paragraph of the statement argued that Labour was committed to active British involvement in the process of closer economic cooperation in the EC. Thus,

> "we argued for the entry of the Pound into the ERM. We support the process of the Single Market, and strongly endorse the Social Charter. We would there-fore negotiate positively with EC partners to achieve further economic and

---

82) CSPEC, Leaders' Declaration on the Intergovernmental Conferences (Madrid, 10 December 1990), p. 6. See also Patrick Wintour, "Euro-Socialists Set Agenda for IGC Talks", *The Guardian*, 11 December 1990.

83) CSPEC, Leaders Declaration on the Intergovernmental Conferences, Madrid, 10 December 1990, p. 1.

84) CSPEC, Leaders Declaration on the Intergovernmental Conferences, Madrid, 10 December 1990, pp. 2-3.

monetary integration in a manner which best serves the long term interests of Britain and the Community."[85]

In this connection the NEC proposed an evolutionary approach to EMU in which a steady hardening of the ERM would constitute the key element, by necessity to be paralleled by increasingly close monetary coordination. Here "it would be quite wrong to abdicate European monetary policy to the Bundesbank whose responsibility is purely national, even though its importance is Community-wide".[86] Consequently, the Council of Finance and Economy Minsters, ECOFIN, was to be given the responsibility for monetary coordination.

The statement argued that increased monetary integration would not require the creation of a single currency, but several other EC states had made clear that they wanted this. In this situation

"Labour believes that it would not be in the national interest if Britain allowed itself to be excluded from such developments. In a period of critically important negotiations all options for the UK must remain open. There can be no question of accepting 'Division Two' status for our country in the Community of the future."[87]

Nevertheless, while the desirability of progress towards monetary union according to the statement relates to the intentions of other EC states, it also depends on "an assessment of the costs and benefits such a move may entail". The NEC listed definite monetary stability as an advantage which was difficult to overestimate, particularly as free capital movements in the Single Market were seen to place considerable strain on the ERM and would possibly destabilise the weaker currencies.

The potential costs included the elimination of the possibility of currency realignments, a fact which reinforced the need for supply side policies at national as well as EC levels. A single currency would also mean the transfer to EC monetary authorities of "what monetary powers still remain with the national central banks".

This was not seen as a particularly important cost, however, since "even before ERM entry it was clear that monetary 'sovereignty' was constrained by the relationship between the pound and the Deutsche Mark".[88]

---

85) The Labour Party, "NEC Statement on Economic and Monetary Union", *Tribune*, 14 December 1990.
86) *ibid.*
87) *ibid.*
88) *ibid.*

The statement argued that if formal monetary sovereignty were to be transferred to Community institutions, there had to be democratic accountability, entailing that the ECOFIN-Council should have the last word on the European Central Bank's monetary policy as well as on the union's exchange rate policy. Furthermore, "it would be an error to attempt to establish a rigid time table for monetary union", as what was needed was real convergence between the economies involved rather than purely nominal convergence of inflation rates. By "real convergence" the NEC means convergence in the growth rates which the different economies can achieve without incurring an unsustainable current account deficit. A convergence of this sort in turn necessitates comprehensive industrial and regional measures on an EC scale.

Finally, the NEC statement declared that a monetary union should not require a uniform economic policy throughout the whole Community and that decisions on fiscal and budgetary policies had to remain the responsibility of the member states.[89]

From early 1989 to late 1990, then, Labour's policy had developed from opposing full British membership of the EMS unless fundamental reforms of the system were made to - in principle - favouring British membership of a prospective Economic and Monetary Union in the EC. The acceptance of British membership was conditioned, however, on a number of significant and presumably not very realistic demands which aimed to strengthen the economic as opposed to the monetary aspect of the Union, involving increased redistribution within the Community as well as an insistence on direct political control over monetary policy.

CONCLUSIONS: LABOUR AND THE EC 1987-1990

In the period from the general election of June 1987 to the start of the intergovernmental conferences in December 1990, the EC policies of the Labour Party underwent significant changes. In the 1987 general election manifesto, the explicit policy of withdrawal from the EC had disappeared, but the party did not contemplate the use of EC institutions for the furthering of its general policy goals, and the acceptance of membership was constrained by Labour's will to implement the policies it found necessary, regardless of whether they would conflict with the

---

89) *ibid.*

Community's legal framework. By December 1990, Labour had endorsed institutional reforms of the Community involving the introduction of majority voting in the Council in those areas "where it would help to improve social policy and raise environmental standards", a certain strengthening of the European Parliament, and, in principle, British membership of a future EMU, albeit on a number of conditions.

Social and Environmental Regulation in the EC

The proposition on the internal dynamic of integration expects social democratic parties to attempt to shape an organisation as the European Community according to their own visions at the moment when a fundamental national dependency on membership of the EC is acknowledged. In relation to a predominately market liberalist scheme as the EC this implies a high level of attitude integration, as social democratic parties will then support the adoption of binding supranational market-intervening regulation, particularly in areas where purely national regulation is not efficient or where supranational regulation could guarantee the continued existence of national regulation.

Given fundamental dependency on EC membership, this proposition also expects social democratic parties to reject an increase in supranational decision-making capacity regarding regional market liberalisations. However, if this capacity is increased despite such resistance, social democratic parties will counter with calls for an increase in supranational market-intervening decision-making capacity in areas where it would further the achievement of the parties' general policy goals at the national level.

The development in the Labour Party's EC policies from 1987 to early 1990 provides ample evidence of this dynamic. As it has been argued, large sections and at times a dominant majority of the Labour Party did not accept any fundamental dependency on continued British membership of the EC in the period from British Rome Treaty accession until after the 1983 election. This is so in the sense that large segments of the party saw a net political and economic benefit ensuing from withdrawal from the Community or, alternatively, from overlooking its legal framework.

As the party's manifesto for the 1984 elections to the European Parliament had hinted at, however, and as it was pointed to as early as at the TUC's 1983 Congress, British economic dependency on continued membership was growing, and at the 1988 annual conference the party leadership and rank-and-file appeared to have accepted that there was no realistic alternative to the EC.

Presumably, one of the most significant factors for this acceptance was the steadily growing importance of the markets of other EC states for British exports. EC markets took about half of all British exports in the second half of the 1980s as opposed to between 30% and 40% in the 1970s and less than 25% in the 1960s.[90] These exports would be endangered were Britain to withdraw from the EC or choose to impose policies conflicting with its legal framework. This entailed that a policy of confrontation with the EC would yield no net benefit for the achievement of the party's general policy goals.

Hence, by 1988 seemed clear to the dominant majority of the Labour Party that the European Community had to remain the most important international framework within which the party would operate. The consequences of this basic recognition became apparent at the 1989 annual conference and in the final version of the party's comprehensive policy review adopted here. Thus, in the policy review, existing EC regulation and the possibilities offered by the availability of EC institutions are for the first time considered in depth and incorporated into the party's political and economic strategies. As a consequence, the policy review in a number of areas expressed support for an extension of supranational regulation which could serve to further the achievement at the national level of the party's general policy goals. This applies to consumer protection, where the granting of more powers to the European Court of Justice was also considered, to EC regulation on environmental protection, and to labour market regulation and employee rights. In both his address to the 1988 conference and in his 1989 article on the future of the EC, Neil Kinnock also emphasised the need for a considerable strengthening of the EC's regional policy.

Particularly regarding labour market regulation and employee rights, however, Labour's support for an extension of EC regulation to a high degree constituted a reaction to the Community's Single Market programme. Thus, the concerns aroused in the British trade union movement by the prospect of advancing regional market liberalisations following the

---

90) Cf. United Nations, *International Trade Statistics, Yearbook 1965, 1970, 1975, 1980, 1985,* and *1989.*

SEA's increase of the EC's decision making capacity in this area prompted the TUC to emphasise the necessity of a "social dimension" to the Single Market, and to call on Jacques Delors to address the organisation's 1988 conference. The Labour Party conferences had paid some attention to the Single Market in 1987, and in 1988 it was explicitly acknowledged by the conference as such, as well as by the leader of the party, that the Single Market process constituted a major challenge to the EC's socialist parties. Subsequently, the conference acknowledged the need to devise a strategy with which to overcome the problems created by it.

It was also to a very high extent the Single Market process which guided Labour's formulation of policies for the 1989 European elections and which underlay the party's eventual May 1990 approval of institutional reforms in the EC in the form of introducing majority decisions in the Council in areas where it would benefit social and environmental standards.

For the Labour Party, the acknowledgement of a fundamental British dependency on continued EC membership thus coincided with the increase in the EC's market liberalising decision-making capacity. In accordance with our proposition on the internal dynamics of integration, the strengthening of market liberalising decision-making capacity in the EC prompted the party to call for increased supranational decision-making capacity for market intervention in areas where it would further the achievement of the party's general policy goals, given the fact that the option of ignoring the EC's legal framework was no longer feasible. To the extent that fundamental British dependency on continued EC membership resulted from EC market liberalisations and the EC's common market, we have therefore identified an internal dynamic of integration.

As mentioned, there are various mechanisms which might be effective in the transition from acknowledged dependency on EC membership and an extension of the EC's market liberalising decision-making capacity on the one hand to social democratic support for extended EC regulation and increased market intervening EC decision-making capacity on the other hand. These mechanisms include the following: (1) EC membership may be seen to provide access to institutions capable of establishing regulation heretofore not perceived to be efficient at the national level or subsequently improving the efficiency of national regulation; (2) EC regulation may be perceived to guarantee the existence of necessary national regulation; (3) advancing EC market liberalisations may be perceived to threaten the efficiency of necessary national regulation, creating the need for supranational replacement regulation or regulation which reestablishes the efficiency of national regulation; or (4) EC market liberalisations may be seen to create or magnify problems whose solution requires new supranational regulation.

Labour's support for extended supranational regulation from 1989 onwards in the fields of consumer protection, environmental protection, and employee rights and labour market regulation, and from 1990 for increased EC decision-making capacity in some of these areas appears motivated by the desire to utilise EC regulation as a guarantee for the existence of national regulation. The crucial issue here is the British labour movement's defensive position in the domestic political system after a decade of Conservative rule, a decade in which market regulation in society was significantly extended. The defensive position of the labour movement seems to have rendered more attractive the idea of adopting certain types of binding supranational regulation which would then be difficult, if not impossible, for later Conservative governments to reverse, witness Ron Todd's remarks at the 1988 TUC conference, George Robertson's statements following the conference, the manifesto for the 1989 EP elections, and the opening statements of the 1989 policy review.

This interpretation implies that the prevailing understanding of the "social dimension" to the Single Market in the Labour Party has been that it involves the question of the future model for economic develop-ment in Western Europe, and that the introduction of majority voting procedures on employee rights and labour market standards could thus place the Community on a path of development involving "offensive" rather than "defensive" labour market flexibility.[91]

The fear of "social dumping" in the Single Market could also have played a certain role for Labour's support for majority voting in the Council. In this sense, the Single Market would be perceived as a potential threat to the efficiency of British labour market regulation, which primarily means collective agreements in a context where

---

91) This understanding of the social dimension is explicit in Labour MEP Glyn Ford's comment on the Maastricht Treaty in "A Political Timebomb", *The House Magazine*, 6 May 1992, p. 11, and was also expressed in a March 1992 personal interview. Similar views were expressed by David Martin, Labour MEP and vice president of the EP, in an interview of November 1992. Note also the TUC's 1988 statement in *Maximising the Benefits*, which claims that the social dimension would improve industry's competitiveness.

regulation of the labour market has traditionally been left to employers and employees to negotiate.

Explicit references to the risk of social dumping were made in the 1989 policy review and by Labour MEP Ian White in March 1990. However, considering the fact that British Labour market regulation is in many respects among the least restrictive in the Community, and that British employment levels would therefore suffer the most if high EC standards were to be imposed, the voicing of Labour's concerns can hardly refer to a direct threat to British standards. Rather, as the 1989 review states, the threat is that Britain will become a "social dumping ground", attracting investment on grounds of low wages and unrestrictive labour market practices, thus entailing a further enmeshment in the economic strategy of "defensive flexibility" opposed by the labour movement.

The call for the introduction of majority voting procedures in the Council on environmental protection measures may similarly be seen as the result of the wish to make use of EC institutions to guarantee the existence of national regulation. At the same time, however, the reference in the May 1990 policy document to the need to decide upon environmental protection measures at the most appropriate administrative level suggests that for the Labour Party, EC membership had also provided access to institutions capable of establishing regulation which would be inefficient if implemented in isolation at the national level.

Finally, to the extent that a significant strengthening of the EC's regional policy would involve an increase of supranationality in the Community, this element Labour's EC policy, as it was emphasised by Neil Kinnock in 1988 and 1989, seems motivated by a desire to use Community regulation to subsequently improve the cost-efficiency of national regulation. Thus, Britain would undoubtedly reap a net benefit from a strengthened EC regional policy and increased EC transfers would therefore improve the resources with which the British state could pursue its own regional or other policies.

Against the above arguments, the claim could be made that purely domestic developments have played a far more important role for Labour's recent EC policies. After all, Labour's approach to the Community developed in a context where a growing rift between the Thatcher Government and the electorate had emerged on the question of Britain's relations to the EC and the Community's future direction. Whereas the Thatcher Government remained hostile to any supranational regulation and increased supranational authority going beyond regional market liberalisations, a clear majority of the British electorate endorsed a "social dimension" to the Single Market. At the same time, the electorate's support for British membership of the EC had been growing steadily from the early 1980s.[92]

Would it not, then, be more appropriate to view the changes in Labour's EC policy regarding some types of social and environmental regulation as an instance of purely domestically induced vote-seeking behaviour? Most likely, concerns for the party's electoral appeal have played a role in the development of Labour's new approach to the EC.[93] However, the British electorate's strong support for a Social Charter in the EC as well as the steadily growing positive evaluation of British EC membership cannot be seen in isolation from the Community's activities and plans for the future and its general impact on British society. Clearly, the proposal for a Social Charter and the electorate's support for it followed from the Single Market process, just as the steadily growing support for British EC membership can be interpreted as a reaction to the ever growing economic dependency on membership as well as to other of the Community's activities.

In other words, vote-seeking seems to have played a role in changing Labour's EC policies, but in this instance the presence of vote-seeking does not mean the existence of a purely domestic development. Rather, to the extent that growing British dependency on EC membership results from the EC's common market and custom's union, the consequences of advancing regional market liberalisations seem to translate into a change of Labour's EC policy conditioned by the party's concerns for obtaining electoral support (see figure 2.2).

Nevertheless, purely domestic developments appear to have influenced Labour's policy on the social dimension to the Single Market in other ways. It seems doubtful whether the party would have endorsed the EC Social Charter and the social dimension had it not been for the Thatcher Government's trade union policies during the 1980s: The enactment of a series of industrial relations laws (the Employment Acts of 1980, 1982,

92) Thus, three opinion polls conducted in spring, summer, and fall 1989 showed support for a Social Charter in the EC from, respectively 65%, 63% and 67% of the British electorate. See Commission of the European Community, *Eurobarometer*, no. 32 (December 1989), which also contains data on support for British EC membership.

93) This has been confirmed by MP and EC spokesman George Robertson, Senior International Officer Mike Gapes, and NEC member Tony Clarke, all of whom were interviewed in October 1990.

1988, and 1990 and the Trades Union Act of 1984), which created a strictly defined legal framework for labour-management disputes, has produced a drastic shrinking of the "protected space" around trade unions.[94] This is particularly so when considering that British labour market relations had previously been among the world's most minimally legally regulated.[95] As the discussion on the social dimension of Community regulation became topical in 1988-89, British trade unions thus had little to lose from supporting it, as their national position had been seriously undermined, and their possibilities for influence via the political channels of the national political system virtually eliminated, cf. again the statements of Ronn Todd at the 1988 TUC Congress as well as George Robertson's subsequent remarks. This is true even when considering that the legal enactment of the contents of the Social Charter could mean the elimination of "closed shop" collective agreements in Britain.

With respect to employee rights and labour market regulation, the internal dynamic of integration was thus conditioned by purely domestic developments which had significantly weakened the British trade unions. Furthermore, in terms of the previously formulated propositions we may also cite the blocking of national channels for influence as having strengthened the British labour movement's willingness to consider supranational options.

The Labour Party and European Monetary Integration

From mid-1989, Labour gradually toned down the very strict conditions it had set for party support for British ERM-entry. Eventually there appeared a barely disguised unconditional approval of ERM membership. This development primarily constituted a reaction to domestic developments. With a general election approaching, a Tory party bitterly divided over the issue, and high and rising inflation and interest rates, there were good reasons for Labour to take the position it did.

First of all, a policy advocating ERM membership would strengthen the party's image as an economically responsible party, an area which

---

94) Cf. David Marsh, *The New Politics of British Trade Unionism. Union Power and the Thatcher Legacy* (London: Macmillan, 1992), pp. 64-138, and Peter Riddell, *The Thatcher Decade* (Oxford: Basil Blackwell, 1989), pp. 43-68.
95) John McIlroy, *Trade Unions in Britain Today* (Manchester: Manchester University Press, 1988), pp. 67-96.

since the currency and inflation crises of the 1970s had been the party's Achilles' heel. Following ERM entry the economic policies pursued by a Labour Government would henceforth have to operate within the confines of retaining a stable exchange rate as well as an inflation rate close to the average of the other ERM states. The party's growing emphasis on ERM membership as a means of controlling inflation is also visible from the fact that Neil Kinnock, in June 1989, stated that he wanted Britain to join the ERM on condition of a competitive exchange rate, whereas in its May 1990 policy document, Labour favoured ERM entry at an exchange rate "avoiding competitive disadvantage but also furthering an anti-inflationary policy". In terms of the previously formulated propositions, it is therefore plausible that the Labour leadership in 1989-90 made instrumental use of the ERM issue in order to broaden the party's electoral appeal.[96]

The domestic concern for electoral appeal and credibility was also at the basis of Labour's ERM policies in other ways. Thus, if the experiences from other countries in switching to a policy of stable exchange rates within the ERM could be expected to be valid for the UK as well, ERM entry would mean immediate economic benefits in terms of an externally induced monetary expansion, thus entailing lower British interest rates,[97] just as a credible fixed rate policy may make the attainment of low inflation less costly. Evidently, Labour could not oppose a development like this and still constitute an attractive alternative to the Conservatives.

Yet, electoral concerns were not the only reason for the Labour Party to endorse ERM entry. There is also evidence of a learning process during which the usefulness of macroeconomic instruments was toned down. As opposed to earlier approaches, including the AES, the comprehensive 1989 policy review placed little emphasis on macroeconomic management as the means of solving Britain's problems. On the contrary, the review stressed that the country's economic problems lay with the supply side of the economy and that they had to be solved here. This "supply side socialism" involved measures such as increased investment in infrastructure and training and the creation of investment funds aimed at

---

96) This interpretation is also presented by Stephen George and Ben Rosamond, "The European Community", in Martin J. Smith and Joanna Spear (eds.), *The Changing Labour Party* (London: Routledge, 1992), p. 174 and pp. 181-182.

97) See, for example, C. Goodhart, "An Assessment of EMU". This has been the effects of a switch to a credible policy of stable exchange rates in the ERM for Denmark and Spain.

long term profitability projects. As a consequence of the analysis, it is not any longer deemed particularly important by the Labour Party whether or not the British Government formally has free hands in setting the exchange rate it wants.

Whereas the experiences from the attempts to modernise the British economy in the 1970s and 1980s form the elements in this learning process, structural economic developments have also strengthened the rationale for stable or fixed exchange rates between Britain and the other EC states. Hence, as the EC share of total British trade has increased along with the openness of the economy from 1973 and onwards, so has the inflationary risk of depreciation vis-à-vis other EC currencies.[98] This led the Conservative Government to shadow the German Mark already prior to ERM entry, and there is some evidence that these developments also influenced Labour's position on the ERM question; witness Neil Kinnock's statement in the Commons on 21 November 1989.[99] To the extent that these structural developments have influenced the party leadership's position and insofar as they follow from EC membership, we may then speak of an internal dynamic in which regional market liberalisations have reduced the efficiency of a national policy instrument, namely currency realignments, and contributed to the Labour Party's endorsement of ERM membership. Structural economic developments thus reduced the perceived value of the absence of formal international constraints in this policy area, rendering more important the benefits that could follow from subjecting the British state to the discipline of the ERM.[100]

Not long after it had endorsed British ERM membership, the Labour Party moved on to accept British participation in a prospective Economic and Monetary Union in the EC, albeit on a number of conditions. Labour's acceptance is largely the result of one factor: The threat of national exclusion in a situation where a number of important West European states had expressed their firm wish to strengthen the supranational framework of the European Community. Roy Hattersley stated this concern very clearly in the beginning of December 1990. Complete

---

98) In 1960-72, imports amounted to between 21% and 22% of British GNP. This share was 33.0% in 1974, 27.7% in 1979, and 28.7% in 1984. Cf. Organization for Economic Cooperation and Development, *OECD National Accounts, 1960-90*, vol. 1: *Main Aggregates*, tables 13 and 18.
99) In an interview of October 1990 George Robertson also stated that in his opinion the benefits of exchange rate flexibility had largely disappeared.
100) Again Neil Kinnock's remarks in the Commons on 29 November 1989 serve as evidence, along with his statements of April 1990.

British refusal to contemplate reforms of the Rome Treaty, he said, involved the risk that others would move ahead, creating, for instance, a new legal framework for cooperation in which Britain would not be a member. To Hattersley, this implied the danger that Britain would later have to apply for membership, then being obliged to accept institutions and policies on which it had no influence whatsoever. The same point was made by Labour's foreign policy spokesman, and the NEC's statement on EMU prior to the start of the intergovernmental conferences emphasises that Britain should not allow itself to be excluded from the upcoming negotiations.

It could be argued that a threat of national exclusion in the British context is not sufficient to make a party in opposition change its policies. Hence, as mentioned previously, opposition parties have few possibilities of influencing government policy in the British political system, for which reason external developments would create few repercussions outside the governing party.

In the British political scenario of late 1990 a general election was approaching, however. In order to portray itself as a party fit to govern, Labour needed to formulate detailed policies as well as react to external developments as if it were already in office. In this sense, the importance of the threat of exclusion regarding the question of an EMU has been conditioned by a domestic factor; namely the approaching general election.

A contextual interpretation of the events within the entire British political establishment in the months prior to the start of the intergovernmental conferences also points to the significance of the threat of exclusion. Even if other factors contributed to the crucially important downfall of Margaret Thatcher, the Prime Minister's unwillingness to compromise in the intergovernmental conferences in order to avoid British exclusion was the most immediate spark behind the revolt in the Conservative Party. The threat of exclusion thus influences the attitudes to supranational institutions of parties across the political spectrum. This supports the argument that where this dynamic applies, political parties act as statist actors rather than actors pursuing policy goals as defined narrowly by their social basis.

The Labour Party's concrete proposals for the outlook of an EMU nevertheless took a distinct form, reflecting the belief in Keynesian demand management if implemented at the EC level: The party's concrete proposals for economic and monetary union, as formulated in the

NEC's December 1990 statement, were clearly aimed at strengthening the "reflationary" possibilities of Economic and Monetary union.

An external development, i.e. the desire of other important EC states to move towards EMU, is thus the most important factor underlying Labour's changing policies on Monetary Union. The other external development which we previously argued could be significant in the European scenario of the late 1980s and early 1990s - namely security concerns following superpower withdrawal and German unification - has been of minor importance. The need to strengthen the EC as a response to German unification was mentioned only in the passing by the May 1990 policy document. Conclusions on the virtual absence of security political concerns in the Labour Party's EC policy must remain tentative, but this absence is a fact which corresponds to the long-standing British tradition for security political "Atlanticism", a tradition which affected British policies even as the EC was founded in the late 1950s, and which in itself reflects the impact on perceptions of fundamental geopolitical conditions.

Even if the threat of national exclusion was the most important factor working to increase the Labour Party's willingness to consider British participation in an EMU, other factors have to some extent influenced the course of developments as well. The growing rationale for British exchange rate stability vis-à-vis the other EC states has been touched upon above. In addition, the functioning of the existing European Monetary System was mentioned in various instances as the Labour leadership motivated its conditional support for EMU. Thus, the party's statements on EMU in 1989-90 referred in several instances to the reduced possibility of pursuing a monetary policy different from that of the German Bundesbank; compare John Smith's statements in June 1989, Roy Hattersley's remarks in early December 1990, and the CSPEC-declaration and the NEC-statement from the same month.

As mentioned, the importance of the Bundesbank for monetary policy in Western Europe follows from the simultaneous existence of a system of stable exchange rates, the EMS, and free capital movements in this system. In this situation, Germany's reputation for giving priority to price stability has led financial markets to consider the Mark the anchor of the EMS system, effectively allowing the Bundesbank to determine the level of interest rates throughout the EMS. To the extent that the liberalisation of capital movements is an element in the EC's Single Market process, we could thus identify a dynamic internal to the integration process: The Single Market could create new incentives for national political forces to support extended supranationality. This is so in the sense that given British ERM membership, capital liberalisations all but eliminated the possibility of an independent British monetary policy. This could again create incentives for a supranational body containing British participation on it for the conduct of EC monetary policy.

Yet, even if capital liberalisations clearly constitute a part of the Single Market programme, and even if a 1988 EC directive incorporated regulation on free capital movements into EC law,[101] the British liberalisations preceded "project 1992" by many years. As all British exchange controls were removed in October 1979, it constituted one of the first actions of the then recently elected Conservative government.[102] To the extent that the diminished possibility of pursuing an independent British monetary policy has contributed to Labour's willingness to consider EMU, Labour reciptivity therefore derives from a domestic development rather than from regional market liberalisations. In terms of the previously formulated propositions, seemingly irreveribly domestic developments have diminished the efficiency of the national monetary policy instrument, thereby strengthening the incentives for supranationality in the monetary area.[103]

---

101) European Communities, Directive 88/361/EEC of June 1988

102) Cf. Francesco Giavazzi, "The impact of EEC membership", in R. Dornbusch and R. Layard, *The Performance of the British Economy* (Oxford: Clarendon Press, 1987), pp. 108-112. Technological developments and the development of new financial instruments have in themselves increased international capital mobility and to some extent undermined the efficiency of national capital controls in recent decades.

103) The reversibility of capital liberalisations is low insofar as a fundamental national dependency on trade with other EC states is acknowledged: Reintroduction of comprehensive capital and exchange controls implies a potential threat to free trade; cf. Tommaso Padoa-Schioppa, "The EMS: A Long Term View", in Francesco Giavazzi, Stefano Micossi and Marcus Miller (eds.), *The European Monetary System* (Cambridge: Cambridge University Press, 1988), pp. 375-376. It is also low as liberalisations create an outflow of bonds valued in the national currency. At the moment a deliberalisation is contemplated, these bonds will return, straining foreign currency reserves and entailing an upward pressure on national interest rate levels, cf. Det Økonomiske Råd, *Danish Monetary Policy in Transition* (Copenhagen, 1985), pp. xxxiv-xxxv and 187-188. Finally, the aforementioned development of new technologies and financial instruments contributes to the low reversibility, just as reversibility is diminished by the 1988 EC directive to the extent that a fundamental dependency on national membership of a well-functioning EC is acknowledged.

7

The SDP and the EC
1961-1982

This chapter turns to the Danish Social Democratic Party and its policies on the EC in the period before the SDP left office in mid-1982. As with the British Labour Party, the analysis will focus on positions developed in the parliamentary group, among rank and file party members, and in the trade union movement, just as the policies of the party leadership constitute a fourth object of study. The tension between the party's reliance on state intervention for attainment of basic policy goals and the limitations on such interventionism following EC membership will guide the analysis, and attention will also be paid to domestic developments and external events influencing the party's approach to the EC.

There are several fundamental differences between the British and the Danish context. This is one of the rationales for comparison between the two systems. Hence, if resembling patterns of policy development are found in differing systems, it suggests that these differences are of little relevance in explaining party policies. It is particularly important to establish whether and how the variable of "size" and the factors connected to it have caused the Danish SDP's EC policy to develop differently from the Labour Party's. Denmark's small relative size could be expected to have marked effects on the nature of the Danish EC debate, as small size increases national dependency on the international surroundings regardless of EC membership.

SOCIAL DEMOCRATIC EC POLICY BEFORE 1972

The issue of European integration was only sporadically present in the Danish political debate before the 1960s, and the topic did not become salient until the 1972 referendum campaign on Danish accession to the

Rome Treaty.[1] In this respect, Danish European policy has closely paralleled British policy, a fact reflecting the profound Danish economic dependency on the United Kingdom from the second half of the nineteenth century and onwards. In 1950 exports to the UK constituted 42% of total Danish exports and 57% of the economically important agricultural exports.[2]

Nevertheless, an independent political affinity was also present. As phrased by the social democrat Frode Jacobsen, one of the few Danish parliamentarians of the time seriously interested in "European" matters, in 1949, "the right thing would be to start, as the British suggest, with cooperation between wholly sovereign states, without wasting time constructing a common European constitution."[3] However, in contrast to British policy, Danish opposition to supranational institutions was not unequivocal. Regarding the removal of barriers to trade with agricultural products, the Danish Liberal - Conservative Government showed considerable interest in a supranational solution in 1952-53,[4] and it is also noticeable that the reformed Danish constitution of 1953 contains an article permitting "powers vested in the constitutional authorities [to] be delegated to international authorities ... to such extent as shall be provided for by statute".

In connection with the negotiations on the establishment of the EC in 1957-59, Danish adherence to the British European policy was largely repeated. In February 1957, the social democratic minority government under Prime Minister H. C. Hansen adopted the position that Denmark should support the creation of a free trade area encompassing the whole of Western Europe, but concrete economic interests caused Britain and Denmark to have opposing views on the position of agriculture in this free trade area. As the Prime Minister stated it, the Danish support for free trade followed from the wish to reduce tariff levels and not only

1) For an analysis of the SDP's European policies in the immediate post war years, see Holger Villumsen, *Det danske Socialdemokratis Europapolitik 1945-49* (Odense: Odense Universitetsforlag, 1991).
2) Peter Hansen, "Adaptive Behaviour of Small States: The Case of Denmark and the European Community", in P. J. McGowan (ed.), *Sage International Yearbook of Foreign Policy Studies*, vol. 2, (London, SAGE 1974), pp. 166-168.
3) Frode Jakobsen in *Folketingstidende*, forhandlingerne 1948-1949, 28 June 1949, col. 5198.
4) Peter Hansen, "Denmark and European Integration", *Cooperation and Conflict*, vol. 4, no. 1 (1969), p. 18, and Vibeke Sørensen, "National Welfare Strategies and International Linkages in a Small Open Economy; The Danish Social Democratic Party and European Integration, 1947-1963", in Richard T. Griffith (ed.), *Socialist Parties and the Question of Europe in the 1950s* (Leiden: E. J. Brill, 1992), manuscript, pp. 17-18.

quantitative restrictions on trade.[5] At the same time, the moment was not seen to be opportune for an application for membership in the emerging European Community as membership of the EC's customs union would block Danish participation in a common market among the Nordic countries. Furthermore, the plans of "the Six" on the establishment of the EC contained too many unresolved aspects and aimed at what the Prime Minister saw as "a far reaching harmonisation of economic policy, including finance policy, social policy and wage policy".[6] Subsequently, the party's executive council decided to develop a "standard speech" for the use of its representatives. Here the rejection of EC membership was motivated by the weak positions of the Labour movements in the six founding states.

Resistance to EC membership was also strong in the Danish trade unions. In November 1957, the chairman of the Labour Movement's Economic Council Frederik Dalgaard thus came out against Danish membership on the grounds that "the Six" did not have the same cultural and social traditions as the Nordic states.[7]

The division of Western Europe into two trading blocks following the establishment of EFTA left Denmark in an uncomfortable situation. The EFTA-agreement was minimal in the agricultural area, thus placing agricultural exports to the expanding markets of the EC in a vulnerable position.[8] The direct economic consequences for the country were far from satisfactory, but in the period from 1957 to 1961 the social democratic led coalition governments did not consider an isolated Danish application for EC membership, preferring instead to uphold the idea of a wider European free trade area.[9]

As a consequence of the Danish quest for a comprehensive European trade solution, the Government quickly followed suit when in 1961 Britain voiced interest in becoming EC member. When the British

---

5) Until 1960 Danish trade policy was characterised by low tariffs and comprehensive quantitative restrictions.

6) H. C. Hansen in *Folketingstidende*, forhandlingerne, 1956-57, 6 February 1957, cols. 2393-94. The proposal for a Nordic common market had been discussed since the Second World War, but by 1957 no agreement had been reached, primarily due to Norwegian opposition. In mid-1959 the plans were overtaken by the establishment of the EFTA.

7) Jens Engberg, *I Minefeltet. Træk af Arbejderbevægelsens historie siden 1936*, (Copenhagen: Arbejderbevægelsens Erhvervsråd, 1986), pp. 67-68.

8) On the SDP's positions in the EFTA-negotiations see Jens Engberg, *I Minefeltet*, pp. 71-73.

9) From May 1957 to November 1960 the Government was composed of the SDP, the Radical Liberals, and the tax reform Justice Party. From November 1960 to September 1964 the Government consisted of just the SDP and the Radical Liberals.

membership application was submitted on 10 August 1961 a Danish application followed immediately. The parliamentary decision authorising the Government to initiate negotiations on Danish membership contained three points which came to serve as basic guidelines in the following years: (1) Denmark sought EC membership together with Britain, (2) full regard should be taken to the interests of the other EFTA members, and (3) the importance of continuing and increasing cooperation between the Nordic countries was emphasised.[10]

Within the social democratic movement, however, support for the decision to start negotiations was far from unanimous. The most pronounced resistance came from a number of important trade unions. Thus, in August 1961 the Confederation of Trade Unions, LO, called for an examination of the possibility of an association agreement with the EC as an alternative to membership. Meanwhile, two most important trade unions, the Unskilled Workers' Union and the Metal Workers' Union, uncompromisingly rejected Danish EC membership.[11] Hans Rasmussen, leader of the Metal Workers' Union and deputy chairman of the SDP, forcefully attacked the Government's policy, concluding with an emotional critique on Germany and a call to retain national political independence: "We cannot grant to German ministers the right to decide the level of unemployment in this country", Rasmussen declared.[12]

Hans Rasmussen's critical position was also reflected in a series of parliamentary questions he directed to the Foreign Minister, indicating his concern about the effects of Rome Treaty accession on economic policy, social policy, industry policy, labour market regulation and the movement of labour and capital. The social democratic Foreign Minister's answers took on a reassuring tone: EC membership would not in itself have any impact on Danish social or labour market legislation, and regarding economic policy he stressed that cooperation on macroeconomic management was foreseen in the Rome Treaty, this being a Government priority since "it is evident that the possibilities of pursuing a stabilising economic policy will be greater the more countries effectively participate in it. Particularly for a country like Denmark, with a large and sensitive foreign trade, this is of great and positive interest."[13]

---

10) *Folketingstidende*, forhandlingerne, 1960-61, 4 August 1961, col. 4785.
11) Peter Hansen, "Denmark and European Integration", p. 28.
12) Toivo Miljan, *The Reluctant Europeans: The Attitudes of the Nordic Countries Towards European Integration* (London: C. Hurst and Company, 1977), pp. 167-168.
13) Beretning fra folketingets markedsudvalg [Report of the Folketing's Market Committee],

As for industrial policy, the Foreign Minister stated that the Rome Treaty's provisions in articles 92-94 would not obstruct Danish legislation in any significant manner. If continued economic growth was to be ensured, Danish industry would face far-reaching restructuring in the years to come. This problem would be of a different character should Denmark enter the EC, but it would be even larger if Denmark were to remain outside the Community. Furthermore, the Minister thought it unlikely that EC regulation would impede the continuation of Danish industrial policies, such as state support, as Denmark's state subsidies were considerably less than in most EC member states.[14]

In April 1962 the Confederation of Trade Unions agreed on a statement which made clear that the unions' final position on EC membership depended on the results of the British negotiations. However, resistance to EC membership regardless of the British position remained strong in the ranks of the Unskilled Workers' Union. At the 1962 annual conference, its chairman Alfred Petersen rejected EC membership unconditionally. As he stated it, he would suffer economically as a free citizen in a free country than join the Common Market.[15] The Danish state's loss of control over capital movements in the EC and the possibility that the free movement of labour and increased competitive pressures in the Common Market would pose a threat to Danish employment opportunities and social and labour market standards were among Petersen's primary objections to EC membership. However, he acknowledged that the trade unions might have a stake in supranationality should membership become a reality. Thus,

> "*if* we enter the EC, we may under certain circumstances have an interest in a supranational authority establishing certain rules which must be adhered to by everybody in the Community".[16]

However, the existing EC framework was deemed unfit to adopt such rules, primarily since it did not have the necessary democratic characteristics.

When President de Gaulle obstructed British EC membership in January 1963, the Danish Government declined to pursue its own

---

Folketingstidende, 1961-62, Appendix B, cols. 352-353.
14) *ibid.*, col. 369 and cols. 374-375.
15) The argument baffled foreign minister Krag: "He wasn't joking. He actually meant it." Jens Engberg, *I Minefeltet*, p. 74.
16) *Arbejdsmændenes og specialarbejdernes fagblad*, no. 23 (December 1962), p. 510.

membership application, and the policy response was to keep Denmark within EFTA and to reemphasise its wish for an all-European free trade area. However, Britains 15% surcharge on imports, enacted in 1964 in violation of the EFTA treaty, prompted a reformulation of the Danish Parliament's, the Folketing's, mandate to the Government on the EC issue, hinting at the possibility of Danish EC entry with or without Britain.[17]

The hint remained a hint, however. By 1967 the diversion of Danish EC policy was rectified when Britain renewed its application for EC membership. Again the British initiative was immediately followed by a Danish application. As opposed to the situation in 1961, support for EC membership was overwhelming in the governing SDP and this time also in the trade union movement.[18] This fact presumably reflected the very favourable economic environment in which discussions took place. Western Europe's booming economy had produced a fundamental restructuring of the Danish economy and strengthened the position of industry. By 1967, therefore, the fears that EC membership would lead to the disruption of entire industries had largely vanished.

The SDP lost office following the election defeat of January 1968 and was to remain in opposition until October 1971. Responsibility for negotiating the final entry terms therefore rested with the coalition government of the Radical Liberals, the Liberals, and the Conservatives. Before this was achieved, however, Danish EC policy performed another diversion with the support of the social democrats, as the plans for Nordic economic integration were revived. Yet, before any agreement could be achieved, the 1969 Haag summit declared the EC open for Danish membership, causing the Finnish Government to reserve its position on the project.[19]

THE SOCIAL DEMOCRATS AND THE EC 1972-1982

In May 1971 the former social democratic Foreign Minister Per Hækkerup had made the surprising announcement that the question of Danish Rome Treaty accession should be subject to a referendum. This

---

17) *Folketingstidende*, forhandlingerne, 1964-65, 12 November 1964, col. 719.
18) Peter Hansen, "Denmark and European Integration", p. 29.
19) See Jens Engberg, *I Minefeltet*, pp. 90-98 for an account of social democratic positions in the so called "Nordek"-negotiations.

possibility was offered by the Danish constitution, section 42 of which states that a referendum shall be held on an issue when at least a third of the members of the Folketing call for it.

The social democratic call for a referendum on EC membership was widely seen as a manoeuvre to prevent the question from becoming an issue at the elections scheduled for September 1971, a situation which could lead to a significant defection of social democratic voters to the pronounced anti-EC Socialist Peoples' Party (SPP) on the left wing.[20]

This SDP tactic was a success as the EC issue did not dominate the campaign and as the social democrats gained 3.1 percentage points of the total vote and could return to office as a minority government. However, the election also saw significant gains the SPP. The referendum thereby became a constitutional necessity, since according to the Danish constitution a transfer of sovereignty to supranational institutions without a referendum according requires a by now unobtainable 5/6 majority in the Folketing.[21]

The 1972 Referendum

The 1972 election had an additional consequence of bringing into the Folketing a number of new social democratic MPs, most of whom opposed Danish EC membership. This group formed its own caucus in the parliamentary group, such that the EC issue had provoked the emergence of the first organised oppositional group within the party in its history.

Resistance to EC membership among social democratic MPs had various motivations. One EC opponent, Svend Auken, in explaining his position in December 1971, pointed to the insufficient democratic control with Community institutions and the bleak prospects for EC institutions to further social democratic goals such as political control over multinationals. Regarding social policy, Auken claimed that membership would result in demands that the Danish tax financed social security system should be replaced with employer financed schemes, as the Danish

---

20) Peter Hansen, "Die Formulierung der dänischen Europapolitik", *Östereichische Zeitschrift für Aussenpolitik*, vol. 13 (1973), p. 25, Nikolaj Petersen and Jørgen Elklit, "Denmark Enters the European Communities", *Scandinavian Political Studies*, vol. 8 (1973), p. 202.
21) Withing in the party the SDP leader Jens Otto Krag had motivated the call for a referendum with precisely the concern that the required 5/6 majority for EC entry could not be achieved in the Folketing, cf. Jens Engberg, *I Minefeltet*, p. 101.

system could be seen as distorting competition. This would in turn have profound consequences for incomes distribution and social policy in Denmark.[22]

The central arguments of the SDP's EC opponents were summarised by Karl Hjortnæs in the April 1972 debate on EC membership:

> "[First,] we do not want to participate in the creation of a new block, and we are convinced that EC membership in the longer run will have foreign- and security political consequences. [Second], the establishment of an economic and monetary union will involve the transfer of the most important political instruments to the Community. ... We have no confidence that it will be possible to pursue a sufficiently effective policy of levelling incomes in the Community. [Third], membership will entail forceful attacks on structures we consider valuable. This goes for education, the social area, and on the labour market. [Fourth], we have no confidence that democratic socialism will have a real chance of creating an alternative society within the Community. [Fifth], we do not find that economic concerns justify membership."[23]

The social democratic supporters of EC membership, including all members of the social democratic minority government, primarily emphasised the economic necessity of Rome Treaty accession. As Prime Minister Jens Otto Krag stated

> "I think we must consider the economic aspects, and I have to repeat that undoubtedly great advantages will follow from membership for agriculture and fishery. These advantages will be lost if we do not join, and they cannot be obtained in other ways. ... Neither should we forget that a 'yes' or a 'no' to the Common Market will be decisive for the employment situation and the wage level of Danish workers in the time to come. If we stay outside, wage levels and employment will be lower than if we join."[24]

Besides the constant emphasis on the immediate economic advantages of membership, the social democratic leadership sought to convince the electorate that EC membership would not entail any risks for existing Danish policies and structures deemed valuable by the party. Both Minister for EC affairs Ivar Nørgaard and spokesman on EC affairs Poul Dalsager stated that there was no obligation to harmonise social- and

---

22) *Folketingstidende*, forhandlingerne, 1971-72, 15 December 1971, cols. 1686-1691.
23) Karl Hjortnæs in *Folketingstidende*, forhandlingerne, 1971-72, 26 April 1972, cols. 5316-5317. See also the positions put forward in Hjortnæs' speech to the SDP's special congress on EC membership, quoted in Jens Engberg, *I minefeltet*, p. 118.
24) *Folketingstidende*, forhandlingerne, 1971-72, 16 December 1971, cols. 1746-1747. See also the remarks by EC policy spokesman Poul Dalsager in *Folketingstidende*, forhandlingerne, 1971-72, 15 December 1971, cols. 1627-28. On Krag's positions, see also his speech to the special party conference on 10 September 1972, quoted in Jens Engberg, *I minefeltet*, pp. 116-118.

labour market policies in the Rome Treaty, just as the claim that the Danish social security system provided Danish employers with a competitive advantage was rejected. In connection with social policies, Dalsager also stressed that the economic advantages of membership would actually provide better possibilities for improving conditions in the future. Furthermore, Nørgaard argued that the Rome Treaty would not stand in the way of Danish regional policies, and in a subsequent debate Prime Minister Krag reiterated that Danish industry policy as pursued by the Government would not be affected by membership.[25]

As to those policy areas in which EC membership meant the immediate transfer of powers to the supranational level - trade and tariff policies and agricultural policy - the SDP leadership welcomed the transfer: Krag stated his approval of having as low tariffs as possible in general and viewed the EC's customs union as a partial step in the right direction. As he saw it, the transfer of powers with respect to both trade and agricultural policies was justified by the concrete economic benefits they entailed for the Danish state.[26] The leadership of the SDP also expressed considerable willingness to approach a situation of fixed or very stable exchange rates. In the context of the crumbling Bretton Woods system, the Minister for EC affairs thus pointed to the need for international cooperation on exchange rate stabilisation:

> "[T]he experiences of the last few years have made clear that there is a strong need for and a marked Danish interest in having international cooperation [on exchange rate policies] put into a firm framework. Denmark gains more when the decisions of the different states are made by international cooperation than when we retain the purely formal freedom to make decisions on our own".[27]

In response to critics who maintained that far-reaching integration on exchange rate policies would eliminate an important instrument for economic policy, Ivar Nørgaard stressed that Denmark had never made use of exchange rate realignments unless being forced to do so by other states' policies. He also emphasised the government's wish to actively engage in international cooperation on macroeconomic management within the EC: "Naturally, Denmark must support extensive cooperation

---

25) Ivar Nørgaard in *Folketingstidende*, forhandlingerne, 1971-72, 15 December 1971, cols. 1492-93, and *Folketingstidende*, forhandlingerne, 1971-72, 15 December 1971, col. 1764, and Poul Dalsager in *Folketingstidende*, forhandlingerne, 1971-72, 26 April 1972, cols. 5281-5282.
26) *Folketingstidende*, forhandlingerne, 1971-72, 26 April 1972, cols. 5460-5461.
27) *Folketingstidende*, forhandlingerne, 1971-72, 15 December 1971, col. 1488. See also *Folketingstidende*, forhandlingerne, 1971-72, 26 April 1972, cols. 5431-32.

on economic policy, as we are particularly dependent on the decisions made by other countries, and therefore have an interest in these matters being discussed internationally".[28] At the same time he pointed to an earlier Government declaration stating that economic policy cooperation in the EC framework must not stand in the way of the Folketing's ability to pursue the distributional policy, including social and tax-policies, that the Folketing wanted. Distributional policies were and should remain a national responsibility.

Finally, on the future institutional development of the Community, the Minister for EC affairs argued that it could not be an aim in itself to strengthen institutions in Brussels. However, if the issues of cooperation demanded it, a strengthening of Community institutions would remain a possibility:

> "To the extent that we have accepted objectives for cooperation which turn out to be more easily achieved through a strengthening of institutions in Brussels, naturally we must consider this possibility."[29]

In sum, and as opposed to the social democratic EC-opponents who to some extent viewed EC membership in a longer time perspective, the SDP leadership did not see any threats to efficient national regulation of Danish society following from EC membership. The problems that could ensue from EC membership were deemed much too insignificant to overshadow the direct economic advantages of entry. This was the position expressed by the party leadership in connection with the first British applications for EC membership, and the same argument was repeated in numerous instances in the period preceding the 1972 referendum.

From 1970 to 1972, opposition to EC membership increased significantly among the Danish electorate. In the 1960s less than 10% had rejected membership but during 1970 opposition increased to 20% of the voters, growing to approximately 30% in 1971 and remaining at that level until the October 1972 referendum. The most dramatic shift of opinion occurred among the SDP voters. In the period from 1961 to 1966, opposition to EC membership averaged 8% among social democratic voters, but in May 1971 it appeared that a clear majority had turned against EC entry with 44% opposing and only 22% approving of it. During the remaining months of 1971 and in 1972 this condition

---

28) *Folketingstidende*, forhandlingerne, 1971-72, 15 December 1971, col. 1487 and col. 1757.
29) Ivar Nørgaard in *Folketingstidende*, forhandlingerne, 1971-72, 15 December 1971, col. 1489.

gradually changed as to give the EC proponents a slight majority of 41%
to 38% in September 1972.[30] According to a 1979 poll, 57% of social
democratic party conference delegates at the 1979 party conference had
voted for EC membership in the 1972 referendum with 41% opposing
it.[31]

In April 1972, the trade union movement as a whole had decided in
favour of Danish EC membership. Delegates to the congress of the
Confederation of Trade Unions voted 524 for and 406 against, with 38
abstentions.[32] Two of the most important trade unions, the Metal
Workers' Union and the Unskilled Workers' Union, remained opposed to
membership. Despite widespread opposition to the EC in the broader
social democratic movement, a clear majority of the parliamentary party
voted for Danish membership: on 8 September 1972 Parliament with 141
votes 34, passed the legislation necessary to enact a Danish affiliation to
the Community. Apart from all 17 SPP members, opposition to EC
membership in the final vote came from one of the small centre parties,
the Radical Liberals, and from 12 of 70 social democrats, predominately
associated with the party's left wing. Two days later, a special SDP party
conference on the EC decided by a vote of 272 to 95 to recommend EC
membership.[33]

In the context of growing opposition to Danish EC membership during
1971 and 1972, the campaign preceding the referendum became both the
most comprehensive and the most intensive political campaign ever
undertaken in Denmark. As in the British referendum, the proponents
very much represented the "establishment", and the anti-EC side the
"anti-establishment".

The organisations active in the campaign against EC membership
included the "Social Democrats against the EC".[34] Supporters of EC
membership appeared to be on the defensive during most of the
campaign, often compelled to reply to accusations that membership would
entail a large scale loss of Danish sovereignty and the demise of Nordic
cooperation.

---

30) Nikolaj Petersen and Jørgen Elklit, "Denmark Enters the European Communities", p. 202.
31) Ib Faurby, "Danish Party Attitudes on European Integration", Institute of Political Science,
    University of Aarhus. Paper presented to the ECPR Conference, March 1980, p. 5.
32) Jens Engberg, *I minefeltet*, p. 116, and Alastair H. Thomas, "Danish Social Democracy and the
    European Community", *Journal of Common Market Studies*, vol. 13, no. 4 (June 1975), p. 461.
33) Jens Engberg, *I minefeltet*, p. 119.
34) Hans Martens, *Danmarks ja, Norges nej. EF-Folkeafstemningerne i 1972* (Copenhagen: DUPI
    and Munksgaard, 1979), pp. 88-89 and p. 138, and Jens Engberg, *I minefeltet*, p. 111.

In the context of massive resistance to EC membership among its own voters, the SDP's leadership appeared to act particularly cautiously, emphasising the direct economic benefits and playing down the wider effects of Danish EC membership.[35]

Despite the opposition's offensive posture in the campaign and the Norwegian electorate's rejection of EC entry a week earlier, the Danish referendum on 2 October 1972 resulted in a clear victory for the pro-EC forces. With a record turnout of 90.1% of the electorate 63.3% voted for Danish membership with 36.7% rejecting it. Among SDP voters, however, support for membership was less pronounced; 55% voted for and 45% against Danish accession to the Rome Treaty.[36] Following the vote, social democratic Prime Minister Jens Otto Krag surprisingly announced his retirement, passing the party leadership and the post as Prime Minister on to the trade union leader Anker Jørgensen.

Within the Community: The 1973 Policy Development

The very divisive referendum and the emergence of widespread opposition to the party leadership's policy on the EC had caused damage to the Social Democratic Party, and the years after 1972 were therefore a period in which attempts were made to heal the wounds inflicted in the early 1970s. One response of the leadership was to play down the importance of EC issues, hoping that the passing of time would in itself repair the rifts.

However, the leadership also acted in other ways to EC membership. Immediately following the referendum, the SDP actively engaged itself in attempts to formulate an offensive and coherent EC policy containing elaborate policy recommendations. The offensive social democratic approach to policy formation in the Community framework was first elaborated as early as the parliamentary debate following the October 1972 EC summit in Paris. A further development of social democratic EC policy was evident in the May 1973 parliamentary debate on the Community and in the comprehensive policy document on the EC released in June the same year by a group of social democratic MPs and party officials.

---

35) Nikolaj Petersen and Jørgen Elklit, "Denmark enters the European Communities", p. 206.
36) Torben Worre, "Europavalget", Økonomi og Politik, vol. 53., no. 3 (1979), p. 260.

Following the Paris summit, the new Prime Minister Anker Jørgensen
told the Folketing that it was the Government's highest priority in the
EC to work for the creation of "the best possible external conditions for
social improvement in each EC member state".[37] Regarding industrial
policy in the Community, Jørgensen stated that this policy should not
just aim at improving the competitiveness of EC companies but should
also "serve to improve the working and living conditions of the individual
employee". Finally, on environmental policy the Community should
ensure that no member state would fall behind in environmental protection at the same time as it should never stand in the way of environmental progress in each member state.

The party's spokesman on EC affairs, Poul Dalsager, motivated the
SDP's approach to the Community in pointing to its general policy goals.
Thus, the goals of the party, "equal opportunity for education, social
justice, employment opportunities, a better environment, and democracy
and co-decision also in the work place", had not changed with EC entry,
and "as internationalists it is not enough for us that these goals are
fulfilled nationally. It is our wish that they should also be achievable ...
for our partners in the Community."[38]

In the May 1973 parliamentary debate and especially in the June
policy report the SDP detailed its EC strategies further in a wide range
of policy areas. The comprehensive 115-page policy would constitute the
party's most explicit EC policy for the next 13 years.

The policy document, developed by both proponents and opponents of
Danish EC membership, addressed the questions of what to do in the
Community, now that Denmark had become a member. As a starting
point the report noted that in many respects the existing EC did not
accord with social democratic visions. As party leader Anker Jørgensen
saw it, the Community of 1973 was "built on a traditional liberalist
model, according to which free competition is supposed to lead to the
greatest possible happiness".[39] This had prompted many social democrats to oppose Danish membership, "[b]ut the Community must be
further developed, and the Treaty is not in itself a liberalist templet".

The report's analysis of the political situation noted the necessity for
social democrats to actively engage with other representatives of the

---

37) *Folketingstidende*, forhandlingerne, 1972-73, 8 November 1972, cols. 928-930.
38) *ibid.*, cols. 971-972.
39) Anker Jørgensen, preface in Ole Andersen et al., *EF: Hvad Nu? Et debatoplæg til en
Socialdemokratisk EF-politik* (Copenhagen: Forlaget SOC, 1973).

European left to prevent the EC from being dominated by political adversaries. It acknowledged that the European labour movement had had a limited influence on the legal and institutional framework of the EC, but precisely for this reason the SDP should support a mobilisation of the social democratic movement across the Community.[40]

On this basis, proposals were put forward for social democratic policy position in a number of areas. Regarding the development of the common trade policy, the authors stated the wish to encourage the liberalisation of international trade. As to macroeconomic policy in the EC the document acknowleged that Denmark, prior to EC membership, formally had considerable national leeway. However, this formal sovereignty was limited in practice, since foreign currency loans for the financing of balance of payments deficit had entailed pressures to adhere to international policy prescriptions, and as Danish dependency on foreign trade had imposed limits on the viable macroeconomic policy options. Following the report, this meant that EC membership in itself merely substituted an unorganised situation with a more explicit set of relations.

Furthermore, particular Danish interests meant that Denmark's and the social democrats' macroeconomic priority in the EC were to be to support the existence of stable but adjustable exchange rates, stable for the sake of the preservation of the Common Agricultural Policy, and adjustable so as to allow for devaluations for the sake of employment. The preference for stable exchange rates did not, however, lead the social democratic government to endorse the proposed "Werner Plan" for economic and monetary union in the EC. In May 1973, Ivar Nørgaard made clear that according to the Government, "[c]ooperation in the second phase [of the Werner Plan] should be focused on extending economic and monetary cooperation where this is possible without legal and particularly institutional reforms".[41]

On monetary policy, the 1973 policy document rejected moves towards an additional liberalisation of capital movements in the EC, as this would render an independent national monetary policy inefficient. Partly as a consequence of these views, the SDP report rejects the creation of a monetary union with a single currency, which would eliminate the possibility of independent exchange rate and monetary policies.[42]

---

40) Ole Andersen et al., *EF: Hvad Nu?*, pp. 24-29.
41) *Folketingstidende*, forhandlingerne, 1972-73, 16 May 1973, col. 6275.
42) Ole Andersen et al., *EF: Hvad nu?*, pp. 38-39.

As to industrial and regional policy in the EC, the report argued that the Rome Treaty's provisions on strict limits to state subsidies should be supported by the SDP. Thus, "it is in the interest of a small country to limit the possibilities of the larger states in this area, to give Danish industry equal terms of competition ... and to prevent that the life of outdated and non-competitive firms is artificially prolonged".[43]

Specifically regarding the policy towards multinationals, the report states that experience with EC legislation has been disappointing so far, but rather than to conclude that the Community is useless, the reaction ought to be that EC regulation should be strengthened in this area. Thus, "[a]s social democrats we have an interest in the strongest possible societal control over and management of large corporations - nationally and at the Community level - and precisely in this area we would welcome a supranational development".[44] The social democratic Minister for EC affairs had elaborated on these views in the May 1973 parliamentary debate. The Government would push for the EC to develop substantial regulation on public access to information on multinationals, on common tax regulation concerning multinationals, for a strengthened EC anti-monopoly legislation, and for regulation of currency speculation by multinational corporations.[45]

With respect to EC social and labour market policy, the report is ambivalent about the consequences of membership, but there is agreement that the SDP should support improvement of social standards in the Community, through the adoption of binding minimum regulations on "safety at work, employment conditions, co-decision, economic democracy etc.", and that Community legislation hence should not stand in the way of national measures improving such standards. The SDP would therefore reject any attempt at harmonising social security levels and the ways of financing social security measures.[46]

As to employee co-decision, the SDP Government during the May 1973 parliamentary debate stated its firm intention to support proposals for EC legislation with this aim.[47] On working conditions and the protection of health and safety at work, the party also expressed its support for the

---

43) Ole Andersen et al., *EF: Hvad nu?*, p. 45.
44) Ole Andersen et al., *EF: Hvad nu?*, p. 61.
45) Ivar Nørgaard in *Folketingstidende*, forhandlingerne, 1972-73, 16 May 1973, cols. 6283-6285. See also Ole Andersen et al., *EF: Hvad nu?*, p. 112.
46) Ole Andersen et al., *EF: Hvad nu?*, pp. 49-54 and p. 111.
47) Ivar Nørgaard in *Folketingstidende*, forhandlingerne, 1972-73, 16 May 1973, col. 6281.

adoption of comprehensive binding minimum regulations in the EC framework.[48] However, the party could not support the establishment of an EC employment agency, as capital and companies in the SDP's opinion should move to employers and not the reverse.

In the May 1973 debate, the Minister for EC affairs also emphasised the Government's wish to support an extension of EC legislation on consumer protection, regarding "prices and competition, marketing and sales methods, ... on declarations of content, packing, date marking, and with respect to dangerous goods".[49] Finally, the 1973 policy report restated the SDP's wish to develop and support an EC policy for the protection of the environment, following the principles stated the previous year. Thus, it is seen as preferable for the Community to establish a number of minimum environmental conditions which must be adhered to by all member states.[50]

In the view of party leader Anker Jørgensen, the contents of the 1973 policy document served as evidence of relatively far-reaching internal social democratic agreement on the goals within the EC:

> "This applies to areas such as control with monopolies and multinational corporations, employee protection and working conditions in general, and environmental policy. A common European policy of minimum standards in these areas constitutes an important support for the realisation of a national social democratic policy. This is why it may very well be that the former opponents of Danish EC membership in certain regards will become zealous integrationists."[51]

For the Danish Social Democratic Party EC entry thus prompted the formulation of offensive policy positions in a number of issue areas. Presumably, the most immediate motivation for the development of an elaborate EC policy was the leadership's wish to reunite the party after the divisive 1972 referendum. In this sense, electoral concerns have clearly played a role. However, the specific contents of the party's EC policies as formulated in the 1973 policy review are not understandable without referring to the party's general policy goals. The party's policies actively sought to make use of EC institutions for market intervention, where this market intervention would further the achievement of the

---

48) Ole Andersen et al., *EF: Hvad nu?*, p. 52, and Ivar Nørgaard in *Folketingstidende*, forhandlingerne, 1972-73, 16 May 1973, col. 6279.
49) Ivar Nørgaard in *Folketingstidende*, forhandlingerne, 1972-73, 16 May 1973, col. 6288-87.
50) Ole Andersen et al., *EF: Hvad nu?*, p. 85.
51) Anker Jørgensen, Preface in Ole Andersen et al., *EF: Hvad Nu?*

party's goals at the national level, implying the extension of binding supranational regulation in several areas. In most instances this regulation should take the form of *minimum* rules so as to enable further moves at the national level, one natural exception being the SDP's support for common legislation on multinational corporations.

The desire to make use of the EC in the furthering of social democratic goals did not translate, however, into support for increased supranational authority to EC institutions or increased decision-making capacity of supranational institutions. Thus, after having discussed the possibility of diminishing the use of unanimous decision-making in the Council or increasing the influence of the European Parliament, the concluding sections of the 1973 policy report defended the dominant position of the Council in the EC as well as the right of veto in this body following the Luxembourg compromise.[52]

However, the insistence on the Luxembourg compromise was questioned in a previous section, where it was argued that the political veto entailed a risk that the EC's development would be determined by the European strong powers, who controlled the resources to utilise the veto.[53] As a means of upholding a parliamentary control with Danish ministers, the position of the Parliament's Market Committee was supported.

The conclusions of the policy report were incorporated into the party's programme following the 1973 congress. The party actively sought to make use of EC institutions and regulation for the promotion of its general policy goals. As a consequence, the SDP endorsed an extension of binding supranational regulation in a number of areas. At the same time it rejected supranational regulation which would inhibit what it saw as progress at the national level. Moreover, the party remained opposed to granting increased authority to supranational institutions and to increasing the supranational decision-making capacity, even if a certain ambiguity on the Luxembourg compromise and its implications for small states was evident.

Underlying the SDP's approach towards the Community in the post-referendum period lay the Danish dependency of EC membership following British Rome Treaty accession, a fact which is illustrated by the closing statement of the 1973 policy report: "For the Social Democratic

---

52) Ole Andersen et al., *EF: Hvad nu?*, p. 104.
53) Ole Andersen et al., *EF: Hvad nu?*, p. 99.

Party it remains a conditions for Danish participation in EC cooperation that Great Britain also remains a member."[54]

Social Democratic EC Policy During Recession: 1974-1982

The first oil crisis and the ensuing economic recession shortly after Danish entrance in the EC had a clear impact on social democratic EC policies. Thus, the Community was seen as the principal international institutional framework for dealing with the effects of economic crisis and energy shortages.

In connection with the "Tindemans Report" on the future development of the EC, the then social democratic Minister for Foreign Economic Affairs, Ivar Nørgaard, in December 1975 assessed that significant progress on EC cooperation would have to await a more favourable economic climate, and that national level solution for problems such as unemployment and inflation presently had priority among the member states. International cooperation, however, would undoubtedly retain its important position at a later point, primarily because many problems simply could not be solved efficiently at the national level. This was notably the case with respect to unemployment and the effects of international economic fluctuations.[55]

Regarding these two problems, the social democratic Government had already taken international initiatives. In the Council of Ministers it had called upon those EC member states with considerable balance of payments surpluses to "take the lead in the economic policy in order to raise economic activity".[56] The Government thus acknowledged the extensive Danish dependency on foreign economic developments, but in anticipation of a foreign-led economic upturn, it nevertheless launched, in August 1975, a unilateral Keynesian expansion. However, as the international upturn to a large extent failed to materialise and as the balance of payments therefore deteriorated rapidly following the expansion, the policy was relinquished.[57]

---

54) Ole Andersen et al., *EF: Hvad nu?*, p. 104.
55) *Folketingstidende*, forhandlingerne, 1975-76, 11 December 1975, cols. 2911-2912. See also Carsten Lehmann Sørensen, *Danmark og EF i 1970erne* (Copenhagen: Borgen, 1978), pp. 275-279.
56) *Folketingstidende*, forhandlingerne, 1975-76, 11 December 1975, col. 2917.
57) For an account of social democratic economic policy following the oil crisis, see Peter Nannestad, *Danish Design or British Disease? Danish Economic Crisis Policy 1974-1979*

On exchange rate policy social democratic EC spokesman, Erik Holst, in December 1975, repeated in strong words the party's commitment to stable exchange rates in the EC. Thus, he called for fixed exchange rates, centralised foreign currency reserves and a common external exchange rate policy. As he put it, the SDP considered this to be particularly important, since "Denmark [would] thereby gain a larger room for manoeuvre for our economic policy. We could thus do even more to reach what we find necessary, namely full employment".[58] In a subsequent debate, he went on to declare that an expansion of exchange rate cooperation and a better coordination of monetary and budgetary policies was necessary "in order to increase the ability to pursue a policy of budgetary deficits".[59] The underlying economic analysis: a pooling of currency reserves in the EC would safeguard against speculative pressures on the Danish currency and would reduce the pressure on states with weak currencies to deflate, since drawing on other states' reserves entails an internal monetary expansion in these states.

As a logical extension of the policies pursued until then, the social democratic Government welcomed the establishment of the European Monetary System in 1979. The EMS did not fulfill all social democratic wishes, and the Government reiterated its wish for a pooling of currency reserves. Yet the then Foreign Minister Kjeld Olesen stated in 1980 that

> "[t]he establishment of the EMS in March 1979 constitutes an important step. It has provided for more stable exchange rate conditions and has thus contributed to diminishing the effects of the international economic downturn."[60]

Apart from the calls for economic expansion in the balance of surplus countries of the EC, and strengthened cooperation on exchange rate stabilisation, social democratic EC policy in the wake of the first oil crisis was dominated by a concern to prevent the undermining of the Common Market and the reemergence of protectionism. Hence, the Danish Government repeatedly stressed the need to control the development of state subsidies to industry.

The SDP persistently opposed institutional reforms of the Community throughout the 1970s, preferring to consolidate and increase the day-to-

---

(Aarhus: Aarhus University Press, 1991).
58) *Folketingstidende*, forhandlingerne, 1975-76, 11 December 1975, col. 2922.
59) *Folketingstidende*, forhandlingerne, 1975-76, 6 February 1976, col. 5452.
60) *Folketingstidende*, forhandlingerne, 1979-1980, 22 May 1980, col. 9901.

day functioning of existing institutional frameworks. As formulated by
Ivar Nørgaard in 1975, "the recent tendencies in some member states to
place far-reaching institutional reforms at the centre of the debate are,
in our view, misguided. They lead to the erroneous belief that the EC will
be able to solve the large economic and social problems by way of institutional reshuffling".[61] The SDP also remained committed to the
Luxembourg-compromise and the political right of veto, but in several
instances the social democratic Government warned against abuse of the
veto. As Ivar Nørgaard saw it in 1976, there had been a tendency since
1972 for the larger countries to be able to block an issue in the Council
simply by declaring that the matter was not ripe for decision. The
Government deplored this abuse of the political veto, and suggested that
"a state should only be able to veto an issue if at the same time it was
willing to claim that the issue is of vital importance".[62]

The proposal for direct elections to the European Parliament was only
very reluctantly accepted by the Social Democratic Party, as promoted
and discussed in 1974-75. The immediate social democratic reaction was
to make acceptance dependent on two conditions: (1) that the members
of the European Parliament should concurrently be members of the
national parliament in the state in which they were elected, and (2) that
direct elections should take place simultaneously with national elections
and not at the same time in all member states. Both proposals were
rejected by a majority in the Danish Parliament and by the other EC
member states. Hence, the party gave in on the conditions and accepted
direct elections as they became a reality from 1979 and onwards.

SDP resistance to direct elections partly reflected the party's long
standing rejection of institutional reforms in the EC. At the same time
the leadership presumably anticipated that direct elections would exhibit
in the public the strong resistance to EC membership among many social
democratic voters and hence the conflict between the party's voters and
leadership on the EC issue.[63]

Nevertheless, the SDP actively participated in the campaign prior to
the 1979 European Parliament elections. Here the party reiterated its
wish to make use of the Community to solve a number of problems which
the party did not consider solvable at the national level. This continued

---

61) *Folketingstidende*, forhandlingerne, 1975-76, 11 December 1975, col. 2920.
62) *Folketingstidende*, forhandlingerne, 1975-76, 6 February 1976, cols. 5438-5439.
63) See e.g. Torben Worre, "Europavalget", p. 264.

a long standing social democratic approach and was a direct extension of
the EC policy statements agreed to at the 1977 party congress. Thus, the
SDP again favoured common efforts against unemployment and economic
crisis, increased control over multinational corporations in the EC
framework, strengthened EC measures for improving employee participation and working conditions, and intensified EC efforts to protect the
environment. At the same time the party rejected any development of the
EC "towards a political union".[64]

For the SDP, the results of the election were very disappointing. The
party won a mere 21.9% of the votes, as opposed to 37% in the last
parliamentary election. The "People's Movement Against the EC", the
primary aim of which was to take Denmark out of the European
Community, won 20.9% of the total vote.

THE SDP AND THE EC 1961-82: CONCLUSIONS

Our proposition on the internal dynamics of integration distinguishes
between social democratic parties' initial attitudes to national
membership of supranational market liberalising arrangemetns such as
the EC and attitudes when a fundamental dependency on continued
membership of such arrangements has been acknowledged. Following
this, we will discuss, first, the SDP's positions on the question of Danish
EC membership and, second, its policies once Denmark had entered the
Community.

The SDP and the Danish Rome Treaty Accession

Danish EC membership meant that the Danish state was subjected to
supranational decision-making procedures and to supranational
regulation in a number of policy areas, implying Denmark's binding to a
project which to a great extent must be characterised as a market liberalising enterprise. Thus, Danish EC entry meant that the Danish state
renounced the possibility of pursuing independent trade policies, tariff

---

64) Socialdemokratiet, "EF-parlamentsvalget 1979, Socialdemokratiets valgudtalelse"
(Copenhagen, May 1979). As the 1979 manifesto of the CSPEC, as mentioned, had been
diluted by the British Labour Party's critical position towards the EC, the Danish SDP had
no difficulties subscribing to it.

policies, agricultural policies and policies involving certain types of state subsidies. In 1971-72, it seemed likely that membership would soon also involve limitations on exchange rate policies. Yet the large majority of the Danish SDP, in particular the parliamentary group, supported EC membership, thereby contradicting the first part of the proposition on the internal dynamic of integration. Following this first part of the proposition, national membership of the EC should be rejected by social democratic parties as it would entail a restructuring of the given nation state's foreign economic relations, implying economic dependency on continued membership. This would in turn mean real as opposed to just formal submission to supranational limits to national state intervention.

How is this contradiction with the proposition on the internal dynamics of integration to be understood? An external event, namely the British application for EC membership, created a considerable risk of Danish exclusion in the form of exclusion of Danisih agricultural exports rom the British markets. While this is not a type of external event in connection with our proposition on externally induced changes in attitude integration, it is appropriate to view the British application as an external event for the Danish political system. At the same time, the British policy meant that, in a sudden and very perceptible way, Denmark had become dependent on EC membership. Given British membership, ensuring Danish access to EC markets came to be of critical importance.

This necessitates a reformulation of the first part of the proposition on the internal dynamic of integration. A contextual interpretation of the SDP's support for EC membership thus suggests that a calculus on the trade-offs between the party's different general policy goals can explain the decision of the party leadership and the parliamentary group. National exclusion from the EC's market in general and its market for agricultural products in particular would in the leadership's perception involve a large direct welfare loss, a loss which would also strike hard at the party's social basis. Compare, for instance, Prime Minister Krag's statements on the economic aspects of EC membership in the December 1971 parliamentary debate.

Moreover, the welfare loss would in the party's perceptions not be offset by the greater formal possibilities for state intervention in the market had Denmark remained outside the Community. Finally, EC membership did not threaten general policy goals which were seen by party leaders to have been largely realised at the national level, and which depended on state intervention in the economy.[65]

In contrast, the social democratic EC opponents judged the direct welfare losses of remaining outside the EC to be smaller than what the party leadership thought to be the case, just as they saw greater long-term risks from EC membership for general policy goals, which to a high degree had been realised in the Danish framework.

It should be noted that according to the party leadership EC membership according did not curtail types of state intervention which had constituted important instruments in the Danish SDP's reform strategy. This was true despite the fact that the Community's formal framework, given the acknowledged Danish dependency on EC membership in the perceptions of the party leadership, had assumed real importance. Hence, after the Second World War, the party had never put much emphasis on trade regulation as a means of managing the general development of Danish society, and since the beginning of the 1960s the SDP had consistently supported an extension of international free trade.

Furthermore, Danish industrial policy had never involved the types of state subsidies prohibited in the Rome Treaty, and direct state subsidies to industry remained at a low level compared to other Western European states. Nor had agricultural policy played any significant role in the party's strategies.[66] The Danish applications for EC membership thus suggest that the value of national state intervention varies from issue area to issue area for social democratic parties. In the case of the Danish SDP, freedom from EC limitations on national state intervention regarding trade and tariffs, agricultural policies, certain types of industrial policy, and also regarding exchange rates was less valued than the direct economic benefits resulting from EC membership.

There are two possible explanations for the SDP's low valuation of the possibility of national intervention in areas where Rome Treaty accession

---

65) This interpretation of the party leadership's decision to apply for EC membership is supported by the fact that Prime Minister Krag had prepared two sets of speeches to be used in the wake of the 1972 referendum: One set, the "white" speeches, in case the Danish electorate approved of membership, were optimistic on the country's economic future and the possibilities of further social improvements. Another, the "black" set, to be used in case of a "no" vote, were pessimistic in these respects. The Government had also developed an action programme in the event of a rejection of EC membership, involving a 15% devaluation of the krone, tax increases and a tightened incomes policy. The "black" speeches and the action programme are reprinted in Jens Engberg, *I minefeltet*, pp. 130-146.

66) It should be noted, however, that the EC's common agricultural policy had from its onset involved a high degree of regulation of markets. Social democratic mistrust of the Community on the grounds that it constituted a market liberalist enterprise could, therefore, hardly be justified in the agricultural sector.

had direct effects: One centres on fundamental structural economic conditions present in the Danish context, and the other focuses on basic Danish political conditions. Regarding the first explanation, the small size of the Danish economy and its correspondent dependency on international trade may have been important.[67] Thus, the fundamental condition of small size may have drastically diminished the possibility of applying any comprehensive and internationally unapproved state intervention in the above mentioned areas with an overall positive effect on the realisation of the party's general policy goals.

Notably, this could apply regardless of Danish EC membership. Hence, public intervention in the economy in the form of unilaterally imposed quantitative restrictions on imports, direct state price subsidies to exports, or devaluations, all in order to secure full employment, does, as argued in connection with the discussion of the British Labour Party's Alternative Economic Strategy, involve the risk of provoking similar measures from other states.

This would in particular a small state in a very difficult situation, as a small state is hit much harder by a larger state's import restrictions than the larger state is affected by similar measures from a smaller state. In the case of direct state price subsidies, the small state risks engaging in a battle on the funding capabilities of the public budget, a battle which it most likely cannot win. Furthermore, protectionist measures in a trade dependent economy may raise the price of intermediate goods and thus undermine the competitiveness of exports in the world markets.

As for the second explanation, a firmly established feature of the Danish political scene since the 1920s is that SDP Governments almost invariably have depended on support from liberal or conservative parties for a parliamentary majority. This fact has led some observers to characterise the situation as agrarian-liberal hegemony.[68] It may thus be possible that the Danish SDP's low valuation of the policy instruments affected by EC membership followed the fact that the use of these instruments was politically impossible anyway, given the Danish Parliament's majority of political forces favouring a high degree of market regulation of society.

---

67) Danish exports amounted to between 28% and 34% of GDP in the period from 1950 to 1970, cf. *United Nations Statistical Yearbook 1969*, and Organization for Economic Cooperation and Development, *OECD National Accounts*, vol. 1: *Main Aggregates* 1960-1990, tables 13 and 17.
68) Gösta Esping-Andersen, *Politics Against Markets*, p. 156 and pp. 205-215.

The arguments put forward by the SDP representatives in the debate on Danish EC membership point to the first of these explanations. The large majority of the parliamentary party never regretted that EC entry would mean the loss of intervention possibilities in areas of trade, tariffs, and agricultural policy, as would have occurred had the party been compelled to renounce the use of these instruments for domestic political reasons. On the contrary, the SDP actively supported further trade liberalisations in the EC and in general; witness, for instance, Prime Minister Krag's statements in April 1972 as well as the 1973 policy report. Even the social democratic EC opponents failed to deplore the loss of formal trade and tariff policy independence.

Furthermore, the party actively supported the strict enforcement of the Rome Treaty's provisions prohibiting certain types of state subsidies, as illustrated by the 1973 policy report's remarks, just as the SDP explicitly cited the vulnerability of the small state in justifying its support for fixed exchange rates and in general for far-reaching economic cooperation in the Community; compare the Foreign Minister's statement on this point as early as 1962, and the remarks of Ivar Nørgaard in April 1972. Finally, it should be recalled that the positive approach of the SDP towards Danish EC membership remained intact, as the SDP and the left wing Socialist Peoples' Party commanded a parliamentary majority between the elections of November 1966 and January 1968.[69]

To sum up, social democratic support for Danish EC membership followed from an external development, namely Britain's application for EC entry. However, the SDP's decision was conditioned by fundamental Danish economic characteristics, primarily the small size of the Danish economy and its dependency on foreign trade. Small size meant that the instruments for state intervention which were formally transferred to the supranational level had never had much value to the SDP.

---

69) The SDP's own experiences pointed to the uselessness of an independent trade policy. In October 1971, the social democratic government tried to impose a 10% surcharge to improve the balance of payments but was forced to exempt most goods as other states threatened to retaliate. See Tage Kaarsted, *Danske Ministerier 1953-72* (Odense: Odense Universitetsforlag, 1992), pp. 474-475. The Norwegian SDP's comprehensive use of direct state subsidies to industry in the 1970s seems to argue against the structural economic explanation; cf. Gösta Esping-Andersen, *Politics Against Markets*, pp. 224-226. However, the anticipated huge oil revenues may distinguish Norway from Denmark; for a period Norway was able to act as if it were a larger state. More generally Peter J. Katzenstein, *Small States in World Markets: Industrial Policy in Europe* (London: Cornell University Press, 1985), pp. 39-47 also argues that small Western European states have supported strong international free trade regimes as a result of their great vulnerability.

Did purely domestic developments influence the SDP's decision to support EC membership? This does not appear to be the case. The only instance in which domestic party-tactical concerns have affected the course of events was when former foreign minister Hækkerup announced the SDP's wish to hold a referendum on Rome Treaty accession, a decision which allowed the party to win an election and avoid open internal disagreement. However, no national development underlay the decision, and it did not influence the substantive content of the party's EC policies. One may speculate, however, what would have happened if the referendum had not been held. The referendum evidently exposed the party's internal disagreement on the EC issue, and perhaps more importantly, it exposed a very significant gap between the views of the great majority of the parliamentary group on the effects of Rome Treaty accession and the much more sceptical views held by the party's social basis and voters or potential voters.

The SDP Within the European Community

The British EC entry meant that to the SDP leadership, Denmark had become dependent on EC membership in a very abrupt and perceptible way. This meant that realisation of the party's general policy goals would be damaged, were Denmark to remain outside the Community.

Following our proposition on the internal dynamics of integration, acknowledged dependency on EC membership should have prompted the SDP to try to shape the Community according to its own visions. This would imply growing support for increased supranational regulation, and possibly, for extended supranational decision-making capacity in policy areas held important by the party. The motive for supporting extended supranational regulation could be either (1) that EC membership provides access to institutions with the capability of establishing regulation not seen to be efficient at the national level or subsequently improving the efficiency of national regulation, (2) that EC regulation serves as a guarantee for the existence of perceived necessary national regulation, (3) that EC membership threatens the efficiency of necessary national regulation, creating the need for supranational replacement regulation or regulation subsequently increasing the efficiency of national regulation, or (4) that EC market liberalisations create or magnify problems whose solution requires new supranational regulation.

Clearly, this dynamic is present for the Danish SDP in the sense that once Denmark had entered the EC, the party - in the post-referendum 1972 and 1973 parliamentary debates and in the comprehensive 1973 policy report - expressed firm support for extending supranational regulation in a number of areas: control over multinational corporations, minimum regulations on environmental protection, consumer protection and working conditions, and other types of labour market regulation. The 1973 policy report is thus a striking illustration of the party's wish to formulate an offensive strategy and to make use of supranational institutions for furthering its general policy goals. Party leader Anker Jørgensen pinpointed the dynamic development of the party's EC policy in his preface to the policy report, restating the mechanism which had been hinted at by the chairman of the Unskilled Workers' Union as early as the 1962 debate on Danish EC membership: Once within the Community, the party, including its former opponents of EC membership, would support the establishment of supranational regulation in a number of policy areas.

The exact cause behind the SDP's support for binding supranational regulation in various areas is difficult to determine, but some clarification results when we distinguish between different issues. Thus, regarding the social democratic desire to strengthen political control over multinational corporations in the EC framework, this proposal most likely constituted an attempt to utilise EC institutions for regulation which almost per definition could not be effective at the national level.

As for the SDP's wish to adopt binding minimum EC regulation for environmental protection and for employee rights and working conditions, the picture is less clear.

On the one hand, party leader Anker Jørgensen's formulation that EC regulation should "support" national improvements in these areas could imply that EC membership was seen to impose certain limits on national regulation as a consequence of increased competitive pressures in the Common Market, that EC membership had thus undermined the efficiency of national regulation, and that a general improvement of standards at the EC level was therefore necessary in order to protect or improve Danish standards.[70]

---

70) This is presumably the argument which underlay the statements of the leader of the Unskilled Workers' Union in 1962 and which was used by the SDP's opponents of EC membership in their campaign against EC entry. Cf. Svend Auken's and Karl Hjortnæs' statements.

On the other hand, the party leadership had consistently rejected the claim prior to the 1972 referendum that EC membership would have significant direct or indirect consequences for Danish social and labour market regulation. Another motivation for the SDP's proposals in this area, therefore, seems more plausible. The proposals may reflect the wish to utilise supranational institutions to effect regulation which would reinforce the cost efficiency of national regulation. Thus, the creation of EC minimum regulations on employee rights and environmental protection could render less costly - in terms of unemployment or falling real wages - effects to improve Danish standards in these areas. If this motive had been important for the SDP, the party had implicitly accepted that labour market and environmental regulation constituted negative competitive parameters and that high standards in the above-mentioned areas would benefit the state with the highest standards prior to EC regulation. In other words, the SDP proposals for EC regulations establishing high minimum levels on environmental protection and employee rights constituted an advanced type of protectionism.

Furthermore, it is possible that the proposed EC minimum regulation could have been motivated by the wish to make use of the EC as a supranational guarantee for national regulation; that is; as minimum regulation which, once adopted, is very difficult to reverse.

Finally, it is a distinct possibility that the proposals could have been caused by a wish to extend desired regulation beyond Danish territory, as it was indeed claimed by Poul Dalsager in the November 1972 parliamentary debate. Hereby the implicit claim is made that the above mentioned types of regulation have productive effects - at least in the longer run and at least to the extent that unemployment is not accepted as the price for higher standards in specific areas. If this motivation was important for the SDP, we transcend the basic analytical assumptions underlying the study; namely, that the parties in question seek to achieve general policy goals only for their national social basis, and that the realisation of general policy goals in other states plays no role in their specific policy formation.

An overall evaluation of the precise motivations underlying the proposals for minimum EC labour market and environmental regulation must remain tentative. It is possible that all types of motivations have been present, as different perceptions and motives for policy may be important for different segments of the party. However, the wish to make use of EC regulation to guarantee the existence of necessary national

regulation does not appear very significant, given the relative strength
of the Danish social democratic movement compared to most other EC
member states.

Furthermore, if may appear contradictory to claim that employee
rights and environmental legislation at the same time constitute a
positive and a negative competitive parameter; that is, may decrease
international competitiveness, as is implied when minimum EC
regulation is motivated as a means to improve the cost efficiency of
national regulation, or increase competitiveness, as it is implied when an
improvement of overall social democratic goal realisation in other states
is claimed to be the motive. However, the contradiction may disappear if
we distinguish between different types of concrete regulation. For
instance, it may be argued that employee co-decision has positive effects
on productivity and competitiveness, whereas strict regulation on
employee working conditions constitutes a burden to competitiveness.

In contrast to the multiple motivations apparently underlying the SDP
calls for EC minimum regulation on environmenal protection and
employee rights, the party's December 1975 proposals for a fixed
exchange rate in the Community, in combination with a pooling of foreign
currency reserves, were clear. Thus, these proposals constituted an
attempt to establish regulation at the supranational level in an area
where internationally uncoordinated national regulation would often be
ineffective. As the experiences from the unilateral Danish economic
expansion in 1975-76 underlined, a Danish economic policy which
deviated from that of the major trading partners in any significant
manner was bound to lead to economic imbalances which would eventually force a policy realignment in accordance with the international
surroundings. In this context, the proposals for fixed exchange rates and
a pooling of foreign currency reserves served to alleviate these external
constraints, i.e. to increase the cost efficiency of national macroeconomic
management. However, depending on which concrete form the SDP's
proposals would have taken, it may be wrong to categorise them as
instances of attitude integration, since they may not have involved
extended supranational regulation or increased supranational decision-
making capacity.

In accordance with the proposition on the internal dynamics of
integration, the perception of dependency on EC membership had turned
the Community into a battleground for the SDP in which a part of the
struggle on regulation of the economy was to take place. However, the

dynamic development foreseen in the proposition is present only to a limited extent. Hence, from 1972 onwards, the SDP supported increased supranational regulation in specific policy areas, but did not support improved supranational decision-making capacity in any policy area. Social democratic attempts to shape the EC's activities according to the party's own visions remained on intergovernmental basis. Why?

The most obvious answer is that reform of the Rome Treaty was simply not on the agenda from the mid-1970s to the mid-1980s. Yet, this does not answer the question of why the party rejected increased supranational decision-making capacity such as extended use of majority voting on minimum regulation in the Council in relevant policy areas from principle, even where in the party's perception it could have furthered the realisation of its general political goals.

One interpretation points to the fact that the party had experienced deep internal disagreements on the question of EC membership. Thus, in spite of the offensive policy proposals advanced in the 1973 report, the issue of membership had not disappeared from the party after the referendum, and that proposals on the introduction of majority decision-making in new policy areas therefore entailed the risk of reopening party-internal rifts, to the detriment of the party's credibility as a governmental party in the electorate. To the extent that this mechanism has been active, it points to the party's EC policies during the 1970s as being utilised instrumentally in order to ensure a broad electoral appeal.

A further tentative explanation would stress the possibility that acceptance of the objective of Treaty reform in the party leadership's perceptions could spur developments beyond the control of the party and, hence, place at risk the possibility of national regulation in highly valued areas. In this connection, it is also likely that proposals for more majority decision-making in the Council could in the party's perception question the status of the Luxembourg compromise, the existence of which had been used to persuade the electorate that no risks followed from EC membership. This last point again points to the concern for the party's electoral appeal as a factor influencing its approach to the European Community in the 1970s.

Furthermore, the existence of unanimity procedures on EC market liberalisations in the Treaty seemed to guarantee that these liberalisations would not advance in a manner threatening to the party's general policy goals, implying that there was little need for increased supranational decision-making capacity in areas where regulation was needed to control and supplement the effects of market forces. This last argument presupposes that the party leadership dod not view EC membership in itself as undermining the efficiency of national regulation in important policy areas. Following the above standing arguments, this seems plausible. Finally, in the first years of EC membership it is possible that the party expected that much could be achieved in terms of desired EC minimum regulation even when the Treaty stipulated the principle of unanimity.

8

The Single Market
and Beyond

For the Danish SDP, the years from 1983 to 1989 marked a turning point. This was so in two respects: the party remained in opposition throughout the entire period; and its EC policy was from 1984 onwards confronted with the challenge of a developing European Community. In this context, the SDP's reaction was to reject the Single European Act and the institutional reforms of the EC contained in it. However, the party subsequently increasingly emphasised its call for strengthening the social and environmental aspects of cooperation in the EC framework, eventually voicing support for institutional reforms in these areas.

TOWARDS THE REFERENDUM ON THE SEA

By mid-1982, and in the context of a new, deep international recession following the second oil crisis, the social democratic Government was facing a level of unemployment unprecedented in the post-war era, an increasing balance of payments deficit, a large and growing foreign debt, and a mounting domestic debt. Confronted with the prospects of deep cuts in public expenditures and staunch resistance to further tax increases in Parliament, the SDP government relinquished power to a coalition government consisting of the Conservative and Liberal parties, the Christian Peoples' Party, and the Centre Democrats.

Social Democratic EC Policy: 1983-84

The Social Democratic Party's first years in opposition entailed no significant reformulation of its long-standing policies on the European Community, even if critique of the Centre-Right Government's handling of EC matters introduced a new element. Thus, as had been the case throughout the 1970s, the SDP's approach to the Community remained result seeking, and the party continued to support Community policies with great importance for the Danish economy such as the CAP. At the same time, steps involving increased supranationality were rejected. In accordance with its firmly established principles, the party, in November 1982, dismissed the "Genscher-Colombo Plan" for institutional reforms of the Community and a strengthening of the EC's foreign policy coope-ration in the EPC system. As EC spokesman Ivar Nørgaard stated, the SDP wanted an extension and an improvement of EC cooperation in a number of areas, but "the institutional framework contained in the [existing] treaties is sufficient for a much more far-reaching cooperation than has been achieved until now."[1] Nørgaard particularly rejected any weakening of the right of veto contained in the Luxembourg-compromise and any strengthening of the European Parliament's authority.

In a May 1984 parliamentary debate a few weeks before the second direct election to the European Parliament, a number of these viewpoints were reiterated:

> "It is the position of the Social Democratic Party that EC policy should aim at those practical problems which the national parliaments and govern-ments cannot solve on their own. This applies primarily to the fight against unemployment, and to effective utilisation of new technology, the fight against pollution and control over multinational corporations".[2]

However, during 1983 and 1984, the emphasis in the party's policy gradually changed so as to direct more attention to the need for a common effort against unemployment in the EC framework. This devel-opment undoubtedly signified the SDP's active participation in the cam-paign for coordinated reflation and a shortening of working hours agreed to by the EC's socialist and social democratic parties. Thus, the SDP had subscribed to the CSPEC European Election Manifesto released in March 1984, a manifesto whose most prominent theme was a proposal for a coordinated economic expansion in the Community, as mentioned previously.[3] The Danish SDP rejected the document's call for increased

---

1) *Folketingstidende*, forhandlingerne, 1982-83, 18 November 1982, cols. 1884-1885.
2) Ivar Nørgaard in *Folketingstidende*, forhandlingerne, 1983-1984, 28 May 1984, col. 7175.
3) CSPEC, "Manifesto Adopted by the XIIIth Congress of the Confederation of the Socialist Parties of the European Community". The call for coordinated reflation had also played a prominent role in the party's EC programme, adopted at a special congress in September 1983; cf. Socialdemokratiet, "EF-valgudtalelse vedtaget på den ekstraordinære kongres i dagene 2.-4. september 1983".

powers to the European Parliament, but in contrast to the British Labour Party it did not reserve its position on a strengthening of the European Monetary System and an increase in the Community's "own resources".

As a consequence, the demand for a coordinated effort against unemployment in the EC constituted the predominant theme in the SDP's manifesto for the June 1984 elections to the European Parliament. In the EP, the SDP declared that it would work for

> "all states to follow a coordinated policy for stimulation of the economy. The economic crisis experienced by large parts of the world cannot be overcome through the one-sided policy of budget cuts, which conservative and liberal governments pursue. It is necessary to increase production and reduce unemployment in cooperation with the trade union movement, avoiding that the states thereby cause each other balance of payments difficulties."[4]

Apart from this, the manifesto contained the by now traditional calls for a more efficient EC policy on environmental protection and control with multinational corporations, just as the SDP favoured among other things a more effective EC policy on energy conservation, and an increase in the Community's "own resources" to the extent this was necessary for stimulating economic growth.

The recession following the second oil crisis was evidently the most important factor underlying the vigourous social democratic calls for coordinated reflation, but the policy was also influenced by other determinants. Hence, social democratic representatives stressed that the experiences of the French Socialist Government in 1981-83 had underlined the urgent need to strengthen the EC states' common efforts to reduce unemployment. As Ivar Nørgaard stated in the May 1984 parliamentary debate,

> "the experiences from France after President Mitterrand took office show that even a large country cannot manage the fight against unemployment if other countries pursue a policy which does not further investments and demand. It is therefore necessary that all member states concentrate on a comprehensive effort against unemployment".[5]

Judging from the SDP statements of 1983-84 and from the manifesto for the 1984 elections to the European Parliament, the party had an approved policy on the EC. However, the seemingly constructive

---

4) Socialdemokratiet, "Socialdemokratiets valgudtalelse til EF-valget Juni 1984", Copenhagen, May 1984.
5) *Folketingstidende*, forhandlingerne, 1983-84, 28 May 1984, col. 7175.

approach to Danish EC membership was far from the complete picture. Presumably as a consequence of the continuing inability of the EC to reach decisions with any substantial bearings on the Western European states' economic and social problems in the early 1980s, resentment towards EC membership in the population remained forceful and indeed grew stronger in the first years of the decade. Polling data has indicated that whereas approval of continued Danish EC membership occured by only a margin of 4% of the electorate in June 1979, the average margin in favour of EC withdrawal in the period 1980-1984 was 12 percentage points.[6]

Various SDP publications released prior to the campaign for the European elections illustrate that the strong and growing hostility towards the Community was taken seriously by the party. Thus, one lengthy pamphlet was devoted to a single objective: arguing that Denmark had substantial advantages from remaining a member. In asserting this, the pamphlet focused almost exclusively on the direct economic advantages of EC membership; i.e. primarily the beneficial effects of the CAP and the EC fisheries policy, as well as the advantages of good access to the markets of other EC states. The importance of more explicitly political aspects was downgraded, and the pamphlet attempted to reassure its readers that the political right of veto and article 236 of the Rome Treaty necessitated the consent of the Danish Parliament to any fundamental changes of the EC.[7]

The result of the 1984 EP election nevertheless continued to reflect the deep scepticism towards the EC in the electorate in general and among SDP voters in particular. With a turnout of 52.4% of the electorate, the party won a mere 19.5% of the total vote, as opposed to 31.6% of the vote at the January 1984 Parliamentary election, and as opposed to 21.9% of the vote in the 1979 EP elections.

The Peoples' Movement Against the EC held on to the almost 21% of the vote achieved in the 1979 European elections. Furthermore, polls indicated that among social democratic voters in 1984, 48% opposed Danish EC membership, whereas only 35% approved.[8] For the SDP, the European Community remained a highly troublesome and divisive phenomenon.

---

6) Torben Worre, "The Danish Euro-Party System", *Scandinavian Political Studies*, vol. 10, no. 1, 1987, p. 81.
7) Socialdemokratiet, "Også solidaritet i fællesskabet" (Copenhagen, October 1983).
8) Torben Worre, "The Danish Euro-Party System", p. 82.

The Intergovernmental Conference and the SEA

As mentioned, the process towards the revisions of the EC contained in the Single European Act was initiated when France's President Mitterrand in May 1984 was endorsing the idea of reforms of the Rome Treaty.

In Denmark the SDP in the same month rejected the idea of Treaty reforms. During parliamentary debate, the party's spokesman again stressed that the party remained committed to preserving the existing distribution of authority among EC institutions. As regards the French President's proposals for an intergovernmental conference, Nørgaard emphasised that "[i]f there is a will to more extensive cooperation, this may perfectly well take place within the limits of the existing treaty". He also made clear that if participation in the conference presupposed that the participants were "positive towards Treaty reforms with more powers to the [European] Parliament and with inclusion of new issue areas under the Treaty, such as education, culture and security policy, we must desist from participating".[9] Subsequently, the Folketing, with SDP support, adopted a motion stating that "the basis for Danish EC membership is a preservation of the right of veto and a continuation of the existing distribution of authority between the Council, the Commission, and the European Parliament".[10]

Prior to the European Council of June 1985 in Milan, which was to decide on the question of an intergovernmental conference, the Folketing again discussed EC developments. In the debate, the SDP repeated its emphasis on the absence of preconditions for participation, and in connection with the emerging debate on a "Europe of two speeds" Nørgaard argued that he saw no dangers in a development where different Western European states participate in different cooperative schemes. Besides this, the SDP devoted much attention to the party's commitment to the preservation of the Luxembourg veto, even if it was also maintained that the veto should not be subject to abuse.[11]

The intergovernmental conference had convened in September 1985, and it had negotiated an agreement 3 months later. During the entire

---

9) Ivar Nørgaard in *Folketingstidende*, forhandlingerne, 1983-84, 28 May 1984, col. 7177.
10) *Folketingstidende*, forhandlingerne, 1983-84, 29 May 1984, col. 7243. The vote was 134 to 30 with 2 abstentions.
11) *Folketingstidende*, forhandlingerne, 1984-85, 23 May 1985, cols. 10425-10426.

negotiating process, the Danish Government had remained in close contact with the Social Democratic leadership. The Folketing's majority had not equipped the Government with any precise mandate for the negotiations in the Market Committee, choosing instead to refer it to the motions on Danish EC policy already adopted by the Folketing's plenum. Nevertheless, the SDP leadership during the whole process informed the Government of its main concerns regarding Danish priorities. As the negotiations proceeded and the tactical possibilities were clarified, it became particularly important for the SDP to ensure that the emerging plans for the completion of a Single Market in the Community would not stand in the way of independent Danish measures on environmental and occupational health issues, and that the balance between EC institutions should remain unchanged.

At the same time, however, the party put forward a number of proposals for concrete reforms of the Treaty, the contents of which were revealed by a policy document issued by the party's so-called Europe Committee which had been established at the party's Congress in September 1984.[12] The document proposed an opening up of the Community in the form establishing far-reaching cooperation between EFTA- and EC- states, and it repeated the SDP's rejection of institutional reforms of Community entailing "a further surrender of sovereignty, a dilution of Danish parliamentary control with EC decisions, reductions in the right of veto, and fundamental changes in the division of labour between the Community institutions". However, *if* the SDP were to accept changes of the Treaty, the Europe Committee proposed that this

> "... would be preferable regarding exchange rate policy, research and technology, energy, the external environment, and the working environment. ... For example, the Treaty could stipulate a number of minimum requirements for the working environment. We could also codify the obligation to pursue an active employment policy in case the unemployment rate exceeded for instance 5%, and we could codify the EMS system and make the ECU an international reserve currency as the dollar."[13]

On the explicit condition that the Luxembourg right of veto should be upheld, the position that the Treaty could be amended so as to formally comprise more areas of cooperation became explicit SDP policy in the fall of 1985, as both EC spokesman Ivar Nørgaard and political spokesman

---

12) The creation of the "Europe Committee" will be discussed later.
13) Birte Weiss, "Ja til Europa - Nej til Union. Materiale til Socialdemokratiets Europa-debat", pp. 2-3.

Svend Auken supported it in newspaper commentaries. In Nørgaard's opinion, such proposals should be in line with the Europe Committee's document, and Svend Auken stated that the SDP agreed to the Government formulating proposals for the codification of new issue areas under the Rome Treaty. However, these proposals were only to serve the purpose of allowing the Government a certain tactical leeway at the intergovernmental conference.[14]

In light of the emerging consensus between the major EC states on Treaty reforms, involving majority decisions in the Council on the establishment of a Single Market in the EC, the SDP and the Government then agreed to put forward a number of concrete proposals for Rome Treaty amendments.[15] To a high extent these proposals reflected the previously revealed social democratic positions. Thus, it was proposed to incorporate into the Treaty an obligation for the member states to promote employment "if unemployment exceeds y%", but the obligation is to be political and therefore not legally binding. Furthermore, at the initiative of the SDP the Danish document also contains a section proposing the introduction of majority decision-making in the Council of Minsters regarding directives laying down "minimum requirements in the working environment". Besides the concern to secure a more prominent position for employment-creating policies and protection of the working environment in the EC, the SDP leadership in the following negotiations attempted to ensure that legislation adopted with a majority in order to establish a Single Market in the EC would not stand in the way of independent Danish measures for improving the working environment or protecting the external environment.

Several of the Social Democratic goals for the intergovernmental conference seemed fulfilled in the SEA, as negotiations had been concluded in December 1985. The SDP's requests had contributed to the incorporation of articles 118A and 100A(4) in the proposed revised Rome Treaty; article 118A introducing majority decision-making on minimum regulation for the working environment, and article 100A(4) allowing a member state to apply national provisions in the single market under the

---

14) Ivar Nørgaard, "Ordet 'Union' vil vi ikke have", *Weekendavisen*, 13 September 1985, and Svend Auken, "Nej til beskæring af veto-retten", *Aktuelt*, 19 October 1985.

15) The four-party Conservative-Liberal coalition government did not have a reliable parliamentary majority which excluded the SDP on questions regarding the EC's development, providing the SDP with considerable leverage in the negotiations. The contents of the proposals are listed in *Europe. Agence Internationale D'Information Pour La Presse*, 18 October 1985, pp. 3-4.

judicial review of the European Court of Justice in order to protect the
working environment or the external environment. However, the obligation to pursue expansive economic policies where unemployment exceeded
a certain level had not been accepted.

The Danish Government reserved its position on the result of the
negotiations, giving the Folketing an opportunity to debate the contents
on 10 December.

In the parliamentary debate, Ivar Nørgaard of the SDP formulated the
SDP's position on the Single European Act in cautious, critical terms.
The negotiating result on the reform of the European Parliament's
powers - the cooperation procedure in the amended Rome Treaty's article
149 - provoked the most critical reactions. As the SDP saw it, the
proposed cooperation procedure did not comply with the Folketing's
preceding motion that Treaty reforms should not alter the distribution
of authority between Community institutions. If the negotiated
agreement on the EP were to be the final result, the party could,
therefore, not vote for its ratification.[16]

The SDP position on the introduction of majority voting in the Council
regarding the establishment of the Single Market was less critical. In a
prior newspaper commentary Nørgaard had emphasised that Denmark
as a small state heavily dependent on international division of labour had
an interest in removing as many barriers to international trade as
possible.[17]

However, both in the commentary and during the parliamentary
debate Nørgaard expressed concern that the coming of the internal
market in the EC, in spite of the SEA's article 100A(4), would stand in
the way of independent Danish measures aimed at the protection of the
external and the working environment. The key problem in this
connection was how the Court of Justice would balance concern for equal
competition with protection of the environment. Consequently, Nørgaard
in the Folketing stated that

> "[i]t is the immediate reaction of the SDP that the perpetuation of the principle
> of unanimity constitutes a better safeguard [for Danish standards of
> environmental protection and protection of the working environment] than
> what the Government claims to have accomplished".[18]

---

16) *Folketingstidende*, forhandlingerne, 1985-86, 10 December 1985, col. 4180 and 4223.
17) Ivar Nørgaard, "Meget står på spil", *Aktuelt*, 1 December 1985.
18) *Folketingstidende*, forhandlingerne, 1985-86, 10 December 1985, col. 4181-82.

The most positive SDP reaction to the result of the negotiations centered upon foreign political cooperation in the EPC system, even if the party saw the codification of the EPC as superfluous.

The 1986 Referendum

After the negotiations on the SEA had been definitively concluded, the SDP parliamentary group, in January 1986, made its final decision on whether to approve Danish ratification. There is evidence that parts of the party leadership including party leader Anker Jørgensen and political spokesman Svend Auken were - in early January 1986 - in favour of approval, as were large parts of the SDP-attached trade union movement. On 5 January Anker Jørgensen had stated that he had a "basically positive attitude towards the [reform] package",[19] and on 6 January a spokesman for LO, the Trade Union Confederation, Bent Nielsen, said that the predominant attitude among the trade unions was positive.

Svend Auken also made clear that he considered the trade unions' position to be very important, and that his primary concern was to obtain legal guarantees that the SEA would not stand in the way of the Danish environmental policy. In contrast, Auken "did not see any significant problems in the bureaucratic rules for the European Parliament" envisaged in the SEA, or in the codification of the EPC.[20]

However, at a meeting of the SDP's parliamentary group on 8 January 1986, where the party's position on the final negotiation result was discussed for the first time, the mood of the group as a whole was overwhelmingly against accepting the SEA. A very clear majority opted for a rejection, apparently handing a spectacular defeat to party leader Anker Jørgensen.[21] The parliamentary group's final decision, made on 14 January 1986, confirmed the spirit of the earlier meeting: the SDP's parliamentary group would not accept the Single European Act.

The group's rejection of the party leadership's position caused tensions with those segments of the trade union movement advocating approval of the reform package. The sceptical position of the trade unions towards

---

19) "Anker siger ja til EF-reformen ", *Politiken*, 7 January 1986.
20) Lars-Bo Larsen and Ingelise Larsen, "LO accepterer EF-pakken", *Politiken*, 6 January 1986.
21) According to Foreign Minister Uffe Ellemann-Jensen, *Da Danmark igen sagde ja til det fælles* (Copenhagen: Schulz, 1987), p. 90, only 3 of the social democratic MPs present at the meeting supported Anker Jørgensen's positive approach.

the parliamentary group's decision was made clear at a meeting of LO's executive committee on 17 January. The statement released following this meeting argued that LO's main concern regarding the SEA was to ensure that the reform would not stand in the way of independent Danish measures on the working environment and the external environment. The EP's new co-operation procedure was not mentioned, and the trade unions' view therefore corresponded closely to the standpoints presented by political spokesman Svend Auken on 6 January, leading some observers to conclude that LO had thereby in effect revealed the party leadership's plan for the SDP's edging towards an approval of the SEA: the party's condition for ratifying the SEA would be for the Foreign Minister to obtain an additional (though most likely legally worthless) guarantee from the other EC states that the Single European Act would not stand in the way of stricter Danish measures on the external and working environment, after which the party would vote for ratification.[22] This seems to be a plausible interpretation of the leadership's intentions, but these intentions turned irrelevant as the parliamentary group revolted.

It has been suggested that the decision to reject the SEA was primarily motivated by the wish to provoke the fall of the Government.[23] In this view, a majority of the SDP's parliamentary group turned against the SEA as it became clear that both left-wing parties, the SPP and the Left Socialists, and one of the centre parties, the Radical Liberals, had committed themselves to rejecting the result of the intergovernmental conference, albeit for very different reasons.[24] The SDP's rejection of the SEA would therefore create a majority against the Government, and as the SEA undoubtedly constituted an important issue, the normal procedure would be for the Government to resign and - most likely - for the Prime Minister to call an election. The SDP could then hope to win the election, take office and accept some symbolically amended version of the SEA.[25]

The possibility of bringing about an election could have played a role in some parts of the SDP's parliamentary group. However, opinion polls

---

22) Henning Fonsmark, "EF-spillet mellem parti og fagbevægelse", *Børsen*, 21 January 1986.
23) This is the position in Torben Worre, "Denmark at the Crossroads", *Journal of Common Market Studies*, vol. 26, no. 4 (June 1988), pp. 361-388.
24) For an account of party positions see Torben Worre, "Denmark at the crossroads".
25) Torben Worre, "Denmark at the crossroads", p. 370, Uffe Ellemann-Jensen, *Da Danmark igen sagde ja til det fælles*, pp. 84-86, and S. Bie, M. Herz, O. S. Pedersen and J. Wagner, "Ny magtbalance efter EF-opgør", *Børsens Nyhedsmagasin*, 20 January 1986, pp. 32-33.

suggest that the party would probably not have been able to form the new government after an election.[26] Furthermore, an interpretation based upon a desire to topple the Government ignores the fact that the rejection of the SEA constituted a logical extension of the party's long standing policies on the EC, as they were indeed expressed as late as in the December 10 parliamentary debate. Since 1972, the party had committed itself to preserving the existing balance between EC institutions, and to preserving the EC as an organisation with limited, clearly demarcated supranational authorities. This position had been formulated in numerous instances, and it also constituted the key element in the statement on the SEA issued by the party's Executive Committee on 1 February 1986:

> "The Social Democratic Party approved of Danish EC membership in 1972. Then and in many subsequent instances, the SDP has made clear that there should be no shifting between the institutions of the EC. This promise has later been confirmed by the Congress of the party. We must therefore reject the granting of new authority to the European Parliament."[27]

Thus, the SDP most likely could not have accepted the SEA without incurring a wave of discontent from the many party members and voters critical of the EC and against the EC's evolution in a more supranational direction.[28] This was despite the fact that the steps in a supranational direction were limited, as were the changes in the distribution of authority between EC institutions following the SEA.

A number of explanations may be offered for the SDP's basic hostility from 1972 onwards towards a strengthening of the European Parliament. Concerns that a strong EP, due to linguistic and cultural barriers, would be incompatible with a functioning democracy may have been of some importance.[29] A more feasible explanation is that the EP in the party's perceptions would display a permanent conservative-liberal bias

---

26) From January 1984 to February 1986, Gallup polls indicated that the SDP would win between 31.6% and 29.6% of the total vote. Even if the left wing SPP were to vote for an SDP Government, this low standing in the polls meant that a future SDP Government needed the support of one or more liberal parties. At this point of time, however, there were no indications that the liberal parties were willing to provide this support.

27) Socialdemokratiet, statement of the SDP executive committee, 1 February 1986. In "Internationale og nej'et til unionen", *Information*, 29 January 1986, p. 6, Ivar Nørgaard also stressed the party's long standing commitments as a justification.

28) Cf. also the explanation of the deputy chairwoman of the SDP's parliamentary group Ritt Bjerregaard in Stig Albinus and Erik Meier Carlsen, "Det bliver ikke nemt", *Information*, 25 January 1986, p. 4.

29) This argument against a strengthening of the European Parliament appears in the 1973 policy report, cf. Ole Andersen et al., *EF: Hvad nu?*, p. 100.

compared to the Danish Folketing, due to political and economic differences between Denmark and other member states.[30] This suggests that
the SDP feared that strengthening the EP would entail the loss of
national control in policy areas deemed valuable by the party, and that
this loss - given the perceived conservative bias of the Parliament - would
work to the detriment of the party's general political goals at the national
level.In this connection there appears to have been worries that even a
modest strengthening of the Parliament would have significant long-term
effects, especially as the SDP expected the Parliament to use its new
powers only to strengthen its power further.[31]

The SDP's decision to reject the result of the intergovernmental
conference pointed to the possibility that the Government would call an
election. However, the four-party centre-right coalition surprised both the
opposition and the public. Immediately following the announcement of
the SDP's final decision on 14 January, Conservative Prime Minister
Schlüter declared that if the majority in the Folketing did not change its
position on the ratification of the SEA he would call an advisory referendum on the issue. In late January it was announced that a referendum would be held on 27 February 1986.

The referendum caught the SDP and others opposed to Danish
ratification of the SEA unprepared, and it exposed to the public the
party's internal disagreements on the SEA. Even though the parliamentary group's decision had been backed by a large majority of the party's
MPs, support for the decision was far from unanimous among trade
unions and SDP local and county mayors. Following the ambiguous
statements of LO in early January and LO's National Executive meeting
on 17 January, many trade unions chose to adhere to the official SDP
position and advocated a rejection of SEA. However, two important
unions as well as the Trade Union Confederation itself eventually made
the decision not to recommend any position to their members.[32]

However, as the referendum campaign got under way, the SDP increasingly united itself behind its parliamentary group. Nevertheless, the

---

30) *ibid.* See also the party's 1986 policy report on the EC, *An Open Europe*, p. 56. This report will
    be dealt with in more detail later.
31) Cf. Ivar Nørgaard's explanation of the party's rejection of new powers to the EP in the SEA,
    Folketingstidende, forhandlingerne, 1984-85, 10 December 1985, col. 4180-4182.
32) Among others the Unskilled Workers' Union and the Female Workers' Union advocated
    rejection. One trade union, the Food Industry Union NNF, openly advocated a "Yes" vote. The
    Trade and Services Union, HK, and the Metal Workers' Union did not make a recommenda-
    tion.

internal strain undoubtedly hampered the "no"-side, and the advocates of Danish ratification of the SEA seemed at some advantage during the campaign. In the final result of the referendum, 56.2% of the participating voters approved the Single European Act with 43.8% rejecting it, overruling a majority of the Folketing. Only 75.4% of the electorate took part in the referendum. Among participating social democratic voters, polls indicated that a clear majority of about 70% had rejected the SEA. This suggests that the parliamentary group had been in broad accordance with its voters, as it decided on 14 January to reject the negotiation result, even if it was also a distinct possibility that many social democratic proponents of ratification abstained out of loyalty to their party.[33]

The leadership of the Social Democratic Party accepted the results of the referendum without reservations.[34] Hence, on 20 May 1986, the Folketing, with only 17 votes against, ratified the Single European Act.

THE SDP AND THE CHALLENGE OF THE SINGLE MARKET

The SDP had lost the referendum on the SEA, albeit with a relatively small margin. Nevertheless, the result of the referendum probably cemented the impression that the majority of the Danish population were opposed to Denmark attempting to act as an obstacle to the development of the European Community, not to mention that a Danish withdrawal from the Community would have never been accepted by the electorate. The release of the party's comprehensive policy report on Europe, in September 1986, to some extent reflected this basic condition.

"An Open Europe": The 1986 Policy Report

However, the development of a policy review on the SDP's European policies was not an immediate consequence of the 1986 referendum. The decision to create a so called "Europe-Committee" had already been made at the SDP's Congress in September 1984. According to the mandate of

---

33) Ole Tonsgaard, "Folkeafstemningen om EF-pakken", *Dansk Udenrigspolitisk Årbog 1986* (Copenhagen: DJØF and DUPI, 1987), pp. 113-139.
34) Cf. *Folketingstidende*, 1985-86, tillæg B, cols. 1547-1548.

the Congress, the task of this committee would be 1) to examine how
Europe economically and politically may become more independent of the
superpowers, 2) to evaluate the prospects for the EC's further development and the possible advantages and disadvantages for Denmark of
such a development, and 3) to consider how Nordic cooperation could be
expanded in a "dynamic European context".

In explaining the party's decision to establish the review committee
both deputy head of the SDP's parliamentary group, Ritt Bjerregaard,
and EC spokesman Ivar Nørgaard cited the party's persistent and
growing need to overcome the internal disagreements on the EC question
which could be traced all the way to 1972. This internal disagreement
had hampered the development of a more assertive posture.[35] Nørgaard
also stressed the altered international context in which the debate on the
social democratic EC policy was taking place. Hence, there was an emerging understanding that improved foreign policy cooperation in Europe
was necessary to reduce superpower dominance, just as there was a need
for technological cooperation in order to face the economic challenges
from the USA and Japan.[36]

The final report of the Europe Committee, which was to serve as the
basis for a continuing discussion of the subject in the SDP at large, was
presented to the party's annual conference in September 1986. Subsequently the conference endorsed its main conclusions. The comprehensive
document, entitled "An Open Europe", does not focus exclusively on the
EC. Other forms of European cooperation such as Nordic cooperation, the
Council of Europe, and the CSCE are also discussed. However, no doubt
is left about the overriding importance of the Community in the European context. Hence, "the EC acts as the leading force in Western
Europe. Creating a more united and independent Western Europe
without the EC is therefore unthinkable".[37]

What is novel in the report compared to earlier statements is primarily the type of arguments put forward to underpin existing and long
standing SDP policies as well as a different emphasis on the various

---

35) Henning Olsson, "Ballade om EF-pakken styrker Ritt", *Politiken*, 26 January 1986; and Vibeke
Sperling, "Nørgaard: Vi kan fremprovokere et valg, hvis regeringen slækker på veto-retten",
Information, 5 September 1985.
36) Vibeke Sperling, "Nørgaard: Vi kan fremprovokere et valg, hvis regeringen slækker på veto-
retten". Presumably, the process towards reforms of the EC following President Mitterrand's
May 1984 speech was a background factor explaining the establishment of the Europe
Committee.
37) Socialdemokratiet, *An Open Europe*, English version (Brussels, 1987), p. 49.

aspects of the party's approach to the EC. In contrast to the 1973 policy review and subsequent SDP statements on the EC, the focus is less on the immediate economic consequences of EC cooperation for Denmark and more on the common European interest in cooperation vis-à-vis the superpowers and principal economic competitors, and on the Danish contribution toward realising these interests. In this respect, the SDP's viewpoint is markedly more "European" and less explicitly "Danish" than what had been the case earlier.

Furthermore, in the context of the tense relations between the Soviet Union and the USA much attention was devoted to the potential benefits of closer foreign policy cooperation between the EC states in the EPC system. The policy of the Reagan administration towards the East Bloc states was seen as important in clarifying the distinct and common European foreign policy interests which existed and which were to be defended.[38]

The perceived conflict between American and European security interests led the report to conclude that "it is our aim that Western Europe should become a politically equal factor vis-à-vis the USA".[39] Strengthened European foreign policy cooperation was to serve two main purposes: (1) to develop a foreign policy which, compared to the policy of the Reagan administration, placed greater emphasis on detente in the relationship with the Soviet Union and which accorded greater importance to political rather than military solutions to international conflicts; and (2) to formulate a policy which more adequately addressed the needs of Third World countries.

Various commentators saw the release of the report as signifying an important reformulation of social democratic EC policy and a step towards a markedly more positive position regarding a further development of EC cooperation than what had previously been the case.[40] This may be justified when assessing the *approach* of the SDP's Europe Committee to the question of the party's EC policy. Instead of accepting the discourse which focused narrowly on the immediate economic or regulatory consequences for Denmark of EC membership, which would confine the party to the discussion on whether or not to remain in the

---

38) *ibid.*, p. 3.
39) *ibid.*, p. 68.
40) E.g. Solveig Rødsgaard, "S får ny EF-profil", *Weekendavisen*, 4 September 1986, p. 2, Gustav Barfoed, "Socialisterne og Europa", *Jyllands-Posten*, 10 October 1986, and Gunhild Nissen, "Slør, sovepude og tvetungethed", *Information*, 6 January 1987, p. 6.

Community, the Committee asked how social democratic EC policy could further common European interests and social democratic values at the European level.

In the wake of the adoption of the SEA and the party's heavy losses in the elections to the European Parliament, the report of the committee thus makes yet another attempt to transcend the frozen positions of the traditional discussion on "yes" or "no" to EC membership, just as the 1973 policy report had attempted. Hoever, unlike the 1973 document, the report explicitly endorsed the concept of a "European interest". In the context of a continuing resistance to the EC among the party's voters and members, this change was a significant one.

Nevertheless, the report's concrete proposals for EC development and policies have few novel elements. As with the 1973 policy report and subsequent documents, the SDP favoured closer cooperation in the EC in a wide range of areas: economic policy, monetary policy, environmental protection, social rights, protection of the working environment, industry policy, and energy policy. As in the 1973 report, this cooperation would entail an extension of binding supranational regulation in some areas in the form of minimum directives or regulations. The 1986 report thus proposed binding EC regulatory measures for multinational corporations, environmental policy, employee rights including minimum rules for employee participation and industrial democracy, and for protection of the working environment.[41] At the same time, the party maintained that the Luxembourg right of veto was a necessary precondition for Danish EC membership; Treaty reforms and changes in the distribution of power between Community institutions were rejected.

That the report could be interpreted as an important modification of social democratic EC policy therefore indicates that opponents of Danish EC membership to a very high degree had seized the initiative in the ongoing debate. The reception of the report illustrates the continuing hostility towards the EC in many circles rather than any important changes in the party's specific policies. The policy review's defense of the institutional status quo in Western Europe, be it the EC or the EPC system, even where changes could work to the benefit of the goals set up in the report, also points to the existence of continued anti-EC feeling

---

41) The specification that certain types of EC regulation of multinational corporations were also to be minimum regulation is new compared to the 1973 report, cf. Socialdemokratiet, *An Open Europe*, p. 118.

among many social democrats. For instance, Danish membership of the Western European Union, WEU, which might have constituted a Danish contribution to creating European independence of the superpowers, is rejected because the WEU "puts more emphasis on confrontation and rearmament than on negotiation and disarmament".[42]

The Single Market and the Welfare State

In 1984-85 the SDP had in principle been in favour of eliminating further obstacles to trade between EC member states. The 1986 policy report reiterated the party's basic support for freer international trade in general and the EC's internal market in particular, albeit on condition that the internal market not interfere with necessary Danish regulation. Thus, on "project 1992" the policy report declared that

> "[t]he Social Democratic Party opposes forms of market regulation which hinder trade and competition between ordinary business undertakings. Arbitrary bureaucracy and protectionism only restrict the scope for reform policy, by causing economic inefficiency and hence reducing prosperity. ... The SDP therefore views with approval the attempts being made to build a more coherent internal market in the EC, but only on condition that the development of the internal market does not act to the detriment of the welfare objectives we in Denmark set ourselves."[43]

Consequently, the authors of "An Open Europe" regarded it as crucial for Denmark to consistently assert its right to implement decisions on the environment and the working environment even where these would diverge from harmonisation measures adopted within the EC framework. Furthermore, the policy review rejected EC harmonisation of policies on VAT and income taxes and excise taxes, as "any contribution such harmonisation might make to freer trade would be outweighed by the costs - notably, a significant restriction of Denmark's ability to pursue an independent policy on the distribution of wealth".[44] Finally, the report argued that a freer market in the EC requires efficient action on monopolies and control with cross-border mergers. Measures were proposed in which the EC framework would prevent multinationals from

---

42) *ibid.*, p. 49.
43) *ibid.*, pp. 101-103.
44) *ibid.*, p. 103.

exploiting their special position for tax transactions.[45] This policy was elaborated in the context of the emerging Single Market, but as we have seen, the proposals are long standing SDP policies, formulated as early as the 1973 policy report. The 1986 policy report therefore signified a primarily defensive reaction to the plans for 1992: the SDP sought to prevent the EC's Single Market from interfering with the possibility of regulation at the national level in areas deemed crucial by the party, such as distributional, environmental, and labour market policies.

The impression of an SDP on the defensive towards the Single Market plans was reinforced in early 1987, as a legal opinion on the meaning of the amended Treaty's article 100A(4) became known. According to this opinion, the scope for independent national environmental measures conflicting with an EC harmonisation directive was more limited than had been implied prior to the Danish SEA referendum. Ivar Nørgaard in an April 1987 commnetary reacted aggressively to the interpretations, stating that if this were the case, the referendum had taken place on false preconditions, and the Folketing should then adopt as much environmental legislation as possible before the SEA took effect.[46]

Following ratification of the SEA and the movement towards the Single Market after the adoption of the Delors-package in February 1988, the SDP's defensive arguments increasingly centered on the potential problems following from "project 1992's" planned removal of EC border controls. Commenting in July and September 1988 and during the Folketing's special debate on the Single Market in November 1988, Ivar Nørgaard argued that the SDP had approved the EC's internal market as an area in which public or private measures distorting competition were to be abandoned. The SDP remained opposed, however, to a market which the citizens had to experience for themselves. The party had approved of a European economic community, "but we have never accepted a harmonisation of our cultural and social life".[47] Furthermore, the social democrats were strongly against the harmonisation of national taxes and duties, which would result from the removal of border controls.

---

45) *ibid.*, p. 105.
46) Ivar Nørgaard, "EF-afstemningens grundlag bortfaldet", *Aktuelt*, 7 April 1987. According to Nørgaard, the legal opinions were presented by the former and present General Directors of the Council's Judicial Service and the General Director of the Commission's Judicial Service. Subsequent interpretations of article 100A(4) have not supported the narrow construction; cf. James Flynn, "How Will Article 100A(4) Work? A Comparison with Article 93", *Common Market Law Review*, vol. 24, no. 4 (Winter 1987), pp. 689-707.
47) Ivar Nørgaard, "Vi har aldrig sagt ja til EF-uniformering", *Det fri Aktuelt*, 16 September 1988.

The only instance where such harmonisation was accepted was where tax rules directly distorted competition.[48] Consequently, in November 1988 the SDP called on the government to work for the preservation of internal border controls so as to maintain differences in tax rates and duties between the member states.[49]

Clearly, the main reason for SDP opposition to tax harmonisation was the party's concern for maintaining the Danish welfare state, with its tax-financed educational, health, and social services. As Ivar Nørgaard stated in the July 1988 commentary:

> "In this country we have created a public service system differing widely from the systems in Germany, Holland, and Belgium. We feel that this is important and that it has been the right thing to do. ... Clearly the adoption of the SEA put these opinions under pressure. In the SEA it is stated that taxes and duties should be harmonised, where they impede the functioning of the internal market. We recommended voting against the SEA and we warned against the risk of common taxes. Then the Government told us not to be worried, and we will remind them of that now. But I must admit that when the Danes approved the SEA, it weakened the defense of the welfare state."[50]

In spite of the pessimistic mood conveyed by these statements, Nørgaard went on to insist that the Danish state had legally maintained the possibility of blocking measures which might threaten the Danish tax system, just as he expressed hope for rapid entry into the EC of other Nordic countries, with their more similar social systems.

The Social Dimension and Environmental Protection

The SDP's approach to the Community's development in the wake of the ratification of the SEA and the accelerating process towards a Single Market during 1988 was, thus, to a high extent defensively motivated. It was an important objective for the SDP to limit the consequences of "project 1992" regarding the possibility of independent national regulation in important policy areas.

However, parallel to the defensive emphasis a more offensive line of argument was increasingly heard, particularly from mid-1988. This line

---

48) *ibid.*, and Jakob Groes, "Velfærdsmodel under pres", *Information*, 30 July 1988.
49) Ivar Nørgaard in *Folketingstidende*, forhandlingerne, 1988-1989, 25 November 1988, cols. 2622-2623.
50) Jakob Groes, "Velfærdsmodel under pres".

of argument stressed the necessity of more efficient EC regulation on protection of employee rights and working conditions in the emerging Single Market. As mentioned, a prominent element in the SDP's approach to the EC since 1972 had been its emphasis on the desirability of common minimum standards in these areas. "Project 1992" for the establishment of the Single Market brought these policy proposals back to the forefront of the discussion.

Social democratic support for binding labour market regulation on minimum standards, seen as explicitly necessitated by the completion of the Single Market, was first alluded to in the 1986 policy review's references to "social dumping":

> "The SDP regards as a highly important task the levelling-out of the differences [in labour market and social standards] by means of the better-off countries acting as levers to help the worse-off. There are two reasons for this. First, we believe that solidarity with the people of the less developed parts of Europe is in itself a central objective. Second, we believe that capital can exploit social differences [making possible] 'social dumping'. This means that countries compete to attract capital by keeping social standards low. There are at present signs that 'social dumping' is on the increase."[51]

Following the adoption of the 1988 Delors-package, the emphasis on the necessity of a social dimension to the Single Market increased markedly, as various leading figures of the SDP movement directed attention to the question. In August 1988 the secretary of the SDP's Europe Committee and later international secretary of the party, Ralf Pittelkow, strongly urged the party and the trade unions to prepare themselves for the struggle on the social aspects of the Single Market. The trade unions were asked to intensify their efforts to influence the removal of technical barriers to trade and related harmonisation measures, as technical specifications in many instances were essential to the working and external environment.

The task was also to secure employee rights in companies operating at the European level. It should not be possible, declared Pittelkow, for these to play out employees in different member states against each others. Finally, the aim of the Danish and the overall European labour movement in the Single Market process was to be the creation of more equal conditions for wage earning groups in the member states. For the richer countries in the EC, this was a question of showing solidarity, but

---

51) Socialdemokratiet, *An Open Europe*, p. 121.

it was also a question of avoiding "social dumping", where some states could attract jobs by keeping social standards low.[52]

The leadership of the trade union movement quickly responded to Pittelkow's appeal. The spokesman of the Confederation of Trade Unions (LO), Bent Nielsen, agreed that trade unions should devote attention to the Single Market process. The aim of the involvement in the process should be to prevent the removal of technical barriers to trade from resulting in worsened conditions for the members: "We cannot accept that Danish wage earners will be exposed to new health hazards or worsened working conditions because harmonisation for the sake of unhindered trade will lower the level [of protection]".[53]

In the same month, chairman of the Metal Workers' Union, Georg Poulsen confirmed his union's strong commitment to the Single Market objective. According to Poulsen, the Single Market was an important means of strengthening Western European economic growth and should be encouraged. However, a strengthening of the Single Market's social dimension constituted a necessary precondition for the creation of real free competition. If the social dimension were to be neglected "[t]here is a risk that the internal market will be destroyed by distorting 'social dumping' in which differences in working and living standards are used to underbid competitors". Consequently, Poulsen called for the adoption of a range of common social minimum standards in the EC framework, just as he argued that provisions for the working environment be incorporated into all directives with potential consequences for this area.[54]

Prior to the SDP's 1988 Congress, Anker Jørgensen had announced his retirement as party leader. The Congress elected political spokesman, Svend Auken, as new leader. In November 1988 Auken participated in a conference of Western European social democratic parties, the topic of which was cooperation between the EC and EFTA states.

In commenting on the discussions and the resolutions adopted at the meeting, Auken stressed the social democratic parties' fundamental desire to improve economic cooperation in Europe, including the creation of an internal market in the EC. According to Auken, European cooperation within and beyond the Community had entered a new dynamic phase with the adoption of the SEA. Unfortunately, however, events had

---

52) Ralf Pittelkow, "Vågn til kamp af jer dvale", *Det Fri Aktuelt*, 11 August 1988.
53) Bent Nielsen, "Vi slår bro fra kyst til kyst", *Det fri Aktuelt*, 17 August 1988.
54) Georg Poulsen, "Terningerne er kastet", *Det fri Aktuelt*, 24 August 1988.

taken place largely on conditions stipulated by conservative political forces, who regarded deregulation and reduction of social rights as a necessary means of improving competitiveness vis-à-vis the USA and Japan:

> "These conservatives clearly oppose the new internal market being made 'rigid' by common rules and common management, based on, for instance, environmental, social, or tax concerns, or on concerns for equal competition. The greatest promise of the new Europe in the eyes of these circles is the golden chance to dismantle the welfare state and return to the laissez-faire policy of past times."

In Svend Auken's view, the social democrats of Western Europe had to react to this situation in order to influence its course and to set the agenda for the future. Thus, "It is a great challenge", he declared, "for all social democratic parties to ensure that the advantages of economic integration will be equitably distributed throughout society and that the gains do not fall solely in the hands of the wealthier regions and peoples."[55]

The chairman of the Unskilled Workers' Union SID, Hardy Hansen, in a February 1989 interview, also made clear his support for strengthened efforts to secure binding minimum regulations on industrial relations within the EC framework. He saw the EC's future development as a question of

> "... who shall exert influence on the policy of the EC. Should it be Margaret Thatcher or Jacques Delors ... who is a socialist. They have widely differing views on European development and regarding the policy on distribution of wealth. Wage earners [should] therefore pay more attention to these matters than has been the case until now."

According to Hansen, the situation thus required the trade union movement to participate actively in the EC framework in order to secure common European minimum wages, high environmental standards and adequate standards for employment security, all in order to "prevent Danish companies from moving abroad."[56]

Finally, the mobilisation of the social democratic movement in the pursuit of a social dimension to the Single Market is illustrated by the fact that both LO and the SID, in spring 1989, published comprehensive

---

55) Svend Auken, "Det ny Europa", *Weekendavisen*, 11 November 1988.
56) Rolf Geckler, "En udfordring til fagbevægelsen"; *Det fri Aktuelt*, 22 February 1989. See also the commentary of a Danish SDP member of the European Parliament, Ejnar Hovgaard Christiansen, "Social Europa eller Kapital Europa?", *Det fri Aktuelt*, 8 February 1989.

analyses of the EC's Single Market plans.[57] The contents of these documents accord with previous statements of trade union leaders. "Project 1992" receives approval on the explicit condition that the social dimension is given full consideration. By "social dimension", LO and SID understood both the implementation of "complementary measures" aimed at maximising the employment effects of freer trade, as well as the adoption of a range of basic social rights in the Community. The need for these social rights is seen as necessitated by the emergence of one market for capital in a situation where there are twelve EC labour markets. As LO's document states it,

> "a company may complain to the Commission ... if it is exposed to what is considered unfair competition, and anti-dumping duties may be levied. Workers do not have the same rights, but can only stand by and watch if production is moved to another country or is pushed out of the market as a result, say, of competitors employing child labour."[58]

Employee rights and conditions were not the only areas in which the SDP movement mobilised its resources in 1988-89. In the wake of the 1992 process, concerns were increasingly voiced regarding environmental protection in the emerging internal market.

As mentioned, the social democratic desire to make use of EC institutions for environmental protection had been present since the very beginning of Danish membership in the Community. At the same time, the SDP did not want EC regulation to stand in the way of independent Danish measures. The 1986 policy review restated this point of view. The SDP would "promote a wide-ranging environment policy offensive in the EC", but would also insist that a more far-reaching Danish environmental policy not be blocked by EC regulation, even after the adoption of the SEA.[59]

The 1986 policy review did not, however, view the SDP's EC environmental policy in direct connection with problems created or amplified by the Single Market. This view changed in the SID pamphlet of February 1989, authored by Ralf Pittelkow:

> "The single market shall pave the way for an increased economic activity in order to create more employment. But if this is to be possible without

---

57) LO, *The Internal Market and the Social Dimension* (Copenhagen, 1989), and SID/Ralf Pittelkow, *Det indre marked og lønmodtagerne. Et debatoplæg* (Copenhagen, SID 1989).
58) LO, *The Internal Market and the Social Dimension*, p. 17.
59) Socialdemokratiet, *An open Europe*, p. 138.

leading to catastrophic environmental destruction, a more profound restructuring of production is needed."[60]

At the same time, environmental pollution is often a problem "which
knows no borders. It can only be fought through international cooperation". In this connection, Pittelkow argued that "it is absolutely necessary
to adopt strict environmental standards in the EC". In recent years the
Commission had advanced a number of potentially valuable proposals in
this area, "[b]ut the Commission's initiatives are often confronted with
resistance from one or more member states - almost always from Margaret Thatcher's Great Britain."[61]

Finally, during 1989, the SDP also reformulated its originally
defensive position vis-à-vis the Community regarding the question of
harmonisation of VAT and income taxes and excise duties. Thus, the
party's far-reaching proposal for restructuring the Danish tax system,
published in spring 1989, was partly motivated by the external pressures
created by the Single Market process. The policy document emphasised
that no EC institutions have the legal authority to force Denmark to a
tax harmonisation. However, "the liberalisation of capital movements,
which has already been implemented, and the future development of the
Internal Market reinforces the economic pressure for greater
homogeneity in taxes and excise duties."[62] In this context, the social
democratic tax proposal consisted of a taxation structure more in line
with other EC member states, implying a reduction in Denmark's high
gross income tax rates and company taxes and an increase in employer
tax contributions.

The 1989 EP Election: Endorsing More Majority Decisions

The SDP's campaign prior to the third direct election to the European
Parliament in June 1989 reflected the arguments formulated in the 1986
policy report as well as the mobilisation during 1988 and early 1989 for
a social dimension to the Single Market and a strengthening of environmental protection in the EC.[63] The policies advocated in the party's

---

60) SID/Ralf Pittelkow, *Lønmodtagerne og det indre marked*, pp. 23-24.
61) *ibid.*
62) Socialdemokratiet, "Gang i 90'erne. Socialdemokratiets bud på en samlet indsats 1990-95"
    (Copenhagen, May 1989), p. 5.
63) Due to internal administrative problems the Danish SDP made a general reservation on the

official European manifesto closely paralleled the arguments of the 1986 policy review, presumably reflecting the slow gradualism in the development of statements involving broad segments of the party organisation. Regarding policies on the future of the EC, emphasis was repeated on each member state's right to pursue differing environmental policies according to article 100A(4). Any strengthening of the Commission and of the European Parliament is rejected, and the Luxembourg right of veto was defended.[64]

However, in the debate preceding the election, the positions of the SDP underwent several changes. The party intensified its campaign against the Peoples Movement Against the EC on the grounds that the referendum on the SEA and the process towards the Single Market had fundamentally changed the situation. The question of Danish EC membership should now be considered as a settled matter.[65] Furthermore, the campaign was characterised by the SDP's vigorous support for the adoption of an EC charter guaranteeing a number of fundamental labour market regulations throughout the Community as well as basic employee and citizen rights. The emphasis on the Social Charter was enhanced as the EC Commission, in mid-May 1989, released the time table for the adoption of the Charter first proposed in May 1988.

Finally, and importantly, the SDP leadership on 21 May 1989, at the launching of the party's election campaign, accepted the idea of Rome Treaty reforms over the longer term. Kirsten Jensen, the party's first candidate, called for these reforms to allow decisions to be made by a qualified majority in the Council of Ministers on minimum regulation for the protection of the external environment and for the adoption of legislation on employee rights. For the short term, however, the party would work under the provisions of the existing treaty for the furthering of the party's goals on environmental protection and social rights.[66]

The proposal for Treaty reforms is understandable as a continuation of the party's mobilisation on social and environmental issues in the 1992

---

contents of the CSPEC manifesto for the European elections, published in February 1989. This document will not, therefore, be considered here.

64) Socialdemokratiet, "Et Åbent Europa", the SDP's manifesto for the June 1989 elections to the European Parliament (Copenhagen, May 1989).

65) E.g. Ritt Bjerregaard, "Vi EF-modstandere havde ret - i 1972", *Det fri Aktuelt*, 22 March 1989, and Ralf Pittelkow, "Folkebevægelsen er fortid", *Det fri Aktuelt*, 4 April 1989.

66) Ole Lorenzen, "S-Kovending", *Det fri Aktuelt*, 22 May 1989, Hans Drachman, "S vil fjerne veto-ret i miljøsager", *Politiken*, 22 May 1989. See also the policy note by the party's political-economic secretariat, "Flertalsafgørelser om miljø-spørgsmål i EF", 25 May 1989.

process. The position that the EC's development from the adoption of the
SEA onwards had been built on an insufficient legal foundation became
a part of the discussions on the social dimension and on the EC's
environmental programme. This position was obvious during early 1989,
but already in connection with the November 1988 meeting of the
Western European social democratic parties, SDP leader Svend Auken
had criticised the post-SEA legal foundations of the Community:

> "Unfortunately it was not possible to find [the right] balance in the SEA,
> which instead of an agreement between Left and Right was formed as a
> compromise between the federalists, Margaret Thatcher, and the London
> City finance world. The Treaty basis for the new Europe thereby became
> insufficient. For example, common rules for the environment may be adop-
> ted by a qualified majority if the aim is harmonisation of technical
> characteristics, whereas environmental measures exclusively aimed at
> fighting destruction of the environment requires unanimity."[67]

The same critique of the EC's legal basis following the SEA was expressed by Ralf Pittelkow in February 1989, and in both of the trade union
analyses of the Single Market. Ralf Pittelkow writing in the SID's
pamphlet declared:

> "The thing is to walk on two legs. We must influence the decisions of the
> EC, and regarding [the environment] it is vital to reach common decisions.
> In this instance the provision for unanimity is an obstacle. It means that
> some of the reactionary states can prevent the decision. The same problem
> is encountered with respect to the social dimension, working conditions and
> employee rights."[68]

The publication of the Danish Trade Union Confederation LO:

> "It is noteworthy that the trade union demands [on a social dimension] are
> supported ... by the vast majority of Member States. The obstacle is that EC
> rules on 'workers' rights' generally require unanimity. This is a provision
> to which the Danish trade union movement has attached crucial importance
> as protection against reductions in Danish pay and working conditions, but
> one which, in a situation like the present where offensive demands are put
> forward, turns out to be a hindrance to developments!"[69]

With its initiative at the launch of the party's election campaign, the SDP
leadership had indicated its approval of Rome Treaty reforms in certain
areas. Yet the proposal for the introduction of majority voting on mini-

---

67) Svend Auken, "Det ny Europa".
68) Ralf Pittelkow quoted from Rolf Geckler, "En udfordring til fagbevægelsen".
69) Trade Union Confederation, *The Internal Market and the Social Dimension*, p. 18.

mum social and environmental regulation failed to play any prominent role in the party's overall campaign, and in a parliamentary debate on 23 May 1989, Ivar Nørgaard even claimed that the proposal had never been made, suggesting that the question was a matter of internal disagreement or that the time was not ripe for stressing the support for Rome Treaty reform.[70]

Nevertheless, the Danish SDP during 1988 and 1989 had adopted a clearly more offensive position on Denmark's relationship to the European Community and on the EC's future development than what had previously been the case, stressing the need for a social dimension to the Single Market, for legally binding minimum legislation on social and employee rights, and the eventual introduction over the longer term of majority decision-making procedures in the Council on minimum regulation for environmental protection and social rights. However, the social democrats secured only a relatively small gain in the June 1989 elections to the European Parliament. With only 46.2% of the electorate participating, the party won 23.3% of the total vote, as opposed to 19.5% at the 1984 European elections and 29.8% in the 1988 elections to the Folketing. In light of the dynamic development of the EC, the anti-EC Peoples Movement had been expected to suffer a significant defeat. Yet it secured 18.9% of the votes, a loss of only 2%, illustrating the persistence of hostility towards the Community among the Danish electorate.

THE DANISH SDP AND THE EC 1982-1989: CONCLUSIONS

In the period from the party's retreat into opposition in September 1982 to the 1989 European elections, the EC policy of the Danish SDP changed in a number of ways.

From the initial emphasis on improved functional EC cooperation and continued rejection of reforms of the Rome Treaty leading to a rejection of the SEA, to recommend institutional reforms of the EC in the longer run. If implemented, these reforms would increase the Community's

---

70) Ivar Nørgaard in *Folketingstidende*, forhandlingerne, 1988/89, 23 May 1989, cols. 10624-10625. The statements on the issue at the launch of the campaign, as well as in the policy note of the SDP's political-economic secretariat, were clear, but Nørgaard argued that the party had favoured only a more flexible use of the Treaty's articles 130S and 100A in the adoption of environmental legislation.

market-intervening decision-making capacity. What factors prompted this transformation?

Towards the SEA

The years from 1982 until after the referendum on the SEA were characterised by (1) the party's consistent calls for an improvement of functional cooperation in the Community framework in a wide range of areas, and (2) its equally consistent commitment to institutional status quo. The call for an expansion of EC cooperation in a number of areas, as we have seen, was a direct continuation of the SDP's EC policy from the early 1970s. Thus, as in the previous decade, the SDP favoured extended efforts in the Community in the areas of environmental protection, political control over multinational corporations, employee rights, exchange rate management, and common efforts to stimulate the economy. On the last point, the SDP's policies took the form of active participation in the Western European social democratic parties' campaign for coordinated reflation.

In some of these areas, such as environmental policy, control over multinational corporations and fundamental employee rights, this approach would imply an extension of existing binding Community regulation in the form of minimum directives or regulations. Regarding the call for coordinated reflation in the EC, it seems likely that this would also have involved the SDP's acceptance of extended supranational regulation had the demand actually had a possibility of resulting in economic expansion in the EC, and had the reflation depended on adoption of such regulation. We cannot make any final conclusions on this question, but the hypothesis is supported by the fact that prior to the 1985 intergovernmental conference, the SDP proposed to incorporate into the Rome Treaty an obligation for member states to pursue "an active employment policy" whenever unemployment rates exceeded a certain level.

If our hypothesis holds, it can be taken as evidence that the party's experiences with unilateral Danish reflation in the mid-1970s, the Mitterrand Government's similar experiences in 1981-83, and the perceived overly tight economic policies of West Germany caused the SDP to adopt a more positive attitude towards supranational regulation in new aspects of the macroeconomic area. This was true as long as such regulation would help achieve one of the party's fundamental general political goals: full employment. In this interpretation, the SDP leadership went through a learning process in the late 1970s and early 1980s. As mentioned, learning cannot can be categorised as being externally induced, as having been caused by domestic developments, or as an instance of the internal dynamics of integration. Rather, learning here appears to result from new experiences with and conclusions on the existing state of affairs as regards macroeconomic management in a small, open economy.

As in the 1970s, those SDP proposals which entailed an extension of existing binding supranational regulation appear motivated by either (1) the wish to make use of Community institutions for adopting EC regulation in areas where national regulation was not seen to be effective, e.g. regarding multinational corporations and environmental protection; or (2) the desire to improve the cost efficiency of national regulation through EC regulation, e.g. in areas such as minimum employee rights and perhaps to a certain extent also regarding environmental protection rules in the EC framework and regulation on macroeconomic expansion in the EC.

In one instance, the 1986 policy report *An Open Europe*, social democratic support for minimum EC regulation on employee rights was also explained with reference to "international solidarity". However, this motivation does not appear to have been particularly important for the party, as is also underlined by the fact that the reference to international solidarity occurs only in close connection with the wish to protect Danish employee standards against "social dumping".

While the European Council in Milan in June 1985 was deciding to convene an intergovernmental conference for reforms of the Rome Treaty, the SDP was rejecting the necessity of such reforms. Yet the party endorsed Danish participation at the conference, albeit on the explicit condition that it not be oblige to accept its results. As the negotiation process got underway, the party put forward a number of concrete proposals for reform of the Treaty. How is this to be understood?

In the most reasonable interpretation, the SDP's behaviour serves as evidence of a threat of national exclusion from a policy arena in which a great number of decisions significant for the possibility of national goal realisation would be made, regardless of Danish participation. Following President Mitterrand's May 1984 speech, it quickly became clear that a majority of EC states, including France and West Germany, actively sought to revitalise EC cooperation by strengthening the Community's supranational character. Had the SDP leadership not granted the Danish Government a certain leeway in the negotiations - e.g. allowing it to put forward proposals for codification of new areas of cooperation and to propose the introduction of majority voting in the Council on minimum regulation for the protection of the working environment - the other member states might have agreed on a reform outside the legal frame-work of the Rome Treaty, leaving Denmark without influence on matters also significant to the SDP. Hence, as the process towards Treaty reform gained momentum, the party put forward proposals which, in seeking to avoid Danish isolation, would also help the party to realise its general policy goals at the national level.

Prior to the June 1985 European Council, the party's EC spokesman had stated that the SDP saw no dangers in a "Europe of two speeds" where different European states participated in different cooperative schemes. This could be seen as a suggestion that fear of exclusion played no role for the SDP. However, the remark presumably indicated that the social democratic leadership was far from willing to accept Treaty reforms which could involve significant threats to those of the party's general policy goals which it considered largely realised in the Danish setting. Hence, the threat of exclusion could not justify putting at risk what the party saw as fundamental social democratic achievements in Denmark, among which were no doubt the social system and the alleged-ly redistributive tax system. The threat of exclusion was important for the party leadership, but not so important so as to force a willingness to compromise on Treaty reforms without a strict evaluation of the contents of such a compromise.

The Rejection of the Single European Act

The parliamentary group's decision to reject the results of the SEA negotiations sharply illustrates that the will to compromise in order to avoid isolation had clear limits. The rejection was largely motivated by concerns that ratification of the SEA would in the short or long term entail a threat to the realisation of general political goals in the Danish context, or would compose a threat to achieved goals. The decision was shaped by anxieties that the introduction of majority voting on the establishment of a Single Market would effectively stand in the way of independent Danish measures to protect the external and working environment, or would undermine existing Danish legislation in these domains. Furthermore, the SDP's rejection of the SEA's provisions on the European Parliament reflected concerns that even a very modest strengthening of the EP's powers would in the long run form a threat, since such powers would only provide the EP with new weapons in the struggle over institutional reform. Moreover, the Parliament was seen to be politically biased against social democratic goal realisation. Concerns that reforms of the EC in a federalist direction would mean a weakening of Danish democracy presumably also played a certain role for the SDP's position on this part of the SEA.

The party's disapproval of the Single European Act in January 1986 is, therefore, understandable as a rejection of a reform which entailed a strengthening of the EC's market liberalist characteristics, in the sense that the SEA improved the EC's decision-making capacity on regional market liberalisations (article 100A) just as in the perceptions of many SDP parliamentary group members the SEA involved a strengthening over the long term of a supranational institution biased towards market regulation of society. In this sense, the SDP's decision accords with the first part of the proposition on the internal dynamics of integration; this states that social democratic political parties will reject a strengthening of supranational market liberalising decision-making capacity, as this would be seen to reinforce external constraints on national state intervention in the economy.

As with the decision to advocate Danish EC membership, however, the great Danish dependency on foreign trade and good access to export markets influenced the party's approach to the SEA. As repeatedly stressed by the party's EC spokesman, and evident in the 1986 policy report, the SDP favoured the creation of a Single Market in the Community, but a Single Market which would not stand in the way of the SDP realising general policy goals at the national level. The SDP's basically favourable opinion on the Single Market plans thus supports the previously formulated conclusion that social democratic parties value the possibility of state intervention differently in different policy areas and that national structural economic characteristics shape this valuation.

Were the desire to protect national achievements and the possibility of national progress on policy goal realisation the only concerns which influenced the SDP decision to reject the SEA? The wish to provoke an election might have been of some importance when the parliamentary group made its decision, but it is unlikely that this factor had significant effect on the outcome, inasmuch as opinion polls suggest that an election in early 1986 would not have resulted in a change of government. Yet concerns for party unity and for the party's overall credibility in the electorate influenced the SEA decision in other ways. An approval of the Single European Act would clearly have constituted a deviation from long standing social democratic principles on the EC's development, primarily as regards the party's commitment to institutional status quo; witness the statement of the party's Executive Committee on 1 February 1986. Given this firm and frequently stated commitment, the SDP voters' strong antipathy towards the EC, and perhaps also the lack of convincing arguments justifying a change of policy, the parliamentary group had most likely concluded that a decision to endorse the SEA would damage the party's electoral appeal in that it would have amplified party internal disagreement even more than was the case following the rejection of the Single Act. In this connection, it is worth remembering that the Prime Minister's decision to call an advisory referendum came as a complete surprise, exposing internal disagreements in the SDP which otherwise wouldt not have not have become so widely known to the public.

To sum up, the SDP's decision to reject the SEA was motivated by the desire to retain the possibility of national regulation of society in policy areas held important by the party, even if concerns for the party's credibility vis-à-vis its voters and potential voters in upholding long standing policy positions contributed to the outcome.

The SDP and the Challenge of the Single Market

Eventually, a majority of the Danish electorate voted in February 1986 to ratify the SEA. Following this, the SDP released its second comprehensive policy report on the European Community. In light of the second EC referendum, the formulation of the report illustrates the party leadership's desire to advance beyond the discussion of whether or not to stay in the EC, towards a debate about what to do in the Community and how to further specific European interests in a superpower dominated world. However, in terms of concrete proposals for social democratic EC policy, the report contains little that is new. Its content and the manner in which it was received are evidence that sizable elements of the party and its voters had still not accepted Danish dependency on EC membership as a fundamental condition on which to proceed. The 1986 policy report thus constitutes yet another attempt to convince the many EC sceptics in the party about the necessity of an offensive approach to the Community in the form of support for EC regulation which would further the realisation of the party's policy goals.

As the process towards the completion of the EC's Single Market got underway from early 1988, the SDP adopted a defensive posture, rejecting the elimination of border controls and the tax harmonisations which would be necessitated by it. As the 1986 policy report states, and as formulated in the November 1988 parliamentary debate, the party continued to reject the kind of regional market liberalisations which would undermine the general political goals which had to a considerable extent already been realised in Denmark. Thus, the primary argument for the refusal to remove internal border controls in the EC was concern that explosive growth in cross-border trade would inhibit the financing of the Danish welfare state with its social citizen rights; witness Ivar Nørgaard's statements in July 1988.

This predominately defensive posture increasingly gave way to a more aggressive approach from mid-1988s. In the perception of a number of prominent figures in the social democratic movement, the accelerating 1992 process constituted a challenge, necessitating a mobilisation of the social democrats' resources in the quest for a social dimension to the Single Market and for a strengthening of the EC's environmental protection measures.

According to our proposition on the internal dynamics of integration, social democratic parties will resist a strengthening of supranational institutions' decision-making capacity on regional market liberalisations. However, where market liberalising decision-making capacity has been strengthened in spite of this resistance, they will subsequently increase their support for a strengthening of supranational interventionist decision-making capacity in areas where it will further the realisation of the parties' general political goals.

This dynamic is indeed present in the case of the Danish SDP from 1988. Thus, when the SDP, prior to the 1989 elections to the European Parliament, endorsed the idea of introducing majority decision-making in the EC's Council of Ministers regarding minimum regulation for the protection of the environment and for employee rights and working conditions, this constituted the culmination of a process initiated with the

SEA in mid-1987 and the launching of the process towards the establishment of the Single Market. In numerous statements by representatives of the social democratic movement during 1988 and 1989, implicit or explicit support for majority decision-making by the Council in new areas was justified with reference to the "imbalanced" nature of the SEA. This imbalance was attributed to the undue influence of the Conservative British Government on the SEA's outlook and the consequent bias of subsequent EC regulation.

As mentioned, there exist several possible motivations for social democratic parties to support extended supranational decision-making capacity in new policy areas once regional market liberalising decision-making capacity has been increased. Thus, accelerating market liberalisations may create new incentives for interventionist political forces in two ways: (1) successive EC liberalisations may threaten the efficiency of perceived necessary national regulation, creating the need for supranational replacement regulation or supranational regulation which subsequently reestablishes the efficiency of national regulation, or (2) successive EC market liberalisations may create or amplify problems whose efficient solution in the perceptions of these parties requires new supranational regulation.

In the case of the Danish SDP, the increasingly vigorous support for a social dimension to the EC's Single Market, culminating in the proposal to introduce majority voting procedures on minimum regulation for employee rights and working conditions, was primarily motivated by concerns that "social dumping" would undermine existing Danish regulation. According to representatives of the social democratic movement, this could become reality in a Single Market within which capital could easily locate production in Community settings where fewer employee demands were made, or where unacceptable social conditions could be utilised by companies or member state governments to increase cost competitiveness; note, for instance, the statements of trade union leaders Georg Poulsen and Hardy Hansen in August 1988 and February 1989, respectively, LO's spring 1989 document, and party leader Svend Auken's November 1988 commentary.

In the perceptions of representatives of the Danish trade union movement as well as several of the leading figures in the SDP the completion of the Single Market threatened the efficiency of necessary national labour market regulation. This led the SDP to increase its support for supranational regulation and to eventually endorse extended supranational decision-making capacity which could make national regulation more efficient. The Community's minimum regulation for the labour market and for employee rights was not viewed as replacing Danish regulation in the area. On the contrary, it aimed at enabling the continuation of efficient Danish regulation, as trade union leader Hardy Hansen put it in "preventing Danish firms from moving abroad" because of cost pressures following from national labour market regulation. Note Hardy Hansen's implicit acknowledgement that labour market regulation often constitutes a negative competitive parameter, whereby it is also admitted that the call for a social dimension, at least in part, constitutes a protectionist strategy.

Other motivations for the proposal to introduce majority voting on employee rights were also of some importance. Thus, if the ideas of the SDP were accepted, the proposed majority voting on minimum labour market regulation would involve the establishment of EC minimum rules on employee information and participation; cf., the 1986 policy report. In other words, majority voting would involve regulation of a kind the economic impact of which is disputed.

To the extent that employee participation does not adversely affect competitiveness, the SDP's proposals in this area might thus be motivated by the desire to make use of binding Community regulation as a guarantee or even as a lever to push forward national regulation. The understanding of the Single Market's social dimension this implies is that it to some degree concerns the question of the model for future economic development in Western Europe, whether it should rely on "defensive" or "offensive" labour market flexibility.

Finally, in the area of employee participation, the proposal to introduce majority decision-making procedures may also have been motivated by the wish to extend highly valued regulation beyond the realm of the Danish state.

As with the social dimension, the SDP proposal for majority voting in the Council on minimum environmental regulation to some extent followed from concerns that the cost efficiency of Danish regulation would decrease in the Single Market, that progressive regional market liberalisations would, given high Danish environmental standards, lead to an outflow of Danish employment opportunities; witness Hardy Hansen's statement in February 1989. Hence, extended supranational decision-making capacity on regional market liberalisations also prompted support for increased supranational decision-making capacity on environmental protection in order to protect the cost efficiency of national environmental regulation.

In addition, Pittelkow's statements in the same month evidenced another dynamic. According to Pittelkow, the Single Market process would aggravate problems which could only be solved efficiently at the supranational level, notably transnational environmental destruction. The logical response would be to allow for the application of majority voting procedures on binding minimum environmental regulations in the Council. Presumably, this added to the SDP's rationale for proposing Treaty reforms on environmental protection. As Auken and Pittelkow formulated it in November 1988 and February 1989, the problem was "to walk on two legs", and to "find the right balance". In this instance, accelerating EC market liberalisations were seen to amplify the kinds of problems which could be efficiently solved only by adopting new supranational regulation, furthering the party's will to endorse majority voting on environmental protection. Hence, both concern for cost efficient national environmental regulation and the desire to make use of supranational institutions to solve problems aggravated by regional market liberalisations were at the core of the SDP's proposals for majority voting on minimum environmental regulation in the EC.

9

The SDP and the New Europe:
1989-1990

The period from the adoption of the SEA and the launch of the 1992-process witnessed a Danish SDP which gradually attempted to take a more offensive position in the debate on the EC's development. The culmination came in May 1989, when the party leadership for the first time endorsed Rome Treaty reforms over the long term. However, the proposal for Treaty reforms occupied no prominent position in the party's campaign prior to the EP elections in June 1989. Rather, the social democratic call for the introduction of more majority voting procedures did not come to the fore until President Mitterrand, in October 1989, proposed an intergovernmental conference on economic and monetary union in the EC. Mitterrand's initiative and German support for it also led to a reformulation of the party's positions towards further monetary integration in the EC.

The SDP and the Political Union

Prior to the December 1989 meeting of the European Council the purpose of which was to decide on the convention of the intergovernmental conference, the Folketing debated Mitterrand's proposal.

The Social Democratic Party's position on economic and monetary union will be dealt with in a later section. However, in the December 1989, debate the party did not focus exclusively on the plans for EMU. Instead the SDP made use of the occasion to officially recommend that the coming intergovernmental conference should aim at introducing majority voting procedures in the Council on minimum labour market and environmental standards. Ivar Nørgaard explained the position in arguing that the conference would be convened regardless of the SDP's decision:

"During the debate in the spring [of 1989] I had the opportunity to express
the position of the SDP: that there was no need for Treaty reforms and thus
nor for a new intergovernmental conference. We know that others have the
same view, but on the other hand we also know that there will be a
majority for convening a conference. We therefore find that naturally we
must participate in such an event, when it is to be held."

He went on to state that the conference should focus on other questions
than solely that of EMU. Thus, "the avalanche-like development in
Eastern Europe, the EFTA-states' desire to gain access to the EC's
internal market, and the need to secure employees and the environment
in a situation of increasing liberalisation of trade are significant changes
which we think should be dealt with."[1] Regarding the last point
Nørgaard explained that

"with the [SEA's provisions for majority voting on the single market] the
free movement of goods, services, and capital was increased. This could
have resulted in our labour market and environmental standards being
jeopardised. We then secured ourselves the so-called environmental guarantee, which means that we can maintain national standards higher than
those adopted by a qualified majority in the Council ... But we did not
obtain the opportunity to press the weaker countries towards higher
standards. This is why the SDP ... wishes to introduce Treaty reforms so
as to permit the establishment of minimum standards for environmental
and labour market conditions via qualified majority."[2]

The motion adopted at the end of the debate, with support from the
government parties and the SDP, included the SDP's call for Treaty
reforms allowing majority decision-making on minimum labour market
and environmental regulation, thus making it official Danish EC policy.
The motion also expressed the wish to establish new forms of cooperation
between the EC and the EFTA states.[3]

In February 1990, SDP leader Svend Auken, speaking at the Berlin
Congress of the CSPEC, argued for a social democratic offensive during
the period leading up to the convention of the intergovernmental conference: "[f]or much too long we have surrendered the initiative to the
conservative forces. The result is that the Community today suffers from
a considerable democratic deficit and lack of concern for the protection
of nature and employee rights".[4] For this reason there was all the more

---

1) *Folketingstidende*, forhandlingerne, 1989/90, 30 November 1989, col. 2576.
2) *ibid.*
3) Dagsordensforslag nr. D 15, *Folketingstidende*, forhandlingerne, 1989/90, 30 November 1989,
   col. 2580.
4) Svend Auken's speech at the Berlin CSPEC Congress, reprinted as "Fællesskabets tiltræk-

reason to consider reforms of the existing Treaty, and the intergovernmental conference should therefore take three actions: First, the
European Parliament's influence over the Commission should be
strengthened and there should be more openness in the Community's
administration. Second, Auken proposed that the conference decide on
the creation of fora in which EC member states could cooperate with non-
EC member states. The integration of the two German states should take
place within the EC rather than outside it as "this was the evident
interest of all of Germany's neighbours". Finally, Auken reiterated his
support for strengthening the EC's decision-making processes regarding
environmental protection and employee rights.

Whereas the importance of the Eastern European revolutions and
Germany's unification for the party's attitude was hinted at by Auken in
February 1990, SDP international secretary Ralf Pittelkow made this
question the focus of the debate in a newspaper commentary a month
later.[5] In a context where, following the GDR elections of 18 March, the
two German states were moving rapidly towards unification, Pittelkow
argued that the explicitly political purposes of the Community were
becoming increasingly important. Thus, the real questions were, "How
can the EC ensure that a united Germany does not become a threat to
other European states? How can the EC contribute to a united Europe in
which the antagonisms between East and West have disappeared?"
Pittelkow's solution was to extend majority decision-making procedures,
as this both would allow an enlargement of the EC and would prevent it
from being dominated by narrow national interests. Thus, "[i]f each
member state in a widened EC has ample possibilities for blocking
common decisions, Europe risks regressing into a mess of national
interests - with a powerful and headstrong Germany as the dominating
power in the middle of it!"

Danish security concerns had, thus, entered the calculus of the SDP
in the formulation of its policies towards the EC. Yet this did not mean
that previous arguments concerning the need to strengthen the EC's
environmental and labour market policies had lost their importance.
Pittelkow compared traditional social democratic attitudes to the SEA
with the new situation:

---

ningskraft", *Weekendavisen*, 16 February 1990. The nucleus of these arguments had already
been put forward in Svend Auken, "Det politiske system og gennemførelsen af det indre
marked", *Politica*, vol. 21, nr. 4 (November 1989), pp. 424-430.
5)   Ralf Pittelkow, "Et fredeligt Europa kræver EF-integration", *Information*, 27 March 1990.

"[T]hen the debate had focused on the question 'How do we limit the EC's power to the highest possible extent, at the same time being able to enjoy the economic benefits of membership?' Today we must raise the debate on the EC as an instrument for tying Europe together and for defending the environment and social welfare against international market forces".

On 18 April 1990, prior to the informal meeting of the European Council later that month, the Folketing again discussed European developments. The Folketing here adopted a motion declaring its support for self-determination for the German people within the framework of the EC and restated its desire to introduce majority decision-making on environmental and labour market conditions. The resolution also called on the intergovernmental conference to strengthen democratic control within the EC and to work for increased openness in the EC's administration, seemingly a continuation of Auken's proposals advanced in Berlin.[6]

In the debate preceding the adoption of the motion, Auken stressed the social democratic will to participate constructively in the intergovernmental conference. At the same time, however, he rejected any grandiose institutional reforms to create a federal Europe, nor did view the emergence of a united Germany as a plausible reason for wide-ranging institutional reforms. The objective of reforms was to make the EC framework flexible enough so that the new Germany could fit into a binding democratic community. However, the creation of a federal Europe would hinder a genuine strengthening of EC cooperation in central areas.[7] The representatives of the Conservative-Liberal-Radical Liberal Government, which had replaced the four-party coalition government following the May 1988 election, expressed basic agreement with the social democratic positions, even though the Liberal Foreign Minister saw German unification as constituting the most important rationale for a strengthening of EC cooperation.[8]

The day after the Folketing's debate, West German Chancellor Kohl and French President Mitterrand issued a common declaration calling upon the European Council to convene a separate intergovernmental conference on political union in the EC. The statement, though

---

6) Dagsordensforslag nr. D 31, *Folketingstidende*, forhandlingerne, 1989/90, 18 April 1990, col. 8481.
7) Svend Auken in *Folketingstidende*, forhandlingerne, 1989/90, 18 April 1990, cols. 8477-8478.
8) Cf. Foreign Minister Uffe Elleman-Jensen in *Folketingstidende*, forhandlingerne, 1989/90, 18 April 1990, col. 8464.

conference on political union in the EC. The statement, though formulated in vague terms, contained proposals for strengthening the Community's efficiency and democratic legitimacy and for enhancing cooperation on foreign and security policy.

The SDP's Ivar Nørgaard reacted sharply to the proposal, stating that "if [the French-German plan] is what we have heard, it is something we must oppose strongly".[9] He also hinted that if the Danish Government stated its intent to accept the Kohl-Mitterrand initiative, it could mean that it would have to resign. However, when the informal meeting of the European Council ended in late April, Svend Auken was quick to dismiss Nørgaard's attacks, stating that "we shall not reject a debate on the content of a political union simply because we dislike the word [union]". Auken noted that "an offensive Danish position is important. We must oppose a federal European state and common military, but approve of increased democratic control and majority decisions on environmental protection and employee rights".[10] Auken thus projected onto the concept of political union those of the SDP proposals for EC reform which were not directly related to the question of economic and monetary union.

In early June 1990, prior to the European Council which was to decide on convening a parallel intergovernmental conference on a political union, the CSPEC then held a meeting in Dublin. Here the Danish SDP agreed to a certain strengthening of the European Parliament as a goal of the conference on political union. Thus, besides calls for the introduction of majority voting procedures on minimum standards for environmental protection and employee rights, the CSPEC-statement issued after the meeting declared its support for the EP's right to initiate legislative proposals for consideration in the Council of Ministers.[11]

THE SOCIAL DEMOCRATS AND THE EMU

As we have seen, ever since EC membership social democratic policy had been to support close monetary and economic cooperation in the EC framework. Both in government and in opposition, the SDP saw inter-

---

9) Terkel Svennson, "S: Nej til konference om politisk union", *Berlingske Tidende*, 26 April 1990.
10) Lars Olsen, "S siger ja til unions-processen i EF", *Information*, 30 April 1990.
11) CSPEC, statement of 6 June 1990. As mentioned this is quite modest, as the EP has granted itself this right years ago. Nevertheless, its codification in the Treaty would strengthen the EP´s ability to influence the Commission.

stable but adjustable exchange rates as the best means of realising one of its basic policy goals: full employment. During the 1970s and early 1980s the party favoured a pooling of foreign currency reserves and further stabilisation of exchange rates as well as coordinated reflation led by the stronger economies. In connection with the SEA negotiations, the party put forward a proposal whereby EC member states would be obliged to pursue expansive policies when domestic unemployment reached a certain level.

This policy certainly reflected the SDP leadership's acknowledgement that independent Danish monetary and finance political measures for economic expansion would be unduly costly and not very effective. Thus, both a pooling of foreign currency reserves and an internationally led reflation would diminish the constraints on an expansive Danish economic policy. At the same time, however, the party saw some leeway for independent Danish macroeconomic measures. This is implied in the motivation for the SDP's rejection of letting macroeconomic coordination proceed beyond purely voluntary cooperation, as expressed in the 1973 policy review and subsequent statements. Economic and monetary union would entail a common economic policy and would eliminate the possibility to pursue an independent exchange rate policy, all of which were seen as undesirable.

The 1986 policy review restated the SDP's commitment to the EMS and to a functional extension of exchange rate cooperation. Thus, the report supports the wider use of the ECU as an international currency, as this would make economic activity in Europe and elsewhere less dependent on changes in US economic policy. With respect to the value of the ECU vis-à-vis third currencies, it also argued that a greater role should be given to the European Monetary Cooperation Fund.[12]

It is acknowledged, however, that the kinds of market interventions which could be implemented by this fund have limited effects on exchange rates, and that the economic policy pursued by each state is more important in determining the relative value of currencies.[13] The report goes on to ask whether in the context of the EMS, where the exchange

---

12) The EMCF was created in connection with the establishment of the EMS in 1979. It was envisaged to gradually take up an important position similar to the International Monetary Fund's role in the Bretton Woods system, when the EMS entered its "final stage". Until now, however, this has not happened. See Det Økonomiske Råd, *Dansk Økonomi* (Copenhagen, December 1988), p. 96.
13) Socialdemokratiet, *An Open Europe*, p. 88.

goes on to ask whether in the context of the EMS, where the exchange rate of the German Mark vis-à-vis third currencies effectively determines the same rate for the other EMS currencies, other EMS countries should have a say in the FRG's economic policy, or "to be more precise, whether the EMS countries should 'pool' their economic policies".[14]

> "The SDP says *no*. There is no basis for taking European monetary coope-ration that far. Moreover, the ends and means of the various countries' economic policies are too far apart. This is the sort of thinking that lies behind the many ambitious plans for a European monetary union which have been put forward throughout the history of the EC. Nobody has tried to hide the fact that such a union requires very close co-ordination of the whole of economic policy. However, these plans have foundered time and time again, because the assumptions were wholly unrealistic."[15]

Thus, the report explicitly acknowledges that Danish policies regarding the exchange rate vis-à-vis non-EMS countries are effectively determined by German economic policies, given the full Danish EMS membership. At the same time, however, steps toward a more binding supranational framework for economic policy coordination in the EC are rejected, both because the means and ends for the economic policies are seen to differ widely between EC states and, although the passage is not quite clear, because monetary union would require an unacceptably close co-ordination of economic policy.

The Delors Report: Social Democratic Scepticism

The question of further monetary integration in the EC came to the fore again after the release of the so called Delors Report in the spring of 1989. As mentioned, the Delors Report envisages the establishment of an EMU in stages, the first stage consisting of relatively cautious measures, primarily the full EMS membership of all EC states. The second stage involves the creation of a system of European central banks. In the third stage, exchange rates are to be locked completely, eventually leading to a common currency.

In the Folketing's debate preceding the June 1989 elections to the EP

---

14) The DM's leading role in the EMS among other things follows from its role as an international reserve currency.
15) The Social Democratic Party, *An Open Europe*, p. 90.

agree to Denmark participating in elaborating the first stage of the
Delors Plan, arguing that a strengthening and extension of exchange rate
cooperation was in the clear interest of a small, export-oriented economy.
However, SDP support for Danish involvement in the work on the first
stage was conditional. It should be made completely clear that "the work
with the first phase neither politically, nor legally obliges to the much
more far-reaching steps in the second and third phases of the Delors
Plan".[16]

Nørgaard went on to state that "[w]e strongly call on the Government
to oppose, at the coming meeting of the European Council, the idea of an
intergovernmental conference, which shall initiate a process towards
reforms of the Rome Treaty". The motivation for this call was provided
later, as the SDP spokesman said that "we oppose relinquishing
sovereignty on the management of economic and monetary policy".[17]

As to the contents of the Delors Report, Nørgaard made clear that it
was decisive for the SDP's position that the concern for employment
would be in focus to a much higher degree than had until then occured
in the Delors Committee's work. He lamented the fact that the central
bank directors' conservative monetary positions had dominated the
Committee's work, and that insufficient attention had been paid to "the
necessity for those countries with large balance of payments surpluses -
and that is of course particularly West Germany - to bring down the
surpluses and secure a larger expansion of the economy. This would
benefit the West Germans themselves and Europe in general".[18] On the
role of the German Bundesbank Nørgaard argued that

> "[the Germans] are so nervous. If only prices go up 0.5-1% they believe that
> there will be hyperinflation. Then they increase the German base interest
> rate and dampen activity in Germany and in all the other countries. I find
> this unreasonable, and that is why we are very critical towards the Bundes-
> bank becoming formally empowered to also manage economic policy in
> Europe, for in reality they unfortunately to a high degree are doing so
> already."[19]

The EC spokesman thus implied, firstly, that the policies of a monetary
union in the EC would be dominated by German preferences. Secondly,

---

16) *Folketingstidende*, forhandlingerne, 1988/89, 23 May 1989, col. 10586.

17) *ibid.*, col. 10624.

18) *ibid.*, col. 10585. The same views are expressed in an internal SDP policy note on the Delors
    Report; see Socialdemokratiet, politisk-økonomisk afdeling, "Notat om Delors-rapporten om en
    økonomisk og monetær union", April 1989.

19) *Folketingstidende*, forhandlingerne, 1988/89, 23 May 1989, col. 10590.

The EC spokesman thus implied, firstly, that the policies of a monetary union in the EC would be dominated by German preferences. Secondly, Nørgaard explicitly acknowledged that formal rather than real and concrete political conditions underlie SDP policies on monetary union.

On future reforms of the Rome Treaty, reforms considered necessary by the Delors Committee's report, the SDP's spokesman said that the party might be able to vote for Treaty reforms allowing but not obliging EC member states to join an economic and monetary union. However, the party could not accept any obligation to enter an EMU, just as "we naturally could not accept that [those states wanting to join an EMU] would create a treaty outside the framework of the Rome Treaty."[20]

The result of the debate was a motion, adopted with support coming from both the SDP and the Government, stating that in the EC "the concern for improved employment, a better environment and a more just distribution [of wealth] must be secured a prominent position in the development of the Single Market and economic and monetary co-operation" and that implementation of the first stage of the Delors Plan does not oblige participation in the second and third stages.[21] During the debate, the Government's position on the Delors Plan had remained vague, and the policies advocated were of a reactive nature, suggesting internal disagreement among the Government parties on the merits of an EMU.

The Folketing discussed the proposal for EMU in a debate prior to the European Council's December 1989 meeting. With the coalition Government of prime minister Schlüter having adopted a strongly positive position on the economic advantages and political necessity of moving towards monetary union,[22] the SDP's spokesman reiterated that regarding EMU, the SDP was against going beyond strengthened cooperation within the EMS system:

> "[W]e support the idea in the Delors Report on strengthening EMS coope-
> ration. ... But we see no reason to go further than this. ... It is true that it
> would be a good thing if the German Bundesbank's dominating position
> could be limited. But we do not for one moment believe that the

---

20) *ibid.*, col. 10624.
21) Dagsordensforslag nr. D 46, *Folketingstidende*, forhandlingerne 1988/89, 30 May 1989, cols. 10587-10588.
22) E.g. Poul Schlüter in *Folketingstidende*, forhandlingerne, 1989/90, 30 November 1989, cols. 2568-2576.

bank influence. However, moves which could further the attainment of this goal, such as establishing a European Central Bank, were rejected since they seemed impossible to obtain. On the other hand, there were also other, more convincing reasons for the party's position on monetary union: "[w]e absolutely oppose removing from the Folketing ... the power to determine the size and content of the national budget, and we hold it dangerous to eliminate the possibility of exchange rate adjustments."[23]

The motion adopted at the end of the debate, with the support of both the Government parties and the SDP, followed the path of the similar motion adopted in May. However, seen in the context of the approaching meeting of the European Council, which was to decide on the establishment of an intergovernmental conference, the motion emphasises in clearer terms Danish support for "stronger cooperation on economic policy and exchange rates" in the EC.[24]

Conditional Support for EMU

As mentioned, the SDP's international secretary Ralf Pittelkow, in a March 1990 feature article stressed the EC's importance in securing peace and stability on the European continent, just as he argued that political rather than purely economic concerns should be given prominence in the Danish EC debate in light of Eastern European developments. In this connection, Pittelkow also argued that an EMU would constitute an important instrument for strengthening the international commitments of the unifying Germany. Thus,

> "[the idea is correct] that central economic areas in which West Germany decides the direction of the development in Europe shall be subject to common EC decisions. Today Denmark ... [is] in a very one-sided way subject to German dominance when it comes to monetary and exchange rate policy. We gain from these decisions becoming subject to common decisions."[25]

However, Pittelkow's support for monetary union was not unconditional, as the concrete shaping of the common decision-making system on monetary and exchange rate policy was extremely important. A system

---

23) Ivar Nørgaard in *Folketingstidende*, forhandlingerne, 1989/90, 30 November 1989, col. 2578.
24) Dagsordensforslag nr. D 15, *Folketingstidende*, forhandlingerne, 1989/90, 30 November 1989, col. 2580.
25) Ralf Pittelkow, "Et fredeligt Europa kræver EF-integration".

However, Pittelkow's support for monetary union was not unconditional, as the concrete shaping of the common decision-making system on monetary and exchange rate policy was extremely important. A system built on the conservative views of various national central bank directors was unacceptable, and concern for low inflation was not to have priority over concern for full employment.

The Folketing again debated European development in mid-April 1990. The Government here reiterated its positive attitude to strengthening the EC in general and to an EMU in particular.[26] However, Svend Auken remained sceptical. Commenting on the views expressed earlier by the party's international secretary, Auken placed much emphasis on the need to secure concern for employment in the EC's scheme of economic cooperation. Referring to the Delors Plan's proposal that a European central bank should have price stability as its sole objective, Auken contended that "[i]n a strengthening of exchange rate cooperation and economic cooperation we still think that the struggle against mass unemployment ... which unfortunately is discussed much to little should have at least the same importance as the fight against inflation."[27] At the same time, Auken reiterated the SDP's clear support for Danish participation in the first phase of the Delors Plan, whereas the SDP would refuse to make national public sector budgets subject to approval of any EC institution. In spite of the differences of opinion on the EMU between the Government and the SDP, the Folketing adopted a motion which largely restated the earlier motion adopted in November 1989.[28]

On 16 May 1990 the Danish SDP members of the EP then approved a preliminary report on economic and monetary union in the EC presented by the EP's Economic Committee.[29] Ejnar H. Christiansen, one of the social democratic MEPs, justified his position by citing the influence of social democratic views on the report: it advocated that the

---

26) E.g. *Folketingstidende*, forhandlingerne, 1989/90, 18 April 1990, cols. 8469-73.
27) *ibid.*, cols. 8478-79.
28) Dagsordensforslag nr. D 31, *Folketingstidende*, forhandlingerne, 1989/90, 18 April 1990, col. 8481. The only substantially new point regarding the EC is the motion's call for the inter-governmental conference to increase democratic control and openness in the development of EC cooperation.
29) Doc. A3-99/90, Interim Report on Behalf of the Committee for Economy, Exchange Rates, and Industry Policy, *Official Journal of the European Communities*, no. C 149, 18 June 1990, p. 57, pp. 66-69 and p. 95.

expansive economic policy in the EC. In order to be effective, this coordination would have to take place within a binding legal framework:

> "[w]e have realised that the EMU will be coming, and that we ought to engage ourselves with our visions, for instance as is now done by the EP. On the part of the trade union movement and the social democratic parties, we have now for more than ten years demanded a common European policy for providing everybody with jobs. But apparently nothing happens without a more binding form of economic cooperation."[30]

At the same time, he stressed that the social democratic MEP's vote in favour of EMU was in accordance with the motion adopted by the Folketing on 18 April. This interpretation of the vote was supported by Ivar Nørgaard, who stated that he personally would accept monetary union if it were under political control. However, he had no confidence whatsoever that this would be acceptable to the Bundesbank, and he remained firmly opposed to delegating the authority to determine monetary or finance policy to a supranational institution unless it was politically controlled, as proposed by the EP.[31] The same views were expressed in a feature article of 20 June 1990 by Svend Auken and Ivar Nørgaard. The SDP leadership here criticised the proposed Central Bank's exclusive objective of price stability.[32]

In September 1990, however, the chairwoman of the SDP's parliamentary group and shadow Foreign Minister, Ritt Bjerregaard, stated her own explicit support for EMU. Following a meeting of EC finance ministers at which the German representative had refused to accept a binding time table for currency union, she expressed concern that the German Government was about to back down from the EMU plans:

> "I am very worried about the German resistance to EMU. ... Today the German Bundesbank decides the monetary policy of Europe, while Denmark and other countries have no substantial influence. It is in Denmark's interest that the plans on EMU are carried through."[33]

By September 1990, the SDP's position had thus evolved towards one of constructive participation in the negotiations on Economic and Monetary Union. Scepticism as to the contents of the Delors Plan was evident, and

---

30) Lars Olsen, "S stemmer ja til møntunion i EF", *Information*, 16 May 1990. See also *Debates of the European Parliament*, no. 3-390, May 1990, p. 159.
31) Lene Frøslev, "Ivar Nørgaard lægger luft til sit partis accept af møntunion i EF", *Information*, 17 May 1990. In a personal interview of September 1990 Ivar Nørgaard confirmed his support for an EMU provided it had the right "reflationary" content.
32) Svend Auken and Ivar Nørgaard, "Europa for Folket", *Politiken*, 20 June 1990.
33) Lars Olsen, "Ritt: Ellemann ødelægger EF-debat", *Information*, 13 September 1990.

the most important objective of the party appeared to be shaping the framework of strengthened monetary cooperation so as to reflect its dominant concern: improving the employment situation. To the SDP leadership this meant that the proposed European Central Bank had to be equipped with a broad "Objectives" clause, including the concern for growth and employment. At the same time, some of the party's spokespersons viewed German unification as a reason to support EMU.

THE 1990 GOVERNMENT MEMORANDUM

Two statements of the SDP-leadership in August 1990 made clear to the public that the party had in fact already decided to reach an agreement with the Government on the Danish position in the upcoming inter-governmental conferences. On 4 August 1990 party leader Svend Auken stated that the party was likely to support Economic and Monetary Union provided that concern for employment was given high priority. The SDP would also support a political union if social democratic demands to strengthen labour market and environmental minimum policies in the EC were fulfilled:

> "[o]n social democratic initiative we have created a unique political agreement on the Danish demands. We want an open EC, where new states can become members. We want a common economic policy, where employment is just as important as price stability. And we want binding majority decisions on environmental protection, health, and social conditions."[34]

According to Auken, this meant that if the other EC member states could agree, the way was paved for Danish approval of an EC Union. Two days later, the chairwoman of the SDP's parliamentary group, Ritt Bjerregaard, followed up, stating that "everything indicates that the SDP and the Government are about to agree on the [Danish position on] the contents of an EC union.[35]

Ivar Nørgaard reacted sharply to Bjerregaard's statements, claiming that it was much to early to announce an agreement, since negotiations with the Government had just begun.[36] Yet his protests brought no results. Rather, in the beginning of September 1990 the Government

---

34) Erik Meier Carlsen, "Auken: Vi er tæt på enighed om union", *Det fri Aktuelt*, 4 August 1990.
35) Jette Meier Carlsen, "Nye EF-toner fra Ritt Bjerregaard", *Jyllands-Posten*, 6 August 1990.
36) Henrik Groes-Petersen, "S-toppen slås om EF-linien", *Politiken*, 7 August 1990.

accepted the social democratic demand that it should develop an official memorandum on the Danish position in the upcoming intergovernmental conferences.

In this connection, on 12 September 1990 - the day after Ritt Bjerregaard had expressed her worries on the German willingness to agree to economic and monetary union - Ivar Nørgaard presented the Government with a list of SDP proposals to be included in the memorandum.[37] As to the political union, this list sums up the positions which had been developed by the party since May 1989. Thus, increased democratisation and openness, both in the EC's administration and regarding decision-making processes was presented as one of the SDP's primary aims. It was proposed that both the meetings of the Council and of the Commission to the highest possible extent shall be open to the public. Also proposed was that the EP be given the right to advance proposals for directives to be considered in the Council, just as the oversight authority of the EP vis-à-vis the Commission's and the member states' implementation of agreed upon measures should be strengthened. In addition the national parliaments were to be given greater influence on decision making in the EC system. Finally, the list contained the by now well-known call for the introduction of majority voting procedures on minimum standards for employee rights and environmental protection.

Regarding the EMU, the SDP's spokesman had made clear that the party had given up demand that concerns for growth and employment should be included as the objectives of a European Central Bank.[38] Instead, the party's list presented to the Government suggested the creation of a permanent political institution under the ECOFIN Council, parallel to the Central Bank. It should be the aim of this institution, a "COREPER" of ECOFIN, to strengthen finance policy coordination in the EC, and it was also to be legally obliged to pursue an active policy for securing employment. Finally, it was to have at its disposal a fund which could even out regional economic imbalances within an EMU.

On 4 October 1990, the Danish Government then presented the official memorandum on the Danish position in the intergovernmental conferences. To a large extent, the document embraces the social democratic proposals, presumably reflecting the Government's wish to secure broad

---

37) Socialdemokratiet, "Notat vedrørende memorandum til regeringskonferencen", Christiansborg, September 1990.
38) Cf. Lars Transbøl, "S-planen for ja til EF-unionen", Land og Folk, 14 September 1990.

securing employment. Finally, it was to have at its disposal a fund which could even out regional economic imbalances within an EMU.

On 4 October 1990, the Danish Government then presented the official memorandum on the Danish position in the intergovernmental conferences. To a large extent, the document embraces the social democratic proposals, presumably reflecting the Government's wish to secure broad agreement of the Danish parliament prior to the initiation of negotiations. Regarding political union in the EC, the memorandum stressed the need to place environmental concerns more centrally in the Treaty:

> "The aim of ensuring environmentally sustainable development should be ... one of the main principles of the Community. ... Solution of problems of the environment should not be made secondary to other considerations. ... Legal instruments in the field of environment policy should be adopted by a qualified majority, while preserving the Member States' right to maintain or to introduce stricter protective measures".[39]

With respect to labour market regulation and social rights, the memorandum stated the Government's desire to strengthen the social dimension as "a means of distributing the benefits deriving from the internal market". Thus,

> "[t]he social dimension is part of the process of achieving the internal market. It should be included among the Community's basic tasks. ... Where the area lends itself to such an arrangement, minimum provisions should be laid down".

The Government also proposed that a series of fundamental principles, including access to work and education, social security, co-determination, freedom of association, and the right to collective bargaining, be enshrined in the Treaty, thereby effectively rendering the Social Charter legally binding. Finally, it proposed that "legal instruments should as a rule be adopted by qualified majority".[40]

Third, the memorandum put forward a number of proposals aiming at strengthening "the democratic basis for EC cooperation". It called attention to the role played by the Folketing's Market Committee, suggesting an increase in national parliamentary control in other EC states, and it proposed to extend the so-called cooperation procedure

---

39) Memorandum from the Danish Government, Copenhagen, 4 October 1990, English version, pp. 2-3.
40) *ibid.*

basis for new policies in the EC framework in the areas of consumer protection, education, and health policy. Regarding education and health policies, the principle of subsidiarity was to be applied, meaning that EC measures were to be implemented only to the extent that they solve problems not solvable at lower administrative levels.

Finally, regarding a strengthening of foreign policy cooperation in the EPC system, the memorandum advocated a cautious approach, presumably reflecting traditional SDP opposition to a strengthening of the EC's role in defense matters. Thus, the Government rejected the idea that foreign policy cooperation in the EPC system include cooperation in defence politics or setting up of common military forces, just as it supported the continuation of unanimity decision-making here.

As to the Economic and Monetary Union, the document, in referring to articles 2 and 104 in the existing Rome Treaty, stated that the concern for full employment should be among the explicit fundamental principles for the EC. However, in an EMU "the Danish Government considers it natural for the European System of Central Banks to conduct monetary policy" and to "ensure price stability while supporting the general economic policy of the Community". As opposed, the Council of Ministers of Finance and Economic Affairs, ECOFIN, "in setting economic policy should take account of the objectives of growth and high employment". The memorandum here argues that ECOFIN must be strengthened, but does not describe how.[42]

Furthermore, the document states that "in the area of financial and budgetary policy of the individual Member States the Treaty must reflect the principle of subsidiarity", meaning that "the Council will not be able to take binding decisions on any Member State's budget surplus or deficit or its revenue and expenditure, just as distribution policy must remain a national matter".

However, the Government accepts a procedure in which "pressure" is brought to bear upon a member state conducting an irresponsible financial and budgetary policy. As a component of this procedure, it should be possible to make economic support from the EC to a member state "conditional upon the observance of agreed requirements concerning budgetary policy".

The SDP reacted favourably to the memorandum, and as the Folketing debated it on 25 October 1990, the party was strongly positive. As

---

42) *ibid.*, p. 9.

brought to bear upon a member state conducting an irresponsible financial and budgetary policy. As a component of this procedure, it should be possible to make economic support from the EC to a member state "conditional upon the observance of agreed requirements concerning budgetary policy".

The SDP reacted favourably to the memorandum, and as the Folketing debated it on 25 October 1990, the party was strongly positive. As Svend Auken stated it,

> "the Danish memorandum is an extraordinarily concrete initiative for a Europe of the citizens where concerns for the environment and employee rights and protection of consumers are not subordinated to profit-led market forces ... The vision of a new EC is to a large extent shaped by our Nordic hopes: to expand the ideals of the welfare state to European cooperation instead of the hopes of the petty bourgeoisie to misuse the internal market for the dismantling of the welfare state."[43]

In the context of the SDP's suport for the Goverment memorandum, it was not difficult for the party to approve the positions on EMU expressed in the CSPEC statement released in December 1990. As mentioned, this statement restated the concern of several of the Community's social democratic parties that a European Central Bank be democratically accountable.

Furthermore, it argued that "the central objectives of monetary policy, ensuring price stability, should be pursued taking due account of general economic policy goals".[44] Neither did the declaration's support for strengthening EP oversight authority and its right to initiate legislation for consideration in the Council pose a problem to the SDP, since the party had endorsed these positions already in June 1990.

THE SDP AND THE NEW EUROPE 1989-1990: CONCLUSIONS

The trends in SDP EC policy which had occurred during 1988 and early 1989 continued throughout 1989 and 1990. At the end of 1989, the party's call for the introduction of majority decision-making procedures in the Council on minimum environmental and labour market regulation

---

43) *Folketingstidende*, forhandlingerne, 1990/91, 25 October 1990, col. 998.
44) CSPEC, Leaders' Declaration on the Intergovernmental Conferences, Madrid 10 December 1990, p. 3.

upcoming intergovernmental conferences, published as an official memorandum. Why did this take place?

The SDP and Political Union

In November 1989 the SDP had officially accepted the proposal for an intergovernmental conference for reform of the Rome Treaty. The party's EC spokesman portrayed this development as purely reactive. Since the conference was to be held anyway, Denmark ought to participate and put forward its ideas, and here he particularly stressed the need to introduce majority voting procedures on minimum regulation for environmental protection and employee rights.

Had this description of the course of developments been correct, the SDP's proposals for Treaty reforms could clearly be seen as externally induced, a development in which a number of major EC states' desire for EC reforms created a threat of Danish exclusion from an important decision-making forum, leading the most significant political forces in Denmark to formulate reform proposals for tactical reasons in order to arrive at a satisfactory compromise. As we have seen, however, the SDP's proposal for the above mentioned Treaty reform had been in the process of formulation already since mid-1988 and always with explicit reference to the implications of the EC's Single Market for highly valued existing Danish regulation. Hence, it is appropriate to view the party's proposals for more majority decisions in the Council as an instance of the internal dynamic of integration, as it was concluded previously.

The possibility that the SDP leadership at an early point had observed and reflected upon the mounting pressure from some of the major EC states for Rome Treaty reforms, and that it sought to formulate social democratic proposals in reaction to this, cannot be completely neglected. It is, however, unlikely given the fact that the proposal on majority voting on employee rights and working conditions to a high extent originated in the social democratic trade union movement, that is: in a setting where the question of possible international isolation has hardly been of preeminent importance.

When in November 1989 the SDP's spokesman described the party's approach to the decision on the establishment of an intergovernmental conference so as to give the impression that it had been fundamentally shaped by external pressures, it therefore served as evidence of the

voting on employee rights and working conditions to a high extent originated in the social democratic trade union movement, that is: in a setting
where the question of possible international isolation has hardly been of
preeminent importance.

When in November 1989 the SDP's spokesman described the party's
approach to the decision on the establishment of an intergovernmental
conference so as to give the impression that it had been fundamentally
shaped by external pressures, it therefore served as evidence of the
leadership's acknowledgement of persistent hostility towards the EC
among many of its voters and rank and file members. The emphasis on
external pressures served the purpose of placing the party's policy in a
light which underlined its consistency with long-standing SDP principles
on the EC's nature and development.[45]

Following initial internal disagreements, the party's reaction was
positive, as Chancellor Kohl and President Mitterrand called for the
summoning of an additional intergovernmental conference on political
union in the EC. However, the initiative - an external development from
the viewpoint of the SDP - did not lead to any significant reformulation
of the party's positions. Rather, the leadership transferred its previously
formulated proposals on more majority decision-making to the emerging
debate on the contents of a political union.

Yet a new justification for these proposals emerged in the wake of the
March 1990 GDR elections and the subsequent rapid development
towards German unity. In late March, the party's international secretary
emphasised the need for more majority decision-making in the EC as a
means of preventing the emergence of a security threat from the new
Germany, suggesting that external developments involving potential
security threats reinforced the will to strengthen the Community.

During 1990, the party also accepted a certain strengthening of the
European Parliament as an element of political union. Thus, the SDP
endorsed the EP's right to initiate legislation for consideration in the
Council as well as improvements in the EP's oversight capacities. Even
if a certain willingness to accept a limited strengthening of the Parliament was evident already in February 1990 - witness the party leader's
statements at the CSPEC Congress in Berlin - the Danish SDP clearly
never actively sought any significant extension of the EP's powers, as it

---

45) Indeed, in a September 1990 personal interview Ivar Nørgaard stressed his personal emphasis
on the elements of continuity in the party's EC policy.

At the same time, however, it seems of some importance that the EP, from the 1989 election onwards, had a "red-green" majority consisting of social democratic, socialist and ecological parties, and that its proposals therefore most often had attempted to influence EC regulation in a direction favourable to Danish social democratic goals. Thus, the traditional SDP position that the EP was inherently biased in a conservative direction had been disproved, for which reason it is also justified to view the eventual acceptance of a certain extension of EP powers as evidence of a learning process.[46]

The SDP and the Economic and Monetary Union

As we have seen, the conclusions of the 1986 policy review were quite clear: the SDP rejected Economic and Monetary Union in the EC, even if the party approved of far-reaching voluntary coordination of economic policies. Nevertheless, via the Government memorandum of October 1990, the Danish SDP endorsed Danish participation in a future EMU, signifying a clear instance of attitude integration in the form of growing support for increased supranationality in the EC.

In the parliamentary debates of May and November 1989, the party's spokesman hinted at a certain willingness to consider increased monetary integration. In several instances he lamented the dominance of the German Bundesbank on monetary policy in the EC and made clear the desire to reduce this dominance.

As mentioned, the importance of the Bundesbank for monetary policy in most of Western Europe follows from the simultaneous existence of a system of stable exchange rates and free capital movements within it. In this context, German monetary policy has won a reputation for giving priority to price stability and for not allowing depreciations of the currency vis-à-vis other currencies in the EMS. This has led financial markets to consider the Mark the anchor of the EMS system and has permitted the Bundesbank to determine the level of interest rates throughout the EMS zone.

---

46) See the interview with Ivar Nørgaard, October 1991, in Peter Roulund, *Socialdemokratiet og Europæisk Integration*, Master's Thesis, Institute of Political Science, University of Aarhus, 1992, pp. 90-92, which suggests that both external pressures and a learning process were important for the party's eventual acceptance of co-decision authority for the EP in certain areas in the Maastricht Treaty.

in most of Western Europe follows from the simultaneous existence of a system of stable exchange rates and free capital movements within it. In this context, German monetary policy has won a reputation for giving priority to price stability and for not allowing depreciations of the currency vis-à-vis other currencies in the EMS. This has led financial markets to consider the Mark the anchor of the EMS system and has permitted the Bundesbank to determine the level of interest rates throughout the EMS zone.

As argued previously, we could then identify an "internal dynamic" of the integration process. To the extent the liberalisation of capital movements constitutes an element in the EC's Single Market, it could be argued that this development has created new incentives for non-German political forces to support the creation of a supranational body for the conduct of Community-wide monetary policy. This is true in the sense that capital liberalisations, given full Danish EMS membership, have eliminated the possibility of an independent Danish monetary policy.

Even if capital liberalisations clearly constitute a part of the Single Market programme, and even if an EC directive in 1988 incorporated the regulation stipulating free capital movements into EC law, Danish capital liberalisations, as was the case for the similar British legislation, preceded "project 1992" by several years. Thus, in the period from 1983 to 1985, the new four party centre-right Government lifted a range of restrictions on the mobility of capital along with a number of internal credit controls, leaving Danish capital markets as an integrated part of the international money market.[47] To the extent that these capital liberalisations have worked to increase social democratic acceptance of Economic and Monetary Union in the EC, they should therefore be viewed as a domestic development which in a way which is difficult to reverse has weakened the efficiency of national regulation.

Furthermore, it is unlikely that considerations of this kind have constituted the most important factor behind the eventual SDP support for EMU. The most significant developments in the social democratic positions on EMU occurred from March 1990, that is: in a European context dominated by the process of German unification and the upcoming intergovernmental conference.[48] In this connection it is impor-

---

47) See e.g. Det Økonomiske Råd, Formandskabet, *Danish Monetary Policy in Transition*, pp. 23-50 and 230-244.
48) Erling Olsen, an economist and experienced social democratic MP, has often expressed support

fact which in itself suggests that either national security concerns or the threat of national exclusion have been important, and only few days after the 18 March 1990 East German elections, which made clear the inevitability of a rapid German unification. Concerns on the importance of German unification were also very significant for the position of the chairwoman of the SDP's parliamentary group, Ritt Bjerregaard, as she in September 1990 expressed her full support for EMU.[50]

However, for a number of the party's other leading figures, including Svend Auken, Ivar Nørgaard, and the SDP members of the European Parliament, external events prompted the policy change in a more indirect way. For these parts of the party, the forceful dynamic towards Treaty reform during 1990 confronted the SDP with an imminent threat of Danish isolation in the event that the party would hold on to its traditional rejection of EMU. Thus, as made clear by Ivar Nørgaard in the May 1989 parliamentary debate, a situation in which the Rome Treaty would be "outflanked" by the creation of a parallel treaty would be unacceptable. Furthermore, SDP rejection of involvement in the project could only strengthen the position of the views of political adversaries in the legal constructions which would provide the future framework for macroeconomic policy in an EMU.

For these reasons, these parts of the SDP actively sought to influence the basis for the Union so as to strengthen its "reflationary" possibilities. This was first done in attempting to equip the European Central Bank with broad objectives. As this turned out to be impossible in light of strong German resistance, the party sought to strengthen the finance political instruments of a future EMU.[51] Influence was first of all sought in the negotiations with the Government on the Danish memorandum, but the party also worked through its representatives in the EP and in the framework of the CSPEC.

Thus, in the case of the EMU negotiations, access to decision-making in an emerging supranational institution with the capability of establishing regulation not seen to be cost efficient at the national level - i.e. macroeconomic policies deviating from the policies of major trade partners - created incentives for the party to attempt to shape this institution. Here it is also justified to speak of a continuation of the

---

50) This impression was confirmed in a September 1990 personal interview with Bjerregaard.
51) This interpretation is supported in a personal interview with one of Ivar Nørgaard's close aides, Kurt Petersen, in September 1990.

but the party also worked through its representatives in the EP and in the framework of the CSPEC.

Thus, in the case of the EMU negotiations, access to decision-making in an emerging supranational institution with the capability of establishing regulation not seen to be cost efficient at the national level - i.e. macroeconomic policies deviating from the policies of major trade partners - created incentives for the party to attempt to shape this institution. Here it is also justified to speak of a continuation of the learning process which presumably contributed to the party's proposal in the SEA negotiations to incorporate into the Rome Treaty an obligation for member states to pursue expansive economic policies when unemployment increases. As the EMU endorsement of the SDP's MEPs illustrates, and as acknowledged by both the MEPs and implicitly also by Ivar Nørgaard, the long sought coordinated reflation seemingly required more binding forms of economic cooperation in the European Community.

To sum up, the growing social democratic support for monetary union in the EC in 1989 and 1990 resulted primarily from external developments. On the one hand it emerged as the reaction to a forceful dynamic following agreement among a number of major EC states on the preference for increased monetary integration. Here SDP sought to influence the shaping of an EMU's legal framework so as to allow more expansive macroeconomic policies at the national level. On the other, hand it was also motivated by the process of German unification and the potential security threats this created in the perceptions of some parts of the party. Finally, constructive involvement in the discussion on EMU was influenced by a learning process on the necessity of a binding economic framework if coordinated reflation were to be realistic.

Overall Evaluation

The SDP's support for significant reforms of the European Community was primarily the result of two types of factors. First, the party's promotion of the introduction of majority voting procedures on minimum EC regulation for environmental protection and employee rights was prompted by the EC's Single Market process following the adoption of the SEA. This suggests an internal dynamic of integration: increased supranational market-liberalising decision-making capacity led the SDP the EMU in a direction which would further the realisation of one of the party's major general political goals: full employment. At the same time, however, the experiences with the failed campaign for coordinated reflation in Western Europe increased the party's willingness to consider more binding forms of macroeconomic cooperation. The party had thus undergone a learning process during the 1980s.

It must also be considered that domestic factors have shaped the development of the party's EC policies from the late 1980s onwards. The lost referendum of February 1986 may have conveyed to the party leadership the impression that elections or referenda in which the SDP played the role as an obstacle to European integration could not be won, and that SDP antipathy towards strengthening the EC would therefore serve only to humiliate the party in the electorate and weaken its credibility as a future government party. Party leader Svend Auken and chairwoman of the SDP parliamentary group Ritt Bjerregaard both voiced such concerns in personal interviews and argued that they had influenced the party's approach to the intergovernmental conferences.[52] However, concerns for the party's future electoral or governmental prospects cannot explain the actual *content* of SDP policies on the EC's development. The 1986 referendum may have weakened the hand of the SDP in the negotiations with the Government on the Danish position towards Rome Treaty reform, just as it may have weakened the Danish negotiating position vis-à-vis the other EC states. Yet this is a problem of negotiating leverage and not of substantive content of policies advocated by the party.

---

52) Interview with Svend Auken of August 1991 and interview with Ritt Bjerregaard of September 1990.

PART III

Social Democracy and European
Integration: Conclusions
and Perspectives

10

The EC Policies of the Labour
Party and the SDP

This study has analysed the EC policies of two political parties. It has focused on the dynamics of what we have defined as attitude integration; i.e., on factors affecting the degree to which the Danish SDP and the British Labour Party have directed their expectations and activities towards the supranational organisation of the EC, including (1) the degree to which support is expressed for national membership of the EC, and (2) the degree to which support is expressed for increased supranationality in the organisation.

The first part of this chapter summarises the findings. It evaluates the explanatory strengths of the propositions on the dynamics of social democratic parties' EC policies. The British and Danish cases are compared, thereby highlighting the importance of systemic differences. The first part also discusses the relative significance of mechanisms translating changes in the parties' surroundings into changes in their EC policies: through changing voter preferences and conditioned by electoral concerns, or conditioned by the general policy goals of the party, cf. figure 2.2 on p. 39 above. Thus, we provide some answers to the question of whether the two parties in their behaviour towards the EC have acted as vote-seeking or as policy-pursuing political actors.

The second part of the chapter evaluates the degree to which the basic assumptions underlying the formulation of our propositions on the dynamics of EC policy change have provided a comprehensive understanding of the two parties' policies. Are the EC policies of the Labour Party and the SDP understandable as instances of what we have termed national-instrumental actions, as the analytical starting point presupposes? Or do they display elements of nationalism or of internationalism, either in the sense that intrinsic importance is accorded to the institutional level at which a given policy goal is pursued, or in the sense that the two parties have pursued goal realisation for groups defined independently of nationality? Finally, what does this tell us about social democratic parties' perception of international cooperation and supranational institutions?

SOCIAL DEMOCRACY AND EUROPEAN INTEGRATION: WHY POLICY CHANGES OCCUR

This study began with three propositions on social democratic parties' behaviour towards the European Community. According to the first proposition, social democratic parties' EC policies are driven by what has been termed the internal dynamic of integration. In the neofunctionalist tradition, the internal dynamic here refers to national political actors' relocation of expectations and activities towards a supranational decision-making centre *as a result* of preceding regional market liberalisations.

More specifically, the internal dynamic is a process in which regional market liberalisations gradually render the nation-state of a given social democratic party dependent on continued membership of the market liberalising scheme. Thus, although social democratic parties are expected to initially reject membership in the European Community, since it could constitute a threat to the possibility of national state intervention, acknowledged dependency on continued EC membership generates profound effects. It causes social democratic parties to view the supranational level as an additional arena in which the struggle over regulation of society is fought. In relation to a predominately market liberalist EC, the perception of dependency on EC membership entails social democratic support for extended supranational market-intervention and/or market-intervening decision-making capacity, where it facilitates the achievement of general policy goals at the national level. If implemented these policies would take the EC beyond the point of being an institution primarily concerned with instituting regional market liberalisations.

As a second possibility, the potential significance of purely domestic developments for changes in social democratic parties' EC policies has been pointed to. In one scenario, developments initiated at the national level and not constituting an effect of regional market liberalisations or of actions of supranational bureaucracy erode the efficiency of national policy instruments in a given issue area in a manner which is difficult to reverse. This erosion may prompt social democratic parties to endorse increased supranational regulation and possibly increased supranational decision-making capacity as a replacement for the vanished possibilities of national regulation in this area. Likewise, a party's perception of blocked national channels for influence may prompt it to turn to the supranational setting for the enactment of desired regulation and to possibly also endorse extended supranational decision-making capacity. Finally, a political party may make instrumental use of support for extended or diminished supranational regulation or supranational decision-making capacity to increase its electoral appeal.

The third proposition focuses on the possibility that events which are external to the nation-state within which a given party operates may produce changes in social democratic policies. Thus, to the extent that there is an acknowledged dependency on continued membership in institutions such as the EC, the desire of other EC states to strengthen the framework's supranational characteristics may create a threat of national exclusion: if such desires are confronted with an outright refusal, the most radical scenario could be that these other states create alternative supranational frameworks, leaving the excluded state with no influence in questions which may affect it regardless of membership. A second type of external development prompting changes in national - and hence not only social democratic - political forces' position towards EC institutions may emerge when the security political significance of these institutions is perceived as growing. Where such developments threaten to reactivate traditional international conflict lines - which it may be argued has been the case in Europe after 1989 - new incentives for enhanced supranationality may arise and influence the positions of a broad spectrum of political parties.

Social Democratic EC Policies: The British Case

Evidently, no single factor accounts for every development in the EC policies of the two parties studied here. The approaches of the British Labour Party and the Danish SDP to the EC have been influenced by most of the above-mentioned factors, to a differing degree and in different connections. In addition, learning processes have played a role for the development of policies over time. Nevertheless, there are a number of similarities in the development of the two parties' positions which justify the evaluation in more general terms of the formulated propositions.

Except for a brief period in 1967-69, the EC policies of the Labour
Party until the mid-1980s were characterised by profound internal disagreement and by broad disapproval of EC membership. The consensus
on the strategy of renegotiation and referendum from 1971 to 1974 did
nothing to remove the substantial disagreement underlying it, and strong
resistance to membership among party activists and trade unions
continued to influence the party throughout the 1970s, causing conflict
with the party leadership's commitment.

The Labour Party's initial scepticism towards the EC is to a great
degree in accordance with the expectations of the proposition on the
internal dynamic of integration. When the Labour Government under
Clement Attlee rejected British participation in the establishment of the
EC's predecessor the ECSC, it was partly based on a fear that regional
market liberalisations in the coal and steel area would "result in chaos".
The Labour Government thereby expressed the party's mistrust in
market regulation of society and the strengthening of this regulation on
an international basis in particular. Similarly, when the Labour Party,
in 1962, adopted a very sceptical attitude towards British membership
of the European Community, it was an important argument that the
Treaty of Rome was "anti-planning" and that EC membership would
stand in the way of independent British management of the economy.

When the Wilson Government reversed these policies in 1967 and
actively pursued EC membership, it was a result of a combination of
external developments and domestic events involving learning processes.
Externally, the erosion of international decision-making fora previously
of central importance to British foreign policy implied a threat of real
national exclusion. To the extent that the dynamically evolving EC was
what threatened the "special relationship" with the US and to the extent
that this EC dynamism resulted from progressive regional market
liberalisations, we may here identify an "internal dynamic of integration".
It is, however, a different dynamic than that outlined previously, as
regional market liberalisations here work by affecting the relationship
between two non-EC member states, entailing the threat of real exclusion
one of these states.

Domestically, experiences with attempts at introducing comprehensive
economic planning in the British economy as well as Mr. Wilson's
personal experiences with the functioning of the Community led the
Labour leadership to upgrade the direct economic value of EC
membership and to downgrade the importance of the formal limits to

national state intervention following Rome Treaty Accession. Both of these processes can be described as learning processes. Finally, there is some evidence that the Wilson Government's approval of the policy of applying for EC membership was used instrumentally in order to broaden the party's electoral appeal.

The Wilson Government's policy thus prompts us to qualify the first part of the proposition on the internal dynamic of integration. The policy reversal suggests that for social democratic parties, the possibility of state intervention in the national market economy unimpeded by international constraints is not an absolute imperative but, rather, something to be held up against other concrete political or economic benefits of subscribing to binding international agreements.

The availability of new knowledge was also important in the broader Labour Party's swing towards rejection of EC entry on the terms negotiated in 1970-71. Thus, the information on the direct economic costs of EC membership contained in the White Paper on the consequences of British Rome Treaty accession contributed to the growing opposition to EC entry in the trade unions as well as among many Labour Party activists and MPs. The release of the White Paper and other assessments of the direct costs of membership also seem likely to have influenced public opinion on the issue, rendering opposition to EC membership an attractive issue for campaigning against the Conservative Government.

The compromise on Britain's relationship with the EC, achieved when Harold Wilson took to the call for a renegotiation of the terms of entry and a referendum on the question of membership, allowed an apparent internal agreement on the issue to emerge. However, this consensus was purely procedural, and consequently, it disappeared in 1974-75. The leadership recommended an approval of the renegotiated terms of entry, but the bulk of the party at large rejected continued EC membership, the trade unions and the left wing increasingly voicing support for an economic strategy which conflicted fundamentally with the Rome Treaty, as it involved a recourse to undisguised protectionism.

It is thus clear that while the leadership of the PLP favoured EC membership, the majority of the larger Labour Party had never accepted it. The left wing remained hostile particularly to those aspects of the EC's legal framework perceived as hindering necessary state intervention in the economy. Strong resistance to formal constraints on independent national policies was also voiced in connection with the debate on full British membership of the European Monetary System in 1979, as the majority of the party rejected it and forced Prime Minister Callaghan to negotiate a British "half-way house".

The continuing and even growing hostility to British EC membership in the Labour Party would appear to contradict our proposition on the internal dynamic of integration. This proposition contends that the extension of regional market liberalisations so as to cover the state of a given social democratic party will prompt this party's support for extended supranational market-intervening regulation and possibly also for increasing supranational decision-making capacity regarding market intervention. However, this dynamic is expected to take place first when a fundamental dependency on continued membership in the EC is acknowledged, in the sense that no net-benefit is seen to ensue from ignoring EC regulation or leaving the EC entirely. In this connection, a majority of the Labour Party had never acknowledged any such fundamental dependency, even though the party leadership until 1980 certainly had a different opinion. Hence, the events of the mid- and late 1970s are evidence of a strong belief that a Britain entangled in fewer formal international constraints had better possibilities to solve British problems.

In the early 1980s this view came to dominate the official party line, as Labour adopted a policy of withdrawing Britain from the Community. The immediate cause for this radicalisation of the party's EC policies was the growing strength of its left wing, which culminated at the party conferences of 1980. The rise of the Labour left, althoug a domestic development, did not involve the mechanisms referred to in the proposition on domestic causes for changes in attitude integration. Rather, the growing strength of the left's viewpoints resulted from experiences with the Wilson and Callaghan Governments as well as from members' reflection on the failed policies of the past and conclusions that radically new strategies were needed.

In adopting a policy which endorsed formal British withdrawal from the EC in order to enable the implementation of the Alternative Economic Strategy, the Labour Party also pursued a policy marred by logical inconsistencies. If a net economic-political benefit is seen to ensue from implementing policies which conflict fundamentally with the Community Treaties, then it makes little sense to formally apply and negotiate to withdraw from the EC. The most significant threat possessed by other EC states when confronted with systematic violation of the Community's legal framework is expulsion. Howver, if there is a net benefit from leaving the EC, expulsion would be no threat. Furthermore, to the extent that the implementation of the AES would provoke foreign economic retaliation in response to measures such as import controls, this remained a possibility regardless of British EC membership. Labour's response to the latter problem was "negotiated withdrawal": in order to lend credibility to the argument that Britain's now increasingly close trade relations with the other EC member states would not be hurt by EC departure, the party's 1982 programme and 1983 general election manifesto argued that negotiations with the rest of the Community would lead to the establishment of new favourable trading agreements as a replacement. However, this response only created new logical inconsistencies as "negotiated withdrawal" meant that the rationale for withdrawal - the restoration of Parliament's freedom to deploy import and investment controls - had to be relinquished in order to facilitate the withdrawal itself.

Thus, the policy of withdrawal, intended to facilitate the implementation of the AES, indicates that parties may formulate incoherent policies, and that misperceptions may influence the contents of specific party positions. "Nationalist" rejections of the principle of supranationalism as such may have been of some importance for the policy, as we shall discuss below, and the desire to evade the direct costs of Britain's net budget contribution added to the wish for withdrawal. Both these motivations would render the policy understandable as instrumental-rational. Yet the concern for the implementation of the AES clearly provided the basis for Labour's position.

The incoherence of the policy of withdrawal contributed to Labour's devastating 1983 electoral defeat. This defeat again lead the party to gradually adopt a less radical policy of "keeping its options open" on the EC. At the same time, and in the wake of the French Socialist Government's failed attempts at sustaining a unilateral Keynesian reflation in an international environment giving priority to low inflation, Labour's leadership increasingly emphasised the need for international coordination of measures to improve growth and increase employment. This policy signified a learning process in which the French experiences, pointing to the need for import controls in order for uncoordinated reflation to be sustainable, appeared to combine with the ever-growing British dependency on access to the markets of other EC states, in turn leading the Labour leadership to stress the merits of international cooperation.

In terms of the proposition on the internal dynamics of integration, there is thus some evidence that dependency on continued EC membership was increasingly acknowledged and reflected upon, but at this point in time - 1984-85 - no economic strategy had been developed to replace the AES. Labour therefore maintained its call for the introduction of managed trade in the EC, just as it reserved its right to demand exemptions from the EC's legal framework so as to enable the implementation of its economic strategy. A persistent "nationalist" hostility to the principle of supranationalism presumably contributed to this continuing rejection of the existing Community framework, a policy position illustrated by Kinnock's proposals for EC reforms in his 1984 article "New Deal for Europe", amounting to the Community's effective abolishment.

Labour's rejection of the Single European Act in early 1986 accords with the proposition on the internal dynamic of integration, whereby social democratic parties will reject any strengthening of supranational decision-making capacity on regional market liberalisations. Thus, the party's representatives repeatedly stressed their mistrust of regionally based market liberalisations as a solution to Western Europe's enduring economic problems. But at the same time, the predominant attitude towards the SEA was one of indifference, a fact which presumably reflected that the party saw few immediate threats to existing and highly valued British regulation to follow from the SEA. Neither was the party leadership convinced that the SEA would actually improve the EC's decision-making capacity, for which reason there was little cause for alarm regarding its longer term consequences.

Nevertheless, the statements of Labour's spokesman during the debates on the SEA in early 1986 testifies to a growing willingness to make practical use of Community institutions. This development most likely reflected the first concrete consequences of the growing acknowledgement that any fundamental restructuring of Britain's relationship with the EC had become less appealing to the party.

The EC question played virtually no role in the 1987 general election, but in the period from the June 1987 elections to the start of the intergovernmental conferences leading to the agreement on the Maastricht Treaty, the party's EC policies underwent three significant changes.

First, the party's 1988 conference accepted that "Britain was economically and politically integrated into the EC". The party subsequently incorporated the existence of EC institutions and the EC's legal framework into its overall strategies, as is evidenced by its comprehensive policy review report approved at the conference in 1989. Here Labour voiced support for an extension of supranational regulation in areas such as consumer protection, environmental protection, employee rights, working conditions, and regional policy.

The second change was that from 1987, the party directed increasing attention to the EC's Single Market programme and the challenges this was seen to pose to the British labour movement. Following the 1988 TUC conference and the annual Labour Party Conference shortly thereafter, this resulted in the adoption of a policy which supported a social dimension to the Community's internal market. The measures which the Labour Party wanted to include in a social dimension involved most of the proposals which had been approved of once the party had acknowledged that withdrawal from the EC was out of the question. However, party policy development in 1989 and 1990 also resulted in the endorsement of institutional reforms in the Community so as to extend majority voting in the Council to "those decisions where it would help to improve social policy and raise environmental standards". This policy was comprised in a campaign document released in May 1990, "Looking to the Future".

Third, the Labour Party during 1989 and 1990 adopted a new approach to the question of monetary integration in the EC. As late as the 1989 policy review, the party had rejected British membership of the Exchange Rate Mechanism unless a number of fundamental reforms of the system were agreed to. During late 1989 and early 1990, the importance of these reforms was gradually toned down, removed, or reinterpreted so as to have less far reaching implications, and in April 1990 the party leadership made clear that the case for British entry was now overwhelming.

At the same time, the party's positions on British membership of a future economic and monetary union in the EC developed. Thus, in late 1989, Neil Kinnock pointed to a number of broad conditions which could make British membership of an EMU acceptable to the Labour Party, and during 1990 the party leadership increasingly emphasised its desire to keep Britain in the "centre" of the EC, including within a monetary union. The party's final position on EMU prior to the start of the inter-governmental conferences was contained in the detailed NEC statement published in December 1990. The party here argued for an evolutionary approach to Economic and Monetary Union including a strengthening of the Community's regional and industrial policies as well as for an accountable European Central Bank.

The development of the Labour Party's EC policy culminating in its calls for extended supranational regulation and institutional reforms in the EC to a high extent appears as an instance of the internal dynamic of integration. Thus, at the moment where a fundamental British dependency on continued membership in the EC had been acknowledged, the party formulated policies implying the active use of Community institutions for furthering of it's general policy goals. Moreover, as this development took place in a setting in which the Community's market liberalising decision-making capacity had previously been strengthened, the call for an extension of binding supranational regulation in certain areas was soon followed by the party's call for an extension of supranational decision-making capacity in some areas of market intervention.

The proposition on the internal dynamic of integration contends that acknowledged dependency on continued membership of a supranational organisation such as the EC will follow from the structural economic effects of regional market liberalisations. National membership in a regional market liberalising scheme will gradually render the nation-state in question economically dependent on continued membership, in the sense that no net economic-political benefit is seen to ensue from ignoring supranational regulation or leaving the organisation.

EC membership has affected the workings of the British economy in many ways, but one trend stands out as particularly important; namely, the effect of the EC's customs union and (partial) common market for British export patterns.[53] Evidently, it is difficult to draw many very firm conclusions on the political importance of developments like this. Thus, they raise the question of how to determine the effects of structural evolutions at the level of political actors. It is nevertheless justified to point to the restructuring of British trade patterns as a fundamental factor shaping the Labour Party's perceptions of viable political-economic strategies: growing dependency on access to the markets of other EC states has rendered strategies involving conflicts with other EC members

---

53) The effect of EC membership is discernable in figure 10.1 as the higher growth in the EC share of total British exports after EC entry. Evidence that EC membership has affected considerably British trade patterns is also provided by Alan Winters, "Britain in Europe: A Survey of Quantitative Trade Studies", *Journal of Common Market Studies*, vol. XXV, no. 4 (June 1987), pp. 315-335, and Francesco Giavazzi, "The Impact of EEC Membership", in R. Dornbusch and R. Layard, *The Performance of the British Economy* (Oxford: Clarendon Press, 1987), pp. 97-130, esp. pp. 106-108.

less and less appealing to the electorate, as well as less and less likely to be seen as furthering the achievement of the party's general policy goals.[54]

As mentioned, there are several mechanisms which could translate a social democratic party's acknowledgement of a dependency on EC membership into support for extended supranational regulation or enhanced supranational decision-making capacity in specific policy areas.

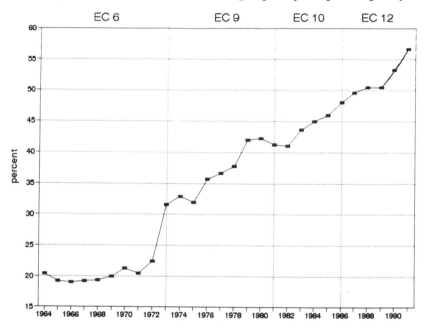

Figure 10.1: EC Share of Total British Exports.

Thus, in the perceptions of social democratic parties (1) EC membership may provide access to institutions capable of establishing regulation heretofore not seen as efficient at the national level or subsequently improving the efficiency of national regulation; (2) EC regulation may serve as a guarantee for the existence of necessary national regulation;

---

54) Sources in figure 10.1: United Nations, *International Trade Statistics, Yearbook* 1965, 1970, 1975, and 1980, 1985, and 1989, and Eurostat, *External Trade and Balance of Payments, Statistical Yearbook 1992* (Luxembourg: Statistical Office of the European Communities, 1992). As the EC share of total exports has risen, so has the importance of exports in the total economy: exports amounted to around 20% of British GDP in the 1950s and 1960s as opposed to between 24% and 29% in the 1980s, cf. Organization for Economic Cooperation and Development, *OECD National Accounts*, vol. 1: *Main Aggregates, 1960-1990*, tables 13 and 17, and *United Nations Statistical Yearbook*, 1964.

(3) advancing EC market liberalisations may threaten the efficiency of necessary national regulation, creating the need for supranational replacement regulation or regulation which reestablishes the efficiency of national regulation; or (4) EC market liberalisations may create or magnify problems whose solution requires new supranational regulation.

Labour's call from 1989 onwards for extended supranational regulation and its subsequent adoption of a policy calling for the introduction of majority voting procedures in the Council in new areas seemed motivated by the wish to utilise the EC framework to guarantee the existence of what was seen as necessary regulation at the national level. Particularly in connection with the so-called "social dimension" to the EC's Single Market, it is important that the British labour movement had been pressed into a very defensive position nationally following a decade of Conservative neo-liberal rule. Thus, when the Labour Party had accepted the permanency of EC membership, it proceeded to make use of the Community as a "second front" against the Thatcher Government, EC regulation in this respect appearing particularly attractive as it would be difficult for future Conservative Governments to reverse. In this sense, the internal dynamic of integration has been conditioned by domestic British developments following the coming to power in 1979 of a Government with a radical programme for liberalist reforms.

The conception of the "social dimension" which the above arguments imply is that EC labour market and social regulation should serve as instruments for promoting a model for economic development in Europe involving "offensive" rather than "defensive" labour market flexibility. A contextual interpretation of the Labour Party's arguments for EC labour market regulation as a protection against social dumping also points to this motivation.

A different mechanism has been active regarding Labour's call for majority voting on environmental protection measures in the EC framework. While the wish to use EC regulation to ensure the existence of necessary national regulation may also have been of some importance here, it is more likely that this aspect of Labour's EC policy has been motivated by the desire to take decisions at the most efficient institutional level. In this instance, EC membership provided access to institutions capable of establishing regulation which would have been inefficient had it been adopted in isolation at the national level.

Purely domestic developments have also constituted an independent factor in shaping Labour's new approach to EC institutions. The blocking of national channels for political influence following the Thatcher Government's complete rejection of corporatist political solutions contributed to the labour movement's willingness to consider supranational options. However, it would not be accurate to describe the Labour Party's new EC policy in the late 1980s as the result of independent changes in the preferences of the electorate and, hence, as domestic vote-seeking behaviour. Labour certainly took advantage of the widening rift between the Conservative Government and the majority of the electorate on the EC issue, and concerns for the party's electoral appeal thus contributed to shaping the party's policies. But the development in the preferences of the electorate cannot be seen in isolation from the effects of the actions of supranational bureaucracies or regional market liberalisations.

Whereas the proposition on the internal dynamic of integration thus enables us to understand Labour's EC policies in areas such as labour market policy, environmental policy, consumer protection and regional policies, the dynamics of policy change in the monetary realm is very different. When the party leadership in April 1990 endorsed British membership of the Exchange Rate Mechanism, having shedded most of the conditions which until mid-1989 were fundamental for advocating entry, it constituted an instrumental use of the issue in order to broaden the party's electoral appeal. Thus, immediate economic benefits were seen to follow ERM entry, strengthening the incentives for the party to support it. Moreover, in a situation where the Conservatives were deeply divided over the issue and where Labour's economic credentials were the weak point in the electorate's perceptions of it, advocacy of ERM entry was a potentially efficient way to strengthen the credibility of Labour as an economically responsible party committed to low inflation and sustainable growth.

While the domestic concern for electoral appeal was therefore the most important reason for the party endorsing full membership of the EMS, other factors were also significant. Labour's new reliance on supply side economics from the 1989 policy review onwards, which must be characterised as the result of a learning process, meant that less importance was accorded to macroeconomic management for the solution of Britain's economic problems. This fact presumably again facilitated the willingness to surrender the formal freedom to pursue exchange rate policy independently of the other member states of the EMS. Further-more, structural economic developments had gradually increased the inflationary risks of currency depreciations vis-à-vis other EMS currencies, as both the EC share of total imports and the openness of the British economy had increased during the 1970s and 1980s. There is some evidence that this influenced the party leadership's position on ERM entry. To the extent that these structural economic developments have resulted from British EC membership, we can therefore identify an internal dynamic of integration in which regional market liberalisations gradually diminish the efficiency of a national policy instrument, thereby increasing the incentives to support British ERM membership.

Finally, the party's policies on a prospective economic and monetary union in the EC were to a very high extent shaped by the perceived threat of national exclusion from an important international decision-making forum. This is evidenced by a number of statements made by the party leadership during 1990, and the case for constructive participation in the EMU negotiations in order to avoid national exclusion was also emphatically stated in the NEC statement published in December same year. In this connection, it should be mentioned that the importance of the threat of exclusion appears to have been partly conditioned by the approaching general election. This fact strengthened the incentives for the Labour Party to act as if it were already in office in order to portray itself as "fit to govern".

The significance of the threat of exclusion for the debate on economic and monetary union in the EC is also underlined by the fact that it was a concern shared by a broad spectrum of political forces in Britain, and a concern which presumably constituted the sing.e most important factor in ousting Margaret Thatcher from 10 Downing Street in November 1990.

Even if the threat of exclusion created by the French-German agree-ment to push for closer monetary integration thus constituted the most important factor shaping Labour's policies on the issue, a domestically based erosion of a policy instrument contributed to the party's willingness to consider a monetary union. Thus, in combination with the growing preference for stable exchange rates vis-à-vis other EC curren-cies and the institutionalisation of this preference in British ERM-membership, the liberalisation of capital movements undertaken by the newly-elected Conservative Government in 1979 had effectively removed the possibility of an independent British monetary policy. There is some evidence that the diminishing possibilities for independent British policies and the effective dominance of the German Bundesbank in West European monetary policy combined to render the idea of a supranational monetary institution more appealing to the party leadership.

Social Democratic EC Policies: The Danish Case

The Danish SDP's attitudes towards the European Community were shaped fundamentally by national dependency on good economic relations with Britain as the question of Danish and British membership in the EC became topical in the 1960s. For the SDP, prospective Danish Rome Treaty accession was always seen in connection with future British EC membership, and Danish membership applications therefore immediately followed on both occasions when Britain approached the EC in the 1960s, as well as when the British application was finally welcomed in 1970.

Danish EC membership meant that the Danish state agreed to forego the use of a number of instruments for national state intervention in the economy. Following Rome Treaty accession, Denmark renounced the possibility of pursuing independent trade, policies, agricultural and certain types of industry policies. In the early 1970s it also seemed likely that EC membership would soon involve supranational limitations on national exchange rate policies. Yet the great majority of the SDP's parliamentary party actively supported Danish EC membership and recommended that the electorate approve EC entry in the 1972 referendum. The imminent threat of Danish exclusion of a very tangible kind - in the form of partial Danish exclusion from access to the British markets, for Danish exports in general and for the economically important export of agricultural products in particular - explains this position. This threat of exclusion is not of a type to fit in with the previously formulated proposition on external determinants for attitude integration, but it is nevertheless justified to view the British membership applications as external developments seen from the Danish point of view.

The case of the SDP's attitude to Danish EC membership contradicts the expectation that social democratic parties will reject national membership of supranational market liberalising organisations. This prompts a reformulation of the proposition on the internal dynamic of integration. In evaluating the events surrounding Danish EC entry, it appears that a calculus on the trade-offs between the party's different general policy goals, including prosperity and full employment, provided the rationale for support for membership. National exclusion from the enlarged EC's markets in general and from markets for agricultural products in particular would have involved a large direct welfare loss which also would have hit the party's social basis. Moreover, the welfare loss would have been of a size which could not have been offset by the greater formal possibilities for national state intervention had Denmark remained outside the Community. Finally, EC membership did not threaten those general policy goals which had been achieved to a high extent in the Danish political system and which were seen to depend on state intervention in the economy.

Just as was the case for the Wilson Government in Britain, the SDP's support for Danish EC membership thus suggests that the possibility of state intervention unimpeded by international agreements is not an absolute priority for social democratic parties but one held up against the concrete economic or political benefits ensuing from surrendering this option. The case of Danish EC entry also suggests that the value of formally-unhindered possibilities of state intervention in areas affected by EC entry was less valued than the direct economic benefits ensuing from membership.

There are two alternative possible explanations for the SDP's low valuation of formally unimpeded possibilities of state intervention. Both rest on the fact that the types of intervention affected by Rome Treaty accession had never played an important part in the SDP's reform strategies.

The first explanation points to the SDP's continuing dependency for a majority in the Folketing on parties favouring a high degree of market regulation of society. This factor could have prompted the SDP to pursue policies not involving state intervention in the above-mentioned areas out of domestic political necessity. Thus, the possibility of state intervention may have been of little real significance to the SDP in light of Danish political circumstances.

The second explanation focuses on the fundamental condition of the small size of the Danish economy and its corresponding dependency on international trade. This dependency may have drastically diminished the possibility to apply any internationally unapproved comprehensive state intervention in the areas affected by Rome Treaty accession with an overall positive effect on general policy goal achievement *regardless* of Danish EC membership. A small state which attempts public intervention in the economy involving quantitative or qualitative import restrictions or the strengthening of international competitiveness via direct state subsidies to industry or in the form of currency devaluations, all in order to achieve or secure the policy goal of full employment, risks provoking similar measures from larger states. If such retaliatory measures occured, it would put the small state in a very difficult situation. Thus, the small state is more dependent on access to the markets of larger states than vice-versa, and direct state subsidies to industry could engage the small state in a battle on the funding capacities of the public budget which it cannot win.

The circumstances of the Danish applications for EC membership point to the second of these explanations. The SDP leadership never regretted that EC entry would mean the loss of possibilities for state intervention in the above-mentioned policy areas. On the contrary, it actively supported further trade liberalisations in the EC and in general. Even the social democratic opponents of EC membership did not deplore the loss of formal trade and tariff policy independence. Furthermore, the SDP actively supported the strict enforcement of the Rome Treaty's provisions prohibiting certain types of state subsidies to industry, just as the party leadership pointed to the vulnerability of the small state in justifying its support for fixed exchange rates. Finally, these policies did not change when the SDP commanded a parliamentary majority with the left wing SPP in 1966-67, weakening the argument that domestic party political conditions shaped the SDP's approach to the EC.

As figure 10.2 below indicates, Denmark had become in a very abrupt and perceptible way dependent on membership of the EC when Britain decided to join. As a consequence of British (and to a much lesser extent Irish) EC entry, the share of Danish exports going to member states of the Community rose from 23.3% in 1972 to 44.5% in 1973.[55]

Following the proposition on the internal dynamics of integration, acknowledged dependency on the EC membership of the country within which a social democratic party operates leads this party to attempt to shape the European Community according to its own visions and percep-

---

55) Sources in figure 10.2: see note 2 above. Denmark has been trade dependent for a long period of time. From the 1950s to the early 1990s, exports amounted to between 28% and 36% of GDP, cf. Organization for Economic Cooperation and Development, *OECD National Accounts*, vol. 1: *Main Aggregates, 1960-1990*, tables 13 and 17, and *United Nations Statistical Yearbook*, 1964.

tions. In relation to a predominately market-liberalist EC, this implies
a high level of attitude integration. The Community should then pursue
interventionist policies which the party believes would support the
achievement of its general policy goals at the national level.

Indeed, an acknowledgement that no net political-economic benefit
could possibly ensue from ignoring the legal framework of the EC, not to
mention staying outside or leaving the Community, prompted the Danish
SDP to develop strategies involving the offensive use of Community
institutions.

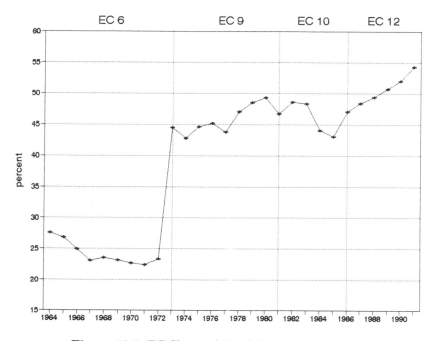

Figure 10.2: EC Share of Total Danish Exports.

Once Denmark had entered the EC, the parliamentary debates in late
1972 and in 1973 as well as the comprehensive 1973 policy report on the
EC showed the party expressing support for an extension of
supranational regulation in a number of areas: control over multinational
corporations and minimum regulations for environmental protection,
consumer protection, working conditions and other types of labour
market regulation.

The precise motivations underlying these policy proposals appear to
vary from one issue area to another. Regarding control over multinational corporations, this proposal almost by definition constituted an

attempt to use EC institutions for regulation which could not be very effective if implemented solely in Denmark. Furthermore, the proposals for minimum labour market and environmental regulation in the EC presumably reflected the wish to use the EC to establish regulation which would subsequently improve the cost efficiency of national regulation in these areas. Minimum EC regulation at a level higher than the lowest existing level in the Community could render improvements of Danish standards less costly here. The call for minimum EC regulation on environmental and labour market standards hence most likely constituted an advanced form of protectionism.

Finally, there is some evidence that the call for certain types of minimum regulation in the EC framework such as that involving employee participation was motivated by the wish to extend highly valued Danish legislation to other parts of the Community.

In addition to the 1973 proposals, the SDP in December 1975 called for the introduction of fixed exchange rates in the Community combined with a pooling of foreign currency reserves. This policy clearly served one purpose, namely to alleviate the external constraints on Danish macro-economic policy, constraints which were becoming painfully clear as the internationally uncoordinated Danish reflation following the first oil crisis resulted in a large balance of payments deficit. The initiative thus aimed at increasing the cost efficiency of national macroeconomic management. However, depending on which concrete form the SDP's proposals would have taken had the initiative gotten off the ground, it may be wrong to see this proposal as an instance of attitude integration, as it may not have involved an extension of the scope of supranational regulation.

Whereas acknowledged dependency on membership of the EC thus led the Danish SDP to call for an extension of supranational regulation in several areas, it did not induce the party to support extended supra-national decision-making capacity in the same areas. There may be a number of reasons for this. First, reforms of the Rome Treaty were simply not on the agenda from the mid-1970s to the mid-1980s. Second, an opening up of the Treaty of Rome might have been thought to release developments the control of the party, putting highly valued national regulation at risk. Third, the existence of unanimous decision-making on regional market liberalisations seemed to guarantee that these liberalisations would not advance in a threatening manner. Finally, it is fundamental that there was considerable internal disagreement about EC membership among the party's members and voters, pointing to the fact that in the electorate perceptions of the implications of EC membership differed from those of the party leadership and the parliamentary group.

The period from the SDP Government's resignation in mid-1982 until after the Danish referendum on the Single European Act in February 1986 was characterised by two developments: the SDP repeatedly called for an improvement of functional international cooperation in the EC framework in a range of issue areas, and the party rejected all attempts at institutional reforms in the EC. The call to improve cooperation in the EC was a direct continuation of the policies formulated by the party in the first half of the 1970s. The social democrats thus favoured extended EC efforts on environmental protection, control over multinationals, employee rights and working conditions, as well as improved exchange rate management and common efforts to stimulate the European economy. In connection with the call for coordinated reflation in Western Europe, the SDP's policy took the form of participation in the campaign of Western European social democratic parties to this end.

In most of these policy areas, the social democratic proposals involved an extension of the scope of binding supranational regulation relative to existing EC regulation. In addition to the previously mentioned issue areas, it seems likely that the SDP's call for a coordinated reflation in the early 1980s would have involved extended binding supranational regulation if the policy had had a realistic chance of resulting in reflationary measures, and if these measures had depended on the adoption of such regulation. If this hypothesis holds, it can be taken as evidence of a learning process in which the party's experiences with unilateral Danish economic expansion in the mid-1970s, the similar experiences of the French Socialist Government in 1981-83, and the perceived overly tight economic policy of West Germany caused the party to adopt a more positive position on binding supranational regulation in new areas of macroeconomic management.

In connection with the intergovernmental conferences in 1985 leading to the agreement on the SEA, the Danish SDP also agreed to present several proposals for reform of the Rome Treaty, including a proposal to introduce majority voting in the Council of Ministers on minimum regulation for protection of health and safety in the workplace. This social democratic desire to become involved constructively in the intergovernmental negotiations reflected the party's wish to avoid Danish isolation in a situation where a number of major EC states had agreed in principle on the need for reforms. In this context, the SDP allowed the Danish Government to put forward proposals which, in seeking to avoid isolation, would also serve to further the achievement or protection of the party's general policy goals. Thus, EC standards on workplace health and safety which exceeded the lowest existing in the EC member states could - again - improve the cost efficiency of Danish regulation in this area, as it would diminish the costs of raising Danish standards further.

Hence, the risk of national exclusion explains the SDP's will to compromise in the SEA negotiations. At the same time, however, the remarks of the party's EC spokesman preceding the negotiations - that a "Europe à la carte" would pose no danger for Denmark - testifies to the clear limits of this willingness to compromise. The SDP was not willing to achieve agreement at the price of putting highly valued existing Danish regulation at risk.

This fact constituted the main reason for the party's rejection of Danish ratification of the Single European Act in January 1986. The rejection was motivated by concerns that, directly or indirectly, in the short or long run, the SEA would form a threat to the party's general policy goals. The party feared that the introduction of majority voting on the creation of a Single Market in the EC would stand in the way of independent Danish measures for the protection of occupational safety and environmental protection or would undermine existing Danish legislation in these areas. At the same time, the concerns caused by the granting of new, albeit limited, powers to the European Parliament reflected worries that the EP would use its new powers only to further its position in the institutional struggle between Council and Parliament. Given the belief that the EP was inherently biased against social democratic goal realisation, granting the EP new powers was seen to contain a threat to the party's policy goals in the long run. Resistance to strengthening the EP was also based upon the belief that development of the EC in a federalist direction would entail a weakening of Danish democracy.

In sum, the SDP's rejection of the Single European Act fits well with our proposition about the internal dynamic of integration: to a high extent, the party rejected the SEA because advancing regional market liberalisations were perceived as a direct threat to highly valued existing regulation and to the possibility of strengthening this regulation in the future, as Danish regulation of the work environment and environmental protection by EC institutions could be seen to involve so-called technical barriers to trade. Furthermore, SDP rejection of giving increased authority to the European Parliament also rested upon the perception that this could work to the detriment of SDP policy goals in the future.

At the same time, the party's approach to the SEA testifies to the fact that national economic conditions were influencing its policy. The Danish dependency on international trade thus meant that the SDP accepted the objective of a Single Market in the EC in principle, a fact which supports the previously formulated conclusion that social democratic parties value the possibility of state intervention differently in different policy areas. Specific domestic political conditions also influenced the decision to reject the SEA, as the strong antipathy towards the EC among many of its voters contributed to the parliamentary group's decision: an approval of the SEA would have revealed considerable disagreements within the party, thereby damaging its electoral appeal.

In September 1986, following its defeat in the 1986 referendum, the SDP presented a comprehensive policy report on the party's European policies. In terms of concrete policies, the report contained little that was new, but its approach and the questions asked involved a markedly more "European" and less explicitly "Danish" perspective. The report therefore illustrated the party leadership's attempt to advance beyond the question of Danish membership in the EC. In many ways replaying the events following the 1972 referendum, indicating continuing strong resistance to EC membership among the party's members and voters.

With the SEA being ratified and taking effect in mid-1987, and with the process towards creating a Single Market under way, the SDP adopted a predominately defensive posture. The party rejected the elimination of border controls within the EC and the associated tax harmonisations. The latter entailed lowering a number of Danish tax rates which would have endangered the financing of the highly valued tax financed social security system in Denmark. However, during 1988 and 1989 this defensive posture towards the EC's development increasingly gave way to a more aggressive approach, in which the party eventually endorsed the introduction of majority voting procedures in the Council on minimum regulation for environmental protecion and employee rights.

This more aggressive posture constituted the culmination of a develcpment initiated with the launch of the process towards a Single Market in the EC. Thus, during 1988 and early 1989, the 1992-programme prompted a number of important trade union representatives and parts of the SDP leadership to mobilise the Danish labour movement in the quest for a social dimension to the internal market, just as the SDP leadership increasingly cited the need to strengthen the position of environmental protection in Community decision-making. Furthermore, in numerous statements during 1988 and 1989, the implicit or explicit support for majority decision-making in the Council in new areas was justified in pointing to the "imbalanced" nature of the EC's legal framework following the influence of the Conservative British Government on the SEA.

This development of the SDP's EC policies accords with the proposition on the internal dynamic of integration whereby social democratic parties will initially reject increased supranational decision-making capacity on regional market liberalisations, but subsequently support increased decision-making capacity on market interventions.

As mentioned, a number of mechanisms can translate increased supranational market liberalising decision-making capacity into social democratic support for greater supranational decision-making capacity in other areas. The Danish SDP's the increasingly vigorous support for a social dimension to the Single Market, culminating in the call for majority voting procedures on minimum regulation for employee rights and working conditions, was motivated primarily by the party's concern for "social dumping" in the form of competitive undermining of Danish labour market standards. Advancing regional market liberalisations were perceived as a threat to the efficiency of necessary national regulation, leading the SDP to support majority voting in the area in order to reestablish this efficiency. The Community's regulation of the labour market was, therefore, not meant to replace national regulation. On the contrary, it was intended to enable a continuation of cost efficient Danish regulation, which also entailed that the call for a social dimension constituted at least in part a protectionist strategy.

Protectionist motivations were also of some importance in the SDP's proposal for majority decision-making on minimum regulation for the protection of the environment. Some trade union representatives cited the need for high environmental standards in the EC in order to prevent the outflow of employment from Denmark to states with less restrictive regulation. However, statements on the issue by the party's international secretary testify to a different dynamic, where progressive regional market liberalisations were seen to amplify problems the efficient solution to which was possible only at the supranational level.

Finally, it should be mentioned that the desire to use Community institutions for the extension of highly valued national regulation to other parts of the EC may have been of some importance in instances where such regulation did not appear to constitute a negative competitive parameter. This could be the case regarding employee participation. The use of EC regulation as a guarantee for the existence of highly valued national regulation may also have been important here.

The SDP's call for the introduction of majority voting in new policy areas in the EC's Council came to constitute the main element in the party's proposals for the content of a political union, as this question became topical following the Kohl-Mitterrand initiative in April 1990. Prior to this, however, the party's international secretary had formulated new justifications for this policy, as security political implications of the Eastern European breakup and German unity strengthened the need for a strong EC.

Whereas external factors in the form of the emergence of new potential security threats may thus have had at least a limited degree of significance for the SDP's approach to the idea of a political union, external developments were of overriding importance when, in October 1990, the party endorsed the proposal for a future Economic and Monetary Union in the Community. For some parts of the party leadership, German unification provided the main justification for the policy reversal, as a pooling of monetary sovereignty was seen to constitute an element for binding the new Germany to supranational institutions. For other leading figures in the party, external events affected their positions more indirectly. The desire of several major EC states to proceed towards EMU created an imminent threat of Danish exclusion, were the party to not relinquish its previous unconditional opposition to EMU and engage constructively in the discussions. For the SDP this meant seeking to increase the Union's reflationary potential. Here we can also identify a learning process as a continuation of the process initiated with the SDP's active involvement in the campaign for coordinated reflation. By 1990, it was acknowledged in many parts of the party that anything resembling a coordinated reflation could not be achieved without more binding forms of economic cooperation.

External events have thus constituted the most significant factors in the development of the SDP's policy on EMU. However, as was the case for the British Labour Party, we can also point to a domestically rooted erosion of a policy instrument as a factor contributing to the party's willingness to contemplate monetary union. Thus, the far-reaching liberalisation of capital movements in the early 1980s meant that the possibility of pursuing an independent Danish monetary policy had all but evaporated in the late 1980s, given the predominant preference for continued full membership of the EMS.

Labour and SDP Policies towards the EC: Some Comparisons

The cases of the British Labour Party and the Danish SDP lead us to a number of more general conclusions. First, the proposition on the internal dynamics of integration must be reformulated. The attitude of social democratic parties towards national membership of an institution such as the EC is not solely determined by the effects of membership on the possibility of national state intervention in the economy. Rather, the initial EC policies of the Danish SDP and the Wilson Government's application to join the Community illustrate that the implications of Rome Treaty accession for the possibilities of state intervention are held up against other potential political and economic benefits flowing from EC membership.

Furthermore, differences in Danish SDP and British Labour Party EC policies in the 1960s, 1970s and early 1980s suggest that fundamental structural economic conditions affect the value which social democratic parties place upon the possibility of state intervention in the areas affected by Rome Treaty accession. The Danish SDP never considered it an important loss to formally surrender the possibility of independent trade policies or industrial policies involving certain types of direct state subsidies. Neither did the possibility of an independent Danish exchange rate policy seem of great value to the party. As we have seen, these aspects of Rome Treaty accession were considered highly controversial among large elements of the Labour Party in all but brief periods from the early 1960s to the mid-1980s.

Underlying this fact is the fundamental factor of the size of the nation-state within which the two parties have operated. Thus, the relative size of the national economy has affected the two parties' perceptions of the possibility of pursuing independent national policies with any net benefit in the above-mentioned policy areas, regardless of EC membership. Small relative size of the national economy corresponds to relatively high dependency on international trade and on access to a limited number of specific foreign export markets.[56] This dependency renders it unlikely that any net benefit can ensue from pursuing independent trade policies: small economies are more dependent on access to the markets of other and larger economies than vice-versa, meaning that foreign retaliatory measures in reaction to, for instance, independently imposed import restrictions will be highly damaging. In addition, small size limits the possibility of pursuing a policy of direct state subsidies to industry as small states most likely have fewer resources at their disposal for such subsidies in a given policy area than do larger states. Finally, small relative size and the correspondent openness and dependency on international trade increases the attractiveness of stable or fixed exchange rates, partly because currency depreciations involve larger inflationary risks for the small and open national economy than for the larger and less open economy.

All of these factors are important in understanding the Danish SDP's and British Labour's different initial approaches to the EC. In the perceptions of the SDP, small relative size of the Danish economy meant that the policy instruments affected by Rome Treaty accession were useless, regardless of EC membership. This was not the case in the perceptions of the British Labour Party. Rome Treaty accession was therefore seen to have more far-reaching real consequences for Britain than for Denmark.

Nevertheless, in evaluating the clear parallels in the development of the two parties' EC policies once a fundamental dependency on membership of the Community had been acknowledged, we can conclude that there indeed exists an internal dynamic of integration for social democratic parties. When dependency on membership is acknowledged, social democratic parties will tend to adopt policies on the EC's development which would take the Community beyond the point of solely adopting and supervising regional market liberalisations.

Furthermore, an internal dynamic has been identified in the sense that an increase in the market liberalising decision-making capacity of the EC was rejected by both parties. However, as increased market

---

56) Peter J. Katzenstein, *Small States in World Markets*, pp. 81-87, summarises the evidence of the small Western European states' economic openness, trade dependency, and dependency on access to a limited number of export markets. As mentioned, the differing levels of Danish and British trade dependency are captured by differences in the export-GDP ratio. Danish exports have normally amounted to significantly more than 30% of GDP since the 1950s, whereas the similar figure fluctuated around 20% in the UK in the 1950s and 1960s.

liberalising decision-making capacity had been agreed to despite social democratic resistance, it was followed by social democratic calls for increased EC decision-making capacity on market intervening regulation. All in all, this conclusion suggests that propositions resting on neofunctionalist understandings of the dynamics of regional integration are relevant in explaining the development of the two parties' policies towards the EC.

Having said this, however, we must note the limits of the proposition regarding the internal dynamic of integration. First, the dynamic has been shown to be of further significance for the British than for the Danish context. In the British case, it was EC membership which in itself, through the effects of the customs union and common market on the structure of British trade patterns, gradually increased Britain's fundamental economic dependency on continued membership. In the perceptions of the Labour leadership and in the party more generally, this rendered any political or economic strategies involving departure from the EC unviable, and precluded systematic violations of the EC treaties or negligence of the EC's legal framework. Labour was thus prompted to attempt to make use of the EC's institutions for the achievement of its policy goals.

In the Danish case, it was not EC entry which gradually created a dependency on continued membership. Rather, dependency emerged abruptly, as a result of the British decision to join, again highlighting the importance of the Danish economy's dependency on trade in the form of dependency on access to specific export markets. To some extent, the British membership application can be ascribed to the threat posed by a dynamically developing EC to the "special relationship" with the United States. In this sense, we can argue that Danish dependency on EC membership constituted an indirect effect of regional market liberalisations within the EC made by The Six. As mentioned, however, the threat to the "special relationship" was only one among several reasons for Britain to pursue EC entry.

The second limitation of the internal dynamic of integration is that it has clearly been conditioned by domestic factors and developments. In the case of the Labour Party, it thus seems doubtful whether it would have endorsed Rome Treaty reforms introducing majority voting in the Council "where it would help to improve social policy" in May 1990, had it not been for the defensive position of the British labour movement following a decade of Thatcherite rule. Labour saw institutional reforms

in the EC as a way of opening a "second front" against the Government
as well as a potential instrument for guaranteeing that future
Conservative governments would be bound in their policies by certain
minimum legislative standards adopted in the EC framework.

In the Danish context, SDP support for the introduction of majority
decision-making on minimum regulation for environmental protection,
employee rights, and working conditions has been conditioned by the
relatively high level of existing Danish standards in these areas. The
concern for the preservation of high Danish standards was significant as
the party rejected the SEA and as the Single Market programme was
getting under way. Protection of Danish regulative standards furthermore constitued the single most important reason for the party to
endorse institutional reforms in the EC in 1989.

This leads to a further conclusion, namely that the agreement between
the Danish SDP and the British Labour Party on the proposals for the
intergovernmental conferences leading up to the Maastricht Treaty has
been based on convergent rather than identical interests. Haas' early
observation that agreement on the creation or development of supranational institutions rests on consensus on specific measures, albeit with
differing underlying motivations, remains valid in the current case.[57]
With respect to the question of a social dimension to European integration, the basis in convergent interests may have consequences in the
longer term when concrete proposals must be formulated, removing the
possibility of "cheap talk" and highlighting the potential conflicts of
interests between Danish and British employees: EC labour market
standards higher than those existing in Britain would benefit Danish
employment levels to the detriment of British levels. This is true at least
in the short run, and to the extent that the regulation in question
constitutes a negative competitive parameter.[58]

Finally, we must stress that our proposition regarding the internal
dynamics of integration cannot account for all aspects of the two parties'
EC policies. In both the British and Danish cases, external developments
have played a significant role for the growing acceptance of an Economic

---

57) Cf. Ernst B. Haas, *Beyond the Nation State*, p. 34, and Ernst B. Haas and Philippe C.
    Schmitter, "Economics and Differential Patterns of Political Integration", *International
    Organization*, vol. 18, no. 4 (Fall 1964), pp. 712-713.
58) On the importance of "cheap talk" in the debate on a social dimension to the single market,
    see Peter Lange "The Politics of the Social Dimension", in Alberta M. Sbragia (ed.),
    Europolitics, pp. 225-256.

and Monetary Union in the Community. A threat of national exclusion from important international decision-making fora prompted willingness to engage in concrete negotiations and to compromise. In addition, the unification of Germany was viewed by some parts of the Danish SDP as constituting a potential security threat, leading these sections of the party to call for increased supranationality in the form of an EMU.

Threats of national exclusion furthermore led the Danish SDP to formulate proposals for Rome Treaty reform in connection with the negotiations on the SEA, resulting in the revised Rome Treaty's article 118A. As mentioned, threats of real national exclusion also played a significant role for the Wilson Government's application to join the EC in the late 1960s, just as it was a threat of exclusion from access to an important export market which led the Danish SDP and several other important Danish political parties to endorse EC membership.

Purely domestic developments have also played a role in the development of both parties' policies, but has been more important in the British than in the Danish case. The Labour Party has made instrumental use of the issue of EC membership as a means of broadening the party's electoral appeal in a number of instances. The "five conditions" policy in the early 1960s was partly a result of the party leadership's wish to formulate policies on the issue which differed from the Conservative Government's, implying that it saw this as a way to enhance Labour's electoral support. The swing in public opinion against British EC entry in 1970-71 also influenced the Labour Party's EC policies, as a number of MPs and party activists saw the EC question as an attractive issue for campaigning against the Heath Government.

The ascendance of the party's left wing in the second half of the 1970s and the dominance of left positions in the party in the early 1980s must also be seen as a domestic British development, even though a development like this is not contained in the proposition on domestic determinants of attitude integration.

Furthermore, the Thatcher Government's complete blocking of corporatist channels for political influence eventually increased the British labour movement's willingness to consider the supranational option. Given the preference for stable exchange rates, the Conservative Government's liberalisation of capital movements also added to Labour's willingness to consider strengthening European monetary integration, as these liberalisations have limited the possibility of an independent national monetary policy.

This last type of domestic development has been of a certain, albeit limited importance for the Danish SDP's positions on an EMU in 1989-90 as well. Similarly, the party's defeat in the referendum on Danish ratification of the SEA was a domestic development which influenced the general approach of the SDP to the question of EC reforms, inasmuch as it suggested that future referenda on the subject in which the party played the protagonist's role would see the SDP in a losing position.

Vote Seeking vs. Policy Pursuit

A final question regarding the dynamics of EC policy change in the two parties concerns the precise mechanisms which translate changes in the parties' societal environment into changes of specific party policy positions. In other words, have changing surroundings translated into policy change via changing voter preferences, conditioned by the concern for electoral appeal, or directly as conditioned by the concern for achievement of general policy goals (cf. figure 2.2)? And what does the answer tell us about the importance of political institutions for the dynamics of party policies?

A situation in which electoral concerns constitute the main conditioning factor implies that the party leadership is reacting to changes in the electorate's preferences on a given issue. Correspondingly, a situation in which the party's immediate concern for general policy goals is predominant implies that the formulation of proposals for policy change have been initiated in organisations representing larger or smaller segments of the party's social basis. Furthermore, the specific contents of policy proposals may preclude any substantial public involvement, implying that the perceived interests of the party's social basis underlie the proposal. Finally, explicit motivations as expressed by party leaders may point to concern for votes or general policy goals as conditioning factors.

In assessing the development of the Labour Party's and the SDP's EC policies, it seems clear that instances of vote seeking behaviour are found more frequently in the British than in the Danish case. In the early 1960s and in connection with the Wilson Government's application to join the EC, there was evidence that parts of the party viewed the policy shift in each instance as a means of broadening the party's electoral appeal. The same may clearly be said of Labour's hardening position against

British EC entry in 1970-71, notably following a swing towards opposition to British EC membership in public opinion. Furthermore, given the
fact that opinion polls in the late 1970s and early 1980s also showed a
majority of the British electorate to be against continued British EC
membership, a belief that the policy of EC withdrawal could strengthen
the party's electoral appeal has most likely been present in some cases
and played a certain role, even if this belief was evidently not shared by
important sections of the party leadership.

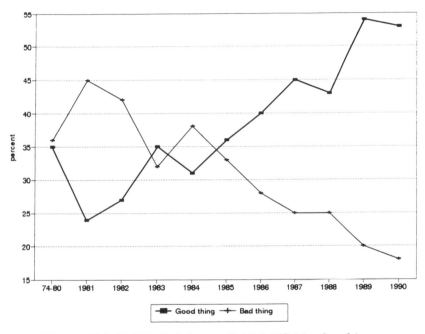

Figure 10.3: Public Opinion on British EC Membership.

The 1983 general election and the opinion polls conducted in this
connection appear to have strengthened the impression that policies
involving withdrawal from the EC would not be accepted by a majority
of the electorate. This again renders it plausible that vote-seeking was
an important factor in the party's subsequent move towards a more
pragmatic line of "keeping options open" vis-à-vis the EC.

Labour's final acknowledgement in 1988-89 of the permanency of
British EC membership, and the party's subsequent incorporation of
existing EC legislation and the availability of EC institutions into its
strategies also coincided with a historically high degree of approval of EC
membership by the British public, as shown in figure 10.3. This suggests

that electoral concerns have been of significance.[59] Finally, we have previously argued that the question of Labour's credibility as an economically responsible political party was decisive for the approval of a policy in 1989 arguing that Britain should enter the Exchange Rate Mechanism of the EMS.

In this connection, it is also relevant that the development of the party's new policies on the EC in the late 1980s took place in the context of a wide-ranging review of past policies, policies which were a major cause of the party's successive election defeats. Hence, a contextual interpretation of the development of the Labour Party's EC policy in the final years of the 1980s also points to the possibility that electoral concerns have played a significant role.

However, even if vote-seeking has been of importance in a number of instances, this does not preclude the significance of concerns for general policy goals as defined by the perceptions of the party's social basis. The Labour Party's EC policy is clearly understandable only if the perceived interests of its social basis are taken into account. The party has not been floating freely in policy space on the hunt for the median voter. Rather, with respect to the question of the European Community and its development, Labour formulated policies which reflected the opportunities and dangers the EC was seen to constitute for its social basis.

The policy of EC withdrawal in 1980-84 was undoubtedly an integral part of the Alternative Economic Strategy, a strategy which to a high extent originated in the trade union movement, thus indicating that the party's social base was deeply involved in its development. Furthermore, the importance of the TUC's endorsement of Jacques Delors' approach to the 1992 programme and of the concept of the social dimension for subsequent developments in the Labour Party can hardly be overstated. This again points to the significance of the social basis' general policy goals as a conditioning factor.

Finally, even if the desire to engage constructively in the discussions on the EMU may to some extent have been influenced by electoral concerns, the threat of national exclusion was the predominant factor underlying this policy, pointing to the concern for the effects of exclusion for the realisation of general policy goals.

---

59) Sources in figure 10.3: Opinion polls reported in Commission of the European Communities, *Eurobarometer*, 1988 and 1990. The question asked was: "Generally speaking, do you think [Britain's] membership of the European Community is 1) a good thing, 2) a bad thing, 3) neither good nor bad/don't know". The graph excludes category 3) answers.

In the Danish case, evidence pointing to the significance of electoral concerns as a conditioning factor is more scarce. Even if the 1960s, as mentioned, witnessed a clear majority of the Danish electorate in favour of Danish EC entry, the drive for Denmark's applications to join was clearly initiated by the Government and the Folketing as a response to external events, and not as a response to changes in public opinion. Furthermore, we can reasonably assume that the apparently overwhelming public majority in favour of EC entry was perceived as fragile and volatile by the SDP's parliamentary group, given the low level of information on the character of the EC in the population at this point.

A defensive type of vote-seeking influenced the SDP leadership's decision to call a referendum on the question of EC membership, as the leadership sought to avoid exposingf internal disagreement on the EC prior to the 1971 election to the Folketing. Exposing internal rifts would have caused considerable damage to the party's credibility and lowered its electoral appeal. Yet the decision to hold a referendum did not influence the party's substantive policies on the EC, which renders this instance of vote-seeking relatively insignificant.

To some extent, the same form of vote-seeking was involved in the SDP's very reluctant acceptance of direct elections to the European Parliament. Given the degree of internal disagreement revealed in the party in connection with the 1972 referendum, the party leadership, in seeking to prevent direct elections, or alternatively to have them coincide with national elections and be conditioned on the "double mandate", sought to avoid open exposition of this disagreement in recurrent European elections.

As the SDP chose to reject Danish ratification of the Single European Act in January 1986, such concerns seem likely to have played a certain role as well. Inasmuch as Prime Minister Schlüter's decision to call an advisory referendum came as a complete surprise to the party, it is plausible that the decision to reject the SEA was an attempt to avoid renewed open rifts in the party. Thus, it seems to have been a predominant attitude that a "Yes" to the SEA would have prompted more turmoil in the party than a "No".

Finally, and as mentioned previously, the lost referendum of 1986 has most likely conveyed to the party leadership the impression that the Danish electorate would not be prepared to obstruct future reforms of the EC, and particularly not in light of the threat of national exclusion this would involve. However wrong this impression may seem today, taking into account the Danish "No"-vote in the June 1992 referendum on the Maastricht Treaty, it is nevertheless plausible that concerns of this type influenced the SDP's approach to the question of EC reform after 1986. In adopting a more accommodating approach, the party leadership may also have been guided by the growing public support for continued Danish EC membership in the late 1980s (cf. figure 10.4), even if acceptance of EC membership is evidently not the same as acceptance of, say, increased supranationality in the EC.[60]

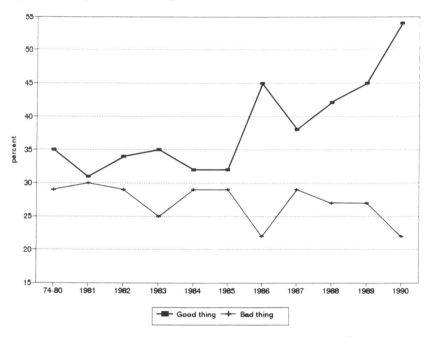

Figure 10.4: Public Opinion on Danish EC Membership.

Vote-seeking thus appears to have been of some importance in the post-1986 period. Similarly, a particularly defensive version of vote-seeking behaviour affected the SDP's policies in some instances prior to 1986. Nevertheless the party's general approach to the European Community has been predominately steered by the policy interests of its social basis. The proposals contained in the 1973 policy report clearly reflected the wish to make use of the Community framework for the pursuit of the party's general policy goals, just as the movement towards an offensive

---

60) Sources in figure 10.4: Opinion polls reported in Commission of the European Communities, *Eurobarometer*, 1988 and 1990, cf. note 59 above.

involvement in (and reaction to) the EC's 1992 programme in the period after 1987 originated in the trade union movement or in the interaction between SDP representatives and trade union officials. Likewise, the party's approach to the proposals for an Economic and Monetary Union was primarily determined by the wish to avoid national exclusion, to increase the reflationary potential of an EMU, and by the wish to bind the unifying Germany, reflecting the concern for the achievement or protection of general policy goals and not any enthusiasm for a single currency in the electorate at large.[61]

In sum, both electoral concerns and the concern for achievement of general policy goals have conditioned the way in which changes in the two parties' surroundings have translated into specific policy changes. However, vote-seeking has clearly been of greater importance in the British than in the Danish case, supporting the proposition, derived from Ström's arguments, that parties in the Westminster political system will be vote-seekers to a higher extent than parties in the Danish political system. Hence, as strategic interaction disappears in what is essentially a two-party system, legislative weight equals bargaining weight in the British system. Victory in the next general election becomes the fundamental prerequisite for the realisation of any intrinsically valued policy goals. In the Danish system, legislative weight does not necessarily equal bargaining weight. This provides parties with stronger incentives to pursue policy goals, with less regard being paid to whether this policy pursuit yields electoral support.

Furthermore, and in contrast to the implicit understanding of political parties in the economic approach as pure vote-seekers, it should be emphasised that general policy goals in the form of perceived interests of the parties' social basis have been crucial in setting the broader limits within which vote-seeking takes place. Thus, neither of the two parties have been willing or able to formulate policies which would conflict with the perceived interests of their social base, even if a broadened electoral appeal might have resulted.

The experiences of the Labour Party in the years prior to the 1983 general election also point to the possibility that perceptions as to what constitutes the best policy for maximising electoral support may vary

---

61) Commission of the European Community, *Eurobarometer* no. 34 of December 1990 records a clear majority in the Danish electorate against a single currency in the EC: 35% in favour, 50% against and 15% undecided.

widely in different parts of the party. The left wing's insistence on radical political and economic strategies in the early 1980s appears to derive from the fact that it actually believed in these strategies' potential electoral appeal. This last conclusion opens up the possibility that the imperative need for electoral support may be seen as less of a straitjacket for political parties than one might expect, as the belief in the power of persuasion and of rational argument enables a wider range of policies to be seen as electorally viable.

THE ANALYTICAL FRAMEWORK: FRUITFULNESS AND FLAWS

In analysing the dynamics of two parties' relationships with the EC this study has also tried to highlight the fruitfulness of studying social democratic EC policy using several basic assumptions about the nature of political parties in this context. In developing the propositions, the explanatory strengths of which have been evaluated above, it was assumed that social democratic parties are neither nationalist nor internationalist, but might instead be termed national-instrumental actors.

As we have defined this term here, national instrumentalism involves (1) that parties have a national social basis, and parties' patterns of general policy goals reflect the perceived common interests of this basis; (2) that the realisation of general policy goals is sought only for this national basis; (3) that parties seek to achieve their general policy goals at the most efficient institutional level, i.e., at the level where goal achievement for the national basis involves the lowest costs; and (4) that political parties are guided by a real rather than a formal understanding of international political institutions: such institutions are considered significant only insofar as they reflect real power structures or structures of interest.

As mentioned, the fruitfulness of this approach may be assessed by considering whether the propositions based on this conceptual foundation have provided a comprehensive understanding of the two parties' EC policies and their evolution.

The propositions pointing to (1) an internal dynamic of integration; (2) domestic developments; and (3) external events have enabled us to elucidate different aspects of the evolution of Labour and SDP positions towards the European Community. Thus, all three categories of factors were necessary in order to achieve a satisfactory understanding of the dynamics of policy change.

Learning Processes and Policy Development

This having been said, however, the analysis of the two parties' EC policies has pointed to a number of developments which cannot be understood as the product of one or more of the above-mentioned factors. Learning processes, in the form of the availability of what is perceived as new knowledge or as reflection upon the existing state of affairs on the basis of previous experiences, appear to have influenced both parties in various instances. Both the SDP's and Labour's willingness to consider the EMU have to some extent been influenced by the experiences of the Mitterrand administration in the 1980s and for the Danish SDP by the experiences with unilateral reflation in the mid-1970s. These events pointed to the necessity of international coordination of macroeconomic policies. Furthermore, the vain attempts to subsequently achieve coordinated reflation in Western Europe also increased the two parties' willingness to consider Economic and Monetary Union.

For the Labour Party, both the Wilson Government's change of policy on the EC in the second half of the 1960s and the rise of the party's left wing appear to be the result of learning processes as well. In the case of the Wilson Government, learning resulted from the failed attempts to implement the National Plan in light of the wish to preserve the parity of Sterling and its status as an international reserve currency. In the case of the ascendancy of Labour's left wing in the late 1970s and early 1980s, the experiences with the Wilson and Callaghan Governments during the 1970s and with the continued relative economic decline of Britain prompted a reconsideration of political and economic strategies.

The result of these learning processes were conflicting, however. Whereas the Wilson Government's experiences in the 1960s led it to endorse the policy of EC membership, the left's experiences and reformulation of strategies prompted it to adopt the opposite policy. The evidence from this study thus suggests that learning processes constitute a part of the ongoing political discourse on the development of society, a factor which may influence the relative strength and the contents of differing political discourses, but which does not point in any particular direction, as one might expect if taking an outset in the increasing rationalisation of society. Learning processes do not direct political behaviour towards a single definable goal.[62]

In the previously developed framework for analysis, learning must thus be added as a factor which may influence the development of specific party policies. Nevertheless, it should be emphasised that the possibility of learning processes does not in itself conflict with the propositions underlying the framework. Rather, it introduces the possibility that the behaviour of political actors is reflexive in the sense that it is affected by their *ex post* evaluation of prior implicit or explicit assumptions.

Nationalism, Internationalism, and Formalism

In contrast, both nationalism and internationalism conflict directly with the framework for analysis which has been applied here. The contents of Labour's and the SDP's EC policies are to a great extent understandable as instances of what we have termed national-instrumental behaviour. This is true in the sense that policy goal achievement has been sought only for the party's national social basis while little importance has been accorded the institutional level at which a given general policy goal is pursued. Regarding the last point, witness the remarks of the SDP's EC spokesman in 1971 on the future institutional development of the EC (quoted on page 177 above).

There are, however, some exceptions. In several instances, the Danish SDP motivated its specific policy proposals by invoking "international solidarity", by its desire to extend highly valued existing Danish regulation beyond Danish borders and to support the adoption of social democratic policies in other countries. However, where international solidarity has been invoked, such as with SDP appeals for EC minimum regulations on employee information and participation and in general for minimum labour market regulations in the EC framework, these calls have been entirely without costs for the SDP in terms of concrete interests of its national basis. As argued previously, wage levels,

---

62) For a generalised description of learning processes see Chris Argyris and Donald Schon, *Organizational Learning: A Theory of Action Perspective* (Reading, Mass.: Addison-Wesley, 1978). On learning processes in international relations see e.g. Peter M. Haas, "Do Regimes Matter? Epistemic Communities and Mediterranean Pollution Control", *International Organization*, vol. 43, no. 3 (Summer 1989), pp. 377-403.

employment opportunities, and general working conditions of Danish employees could only benefit from high EC-imposed standards in these areas, given the existence of relatively high Danish standards, and assuming that high standards in these areas constitute negative competitive parameters. Furthermore, it should be noted that in contrast to the Labour Party, the SDP never devoted much attention to strengthening the EC's regional policy, which would involve increased transfers from affluent to less affluent regions. The "internationalist" elements in the Danish SDP's EC policies have thus been of symbolic rather than of real importance.

Nationalist elements have been of somewhat greater significance. In the very earliest phases of both the British and Danish discussions on EC membership there is evidence of anti-German feeling having played a role for policy positions (cf. Robin's interpretation of Labour's policy of the five conditions in 1962-65 and the statements of trade union leader Rasmussen in 1961 in the Danish case). Furthermore, the reference in the early 1960s to cultural differences between Denmark and "the Six" as a reason to reject EC membership may be interpreted as a nationalist position, and trade union leader Alfred Petersen's rejection of supranationalism *per se* in April 1962 was clearly a nationalist argument. The SDP's EC spokesman's rejection of "harmonisation of our cultural and social life" and of a Single Market "in which the citizens must experience for themselves that they live in it" in mid-1988 (cf. page 216 above) also points to the existence of nationalist values. The idea of common policies or harmonisation in specific areas is opposed on the grounds that the institutional level at which such policies would be adopted is supranational. However, opposition to a "Citizens' Community" was motivated largely by the planned elimination of border controls in the EC and the presumed effects of open borders on the Danish welfare state, thus again highlighting a national-instrumental motivation.

Nationalist rejection of the principle of supranationality *per se* may also have played a certain role in the Labour Party's continued and growing hostility towards the EC during the 1970s and in the early 1980s. Yet it is difficult to isolate what we have defined as nationalist motivations from what is termed national-instrumental motivations in this respect, particularly as the call for EC withdrawal was always very closely connected with the perception that EC departure was necessary in order to implement the Alternative Economic Strategy. Nevertheless, the dissident cabinet members' motivation for objecting to continued

British EC membership in 1975, where membership meant "denying the British people the right to democratic self-government", points to a nationalist motivation: the argument implied that democracy must be confined to the nation-state and its institutions.

Neil Kinnock's persistent unwillingness to accept the principle of supranationality in his 1984 article, even after the inherent weaknesses of the AES had been demonstrated, may similarly be interpreted as nationalist, just as resistance to EC membership by leading Labour figures who were *not* attached to its left wing could suggest the presence of nationalist motivations.

In an overall evaluation, neither nationalism nor internationalism have constituted predominant features of the Labour Party's or the SDP's approach to the European Community, suggesting that in this respect, our framework for analysis has been a fruitful point of departure.[63]

In contrast, formalism in the two parties' understanding of international relations seems to at times have influenced their policies significantly. This is so especially regarding the Labour Party's policy of withdrawal from the EC in the period from 1980 to 1983. As we have argued, EC withdrawal, in order to allow the implementation of the AES, did not constitute a logically coherent policy. A policy involving systematic violation of the Rome Treaty's provisions on import controls and state subsidies to industry would have risked provoking retaliatory measures from other states, regardless of whether or not the violating state had formally subscribed to the Treaty's provisions.

In mistaking formal for real constraints on policy making, Labour's policy violated the assumption that parties accord importance to international institutions only to the extent that these reflect genuine underlying power structures or structures of interest. The policy of EC withdrawal in order to allow for the implementation of the AES constituted a projection of a national understanding of political institutions to the international level, a projection which failed to account for the distinct nature of international relations where no superior institution can guarantee compliance with treaties or other formal agreements. The policy reflected an understanding of national law which assumes punishment only as response to violations of formal rules.

---

63) For the Danish SDP this conclusion corresponds well with foreign minister Krag's complete rejection, in 1962, of trade union leader Alfred Petersen's nationalism.

We can suggest only tentative answers as to why this formalism came to dominate Labour's approach to the Community for several years. One explanation could be the grass roots character of the left wing ascendancy. The revolt against the established party leadership may have entailed involvement in the party's policy making process of persons unfamiliar with the realities of international politics, facilitating the projection of national understandings of political institutions to the international level.

A related explanation may account for the formalism in the EC policy exhibited by the Danish SDP. While this formalism was less important for the party's overall approach to the Community than was the case for Labour, it is nevertheless clearly present in the SDP's position on an EC Economic and Monetary Union in the EC. This was explicitly acknowledged by the EC spokesman in the May 1989 parliamentary debate where he objected to the German Bundesbank "formally becoming able to manage economic policy in Europe for in reality they unfortunately do that already" (cf. page * above).

This formalism cannot be ascribed to Ivar Nørgaard's own projection of national conditions to the international level, as he conceded the real influence of the Bundesbank regardless of formal international agreements. Moreover, as early as in the December 1971 parliamentary debate, Nørgaard had argued that Danish independence in exchange rate policy was purely formal and without any real content. Rather, his remarks could reflect an acknowledgement of the difficulties the party would be expected to have in explaining the difference between formal and substantive importance of international institutions to the public, especially as concerns the party's own EC-sceptical voters. It thus seems likely that the SDP leadership was fully aware of the hurdles it would face in making clear the real as opposed to the formal importance of any future reforms of the Rome Treaty, including the establishment of an EC Central Bank.[64]

In general, analysing the EC policies of Labour and the SDP using the basic assumptions summarised in the concept of national instrumentality

---

64) The difficulty in explaining the differences between the formal and the substantive importance of international agreements may also help to account for the gap in the late 1980s and early 1990s between the SDP parliamentary group's approach to the EC and its voters, most lucidly illustrated in the 1992 referendum on the Maastricht Treaty. In this connection, various opinion polls reported that between 61% and 67% of the SDP's voters voted against Danish ratification in spite of the party's recommendation. See Karen Siune, Palle Svennson, and Ole Tonsgaard, *Det blev et nej* (Aarhus: Politica, 1992), pp. 71-72.

has thus proved useful. The propositions emanating from in these assumptions have all been relevant for understanding different aspects of the development of the two parties' policies on the Community and its development. At the same time, however, the possibility of learning processes should be taken into account, and the assumption that parties operate using a real rather than a formal understanding of the significance of international institutions has proven wrong in several instances, at times leading the SDP and Labour to adopt policies and commence actions which conflict with national-instrumental behaviour.

11

Internal Dynamics and External Determinants in the EC Integration Process

The preceding chapter summarised the conclusions of the study and evaluated the fruitfulness of the analytical framework underlying it. This chapter places the findings in a wider perspective in two ways.

First, it relates the conclusions on factors affecting Labour and SDP EC policies to factors having influenced the policies of other social democratic parties in the European Community. Space does not permit a thorough analysis of other parties, but some tentative conclusions will be suggested and fruitful areas for future research proposed as we briefly discuss the EC policies of the French PS and the German SPD.

Second, we will relate the findings of this study to the general discussion on the dynamics of European integration. We have pointed to the existence of an internal dynamic in the integration process, even though both domestic and external developments have also been significant. How does this conclusion correspond to other studies of political developments within the EC? What is the validity of neofunctionalist and intergovernmental understandings of integration processes have in this connection?

Furthermore, to what extent do processes which appear external from the viewpoint of the Danish or British political systems actually constitute a direct or indirect result of regional market liberalisations or the actions of supranational bureaucracy? If important developments such as the movement towards the SEA and the proposal for an Economic and Monetary Union in the EC can be traced to the effects of foregoing regional market liberalisations or the actions of supranational bureaucracy, it suggests that the internal dynamic of integration is more far-reaching than the cases of the British Labour Party and the Danish SDP in themselves point to.

THE EC POLICIES OF THE FRENCH PS
AND THE GERMAN SPD

Since the overall development of the European Community depended on
the positions of the French and the (West) German Governments,
attention should be directed to the EC policies of the French Parti
Socialiste (PS) - prior to May 1969 the SFIO - and the German SPD. To
what extent have the policies of these two parties displayed the same
patterns as the British Labour Party and/or the Danish SDP? Does this
pattern point to the existence of an internal dynamic of integration?

The French Parti Socialiste and the EC

While conclusive evidence must await further research, the European
policy of the French Socialist Party certainly contains elements which can
be found in both Labour's and the SDP's approaches, just as the
dynamics of this policy displays in several respects a familiar pattern.

As described by Haas, the SFIO's initial response to the proposal for
the European Coal and Steel Community was sceptical. The party
ultimately accepted the treaty establishing it as a means of promoting
higher living standards, but the French misgivings were plentiful, and in
the party it was a widely held view that "everything must be done to
interpret the ECSC Treaty so as to permit special protection for French
coal production during the transitional period".[1] As opposed to this, the
EEC Treaty was eventually signed by the Socialist Government under
Guy Mollet, and during the remainder of the 1950s and in the early
1960s the SFIO maintained a centrist position and voiced few objections
as to the content of EC cooperation.[2]

This situation changed in 1969 with the replacement of the electorally
declining SFIO with the Parti Socialiste. Even if the more critical
approach of the PS to the Community, as illustrated in the 1973
"Common Programme of the Left", may to some extent be ascribed to the
influence of the French Communist Party (PCF), it is noticeable that the
programme contains positions much in line with the Labour Party's

---

1) Ernst B. Haas, *The Uniting of Europe*, p. 116.
2) Kevin Featherstone, *Socialist Parties and European Integration*, pp. 116-119.

policies in the 1970s. For example, it insists on the freedom to pursue the national policies deemed necessary as the representatives of the Left would seek to "preserve at the heart of the Common Market their liberty of action for the realisation of their political, economic, and social programme."[3] At the same time, however, the policies of the Left contained positions close to those formulated in the Danish SDP's 1973 policy report. As with the Danish SDP, the Programme stated the wish to make use of Community institutions for the furthering of the Left's general policy goals, pointing to a possible extension of the scope of existing supranational regulation. The left would

> "participate in the construction of the EEC, ... in its common policies seeking to free it from the domination of monopoly capital, democratising its institutions, supporting the workers' demands by orientating Community objectives in the direction of their interests."[4]

The European policy formulated at the party conference shortly before the first direct elections to the European Parliament in 1979 emphasised the critical approach to the EC. A resolution adopted here thus stated that "[t]here is no way that the present Common Market - the market of 'big capital interests' - can be acceptable to us. We want, rather, a Europe of working people." It also rejected more powers to the European Parliament. In adopting a "Socialist Project for France in the 1980s" the March 1980 PS National Convention reiterated the party's critical position towards the existing EC, concluding that the course of the Socialist Project required "the preservation of our room for manoeuvre as well as its extension" in the EC. Nevertheless, it also stressed the belief that fundamental change of the existing Community was possible:

> "Undoubtedly, the perspective of socialism is not the hallmark of the [Rome] Treaty ... [But] the realisation in France of a socialist project will be a shock to our European environment, which will cause it to be less marked by liberalism and Atlanticism. Engaged in the construction of a socialist society, France will contribute to the democratisation of the Community. She will utilise the institutions [in the struggle] against unemployment, for the reduction of working hours, for control of the multi-nationals, for the defence of liberties and the extension of democracy."[5]

---

3) *ibid.*
4) *Le Programme Commun de Gouvernement de la Gauche* (Paris: Flamarion, 1978), here quoted from Kevin Featherstone, *Socialist Parties and European Integration*, p. 119.
5) *Projet Socialiste Pour La France Des Années 80*, Paris: Club Socialiste de Livre, 1980, p. 352, here quoted from Kevin Featherstone, *Socialist Parties and European Integration*, p. 125.

Francois Mitterrand's programme prior to the 1980 presidential election also implicitly stressed the desire to preserve or a widen the national political-economic room for manoeuvre in the EC framework. His 120 pre-election "propositions" included the goal of "recapturing the home market", that is, halting import penetration and a subsequently rolling it back so as to reduce the share of trade in gross domestic product to 20 per cent by 1990. Presumably, however, this was to be achieved via an active industrial policy rather than direct protectionism, as the programme also pledged strict enforcement of the Treaty of Rome.[6]

The redistributional reflation launched by the Socialist Government when it took office quickly ran into trouble. It failed to achieve the promised results in terms of significantly reducing unemployment, and it was followed by a rapidly growing balance of payments deficit necessitating repeated devaluations of the Franc in the ERM. The Government responded with austerity measures in June 1982, but these proved insufficient in stemming the Franc's downward drift. The Mitterrand administration was faced with a choice between departure from the ERM and recourse to open protectionism in the form of import controls to improve the trade deficit, as advocated by the party's left wing, versus a full scale abandonment of the reflation. In March 1983 Mitterand decided in favour of continued membership in the ERM and agreed to the second wave of deflationary measures.[7]

Eleven months later, speaking to the European Parliament, Mitterand came out in favour of reforms of the Rome Treaty including the extension of majority voting procedures in the Council, thereby initiating the process which would lead to the adoption of the Single European Act.[8] Since this statement, the Socialist party's EC policy has persistently advocated strengthening of the "European construction", even if the original reservations on the role of the European Parliament have remained intact. As mentioned, it was the French Finance Minister Balladur who in 1987 took the initiative to a strengthening of European monetary integration,[9] just as the French Socialists have been among

---

6) Peter Holmes, "Broken Dreams: Economic Policy in Mitterrand's France", p. 35.
7) Peter Hall, *Governing the Economy*, pp. 199-202.
8) For an account of French EC policy from 1983 to 1986 see e.g. Andrew Moravczik, "Negotiating the Single European Act", pp. 29-30, and Hans-Peter Fröhlich, "Die französische Wirtschaftspolitik unter Präsident Mitterrand aus europäischer Perspektive".
9) Balladur's initiative was taken in the 1986-88 "cohabitation" period, for which reason the Finance Minister was a Conservative. Yet Mitterrand must clearly have known and approved the initiative.

the forces calling for a strong social dimension to the Single Market. Finally, French leadership was essential for convening the two inter-governmental conferences in December 1990.

The failure of the unilateral reflation in 1981-82 therefore seems to have had far-reaching consequences for the PS' relationship to the European Community. Whereas there are a number of reasons for this failure, the increasing openness of the French economy during the 1960s and 1970s contributed considerably, magnifying the reflation's import leaks and adding to balance of payments sensitivity. From 1960 to 1981 imports as a percentage of the French GDP nearly doubled, from 12.4% to 23.5%.[10] In this connection, it remains a clear possibility that this increased openness has followed from the long-standing French member-ship of the EC and its Common Market.

At the same time, French economic dependency on continued EC membership remained at a high level from the early 1970s and onwards, EC markets accounting for between 48.2% and 56.4% of total French exports.[11] As with the British Labour Party in the second half of the 1980s, acknowledged dependency on continued EC membership therefore seems likely to have influenced the Government's decision to reject comprehensive protectionist measures, as would have been necessary to sustain the reflation over a longer period of time.[12] In combination with the failure of the reflation, dependency on continued membership left the Socialists with few viable alternatives in its EC policy to a development of EC institutions and the content of EC regulation in the longer run so as to work to the benefit of the Parti Socialiste's general policy goals at the national level. This would again entail PS support for extended supranational regulation and decision capacity in several areas.

---

10) Cf. Organization for Economic Cooperation and Development, *OECD National Accounts*, vol. 1: *Main Aggregates, 1960-1990*, tables 13 and 18. The sensitivity of the balance of payments depends on the marginal import quota, but the average import quota provides a rough indication of the size of import leaks. Peter Hall, *Governing the Economy*, pp. 195-197; Peter Holmes, "Broken Dreams: Economic Policy in Mitterrand's France", pp. 37-48; Pierre-Alain Muet, "Economic Management and the International Environment, 1981-1983", in Howard Machin and Vincent Wright (eds.), *Economic Policy and Policy Making Under the Mitterrand Presidency 1981-1984* (London: Frances Pinter, 1985), pp. 70-84, all point to the current account effects of "Keynesianism in one country" as the main reason for the failure of the reflation. These effects would have been smaller in a more closed French economy.

11) Cf. *United Nations International Trade Statistics*, Yearbooks for 1974, 1977, and 1981. To this must be added French agricultural dependency on EC subsidies for exports to third countries.

12) However, the Government introduced some import controls in certain areas, just as state subsidies to the steel and textile industries provoked investigations from the EC Commission, cf. Michael Newman, *Socialism and European Unity*, p. 116.

To the extent that the unilateral reflation failed because of the structural effects of French EC membership, we can therefore identify an internal dynamic of integration in the case of the French PS. However, unlike the British case, this dynamic has not taken the form of steadily increasing dependency on access to EC export markets, as this dependency was already high in France. Rather, it seems likely that regional market liberalisations have increased the openness of the French economy, undermining the long-term viability of macroeconomic measures deviating in their trend from the international surroundings.[13]

Nevertheless, the Mitterrand Government's support for the SEA and the ensuing 1992 programme appears to conflict with our general expectation that social democratic parties will reject increased supranational market liberalising decision-making capacity.

While an explanation for this contradiction must remain tentative, it is clear that the Single Market was not Mitterrand's first priority. Neither was it seen as an end to itself. For the French leadership the SEA and "project 1992" rather constituted a first step towards a revitalisation of the EC, a necessary concession to the British Government in order to obtain its support, and a step to be followed by others such as further monetary integration and strengthened cooperation on other aspects of macroeconomic policy.

Most likely, the dynamism of "project 1992" has also increased pressure on the French Government to strengthen social regulation within the EC framework, suggesting that in this instance, as in the British and Danish cases, advancing regional market liberalisations may have led to calls for introducing majority decision-making in the Council in areas of market intervention. In this respect, there exists an internal dynamic of the integration process which is equally valid for the French PS, the British Labour and the Danish SDP.

At the same time, security political considerations have clearly played a significant role for president Mitterrand's European policies from 1989 and onwards. French EC policy in the period prior to the commencement of the two intergovernmental conferences in December 1990 is hardly understandable without taking into account German unification. As in other Western European states, unification lend an air of urgency to the

---

13) In terms of the proposition on the internal dynamic of integration, advancing regional market liberalisations may have undermined the efficiency of national policy instruments, prompting support for supranational replacements.

call for Economic and Monetary Union as a way to render Germany's commitment to supranational European structures irreversible.[14]

The EC Policy of the West German SPD

Security considerations in the form of historical experiences with national rivalries have influenced the EC policies of the German SPD to an even greater extent than the French PS. Thus, the SPD's initial rejection of the ECSC followed primarily from Kurt Schumacher's suspicion that the Schuman-Plan would become a vehicle for the rearmament of West Germany. At the same time, however, the SPD's rejection of the Treaty in the Bundestag was motivated among other things on the grounds that it would be difficult for any government to have an economic policy which was not ultimately dependent on the prior decisions of the High Authority, the ECSC's counterpart to the EC Commission.[15]

This last point is much in line with our general expectation that social democratic parties will initially adopt a sceptical position towards regional market liberalisation in a supranational framework on the grounds that it will stand in the way for national state interventionism.

When the ECSC Treaty had been ratified in 1952 in spite of the SPD's vote, the party gradually increased its support for the Coal and Steel Community, and by late 1954 the SPD was pressing for more, not less, power for the High Authority in the areas of investment, social affairs, and full employment policies.[16] However, whereas this development clearly reflected the wish to make use of supranational institutions for the furthering of the party's general policy goals at the national level, thereby paralleling subsequent developments in the Danish SDP's and the British Labour Party's EC policies, the SPD's growing commitment to European integration - its increasing acknowledged dependency on membership in supranational organisations - was not a structural economic dependency directly or indirectly reflecting the effects of regional market liberalisations. Rather, it reflected an emerging belief in

---

14) For an account and analysis of French foreign policy in 1989, see e.g. Ole Wæver, "Three Competing Europes: French, German, Russian", *Foreign Affairs*, vol. 66, no. 3 (July 1990), pp. 481-484.

15) William Paterson, *The SPD and European Integration*, pp. 61-65.

16) William Paterson, *The SPD and European Integration*, p. 118, and Ernst B. Haas, *The Uniting of Europe*, p. 137.

the possibility that supranational European institutions could provide a
bulwark against a repetition of the monstrosities of two world wars. This
belief was in itself important for the party leadership. Moreover, it meant
that the European ideal was tremendously popular in the German
population, providing strong incentives for the SPD leadership to change
its course for electoral reasons.[17]

The growing SPD commitment to European integration was also
reflected in the party's positions on the EEC Treaty, the ratification of
which it decided to support in July 1957. While the party maintained
certain reservations, calling for more ambitious goals regarding common
monetary, financial and investment policies than what was the case in
the Rome Treaty, support for the Common Market was overwhelming.[18]

Following the establishment of the EC, one of the SPD's primary goals
became a strengthening of the Assembly's - later the European
Parliament's - authority in the system, just as it criticised President de
Gaulle's notions of European cooperation for its lack of supranationality.
In the late 1960s it was the SPD's leader Willy Brandt who, as a member
of the Grand Coalition Government, put forward proposals for an
Economic Union in the Community as well as for the development of
foreign policy cooperation between the EC states, repeating them in his
second Governmental Declaration of January 1973.[19] Even if these
initiatives were vaguely phrased, they served to indicate the SPD's
enduring support for the EC and for a strengthening of the Community
framework in the longer term.

The SDP's policies on the EC have been fairly constant since then.
Both in the 1979 and 1984 European Parliament elections the party
expressed support for more powers to the EP. In 1984 the SDP also
pressed for institutional reforms which would increase the Council's
decision-making efficiency, and in connection with the July 1985 meeting
of the European Council in Milan the faction leader of the SPD, Hans
Jochen Vogel, stated that

> "[w]e want the European Council ... to make progress with the Draft Treaty
> of the European Parliament. ... We are in favour of the introduction of a
> comprehensive internal market [and we] are in favour of steps being made
> towards having a European currency."[20]

---

17) William Paterson, *The SPD and European Integration*, pp. 119-120.
18) *ibid.*, p. 127.
19) Kevin Featherstone, *Socialist Parties and European Integration*, p. 154.
20) Hans Jochen Vogel in *Deutscher Bundestag*, 149. Sitzung, July 1985, cols. 11088-11093.

Consequently, the party voted for the ratification of the SEA, although critical voices were raised against the small increases in the powers of the EP. Since 1987, the SPD has been one of the driving forces behind a social dimension to the Single Market.[21] Similarly, it has persistently voiced support for an Economic and Monetary Union on condition that it rests on an independent Central Bank, as this theme became topical again from 1988. The 1989 Eastern European revolutions and the unification of the two German states in 1990 only served to strengthen the SPD's commitment to enhanced EC cooperation.[22]

Thus, since the late 1950s the SPD has been a consistent supporter of strengthening the EC in a wide range of areas. It is difficult to avoid the conclusion that national historical experiences and, hence, security political concerns constitute the fundamental explanation for the SPD's staunch EC support. Nowhere has the legitimacy of the nation-state been so severely questioned as in West Germany after the Second World War, and nowhere has the idea of European unification been so inextricably bound up with questions of peace and internationalism.

The security political approach to the EC is also reflected in the fact that Brandt's proposals for economic and monetary union in 1969 were meant to balance his Ostpolitik, aiming at reassuring France and West Germany's other neighbours of the German Government's continued will to be bound by supranational structures and to avoid German isolation, possibly in the form of unification of the two Germanies in return for neutrality.[23] Similarly, the party's growing emphasis on the need to strengthen the EC in the wake of the East European revolutions and the threat of a new nationalism as a consequence testifies to a security political understanding of the EC's nature and characteristics.

It should be noted, however, that the strength of the West German economy has been a key factor which allowed the SPD to adopt such strongly positive positions on European integration. In the 1970s and early 1980s, the SDP was not facing the kinds of economic problems as

---

21) See for example Entschließungsantrag der Fraktion der SPD zur Erklärung der Bundesregierung zum Europäischen Rat in Kopenhagen, *Deutscher Bundestag*, Drucksache 11/1487, 9 December 1987, and Antrag der Fraktion der SPD, Europapolitik, *Deutscher Bundestag*, Drucksache 11/3851, 19 January 1989.

22) Cf. for instance Peter Glotz, "Gesamteuropa - Skizze für einen schwierigen Weg", *Europa Archiv*, vol. 45, no. 3 (January 1990), pp. 41-51. Peter Glotz is one of the SPD's leading foreign policy spokesmen.

23) Loukas Tsoukalis, *The Politics and Economics of European Monetary Integration* (London: Allen and Unwin, 1977), p. 85, cites this factor among others in explaining Brandt's proposals.

the British Labour Party or the French PS. Hence, fundamental questions on alternative political-economic strategies for economic recovery which might have brought the German state into conflict with its EC partners and with the formal EC framework were not raised.[24]

The ongoing Single Market programme undoubtedly caused concerns in the German trade union movement in the late 1980s, prompting SPD pressure to strengthen EC social and environmental legislation. Those mechanisms shown to have been significant for the Danish SDP in this respect may have been important for the German SPD as well, indicating the existence of a certain internal dynamic of integration in the German case. However, given the SPD's positive attitudes towards increased supranationality in the EC prior to the launch of "project 1992", this dynamic appears of limited significance.

In contrast to the early propositions of Ernst Haas there is therefore little evidence suggesting the presence of an internal dynamic of integration in the case of the West German SPD. The party's support for a social dimension to the Single Market may be the exemption from the general conclusion that direct or indirect security political concerns have provided the main impetus for the SPD's EC policy. In combination with the unique characteristics of the West German economy this leads us to see the SPD as a special case when compared to the British Labour Party, the Danish SDP and the French PS.

THE DYNAMICS OF EC INTEGRATION

Beyond doubt, the two main developments of the EC in the 1980s and early 1990s have been the reform of the Rome Treaty embodied in the Single European Act and the agreement in the Maastricht Treaty to move towards Economic and Monetary Union.

What factors have prompted these developments? To what extent does an analysis suggest that evolutions, which appear as external when seen from Denmark and Britain, result from preceding regional market liberalisations or the influence of supranational political actors? If supranational actors or the effects of regional market liberalisations have

---

24) Even the left wing of the SPD has remained committed to German EC membership and a future strengthening of the Community. Among other things, the EC is seen as the only possible mechanism for controlling multinational corporations, cf. William Paterson, *The SPD and European Integration*, pp. 146-147.

prompted these reforms, it indicates that the internal dynamic of integration is more far-reaching than suggested in the comparison of the British Labour Party's and the Danish SDP's EC policies.

The SEA: Political Actors and Underlying Trends

The debate on the causes behind the adoption of the Single European Act has shed light on the course of developments and on the structural conditions within which negotiations on Rome Treaty reform took place in 1984-85, enabling us to draw some tentative conclusions.

Several earlier studies of the SEA process pointed to the direct and indirect importance of actions taken by the EC Commission, the influence of transnational corporate networks, specifically the so-called European Roundtable of Industrialists, and the initiatives of the European Parliament as factors pushing EC governments towards reforms.[25] Sandholz and Zysman and others call attention to a number of structural economic and domestic political changes which facilitated the movement towards the SEA. These factors include the poor performance of the EC economies in the early 1980s compared to Japan and the USA, the widening technology gap between the same economies, and the weakness of the European Left from the first years of the decade and onwards.

Nevertheless, great significance is accorded to the actions of supranational political actors. The Commission is viewed as the single most important political actor in the process leading to the adoption of the EC's internal market plans, acting as a political entrepreneur and providing crucial leadership in various respects. The Commission is also seen to have acted indirectly through the transnational organisation of the European Roundtable of Industrialists, as it was involved in the very creation of this body of heads of European multinationals and continuously accorded its positions high priority.[26]

Although Sandholz and Zysman criticize the neofunctionalist approach to regional integration processes, the interpretations they offer are hence compatible with neofunctional propositions in all but minor respects: the

---

25) E.g. Wayne Sandholz and John Zysman, "1992: Recasting the European Bargain", World Politics, vol. 42, no. 1 (October 1989), pp. 95-128; Peter Nedergaard, EFs Markedsintegration (Copenhagen: DJØF and DUPI, 1989); and Peter Ludlow, Beyond 1992: Europe and Its Western Partners (Brussels: Center for European Policy Studies, 1989), esp. pp. 27-30.

26) Wayne Sandholz and John Zysman, "1992: Recasting the European Bargain", pp. 113-118.

presence and behaviour of supranational actors is ultimately at the core of their explanation (cf. also figure 3.1 on p. 43 above).[27]

While the importance of the Commission and of transnational corporate networks remains to some extent an unresolved empirical question, Moravcsik has argued convincingly that the main impetus for the process toward the SEA came from the French Government's policy change in 1984. As the German-backed French initiative threatened British exclusion, it extracted willingness from the Thatcher Government to endorse increased use of majority decision-making in the Council in one important area, namely regarding the EC's Single Market. The British Conservatives wanted to open the markets of the other EC states for its highly competitive banking and insurance sectors.

Where Sandholz and Zysman argue that the decisive event at the level of political actors in the process towards the SEA was the Commission's publication of its White Paper on the Single Market in June 1985, Moravcsik thus points to the fact that the British Government, in reaction to French-German moves towards EC reforms, had put forward proposals for further liberalisation of trade, particularly in services, as early as at the Fontainebleau European Council in June 1984. Notably, these proposals included a deadline for these trade liberalisations to be accomplished.[28]

Seen in this light, French leadership was pivotal for the initiation of the reform process, but the result of the negotiations reflected the minimum common denominator emerging from intergovernmental bargaining, as British preferences prevailed in all but a few respects.

The high profile of the EC Commission in subsequent developments is also traceable to a government policy change; namely, Mitterrand's wish to support a *relance européenne*. It was this decision which led him to nominate political heavy weight Jacques Delors as President of the Commission in late 1984. The European Roundtable of Industrialists is not seen to have been of any importance, as it did not participate in the Single Market debate until more than a year after the French presidency.[29]

In this context, it can hardly be maintained that supranational or transnational actors have had more than a very limited influence on the

---

27) This point has also been noted by Andrew Moravcsik in "Negotiating the Single European Act", p. 24.
28) *ibid.*, pp. 34-44.
29) *ibid.*, pp. 45-46.

course of developments leading to the launch of the Community's "1992-programme". In evaluating the SEA process we can therefore reject the validity of that part of neofunctionalist integration theory which emphasises the importance of such actors.[30]

As we have seen, however, the actions of supranational political actors are only one of two fundamental variables cited in neofunctionalist theory as pushing forward the process of relocation of activities and expectations and leading to increased supranationality.

The other is constituted by regional market liberalisations and the effects of such liberalisations on the perceptions and behaviour of national or transnational political actors. As we have argued, it remains a clear possibility that the French Government's decisive U-turn on reforms of the EC in 1984 followed from the failure of national economic-political strategies. This failure may be traced to the increasing openness of the French economy following two decades of membership in the EC's Common Market.

EMU: Actors and Structures

The same complex pattern of structural economic developments and intergovernmental bargaining processes characterised the process towards the agreement in the Maastricht Treaty on the establishment by 1999 of an Economic and Monetary Union in the EC. In addition, however, broader security political concerns have clearly influenced developments to a much greater extent than was the case for the SEA.

The first steps in the 1980s towards closer monetary integration in the Community were taken in the Basel-Nyborg agreement of September 1987. This agreement constituted a reaction to the perceived effects of progressing liberalisations of capital movements in the Community. As has been argued, these liberalisations have resulted partly from the EC's Single Market programme, and the Basel-Nyborg agreement, achieved after French pressure, served to strengthen the credit facilities of the ERM. This again enhanced the ability of national monetary authorities to withstand speculative pressures, the risks of which were seen to grow

---

30) Moravcsik terms that aspect of neofunctionalist theory pointing to the importance of supranational political actors "supranational institutionalism".

following capital liberalisations.[31] When French Finance Minister Balladur in January 1988 reopened the discussion on a further strengthening of monetary integration in the EC, it was primarily a consequence of the perceived inadequacies of the functioning of the existing EMS, inadequacies amplified by the gradual liberalisation of capital movements. The French Government was dissatisfied with the dominance of the German Bundesbank in the system and with the excessively deflationary monetary policies it was seen to impose on other member states, given high and growing capital mobility and a preference for stable exchange rates.

Balladur's proposal was warmly endorsed by the governments of Italy, Belgium, and the Netherlands, but initially the German Government's response was mixed and affected by internal divisions. Foreign Minister Genscher quickly answered approvingly to the French initiative, but Finance Minister Stoltenberg waited four weeks before acknowledging Balladur's speech. The Economics Minister, Martin Bangemann, eventually endorsed the French proposal in principle, but the president of the Bundesbank made clear that EMU could only be a long term objective and that it would require an independent central bank. In February 1988 the West German cabinet finally adopted a position which was close to the Bundesbank's. At the June 1988 European Council in Hanover, the emerging agreement resulted in the creation of the Delors Committee for the study of economic and monetary union.[32]

Even though the German position at this point contained only qualified support for monetary union in the EC, it nevertheless signified a remarkable turnabout in West German foreign economic policy, until then characterised by staunch rejection of institutional reforms in the monetary area.

The German Government's willingness to endorse monetary union was further enhanced as the East European revolutions shook the European political landscape and opened up the possibility of early German reunification. In response to French calls for a speed-up of monetary integration from October 1989 Chancellor Kohl agreed to a rapid

31) Hans B. Feddersen, "Det indre marked og EF's monetære integration", *Politica*, vol. 21, nr. 4, 1989, pp. 416-417.
32) Cf. Hans B. Feddersen, "Det indre marked og EF's monetære integration", pp. 419-420, and David M. Andrews, "From Ad Hoc to Institutionalized Coordination and Beyond: Twenty Years of European Monetary Integration". Paper presented at the Inaugural Pan-European Conference, organised by the ECPR's Standing Group on International Relations, Heidelberg, September 1992, pp. 29-33.

convening of an intergovernmental conference on EMU, and the German Government remained firmly committed to monetary union throughout the negotiations leading to the Maastricht Treaty, while insising on an independent central bank with the overriding objective of maintaining price stability.[33] Given the fact that Germany was the state in Western Europe which had the most substantive monetary autonomy to surrender in the establishment of an Economic and Monetary Union, the intergovernmental bargaining processes in the negotiation of the Maastricht Treaty subsequently meant that the EMU would reflect fundamental German preferences in all areas of importance.

Security political concerns have thus been of considerable significance in the process towards the political agreement on Economic and Monetary Union in the EC. The turning point was the West German Government's decision, in early 1988, to endorse institutional reforms in the monetary area in principle. In the most reasonable interpretation, this decision was aimed at balancing the Federal Republic's very active policy towards the Soviet Union and Eastern Europe and hence to reassure its West European partners of West Germany's continued commitment to multilateral and supranational European structures.

In this sense ,there are very clear parallels between Brandt's Ost-politik and his proposal for economic union in 1969 on the one hand, and Genscher's and Kohl's Ostpolitik and their endorsement of movement towards EMU in 1988 on the other.[34] The marked strengthening of West German support for EMU during 1989 also serves as evidence of the importance of security political developments.[35]

We may also identify other developments which have enhanced pressures for monetary union. First, given the strong credibility of the Deutsche Mark on international financial markets, the liberalisation of capital movements in the Community has limited the national monetary policy autonomy for the non-German ERM member states. This appears to have been important for the original French initiative on EMU in early 1988.

---

33) *ibid.*, pp. 29-35; and Jonathan Story, "The Launching of the European System of Central Banks". Paper prepared for the European Consortium for Political Research, workshop on National Political Systems and the European Community, Essex 1991, pp. 5-12.

34) This interpretation is also offered in Hans B. Feddersen, "Det indre marked og EF's monetære integration".

35) Cf. David M. Andrews, "From Ad Hoc to Institutionalized Coordination and Beyond", pp. 32-33.

Second, it should also be emphasised that the economic rationale for monetary union in the EC has grown during the past two decades. The openness of the EC economies has increased markedly (cf. table 11.1), entailing growing inflationary risk from currency instability as rising import prices will have greater effects on the overall national economy.

Dependency on trade has also increased in the EC (cf. table 11.2), providing additional incentives for fixed exchange rates. Thus, growing trade dependency means that the damaging effects of foreign currency fluctuations on exports become increasingly important. Evidently, monetary union is the ultimate, though not the only viable solution to problems of currency instability.

Table 11.1: Imports as Percentage of GDP. Unweighted Average for the EC12 Member States.[36]

1960	1972	1989
24.5	27.0	37.5

Table 11.2: Exports as Percentage of GDP. Unweighted Average for the EC12 Member States.

1960	1972	1989
23.3	26.3	37.8

Finally, during the 1980s the EC states have become increasingly dependent on imports specifically from other EC states and on exports to other EC members. From 1980 to 1989 the average EC share of total imports increased from 49.7% to 59.8% for the twelve member states of European Community. The average EC share of total exports increased in the same period from 57.9% to 63.1%[37] This trend renders the existence of stability between the currencies of the Community states particularly advantageous.[38]

---

36) Sources in table 11.1 to 11.4: Organization for Economic Cooperation and Development, *OECD National Accounts*, vol. 1: *Main Aggregates, 1960-1990*, tables 13, 17, and 18.

37) Unweighted average for the EC12 member states, computed from United Nations, *International Trade Statistics*, Yearbook 1989. Belgium and Luxembourg have been treated as one economy in the calculations.

38) Jan Fagerberg, "Nedgangen i EFs samhandelsgrad etter 1973", *Internasjonal Politikk*, vol. 48, no. 1 (March 1990), pp. 99-109, notes that the EC6 share of the EC6 states' total trade fell in 1973-84. Yet from 1984 this share has been rising again, and for the enlarged EC the decrease in EC6 trade is more than offset by increasing trade with and among new member states.

To the extent that these three structural developments are traceable to the effects of the EC's Common Market, we may, thus, identify a neofunctionalist dynamic in which regional market liberalisations have strengthened incentives for further supranationality in the monetary area.

Clearly, the above-mentioned developments have not been sufficient causes for the agreement on EMU, but equally clearly they have enabled the the EMU project to constitute an attractive objective. Without them, the proposals for monetary union would not have been even remotely realistic.

Understanding European Integration

In placing the case studies of the Danish SDP's and the British Labour Party's EC policies in a wider perspective, this chapter has analysed the relevance of conclusions from these two cases to other social democratic parties in the EC. It has been especially important whether the cases of the French PS and the German SPD suggest that there is an internal dynamic of integration in which regional market liberalisations shape the political and economic strategies perceived as viable to social democratic parties, eventually leading them to support increased supranationality in the EC.

The chapter has also tried to establish the extent to which important developments such as the adoption of the Single European Act and the the Maastricht EMU agreement have followed from the effects of regional market liberalisations or the actions of supranational political actors. This is important insofar as the study of Labour and the SDP has until now proceeded from the implicit assumption that both developments should be seen as external and, hence, not related the effects of the existing EC.

The analysis of the EC policy of the German SPD provided no evidence of any internal dynamic of the integration process. Rather, the persistently positive approach of the SPD towards the principle of supranationality and towards increased supranationality in the EC from the late 1950s appears directly and indirectly appears to have resulted from its security political understanding of the Community. This understanding again presumably follows from Germany's experiences with nationalism and national rivalries.

In contrast to the SPD "exception", the case of the French PS has in several respects highlighted dynamics of policy change which resemble the Danish and particularly the British case. The tension between the EC's limitations on national state intervention in the economy and the desire of the PS to pursue the interventionist policies deemed necessary characterised the party's reluctant approach to the Community in the 1970s. As the unilateral reflation of 1981-83 became unsustainable, the party shied away from a general recourse to open protectionism, a fact which points to an acknowledged dependency on continued French EC membership. Subsequently, the Mitterrand administration attempted to revitalise the Community so as to benefit the achievement of the party's general policy goals at the national level in the longer run, much in line with the development of the Labour Party's EC policy in the second half of the 1980s.

However, it was not any growing dependency on EC membership which led the PS to adopt a constructive approach to the EC, as this dependency had long been present. Rather, it was the failed reflation in itself which appeared to convince President Mitterrand of the necessity of supranational strategies. The question of whether we can identify an internal dynamic of integration in the French case therefore hinges on whether EC membership and the EC's regional market liberalisations contributed to the failure of the French reflation.

The same question is crucial when evaluating the nature of the process towards the Single European Act. Thus, as Moravcsik has argued, the SEA reform was not a direct or indirect consequence of the actions of supranational political actors. Rather, it reflected the French policy U-turn of 1984, which recreated the Bonn-Paris axis for a strengthening of the EC framework.

As for the process towards the agreement on Economic and Monetary Union in the EC, the decisive event was the German Government's endorsement in principle of the project in early 1988. This policy change appears primarily as the result of a perceived need to balance West Germany's very active foreign policy towards the Soviet Union and Eastern Europe, aimed at reassuring France and Germany's other neighbours of the Government's continued commitment to the EC. Broad security political considerations were therefore at the nucleus of the decision.

Nevertheless, the initial French proposal for Economic and Monetary Union appears partly as the result of the progressive liberalisation of the

French regulations on capital movements, a development which eroded the French Government's monetary autonomy. It is therefore also important whether the French capital liberalisations constituted an independent national measure, as with Britain and Denmark, or whether they have been an integral part of the EC's market liberalisations in which case we can identify an internal dynamic of integration.

Finally, structural economic developments in the EC have constituted necessary though not sufficient conditions for the EMU proposal to be even remotely attractive for national political actors. Increased openness and dependency on trade, as well as increased dependency on trade specifically with other EC states, have added to the incentives for monetary union. To the extent that these developments have resulted from EC market liberalisations, there appears to be operating an integrative dynamic which is internal to the process.

Regarding the French liberalisation of capital movements, this clearly constituted an integral part of the ongoing 1992 process of EC market liberalisations. Thus, the French Gvernment did not agree to the important 4th EC directive on capital liberalisations until after the Basel-Nyborg agreement on a strengthening of the EMS, and only after German pressure.[39] To the degree that diminished national monetary autonomy following these capital liberalisations constituted the main motivation for the Balladur proposal, there is, therefore, an internal dynamic of integration here.

Furthermore, there is evidence that the EC's Common Market has had an independent effect on the increased openness of the French economy, as well as on the more general structural economic developments constituting necessary preconditions for an Economic and Monetary Union As for the openness of the EC states' economies, particularly important for the failure of the French reflation and thereby eventually for the adoption of the SEA, the data in table 11.3 indicate that the average openness has increased significantly more in the EC than in other Western European states, or in North America and Japan from 1972 to 1989.

As for increased trade dependency in general and dependency on trade with other EC states in particular, and regarding the growing importance of imports from other EC states, the data in table 11.4, 11.5 and 11.6 also suggest that the EC's regional market liberalisations have had an impact.

---

39) Hans B. Feddersen, "Det indre marked og EF's monetære integration", p. 417.

The average export share of GDP, the share of total imports from EC states, and the share of total exports to EC states have increased more in the EC10 or EC12 member states than elsewhere in the OECD-area.[40] The last point is particularly significant in relation to the case of the British Labour Party as it indicates that growing dependency on exports to other EC states is not restricted to Britain following British EC membership.

Table 11.3: Unweighted Average Change in States' Import Share of GDP, Percentage Points.[41]

	EC10	EC12	EFTA5	US+Can+Jap
1972-89	11.3	10.5	4.6	3.5

Table 11.4: Unweighted Average Change in States' Export Share of GDP, Percentage Points.

	EC10	EC12	EFTA5	US+Can+Jap
1972-89	12.3	11.5	4.8	2.4

Table 11.5: Unweighted Average Growth in EC12 Share of States' Total Imports, Percentage Points.[42]

	EC10	EC12	EFTA5	US+Can+Jap
1980-89	7.1	10.1	2.9	4.5

Table 11.6: Unweighted Average Growth in EC12 Share of States' Total Exports, Percentage Points.

	EC10	EC12	EFTA5	US+Can+Jap
1980-89	3.2	5.2	1.6	-1.1

The overall picture of the European integration process emerging from the study of four social democratic parties and the SEA and EMU agreements is complex. The analysis has suggested that security political

40) Jeffrey J. Schott, "Trading Blocks and the World Trading System", *World Economy*, vol. 21, no. 4, 1991, pp. 1-17, contains additional data on the growing importance of intra-EC trade.

41) EFTA5 is Norway, Sweden, Finland, Austria, and Switzerland. Data from Iceland has been omitted due to the small size of its economy. EC12 data includes data from Spain and Portugal, excluded from the EC10 figure. Spain and Portugal entered the EC on 1 January 1986. The openness of the French economy increased 7.2 percentage points from 1972 to 1989.

42) Computed from United Nations, *International Trade Statistics*, Yearbook 1989. Belgium and Luxembourg have been treated as one economy in the calculations.

conceptions of the EC are important for the Community's development. Moreover, intergovernmental bargaining shapes the contents of fundamental reforms of the EC framework. However, we must also direct attention to the significance of internal dynamics of integration and the validity of neofunctionalist propositions on international integration processes which this implies.

Existing evidence suggests that the presence and behaviour of supranational political actors has not been very important for the development of the EC in the 1980s and early 1990s, leading to the conclusion that this aspect of neofunctionalist theory has little explanatory power. In contrast, there is evidence that the second fundamental variable of the neofunctional theory, regional market liberalisations, has indeed been important for the way in which the EC has evolved.

As we have seen, the growing British economic dependency on continued EC membership has contributed significantly to the Labour Party's final acceptance of the Community as the regional framework within which to operate, entailing the party's support for extended supranational regulation in new policy areas. This has already had consequences for British EC policy and could be even more significant for the long term. The growing British dependency on trade with other EC states has again to a high extent resulted from the existence of the Community's Common Market.

Secondly, increased supranational decision-making capacity on regional market liberalisations led both the British Labour Party and the Danish SDP to endorse increased supranational decision-making capacity in areas of market intervention, specifically as a reaction to the Community's 1992-programme. Pressures from these two political parties as well as from significant political forces in other member states eventually led to the provisions in the Maastricht Treaty on majority decision-making procedures on minimum regulation for working conditions and employee rights as well as on aspects of environmental protection.

Third, this chapter has pointed to the importance of structural effects of the Community's Common Market for the EC policy of the French PS. Conclusive evidence must await further research, but the growing openness of the French economy in the 1970s clearly contributed to the failure of the unilateral reflation launched by the PS administration. It seems likely that it was this failure which was the single most important factor prompting President Mitterrand to endorse reforms of the EC. The growing openness of the French economy was most likely partly the result of France's long-standing EC membership. Indirectly, then, regional market liberalisations contributed to the pressures leading to the adoption of the SEA.

Fourth, the growing openness of the EC states' economies as well as these states' increasing dependency on trade in general and with other EC states in particular have constituted a necessary though not sufficient condition for an Economic and Monetary Union in the EC to constitute an attractive objective for national political actors. There is evidence that this growing openness and trade dependency has followed not least from the EC's partial - and in the second half of the 1980s deepening - Common Market.

Finally, increasing liberalisation of capital movements in the EC has contributed to pressures for Economic and Monetary Union. In particular this appears to have been of importance for the French proposal on further monetary integration in the EC in early 1988. These liberalisations have in some cases followed from the Community's 1992 programme, even though the British and Danish cases illustrate that capital liberalisations were also implemented independently at the national level in the early 1980s.

The neofunctionalist approach to regional integration should not be dismissed as irrelevant, as was done almost universally in the 1970s and early 1980s. The neofunctional model clearly cannot account for all developments of European integration, as security concerns - which are not an integral part of the neofunctionalist approach - have been shown to be of considerable importance. Similarly, threats of national exclusion and intergovernmental minimum common denominator bargaining have to a large extent determined the specific content of EC reforms. Nevertheless, regional market liberalisations appear to have shaped the incentives and perceptions of available viable policy options for important national political actors, inducing them to support additional supranationality. Not least of all there appears to be long-term structural effects of a Common Market between a number of nation-states working in this direction.[43] For obvious reasons, such effects of regional market

---

43) With some concepts from international relations theory, there seems to be a connection between economic integration, regional interdependence and political integration in Western Europe: economic integration creates growing economic interdependence, which in turn strengthens incentives for further political supranationality. For a discussion of the relation

liberalisations played no role in the original neofunctionalist framework, focusing as it did on the level of political actors, and confining itself to a limited time horizon.

---

between interdependence theory and neofunctionalism see Jens Henrik Haahr, "Regional Integration Theory: Contents and Current Relevance", working paper (Aarhus: Institute of Political Science, 1991).

BIBLIOGRAPHY

BOOKS AND ARTICLES

Allsopp, Christopher, "The Political Economy of EMS", *Revue Economique*, vol. 30, no. 5, 1979, pp. 866-894.

Andersen, Ole et al., *EF: Hvad Nu? Et debatoplæg til en Socialdemokratisk EF-politik*, Copenhagen: Forlaget SOC, 1973.

Andrews, David M., "From Ad Hoc to Institutionalized Coordination and Beyond: Twenty Years of European Monetary Integration". Paper presented at the Inaugural Pan-European Conference, organised by the ECPR's Standing Group on International Relations, Heidelberg, September 1992.

Argyris, Chris and Donald Schon, *Organizational Learning: A Theory of Action Perspective*, Reading, Mass.: Addison-Wesley, 1978.

Auken, Svend, "Det politiske system og gennemførelsen af det indre marked", *Politica*, vol. 21, no. 4, November 1989, pp. 424-430.

Axelrod, Robert, *Conflict of Interest*, Chicago: Markham, 1970.

Bacon, Richard, Wynne Godleay and Alister McFarquhar, "The Direct Costs to Britain of Belonging to the EEC", in *Cambridge Economic Policy Review*, no. 4, March 1978, pp. 44-49.

Benn, Tony, *Arguments for Socialism*, London: Jonathan Cape, 1979.

Beyme, Klaus von, "Theoretische Probleme der Parteienforschung", *Politische Vierteljahresschrift*, vol. 24, no. 3, October 1983, pp. 241-252.

Boyer, Robert, "Defensive or Offensive Flexibility?" in R. Boyer ed., *The Search for Labour Market Flexibility*, pp. 222-251.

Boyer, Robert, "The Search for New Wage/Labour Relations" in R. Boyer ed., *The Search for Labour Market Flexibility*, pp. 252-273.

Boyer, Robert, ed., *The Search for Labour Market Flexibility*, Oxford: Oxford University Press, 1988.

Boxhoorn, A., J. Th. Leersen and M. Spiering eds., *Britain in Europe*, Yearbook of European Studies no. 1, Amsterdam: Rodopi, 1988.

Bradley, Ian, *Breaking the Mould? The Birth and Prospects of the Social Democratic Party*, Oxford: Martin Robertson, 1981.

Budge, Ian and Michael Laver, "Office Seeking and Policy Pursuit in Coalition Theory", *Legislative Studies Quarterly*, vol. 11, no. 4, November 1986, pp. 485-506.

Bulmer, Simon, "Domestic Politics and European Policy Making", *Journal of Common Market Studies*, vol. 11, no. 4, December 1983, pp. 349-363.

Butler, David and Uwe Kitzinger, *The 1975 Referendum*, London: Macmillan, 1976.

Butler, David and David Marquand, *European Elections and British Politics*, Harlow: Longman, 1981.

Butler, David and Dennis Kavanagh, *The British General Election of 1983*, London: Macmillan, 1984.

Butler, David and Paul Jowett, *Party Strategies in Britain. A Study of the 1984 European Elections*, London: Macmillan, 1985.

Buzan, Barry et al., *The European Security Order Recast*, London: Pinter Publishers, 1990.

Buzan, Barry, *People, States, and Fear: An Agenda for International Security Studies in the Post-Cold War Era*, 2nd ed., Hemel Hampstead: Wheatsheaf, 1991.

Byrd, Peter, "The Labour Party and the European Community 1970-1975", *Journal of Common Market Studies*, vol. 13, no. 4, June 1975, pp. 469-483.

Camps, Miriam, *Britain and the European Community 1955-63*, London: Oxford University Press, 1964.

Coates, David, *Labour in Power?* London: Longman, 1981.

Cripps, Francis, Martin Fetherston, and Terry Ward, "The Effects of Different Strategies for the UK Economy", in *Cambridge Economic Policy Review*, no. 4, March 1978, pp. 5-21.

Cripps, Francis et al., *Manifesto. A Radical Strategy for Britain's Future*, London: Pan Books, 1981.

Curran, James ed., *The Future of the Left*, Cambridge: Polity Press and New Socialist, 1984.

Daalder, Hans and Peter Mair eds., *Western European Party Systems: Continuity and Change*, London: Sage, 1983.

Dankert, Piet and Ad Kooyman eds., *Europe Without Frontiers. Socialists on the Future of the European Economic Community*, London: Mansell Publishing, 1989.

Dell, Edmund, *Hard Pounding. Politics and Economic Crisis 1974-76*, Oxford: Oxford University Press, 1991.

Dittrich, Karl, "Testing the Catch-All Thesis: Some Difficulties and Possibilities", in Hans Daalder and Peter Mair eds., *Western European Party Systems: Continuity and Change*, pp. 257-266.

Dodd, Lawrence C., *Coalitions in Parliamentary Government*, Princeton: Princeton University Press, 1976.

Dornbusch, R. and R. Layard, *The Performance of the British Economy*, Oxford: Clarendon Press, 1987.

Downs, Anthony, *An Economic Theory of Democracy*, New York: Harper and Row, 1957.

Duverger, Maurice, *Political Parties*, London: Methuen and Company, 1954.

Elfferding, Wieland, "Klassenpartei und Hegemonie. Zur impliziten Parteientheorie des Marxismus", *Argument Sonderband AS 91*, Berlin: Argument Verlag, 1983.

Elklit, Jørgen and Ole Tonsgaard eds., *Valg og vælgeradfærd: studier i dansk politik*, Aarhus: Politica, 1984.

Elklit, Jørgen and Ole Tonsgaard eds., *To folketingsvalg*, Aarhus: Politica, 1989.

Ellemann-Jensen, Uffe, *Da Danmark igen sagde ja til det fælles*, Copenhagen: Schulz, 1987.

Engberg, Jens, *I Minefeltet. Træk af Arbejderbevægelsens historie siden 1936*, Copenhagen: Arbejderbevægelsens Erhvervsråd, 1986.

Epstein, Leon D., *Political Parties in Western Democracies*, New Brunswick, N. J.: Transaction Books, 1980.

Esping-Andersen, Gösta, *Politics Against Markets. The Social Democratic Road to Power*, Princeton: Princeton University Press, 1985.

Esping-Andersen, Gösta, *Three Worlds of Welfare Capitalism*, Cambridge: Basil Blackwell, 1990.

Fagerberg, Jan, "Nedgangen i EFs samhandelsgrad efter 1973: Tre teorier om årsakssammenhængen", *Internasjonal Politikk*, vol. 48, no. 1, March 1990, pp. 99-109.

Faurby, Ib, "Danish Party Attitudes on European Integration", Institute of Political Science, University of Aarhus. Paper presented to the European Consortium for Political Research Joint Sessions of Workshops, March 1980.

Featherstone, Kevin, *Socialists and European Integration. A Comparative History*, Manchester: Manchester University Press, 1988.

Feddersen, Hans B., "Det indre marked og EF's monetære integration", *Politica*, vol. 21, no. 4, November 1989, pp. 407-423.

Flynn, James, "How Will Article 100A4 Work? A Comparison with Article 93", *Common Market Law Review*, vol. 24, no. 4, Winter 1987, pp. 689-707.

Frey, Cynthia W., "Meaning Business: The British Application to Join the Common Market November 1966-October 1967", *Journal of Common Market Studies*, vol. 6, no. 3, September 1968, pp. 197-230.

Fröhlich, Hans-Peter, "Die französische Wirtschaftspolitik unter Präsident Mitterrand aus europäischer Perspektive", *Europa-Archiv* vol. 41 no. 3, February 1986, pp. 79-86.

George, Stephen, *An Awkward Partner. Britain in the European Community*, Oxford: Oxford University Press, 1990.

George, Stephen and Ben Rosamond, "The European Community", in Martin J. Smith and Joanna Spear eds., *The Changing Labour Party*, pp. 171-184.

Giavazzi, Francesco and Marco Pagano, "The Advantage of Tying One's Hands", *European Economic Review*, vol. 32, June 1988, pp. 1031-82.

Giavazzi, Francesco, Stefano Micossi and Marcus Miller eds., *The European Monetary System*, Cambridge: Cambridge University Press, 1988.

Giavazzi, Francesco "The Impact of EEC Membership", in R. Dornbusch and R. Layard eds., *The Performance of the British Economy*, pp. 97-130.

Glans, Ingemar, "Langtidsudviklingen i dansk vælgeradfærd", in Jørgen Elklit and Ole Tonsgaard eds., *To Folketingsvalg*, pp. 52-83.

Glotz, Peter, "Gesamteuropa - Skizze für einen schwierigen Weg", *Europa Archiv*, vol. 45, no. 2, January 1990, pp. 41-51.

Goodhart, C., "An Assessment of EMU", *The Royal Bank of Scotland Review*, no. 170, June 1991, pp. 3-25.

Gourevitch, Peter et al., *Unions and Economic Crisis: Britain, West Germany and Sweden*, London: George Allen and Unwin, 1984.

Grahl, John, and Paul Teague, "The British Labour Party and the EEC", *The Political Quarterly*, vol. 59, no. 1, January-March 1988, pp. 72-85.

Griffith, Richard T., ed., *Socialist Parties and the Question of Europe in the 1950's*, Leiden: E. J. Brill, 1992.

Groom, A.J.R. and Paul Taylor eds., *Functionalism. Theory and Practice in International Relations*, London: University of London Press, 1975.

Haahr, Jens Henrik, "Regional Integration Theory: Contents and Current Relevance", working paper, Aarhus: Institute of Political Science, 1991.

Haas, Ernst B., and Philippe C. Schmitter, "Economics and Differential Patterns of Political Integration", *International Organization*, vol. 18, no. 4, Fall 1964, pp. 705-737.

Haas, Ernst B., *Beyond the Nation State*, Stanford: Stanford University Press, 1964.

Haas, Ernst B., *The Uniting of Europe*, London: Stevens and Sons Ltd., 1958.

Haas, Ernst B., "Turbulent Fields and the Theory of Regional Integration", *International Organization*, vol. 30, no. 2, Spring 1976, pp. 173-212.

Haas, Peter M., "Do Regimes Matter? Epistemic Communities and Mediterranean Pollution Control", *International Organization*, vol. 43, no. 3, Summer 1989, pp. 377-403.

Hagen, Kåre, *Nasjonalstat, Velferdspolitik og Europeisk Integration*, Oslo: FAFO, 1990.

Hall, Peter A., *Governing the Economy. The Politics of State Intervention in Britain and France*, Cambridge: Polity Press, 1986.

Hansen, Peter, "Adaptive Behaviour of Small States: The Case of Denmark and the European Community", in P. J. McGowan ed., *Sage International Yearbook of Foreign Policy Studies*, pp. 143-174.

Hansen, Peter, "Denmark and European Integration", *Cooperation and Conflict*, vol. 4, no. 1, 1969, pp. 13-46.

Hansen, Peter, "Die Formulierung der dänischen Europapolitik", *Östereichische Zeitschrift für Aussenpolitik*, vol. 13, 1973, pp. 3-31.

Harris, Kenneth, *David Owen*, London: Weidenfeld and Nicholson, 1987.

Heath, Anthony et al., *How Britain Votes*, Oxford: Pergamon Press, 1985.

Hirschman, Albert O., *Exit, Voice, and Loyalty*, London: Harvard University Press, 1970.

Hoffman, Stanley, "Obstinate or Obsolete? The Fate of the Nation-State and the Case of Europe", *Daedalus*, vol. 95, Summer 1966, pp. 862-915.

Holland, Stuart, ed., *Out of Crisis: A Project for European Recovery*, Nottingham: Spokesman, 1983. Abridged version, Roskilde: Institute of Economics and Planning, 1983.

Holland, Stuart, *Uncommon Market. Capital, Class and Power in the European Community*, London: Macmillan, 1980.

Holmes, Peter, "Broken Dreams: Economic Policy in Mitterrand's France", in S. Mazey and M. Newman, eds., *Mitterrand's France*, pp. 33-56.

Johnson, K., and C. Painter, "British Governments and the EMS", *The Political Quarterly*, vol. 51, no. 3, July-September 1980, pp. 317-330.

Jowell, Roger and Gerald Hoinville eds., *Britain into Europe. Public Opinion and the EEC 1961-75*, London: Croom Helm, 1976.

Katzenstein, Peter J., *Small States in World Markets: Industrial Policy in Europe*, London: Cornell University Press, 1985.

Kavanagh, Dennis, "Power in British Political Parties: Iron Law or Special Pleading", *West European Politics*, vol. 8, no. 3, July 1985, pp. 5-22.

King, Anthony, *Britain Says Yes: The 1975 Referendum on the Common Market*, Washington D.C.: American Enterprise Institute, 1977.

Kinnock, Neil, "Facing the Future of the European Community", in Piet Dankert and Ad Kooyman eds., *Europe Without Frontiers. Socialists on the Future of the European Economic Community*, pp. 1-11.

Kinnock, Neil, *Making Our Way: Investing in Britain's Future*, London: Basil Blackwell, 1986.

Kinnock, Neil, "New Deal for Europe", in James Curran ed., *The Future of the Left*, pp. 231-242.

Kirchheimer, Otto, "The Waning of Opposition in Parliamentary Regimes", *Social Research* vol. 24, no. 2, 1957, pp. 127-156.

Kirchheimer, Otto, "The Transformation of the Western European Party Systems", in Joseph Lapalombara and Myron Weiner eds., *Political Parties and Political Development*.

Kitzinger, Uwe, *The Second Try. Labour and the EEC*, Oxford: Pergamon Press, 1968.

Kogan, David and Maurice Kogan, *The Battle for the Labour Party*, London: Kogan Page, 1982.

Kolte, Lars, "Beslutningsprocessen i EF 1985-89", *Politica*, vol. 21, no. 4, November 1989, pp. 376-395.

Kaarsted, Tage, *Danske Ministerier 1953-72*, Odense: Odense Universitetsforlag, 1992.

Kristensen, Jens Pagter, "Den Europæiske Centralbank", *Samfundsøkonomen*, no. 6, October 1988, pp. 31-37.

Lange, Peter, "The Politics of the Social Dimension", in Alberta M. Sbragia ed., *Europolitics*, pp. 225-256.

Lapalombara, Joseph and Myron Weiner eds., *Political Parties and Political Development*, Princeton: Princeton University Press, 1966.

Laver, Michael, "Party Competition and Party System Change. The Interaction of Coalition Bargaining and Electoral Competition", *Journal of Theoretical Politics*, vol. 1, no. 3, July 1989, pp. 301-324.

Lieber, Robert J., *British Politics and European Unity*, London: University of California Press, 1970.

Lijphardt, Arendt, "Comparative Politics and the Comparative Method", *American Political Science Review*, vol. 65, no. 3, September 1971, pp. 682-693.

Lindberg, Leon N., *The Political Dynamics of European Economic Integration*, London: Oxford University Press, 1963.

Lindberg, Leon N. and Stuart S. Scheingold, *Europe's Would Be Polity*, Englewood Cliffs, N. J.: Prentice Hall, 1970.

Lindberg, Leon N. and Stuart A. Scheingold eds., *Regional Integration: Theory and Research*, Cambridge: Harvard University Press, 1971.

Lips, Letje, "The Labour Party and the Common Market", in A. Boxhoorn, J. Th. Leersen and M. Spiering eds., *Britain in Europe*, pp. 99-129.

Lipset, Seymour Martin, *Political Man*, New York: Doubleday, 1960.

Lipset, Seymour Martin and Stein Rokkan, "Cleavage Structures, Party Systems, and Voter Alignments", 1967, reprinted in Peter Mair ed., *The West European Party System*, pp. 91-138.

Lodge, Juliet, ed., *The European Community and the Challenge of the Future*, London: Pinter, 1989.

Ludlow, Peter, *Beyond 1992: Europe and Its Western Partners*, Brussels: Center for European Policy Studies, 1989.

Ludlow, Peter, *The Making of the European Monetary System*, London: Butterworth Scientific, 1982.

Mair, Peter ed., *The West European Party System*, Oxford: Oxford University Press, 1990.

Marsh, David, *The New Politics of British Trade Unionism. Union Power and the Thatcher Legacy*, London: Macmillan, 1992.

Marshall, Thomas H., *Class, Citizenship, and Social Development*, London: The University of Chicago Press, 1977, first edition 1950.

Martens, Hans, *Danmarks ja, Norges nej. EF-Folkeafstemningerne i 1972*, Copenhagen: DUPI and Munksgaard, 1979.

Martin, David, *European Union and the Democratic Deficit*, West Lothian: John Wheatley Centre, 1990.

Marx, Karl and Friederich Engels, *Werke*, vol. 7, Berlin: Dietz Verlag, 1964.

Machin, Howard and Vincent Wright eds., *Economic Policy and Policy Making Under the Mitterrand Presidency 1981-1984*, London: Frances Pinter, 1985.

Maunder, Peter, "International Trade", in Peter Maunder ed., *The British Economy in the 1970s*, pp. 247-278.

Maunder, Peter ed., *The British Economy in the 1970s*, London: Heinemann, 1980.

Mazey, S. and M. Newman, eds., *Mitterrand's France*, London: Croom Helm, 1987.

McIlroy, John, *Trade Unions in Britain Today*, Manchester: Manchester University Press, 1988.

McGowan, P. J. ed., *Sage International Yearbook of Foreign Policy Studies*, vol. 2, London: SAGE, 1974.

Miljan, Toivo, *The Reluctant Europeans: The Attitudes of the Nordic Countries Towards European Integration*, London: C. Hurst and Company, 1977.

Mitchell, Austin, *The Case for Labour*, London: Longman, 1983.

Mitrany, David, *A Working Peace System*, Chicago: Qudrangle Books, 1966.

Molin, Björn, *Tjänstepenionsfrågan: En studie i svensk partipolitik*, Göteborg: Akademiförlaget, 1965.

Moravcsik, Andrew, "Negotiating the Single European Act: National Interest and Conventional Statecraft in the European Community", *International Organization*, vol. 45, no. 1, Winter 1991, pp. 19-56.

Muet, Pierre-Alain, "Economic Management and the International Environment, 1981-1983", in Howard Machin and Vincent Wright eds., *Economic Policy and Policy Making Under the Mitterrand Presidency 1981-1984*, pp. 70-84.

Mundell, R. A., "A Theory of Optimum Currency Areas", *American Economic Review*, vol. 51, no. 4, September 1961, pp. 657-665.

Nannestad, Peter, *Danish Design or British Disease? Danish Economic Crisis Policy 1974-1979*, Aarhus: Aarhus University Press, 1991.

Nau, Henry R., "From Integration to Interdependence: Gains, Losses, and Continuing Gaps, *International Organization*, vol. 33, no. 1, Winter 1979, pp. 119-147.

Nedergaard, Peter, *EFs Markedsintegration*, Copenhagen: DUPI and DJØF, 1989.

Newman, Michael, *Socialism and European Unity: The Dilemma of the Left in Britain and France*, London: Junction Books, 1983.

Nye, Joseph S., "Comparing Common Markets" in Leon N. Lindberg and Stuart A. Scheingold eds., *Regional Integration: Theory and Research*, pp. 192-231.

Nye, Joseph S., *Peace in Parts: Integration and Conflict in Regional Organization*, Boston: Little & Brown, 1971.

Olsen, Erling, "En tysk satellit bliver til en europæisk provins", *Samfundsøkonomen*, no. 2, March 1992.

Padoa-Schioppa, Tommaso, *Efficiency, Stability, and Equity: A Strategy for the Evolution of the Economic System of the European Community*, Oxford: Oxford University Press, 1987.

Padoa-Schioppa, Tommaso, "The EMS: A Long Term View", in Francesco Giavazzi, Stefano Micossi and Marcus Miller eds., *The European Monetary System*, pp. 369-384

Palmer, John, "Britain and the EEC: The Withdrawal Option", *International Affairs*, vol. 58, no. 4, Autumn 1982, pp. 638-647.

Paterson, William E., *The SPD and European Integration*, Farnborough: Saxon House, 1974.

Petersen, Nikolaj and Jørgen Elklit, "Denmark Enters the European Communities", *Scandinavian Political Studies*, vol. 8, 1973, pp. 198-213.

Przeworski, Adam and Henry Teune, *The Logic of Comparative Social Inquiry*, London: John Wiley, 1970.

Puchala, Donald, "Of Blind Men, Elephants and Regional Integration", *Journal of Common Market Studies*, vol. 10, no. 3, September 1972, pp. 267-284.

Puchala, Donald J., "Of Worm Cans and Worth Taxes: Fiscal Harmonization and the European Policy Process", in Helen Wallace, William Wallace and Carole Webb eds., *Policy Making in the European Community*. pp. 237-264.

Rhodes, Martin, "Labour Market Regulation in Post-1992 Europe", *Journal of Common Market Studies*, vol. 30, no. 1, March 1992, pp. 23-51.

Riddell, Peter, *The Thatcher Decade*, Oxford: Basil Blackwell, 1989.

Riker, William, *The Theory of Political Coalitions*, New Haven: Yale University Press, 1962.

Robins, Lynton J., *The Reluctant Party: Labour and the EEC, 1961-1975*, Ormskirk: G. W. and A. Hesketh, 1979.

Roulund, Peter, *Socialdemokratiet og Europæisk Integration*, Master's Thesis, Aarhus: Institute of Political Science, University of Aarhus, 1992.

Sandholz, Wayne and John Zysman, "1992: Recasting the European Bargain", *World Politics*, vol. 42, no. 1, October 1989, pp. 95-128.

Sartori, Giovanni, "The Sociology of Parties: A Critical Review", 1968, reprinted in Peter Mair ed., *The West European Party System*, pp. 150-182.

Sbragia, Alberta M. ed., *Europolitics*, Washington DC: The Brookings Institution, 1992.

Scarrow, H.A., *Comparative Political Analysis. An Introduction*, New York: Harper and Row, 1969.

Scheingold, Stuart A., "Domestic and International Consequences of Regional Integration", in Leon N. Lindberg and Stuart A. Scheingold eds., *Regional Integration: Theory and Research*, pp. 374-398.

Schott, Jeffrey J., "Trading Blocks and the World Trading System", *World Economy*, vol. 14, no. 1, March 1991, pp. 1-17

Seyd, Patrick, *The Rise and Fall of the Labour Left*, New York: St. Martin's Press, 1987.

Siune, Karen, Palle Svennson, and Ole Tonsgaard, *Det blev et nej*, Aarhus: Politica, 1992.

Sjöblom, Gunnar, "Analysis of Party Behavior", *Scandinavian Political Studies*, vol. 2, 1967, pp. 203-222.

Sjöblom, Gunnar, *Party Strategies in a Multiparty System*, Lund: Student-litteratur, 1968.

Smith, Martin J. and Joanna Spear eds., *The Changing Labour Party*, London: Routledge, 1992.

Spence, James, "Movements in the Public Mood: 1961-75", in Roger Jowell and Gerald Hoinville eds., *Britain into Europe: Public opinion and the EEC 1961-75*, pp. 18-36.

Statler, Jocelyn "The European Monetary System: From Conception to Birth", *International Affairs*, vol. 55, no. 2, April 1979, pp. 206-225.

Story, Jonathan, "The Launching of the European System of Central Banks". Paper prepared for the Eureopan Consortium for Political Reseach, workshop on National Political Systems and the European Community, Essex 1991.

Ström, Kaare R., "A Behavioral Theory of Competitive Political Parties", *American Journal of Political Science*, vol. 34, no. 2, May 1990, pp. 565-598.

Sørensen, Carsten Lehmann and Karen Siune, "Is the Theory of European Integration Dead or Alive? The Case of Danish Political Parties". Paper presented at the European Consortium for Political Research meeting in Louvain, April 1976.

Sørensen, Carsten Lehmann, *Danmark og EF i 1970erne*, Copenhagen: Borgen, 1978.

Sørensen, Vibeke, "National Welfare Strategies and International Linkages in a Small Open Economy; The Danish Social Democratic Party and European Integration, 1947-1963", in Richard T. Griffith ed., *Socialist Parties and the Question of Europe in the 1950's*.

Tavlas, George S., "On the International Use of Currencies: The Case of the Deutsche Mark", *Essays in International Finance*, no. 181, March 1991, pp. 1-41.

Taylor, Paul, "The Politics of the European Communities: the Confederal Phase", *World Politics*, vol. 27, no. 3, April 1975, pp. 336-360.

Taylor, Paul, *The Limits of European Integration*, London: University of London Press, 1983.

Taylor, Paul, "The New Dynamics of EC Integration in the 1980s" in Juliet Lodge ed., *The European Community and the Challenge of the Future*, pp. 3-25.

Teague, Paul, "The British TUC and the European Community", *Millenium*, vol. 18, no. 1, Spring 1989, pp. 29-45.

Teague, Paul, *The European Community: The Social Dimension*, London: Kogan Page, 1989.

Thomas, Alastair H., "Danish Social Domocracy and the European Community", *Journal of Common Market Studies*, vol. 13, no. 4, June 1975, pp. 454-468.

Thomsen, Søren Risbjerg, "Udviklingen under forholdstalsvalgmåden 1920-1984" in Jørgen Elklit and Ole Tonsgaard eds., *Valg og vælgeradfærd: studier i dansk politik*, pp. 39-69.

Tonsgaard, Ole, "Folkeafstemningen om EF-pakken", *Dansk Udenrigspolitisk Årbog 1986*, Copenhagen: DJØF and DUPI, 1987, pp. 113-139.

Tsoukalis, Loukas, *The Politics and Economics of European Monetary Integration*, London: Allen and Unwin, 1977.

Villumsen, Holger, *Det danske Socialdemokratis Europapolitik 1945-49*, Odense: Odense Universitetsforlag, 1991.

Wagner, Helmut, "Neues im Westen. Frankreichs späte Hinwendung zu Europa", *Zeitschrift für Politik*, vol. 31 no. 4, December 1984, pp. 351-364.

Wallace, Helen, William Wallace and Carole Webb eds., *Policy Making in the European Community*, 2nd ed., Chicester: John Wiley, 1983.

Ware, Alan ed., *Political Parties: Electoral Change and Structural Response*, Oxford: Basil Blackwell, 1987.

Ware, Alan, "Introduction: Parties under Electoral Competition", in Alan Ware ed., *Political Parties: Electoral Change and Structural Response*, pp. 1-23.

Warnecke, Steven J., "The Study of the Europan Community: A Critical Appraisal", in *Research Resources: The European Community*, New York: Council for European Studies, 1977.

Williams, G. L. and A. L. Williams, *Labour's Decline and the Social Democrats' Fall*, London: Macmillan, 1989.

Winters, Alan, "Britain in Europe: A Survey of Quantitative Trade Studies", *Journal of Common Market Studies*, vol. 25, no. 4, June 1987, pp. 315-335.

Woolley, John T., "Policy Credibility and European Monetary Institutions", in Alberta M. Sbragia ed., *Europolitics*, pp. 157-172.

Worre, Torben, "Europavalget", *Økonomi og Politik*, vol. 53, no. 3, 1979, pp. 259-285.

Worre, Torben, "The Danish Euro-Party System", *Scandinavian Political Studies*, vol. 10, no. 1, 1987, pp. 79-91.

Worre, Torben, "Denmark at the Crossroads", *Journal of Common Market Studies*, vol. 26, no. 4, June 1988, pp. 361-388.

Wæver, Ole, "Three Competing Europes: French, German, Russian", *Foreign Affairs*, vol. 66, no. 3, July 1990, pp. 477-493.

Yin, Robert K., *Case Study Research*, London: Sage, 1984.

OFFICIAL DOCUMENTS

Antrag der Fraktion der SPD, Europapolitik, *Deutscher Bundestag*, Drucksache 11/3851, 19 January 1989.

Beretning fra folketingets markedsudvalg [Report of the Folketing's Market Committee], *Folketingstidende*, 1961-62, Appendix B, cols. 352-375.

Bulletin of the EC, no. 5, 1984.

Commission of the European Community, *Eurobarometer*, various volumes.

Commission of the European Community, "Requirements for the Implementation of the Single Act", Brussels 1987.

Committee for the Study of Economic and Monetary Union, *Report on Economic and Monetary Union in the European Community*.

Conference of Socialist Economists, London Working Group, *The Alternative Economic Strategy*, London: CSE, 1980.

CSPEC, "Manifesto Adopted by the XIIIth Congress of the Confederation of the Socialist Parties of the European Community", Luxembourg, March 1984.

CSPEC, "Manifesto Adopted at the XVIth Congress of the Confederation of Socialist Parties of the European Community", Brussels, 10 February 1989.

CSPEC, Leaders' Declaration on the Intergovernmental Conferences, Madrid, 10 December 1990.

Dagsordensforslag nr. D 15, *Folketingstidende*, forhandlingerne, 1989/90, 30 November 1989, col. 2580.

Dagsordensforslag nr. D 31, *Folketingstidende*, forhandlingerne, 1989/90, 18 April 1990, col. 8481.

Dagsordensforslag nr. D 46, *Folketingstidende*, forhandlingerne 1988/89, 30 May 1989, cols. 10587-10588.

Debates of the European Parliament, various volumes.

Deutscher Bundestag, 149. Sitzung, July 1985, cols. 11088-11093.

Doc. A3-99/90, Interim Report on Behalf of the Committee for Economy, Exchange Rates, and Industry Policy, *Official Journal of the European Communities*, no. C 149, 18 June 1990, pp. 66-69.

Entschließungsantrag der Fraktion der SPD zur Erklärung der Bundesregierung zum Europäischen Rat in Kopenhagen, *Deutscher Bundestag*, Drucksache 11/1487, 9 December 1987.

Europe. Agence Internationale D'Information Pour La Presse, *Europe Documents*, 11 March 1988.

European Communities, Directive 88/361/EEC of June 1988.

European Parliament, "Interim Report of the Committee on Institutional Affairs", Doc. A 3-47/90.

European Parliament, "Resolution on the Intergovernmental Conference in the Context of Parliament's Strategy for European Union", 14 March 1990.

Eurostat, *External Trade and Balance of Payments, Statistical Yearbook 1992*, Luxembourg: Statistical Office of the European Communities, 1992.

First Report from the Expenditure Committee, Session 1978-79, *The European Monetary System*, HMSO, pp. 138-143.

Folketingstidende, forhandlingerne, various volumes.

Folketingstidende, 1961-62, tillæg B, cols. 352-375.

Folketingstidende, 1985-86, tillæg B, cols. 1547-1548.

Hansard Parliamentary Debates, Commons, various volumes.

HMSO, *The European Monetary System*, Cmnd. 7405, November 1978.

House of Lords Select Committee on the European Communities, "European Union" Session 1984-1985, 14th Report, HL 226 July 1985.

Labour Party Conference Reports, various volumes.

Labour Party, *Britain and the European Communities: An Economic Assessment*, London, 1970.

Labour Party, *The EEC and Britain. A Socialist Perspective*, London, 1977.

Labour Party, "Composite Resolution 42 as Approved by Annual Party Conference 1978", *Labour and Europe: Recent Statements of Policy*, London, 1978.

Labour Party, "The European Monetary System", background paper, London, 1978.

Labour Party, "Appeal to All EEC Electors, Declaration Agreed to at the Brussels Congress of the Confederation of Socialist Parties of the European Community", London, 1979.

Labour Party, "Labour's Manifesto for the 1979 European Elections", London, 1979.

Labour Party, "Labour's Manifesto for the 1979 General Elections, The Labour Way Is the Better Way", London, 1979.

Labour Party, "Withdrawal from the EEC". Statement by the National Executive Committee to the 1981 Conference.

Labour Party, "Labour's Manifesto for the 1983 General Election, New Hope for Britain", London, 1983.

Labour Party, "Labour's Manifesto for the 1984 European Elections", London, 1984.

Labour Party, "Labour's Manifesto for the 1987 General Election, Britain Will Win", London, 1987.

Labour Party, "Moving Ahead", NEC Statement to the Labour Party Conference 1987.

Labour Party, "Labour's Manifesto for the European Elections, Meeting the Challenge in Europe", London, 1989.

Labour Party, Campaign Briefing, 9 June 1989.

Labour Party, "Neil Kinnock's Statement at the Launch of Labour's Campaign for the European Parliament Elections", London, 23 May 1989.

Labour Party, *Meet the Challenge, Make the Change: A New Agenda for Britain. Final Report of Labour's Policy Review for the 1990s*, London, 1989.

Labour Party, *Looking to the Future*, Labour Party Policy Review, London, 1990.

Labour Party, "NEC Statement on Economic and Monetary Union", *Tribune*, 14 December 1990.

Labour Party, *Labour's Programme 1973*, London, 1973.

Labour Party, *Labour's Programme 1976*, London, 1976.

Labour Party, *Labour's Programme 1982*, London, 1982.

Labour Party News Release: "The Prime Minister's Letter to the September 1977 Meeting of the NEC about the Common Market", Harvester Microfilms, "Britain in Europe" series.

LO, *The Internal Market and the Social Dimension*, Copenhagen: LO, 1989.

Memorandum from the Danish Government, Copenhagen, 4 October 1990, English version.

NEC, "Labour and the Common Market", London, 1962.

NEC, "Labour and the Common Market", London, 1967.

NEC, "Campaigning for a Fairer Britain", London, 1983.

NEC, Report to Conference 1989.

Official Journal of the European Communities, no. C 297 1980.

Organization for Economic Cooperation and Development, *OECD National Accounts, 1960-90, vol. 1: Main Aggregates*.

Le Programme Commun de Gouvernement de la Gauche, Paris: Flamarion, 1978.

Projet Socialiste Pour La France Des Années 80, Paris: Club Socialiste de Livre, 1980.

SID/Ralf Pittelkow, *Det indre marked og lønmodtagerne: Et debatoplæg*, Copenhagen: SID, 1989.

Socialdemokratiet, "EF-parlamentsvalget 1979, Socialdemokratiets valgudtalelse" Copenhagen, May 1979.

Socialdemokratiet, *An Open Europe*, English version, Brussels, 1987.

Socialdemokratiet, "EF-valgudtalelse vedtaget på den ekstraordinære kongres i dagene 2.-4. september 1983".

Socialdemokratiet, "Også solidaritet i fællesskabet", Copenhagen, October 1983.

Socialdemokratiet, "Socialdemokratiets valgudtalelse til EF-valget Juni 1984", Copenhagen, May 1984.

Socialdemokratiet, Statement of the SDP Executive Committee, 1 February 1986.

Socialdemokratiet, politisk-økonomisk afdeling, "Notat om Delors-rapporten om en økonomisk og monetær union", April, 1989.

Socialdemokratiet, "Et Åbent Europa", the SDP's Manifesto for the June 1989 Elections to the European Parliament, Copenhagen, May 1989.

Socialdemokratiet, politisk-økonomisk afdeling, "Flertalsafgørelser om miljøspørgsmål i EF", 25 May 1989.

Socialdemokratiet, "Gang i 90'erne: Socialdemokratiets bud på en samlet indsats 1990-95", Copenhagen, May 1989.

Socialdemokratiet, "Notat vedrørende memorandum til regeringskonferencen", September 1990.

TUC, *Annual Reports*, various issues.

TUC, *Renegotiation and the Referendum: The TUC View*, London, April 1975.

TUC, *Maximising the Benefits. Minimising the Costs*, Report on Europe 1992, London, 1988.

United Nations International Trade Statistics, various yearbooks.

United Nations Statistical Yearbook, various volumes.

Weiss, Birte, "Ja til Europa - Nej til Union. Materiale til Socialdemokratiets Europa-debat".

Økonomiske Råd, Det, *Dansk Økonomi* Copenhagen, December 1988.

Økonomiske Råd, Det, *Dansk Økonomi* Copenhagen, December 1989.

Økonomiske Råd, Det, *Dansk Økonomi* Copenhagen, May 1991.

Økonomiske Råd, Det, *Danish Monetary Policy in Transition*, Copenhagen, 1985.

INDEX